AF476969

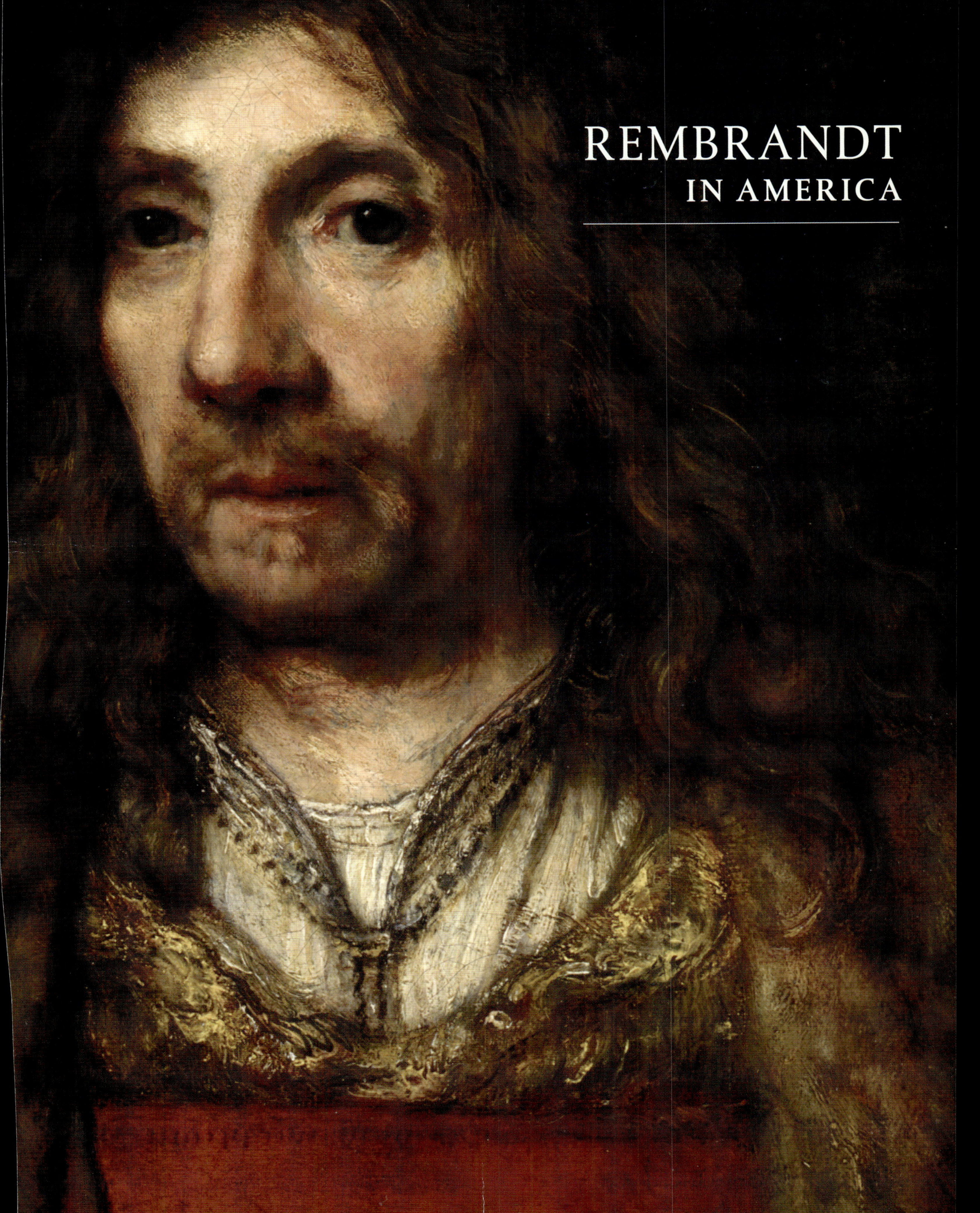

REMBRANDT
IN AMERICA

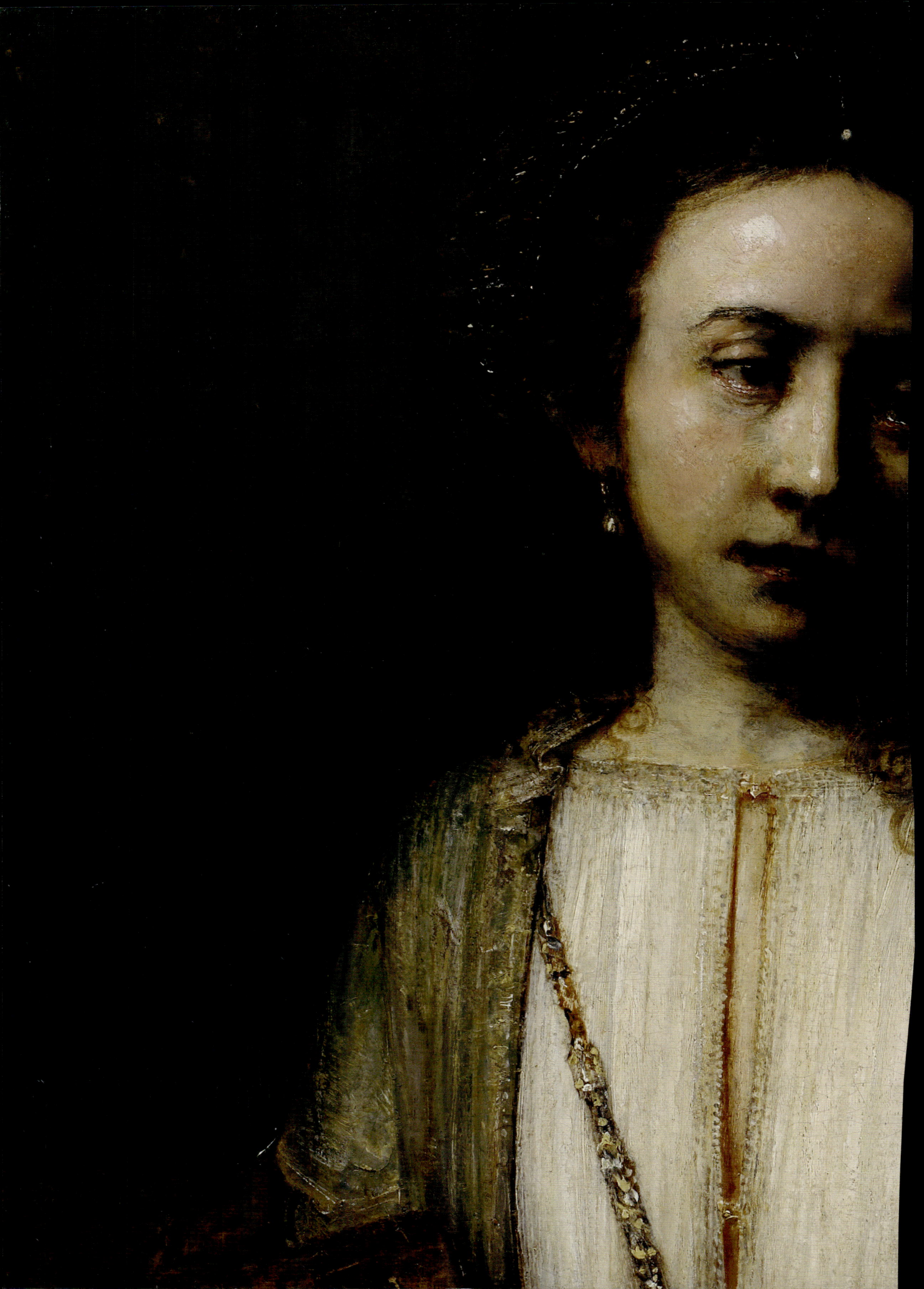

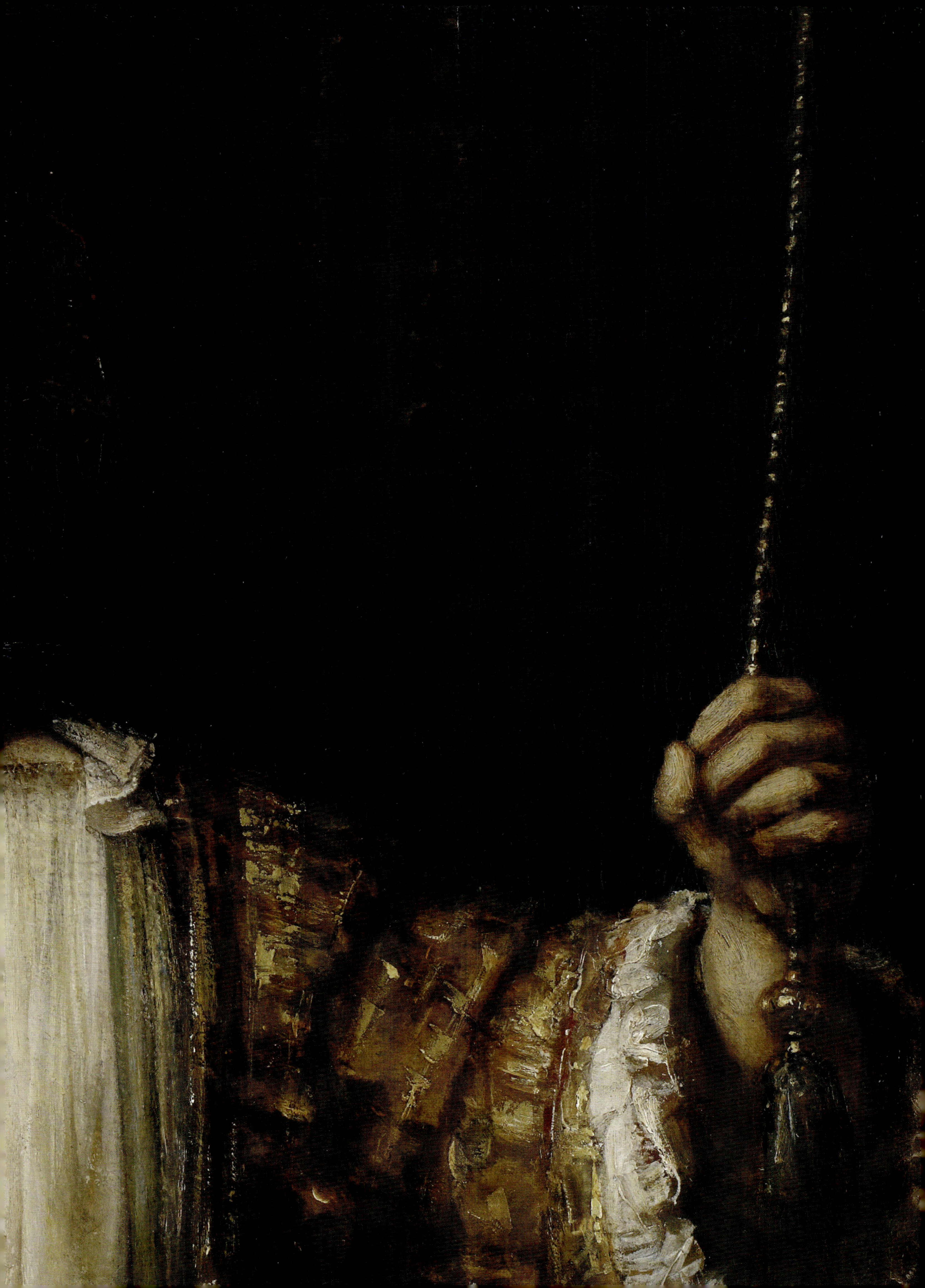

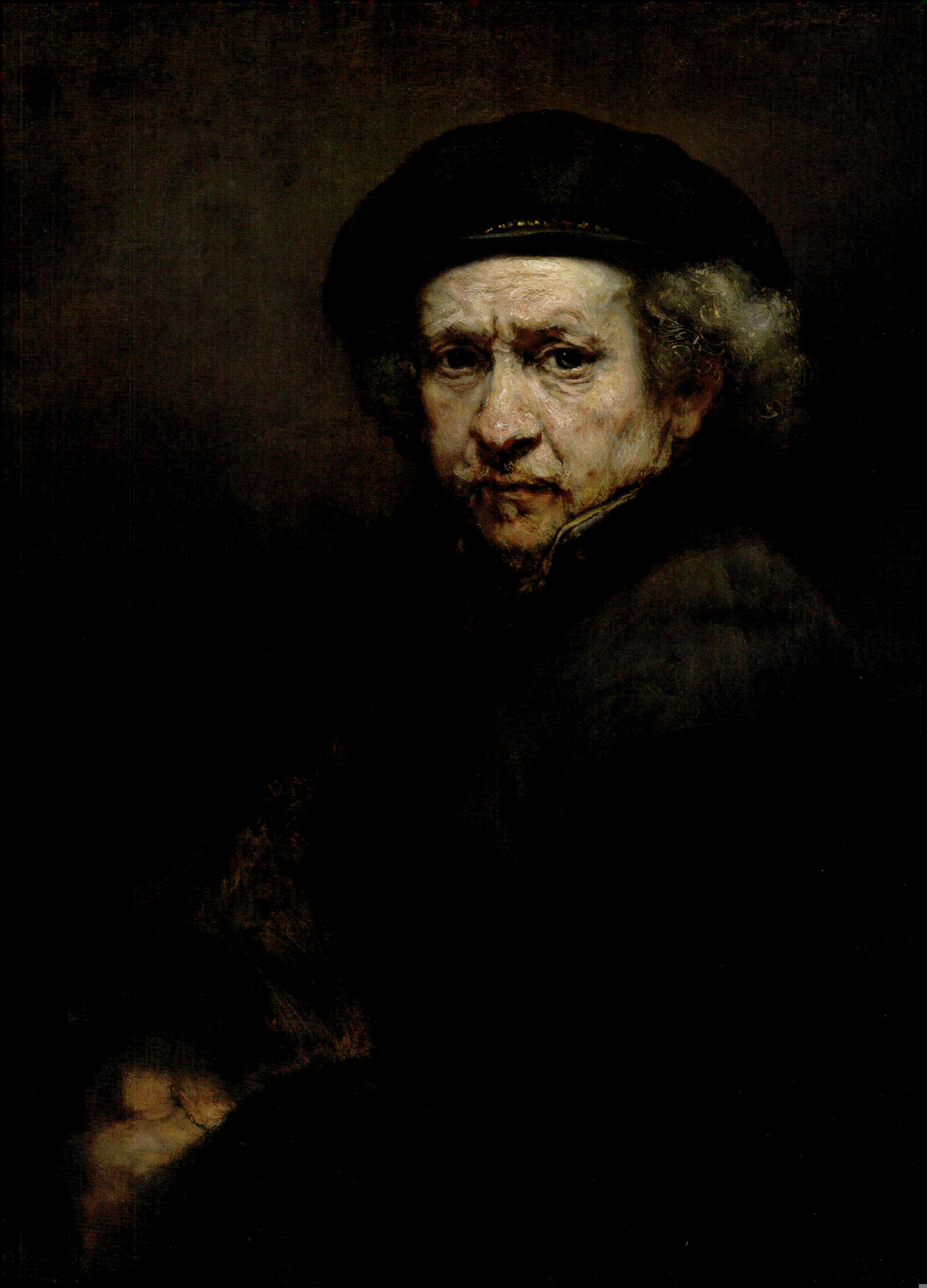

REMBRANDT
IN AMERICA

Collecting and Connoisseurship

GEORGE S. KEYES
TOM RASSIEUR
DENNIS P. WELLER

In collaboration with Jon L. Seydl

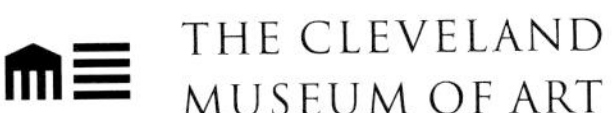

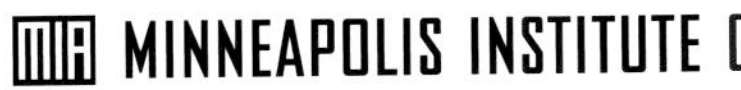

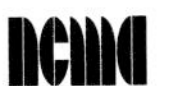
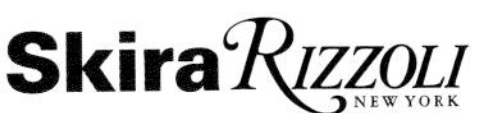

Published on the occasion of the exhibition *Rembrandt in America*, 30 October 2011–22 January 2012 at the North Carolina Museum of Art, 19 February–28 May 2012 at the Cleveland Museum of Art, and 24 June–16 September 2012 at the Minneapolis Institute of Arts.

Organized by the North Carolina Museum of Art, Raleigh, the Cleveland Museum of Art, and the Minneapolis Institute of Arts.

The exhibition is supported by an indemnity from the Federal Council on the Arts and the Humanities.

Organizational support provided by The Samuel H. Kress Foundation.

In Raleigh, the exhibition is made possible, in part, by the North Carolina Department of Cultural Resources, the North Carolina Museum of Art Foundation, Inc., and the William R. Kenan Jr. Endowment for Educational Exhibitions.

The Cleveland Museum of Art is generously funded by Cuyahoga County residents through Cuyahoga Arts and Culture. The Ohio Arts Council helps fund the museum with state tax dollars to encourage economic growth, educational excellence, and cultural enrichment for all Ohioans.

Operation of the MIA and its programs is supported by the citizens of Hennepin County through the Park Museum Fund and by a grant provided by the Minnesota State Arts Board, through an appropriation by the Minnesota State Legislature from the Minnesota arts and cultural heritage fund with money from the vote of the people of Minnesota on November 4, 2008, and a grant from the National Endowment for the Arts.

www.ncartmuseum.org
www.clevelandart.org
www.artsmia.org

First published in the United States of America in 2011 by
Skira Rizzoli Publications, Inc.
300 Park Avenue South
New York, NY 10010
www.rizzoliusa.com

ISBN: 978-1-935294-05-4 The Cleveland Museum of Art (paperback)

ISBN: 978-0-8478-3685-7 Skira Rizzoli Publications, Inc. (hardcover)

Library of Congress Catalog Control Number: 2011929646

This book has been typeset in Albertina MT and DTL Haarlemmer.

Prepared by the Curatorial Publications Department at the Cleveland Museum of Art, Barbara J. Bradley, director; Amy Bracken Sparks, assistant editor; Caroline Smith, proofreader.

Skira Rizzoli Publications, Inc.
Margaret Chace, Associate Publisher
Julie Di Filippo, Editor

Design: Studio Blackwell, Kelsey Blackwell with Martina Hwang

Printed in China

Contents

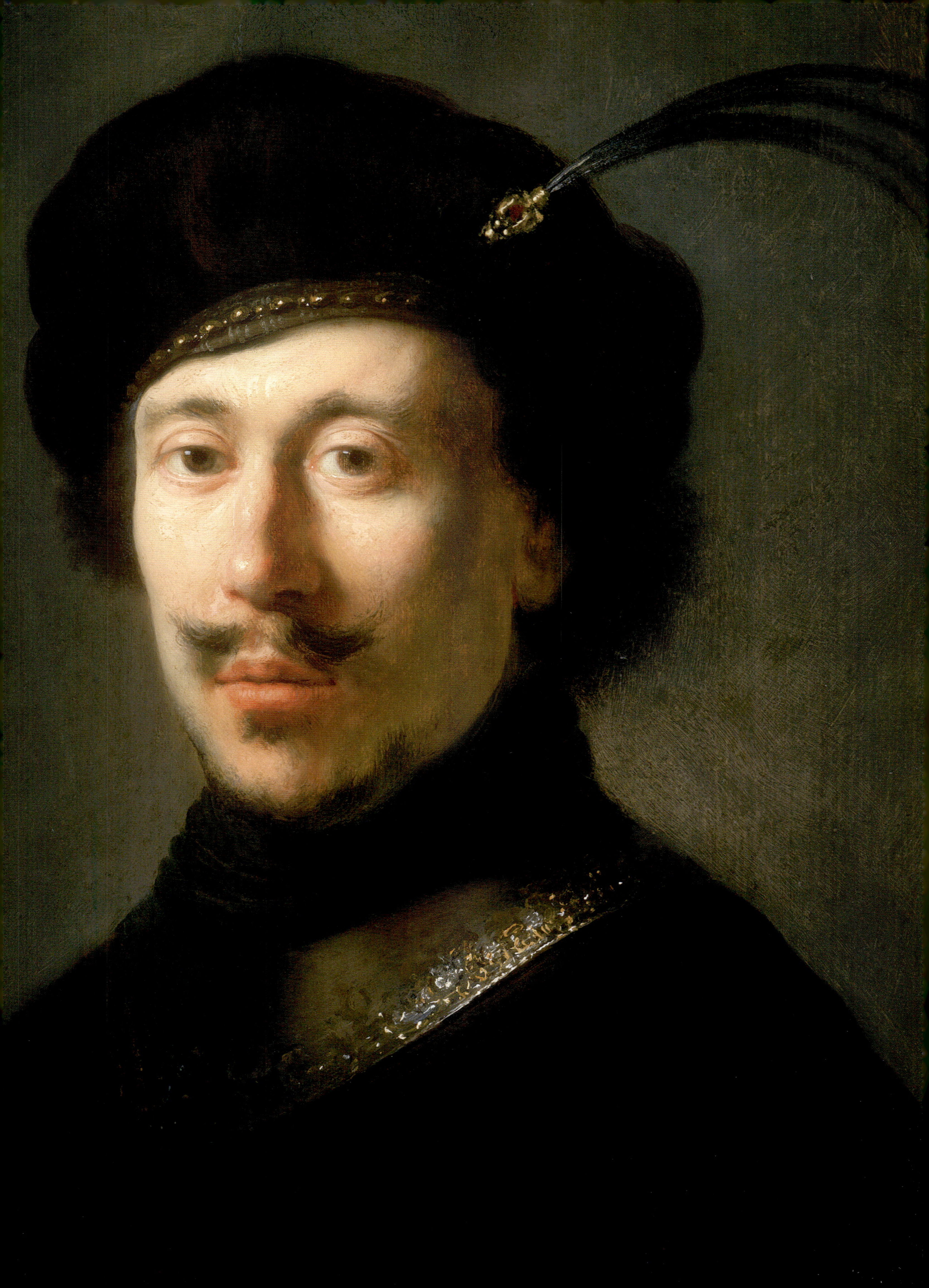

Directors' Foreword

Rembrandt belongs to the pantheon of artists known by a single name: Raphael, Michelangelo, Caravaggio, Rubens, Goya, and Picasso. In America, Rembrandt's name has become synonymous with excellence—so much so that marketers of toothpaste, electronics, and tobacco have appropriated his name or his art to sell their wares. Since the Gilded Age of robber barons, wealthy collectors have eagerly sought his pictures. Largely through their gifts and legacies, dozens of Rembrandt paintings have entered American museum collections. Even today, Americans—both private individuals and major institutions—number among the most aggressive collectors of Rembrandt paintings. The result is a wealth of Rembrandt paintings in America but a dearth of opportunities to see many of them gathered together.

Rembrandt in America brings more than thirty paintings by the master to each of the three participating museums. As such, these will be the largest groups of Rembrandt paintings seen in America in a generation, if ever. The selection allows our audiences to see Rembrandt's trajectory from brash young artist to confident master to timeless student of the human condition. Many of the paintings are portraits, and many of those that are not strictly portraits bear a strong resemblance to portraiture. Among this latter class are imaginary character studies as well as images of biblical and literary figures portrayed with a lively immediacy that brings their historical antecedents to life. Anyone who has wielded a brush will be astounded by the range and subtlety of Rembrandt's touch. From the animated musculature around his sitters' eyes, to the infinitely varied colors of their complexions, to the wisps of their hair, to the starched linen of their clothing, to the evanescent shadows of their surroundings, Rembrandt created countless effects that bring forth his subjects as sentient beings—as alive in our own times as they were in the seventeenth century.

American collectors of Rembrandt paintings were often overly optimistic about the objects that they bought. Many works by his contemporaries were purchased as being by Rembrandt himself. Indeed, many questions still surround pictures that may or may not be by Rembrandt. The exhibition and this volume include many comparative works that were formerly hailed as Rembrandts but are no longer thought to be so. They provide a strong sense of Rembrandt's powerful effect on the art of his time, and they provide a context for appreciating both the similarities and the differences between the art of the master and that of his followers.

We are proud that our three institutions have collaborated so well to bring this extraordinary exhibition and handsome publication before the public. We also wish to underscore that a project as ambitious as *Rembrandt in America* relies on the enormous generosity of lenders of precious works of art and the financial support of sponsors at all three venues. First, we would like to acknowledge the generosity of the Samuel H. Kress Foundation for supporting curatorial research and the publication of this catalogue. The exhibition is also made possible through an indemnity from the Federal Council on the Arts and the Humanities. In Raleigh, the exhibition is presented by Progress Energy with additional support from Quintiles. In Cleveland, the exhibition is made possible, in part, by KeyBank. Delta Air Lines is the official airline of the Minneapolis presentation. To all we owe our enduring gratitude.

KAYWIN FELDMAN
Minneapolis Institute of Arts

DAVID FRANKLIN
The Cleveland Museum of Art

LAWRENCE J. WHEELER
North Carolina Museum of Art

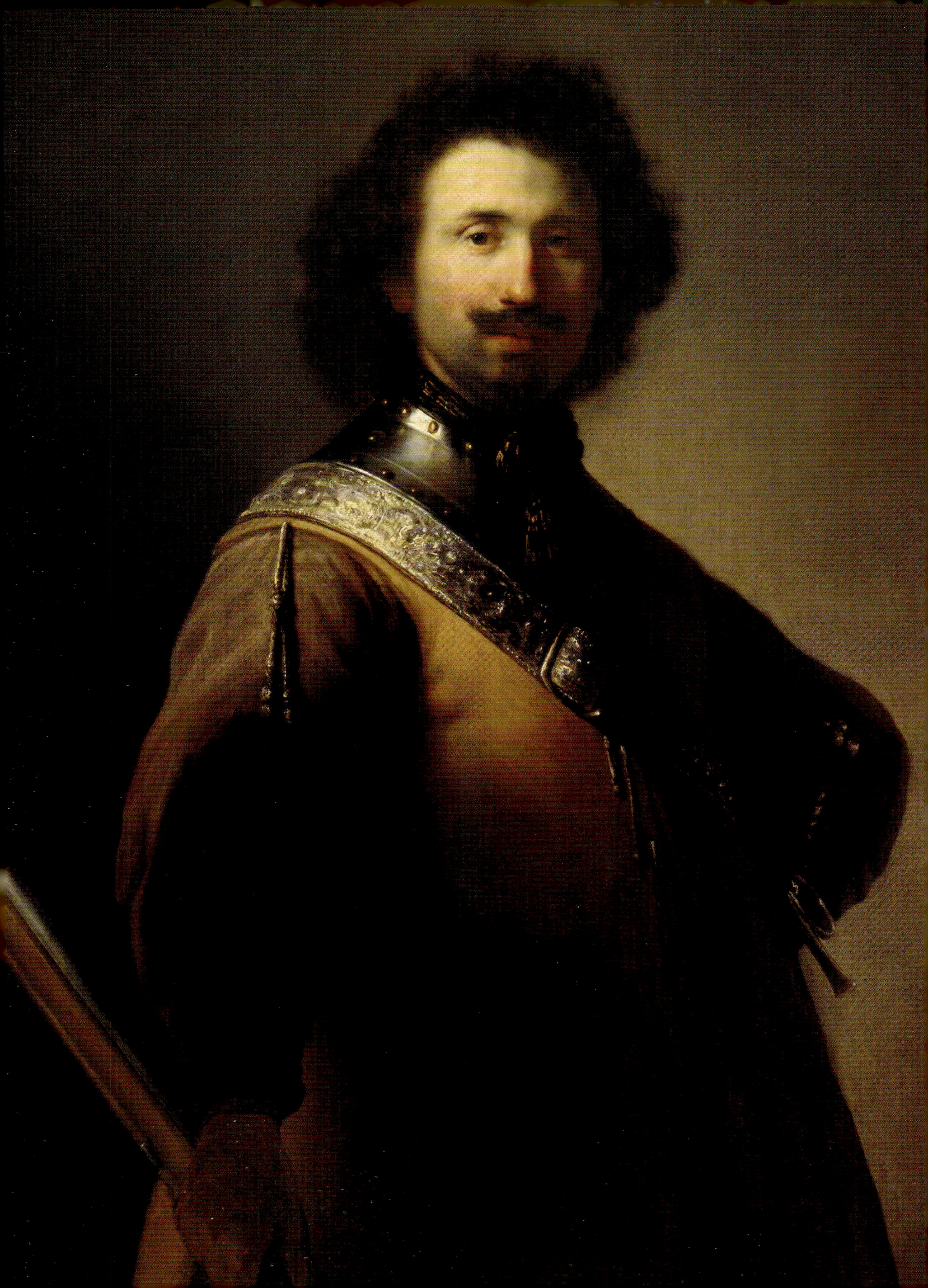

Acknowledgments

American collectors have been fascinated with the myth and reality of Rembrandt and his paintings for well over a century. While their counterparts in the Netherlands, England, France, Germany, and Russia had a decided head start in obtaining his masterpieces, collectors on this side of the Atlantic have, nevertheless, been able to match or in many cases surpass their efforts. Today, between a quarter and a third of Rembrandt's painted oeuvre has found a home in America's public and private collections. Interestingly, an even greater number of pictures previously attributed to the master but no longer accepted by scholars have made their way to our shores since the mid-nineteenth century. Thus, an exhibition devoted to the issues of Rembrandt collecting and connoisseurship in America seems long overdue.

The genesis of the exhibition *Rembrandt in America* began with discussions undertaken with colleagues during a number of CODART (curators of Dutch and Flemish art) meetings and study trips over the years. Recognizing the role played by legendary Rembrandt scholar and American museum pioneer Wilhelm (William) R. Valentiner, we were forced to acknowledge and then question his exceedingly broad acceptance of autograph Rembrandts. More than a half century after his death, Valentiner's controversial attributions still play a role in both Rembrandt connoisseurship and the history of Rembrandt paintings in America.

Rembrandt in America and its accompanying catalogue presented many challenges for its organizers, but we are pleased with the results. While many individuals and institutions are acknowledged below, first and foremost we offer our heartfelt thanks to the private collectors and museums who so generously lent paintings to the exhibition. It is gratifying to realize so many of our colleagues across America embraced the idea of the exhibition and were willing to part with their treasures for nearly a year while the exhibition is shown in Raleigh, Cleveland, and Minneapolis.

Numerous foundations, libraries, and research institutions provided access to resources that were instrumental in supporting the research and funding for the project. They include the research libraries of the National Gallery of Art, the Detroit Institute of Arts, the Philadelphia Museum of Art, the Cleveland Museum of Art, the Sterling and Francine Clark Art Institute, Bowdoin College, the Frick Art Reference Library, and the Rijksbureau voor Kunsthistorische Documentatie in The Hague. The Samuel H. Kress Foundation supported much of our research and has generously contributed to the production of the exhibition catalogue. In Raleigh, a portion of the research was supported by the Andrew W. Mellon Foundation and the Ann and Jim Goodnight fund for curatorial and conservation research and travel. The exhibition was further supported by an indemnity from the Federal Council on the Arts and the Humanities.

Others who have contributed to the success of the project include Jackie Adkins, Lynne Ambrosini, Christopher Apostle, Ronni Baer, Roger Berkowitz, Todd R. Boyette, Tara Cerretani, Ruth Cloudman, Erin Corrales-Diaz, Cynthia Culbert, Laurel Dial, Claudine Dixon, Christopher Etheridge, Jay Fisher, Ivan Gaskell, Sona Johnston, Ronda Kasl, Ian Kennedy, Maria Ketcham, Richard Knight, Friso Lammertse, Alexandra Libby, Walter Liedtke, John Marciari, Mitchell Merling, Otto Naumann, Lawrence Nichols, Lynn Orr, Esmée Quodbach, Richard Rand, Catherine B. Scallen, Scott Schaefer, George T. M. Shackelford, Dominique Surh, Amy Walsh, Arthur Wheelock, John Wilson, David De Witt, Martha Wolff, Stephan Wolohojian, Anne T. Woollett, and Eric Zafran. Thanks also to Barbara J. Bradley at the Cleveland Museum of Art for her masterful editing of the catalogue, as well as to the design and production team at Skira Rizzoli led by Margaret Chace, associate publisher.

Finally, we are grateful to the staff members of the three venues who are presenting *Rembrandt in America*. Both their individual and collective contributions have made the exhibition possible.

At the North Carolina Museum of Art in Raleigh we need to mention Lawrence J. Wheeler, director; Tiara L. Paris, exhibitions manager; Eric Gaard, exhibition designer; Barbara Wiedemann,

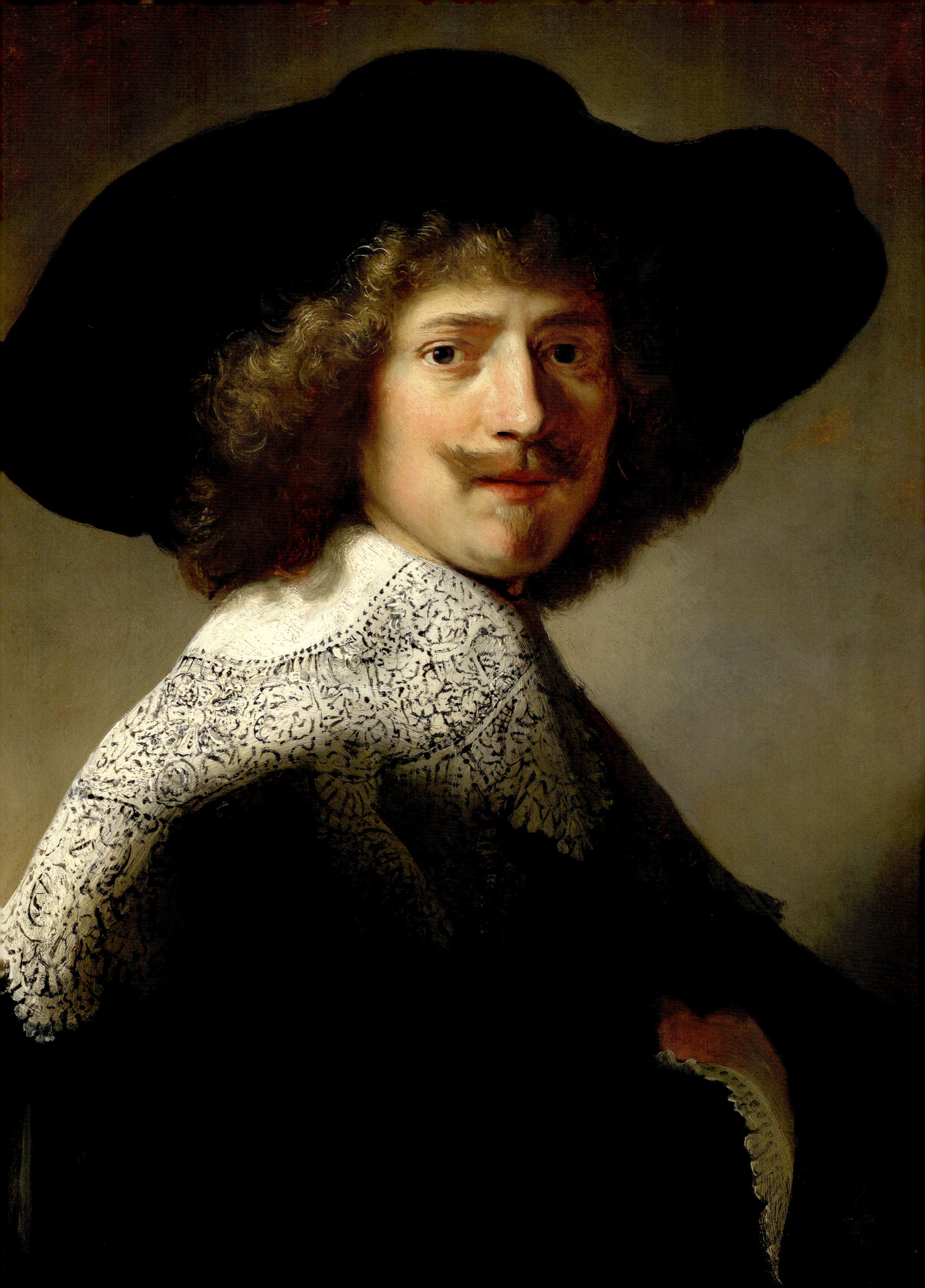

graphic designer; Natalie Lonchyna, chief librarian; Karen Kelly, editor; Maggie Gregory, registrar, and her assistant, Angela Bell-Morris; Tom Lopez, art handler, and his team; Sandy Rusak, head of Education; Melanie Davis-Jones, director of Marketing and Communications; Karen Malinofski, head photographer; and members of our Development Department, led by Ellen Stone.

At the Minneapolis Institute of Arts we wish to acknowledge Kaywin Feldman, director and president; Pat Grazzini, deputy director; Matthew Welch, deputy director and chief curator; Katherine Milton, director of Learning and Innovation; Elizabeth Armstrong, director of CAMP (Center for Alternative Museum Practice); Julianne Amendola, director of Development; Kristin Prestegaard, director of Marketing and Communications and Design and Editorial; Anne-Marie Wagener, director of Public Relations; Elisabeth Brandt, Foundation Relations manager; Sheila McGuire, director of Museum Guide Programs; Susan Jacobsen, director of Public Programs; Garnaette Kuznia, brand communications specialist; Brian Kraft, head of Registration; Jennifer Starbright, associate registrar for Exhibitions; Roxy Ballard, exhibition designer; Jennifer Jurgens, graphic designer for interactive media; Jessica Zubrzycki, graphic designer; Laura DeBiaso, administrator of Curatorial Affairs and Exhibitions; Patrick Noon, Patrick and Aimee Butler Chair of the Paintings Department; and Annika Johnson, research assistant.

At the Cleveland Museum of Art thanks go out to Timothy Rub, director 2006–9, who initially encouraged the project; Deborah Gribbon, the museum's interim director, 2009–10, who supported the show during her tenure; and David Franklin, the museum's current director, who guided the project through its final stages. C. Griffith Mann, deputy director and chief curator, offered his leadership as the project developed; Jon L. Seydl, Paul J. and Edith Ingalls Vignos Jr. Curator of European Painting and Sculpture, 1500–1800, was instrumental throughout; Heidi Strean, director of Exhibitions, shepherded the exhibition and managed the venue negotiations, while Mary Suzor and the staff of Collections Management coordinated and facilitated the loans for Cleveland together with Kim Cook, who also managed the rights and reproductions with the assistance of Jen Hannan. Julia A. Barber provided invaluable research assistance. We appreciate Jeffrey Strean and Jim Engelmann in Architecture and Design for the installation in Cleveland; Marjorie Williams and Caroline Goeser in Education and Public Programs for organizing educational programming; and Betsy Lantz, Louis Adrean, and the staff of Ingalls Library for facilitating library programming.

Other staff members from the Cleveland Museum of Art also deserve mention: June De Phillips and Dana Cowen, in the Department of European and American Art; August Napoli and his Institutional Advancement staff, especially Christina Thoburn and Mary Wheelock; Howard Agriesti, David Brichford, Gary Kirchenbauer, and Bruce Shewitz in Photographic and Imaging Services; Marcia Steele, Dean Yoder, and Eileen Sullivan in Conservation; Mary Thomas, Terra Blue, and Alex Jung in Design; Marty Ackley, Barry Austin, Arthur Beukemann, John Beukemann, Joseph Blaser, Nicholas Gulan, and Tracy Sisson in Collections Management; Robin Roth and the Exhibition Production staff; Cindy Fink, Elizabeth Bolander, and Marketing and Communications staff members; Curatorial Publications staff Jane Takac Panza and Amy Sparks; and Emily Marshall and Sheri Walter in the Exhibitions Office.

GSK, TR, and DPW

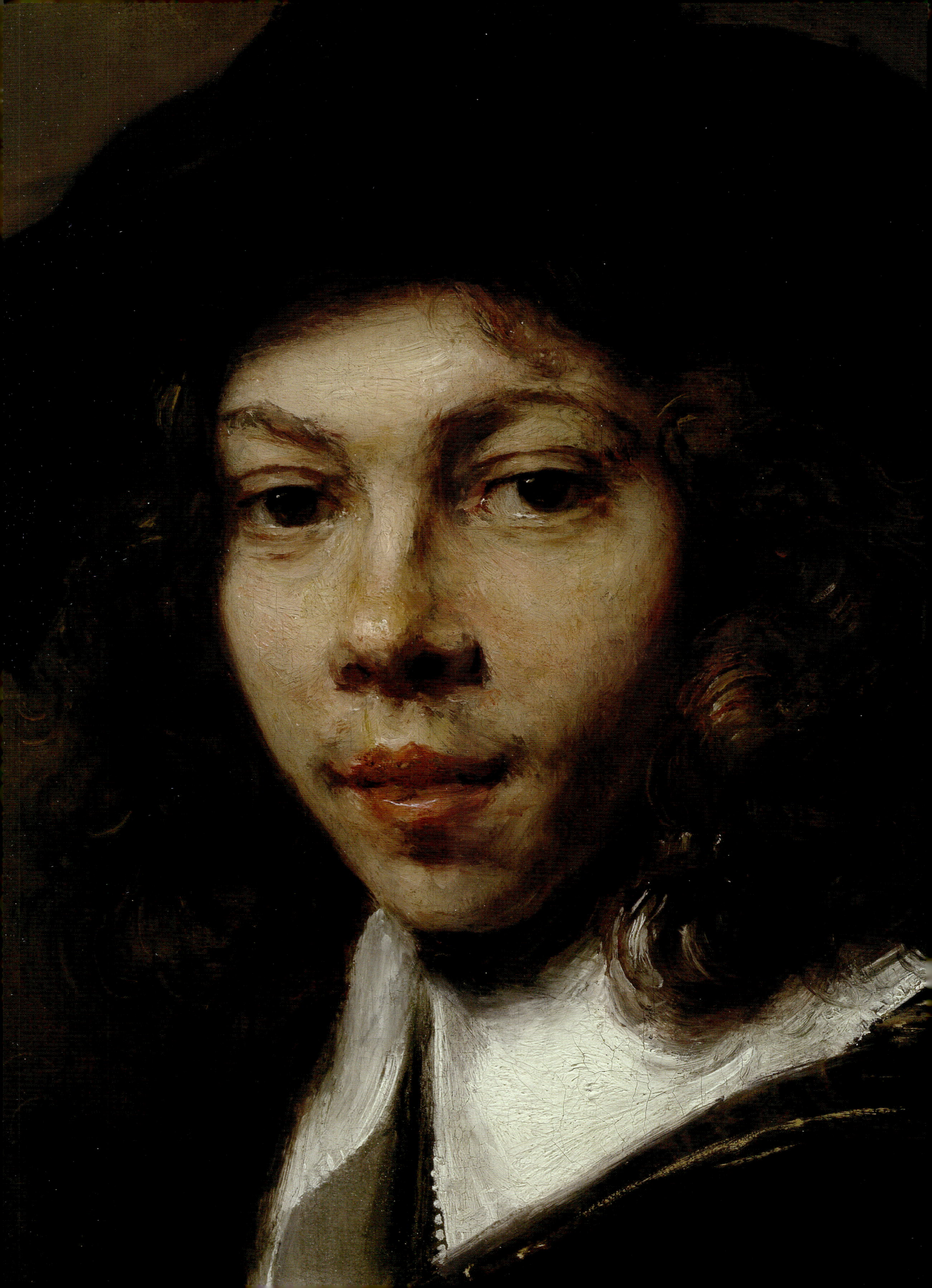

Lenders to the Exhibition

Allentown Art Museum, Pennsylvania
The Armand Hammer Collection, Los Angeles
Baltimore Museum of Art
The Art Institute of Chicago
Collection of Isabel and Alfred Bader, Milwaukee, Wisconsin
The Cleveland Museum of Art
Detroit Institute of Arts
Fine Arts Museums of San Francisco, Legion of Honor
Fogg Art Museum, Harvard University, Cambridge, Massachusetts
Indianapolis Museum of Art
The J. Paul Getty Museum, Los Angeles
The John and Mable Ringling Museum of Art, Sarasota, Florida
Los Angeles County Museum of Art
Memorial Art Gallery, University of Rochester, New York
The Metropolitan Museum of Art, New York
Minneapolis Institute of Arts
Museum Boijmans Van Beuningen, Rotterdam
Museum of Fine Arts, Boston
National Gallery of Art, Washington, D.C.
The Nelson-Atkins Museum of Art, Kansas City, Missouri
North Carolina Museum of Art, Raleigh
Private collection, New York
The San Diego Museum of Art
Shelburne Museum, Vermont
The Sterling and Francine Clark Art Institute, Williamstown, Massachusetts
Timken Museum of Art, San Diego
The Toledo Museum of Art
Wadsworth Atheneum Museum of Art, Hartford, Connecticut

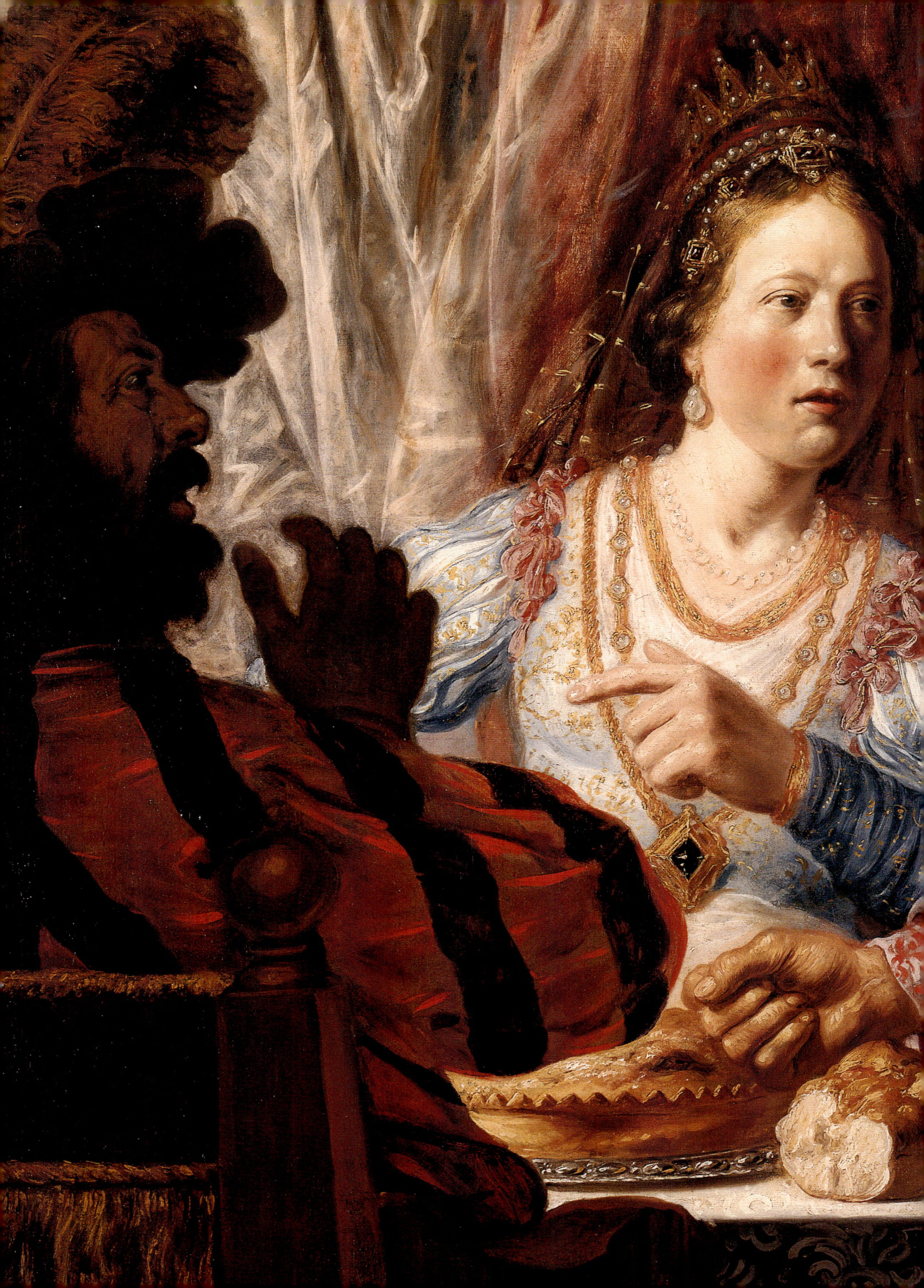

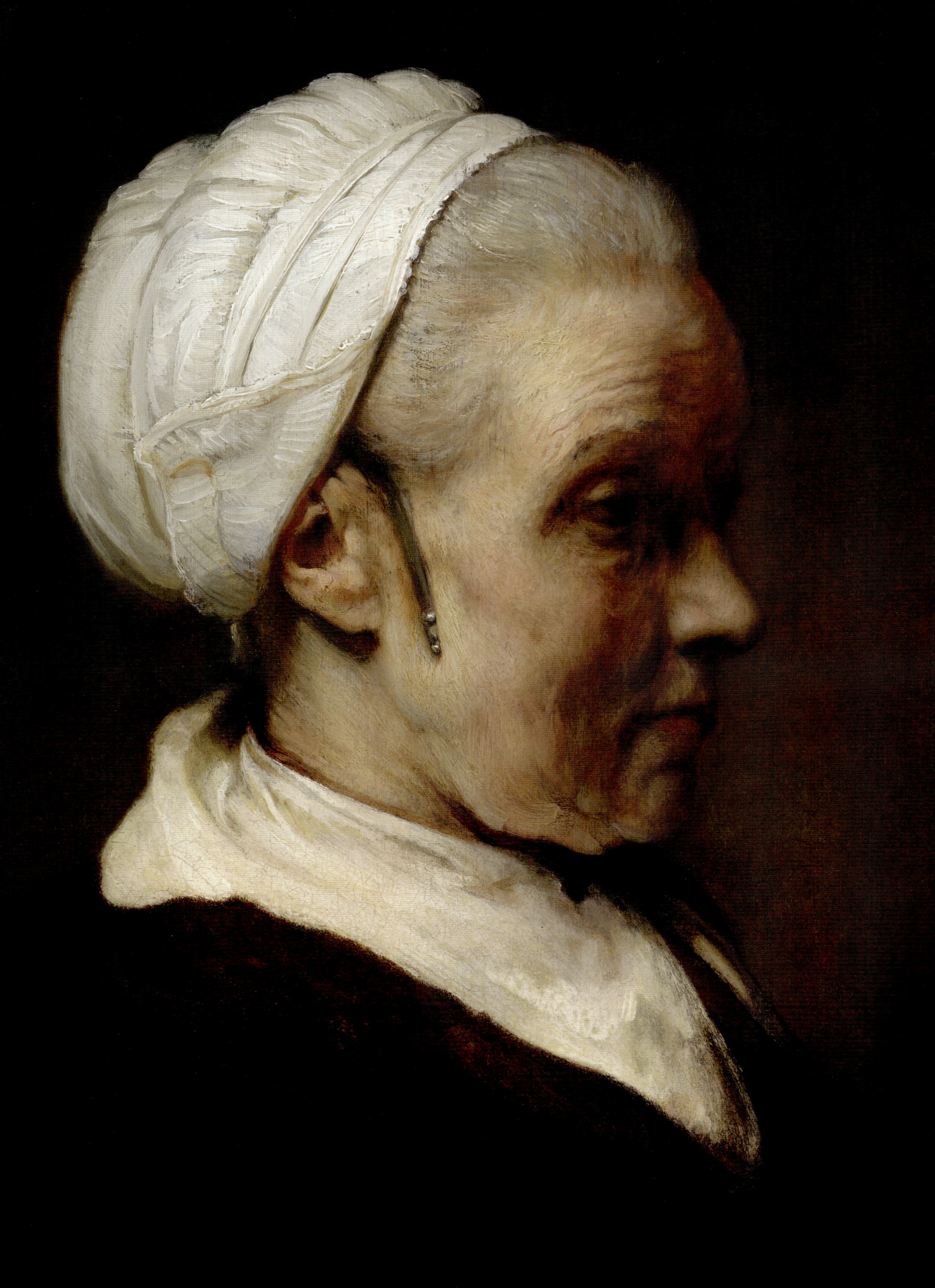

Rembrandt Paintings in America

DENNIS P. WELLER

Eighty years ago, in 1931, the noted scholar and museum director Wilhelm (William) R. Valentiner (FIG. 1) published *Rembrandt Paintings in America*, a compilation of all the known Rembrandt pictures then residing in collections throughout the United States and Canada.[1] This catalogue—large in size and filled with a vast array of paintings—provided readers with a summary of Valentiner's informed, yet flawed, accounting of North America's accumulated share of Rembrandt's painted oeuvre. The 175 so-called Rembrandts illustrated on its pages are certainly unimaginable by current standards, and rightly so. Today, only about one-third of these pictures are generally accepted as autograph works by the master. At the time, however, and in step with the drumbeat of bloated Rembrandt oeuvre catalogues regularly appearing, few dissenting voices would have been heard.[2]

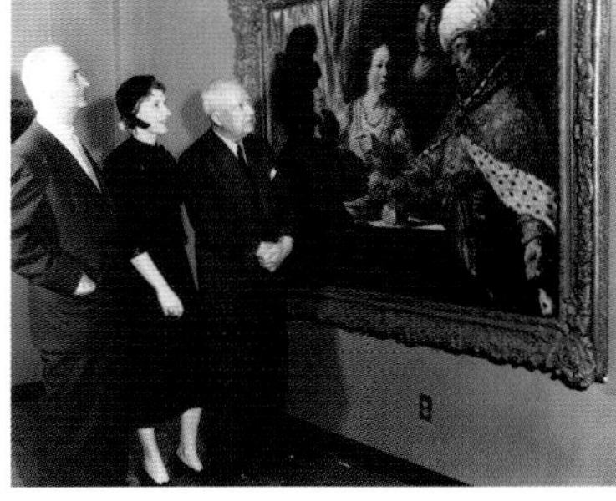
FIG. 1

Valentiner's findings dovetailed with an art world that had become accustomed to newspaper headlines detailing rediscovered Rembrandt pictures with record prices attached to them. America had by then become a significant proving ground for his paintings, for in the decades before the publication of *Rembrandt Paintings in America*, collectors on this side of the Atlantic had fallen in love with both the myth and the genius of Rembrandt and his art. By contrast, the Europeans saw their treasures steaming for New York, Chicago, Philadelphia, and elsewhere, with the power of the dollar virtually unchallenged during the Gilded Age and its aftermath. As Valentiner's book clearly demonstrates, however, the results of this collecting frenzy were mixed at best. Paintings misattributed to Rembrandt had arrived at a rate far higher than his autograph pictures.

Still, by 1931, America could claim an embarrassment of riches of paintings by the master. Soon thereafter, the early and often contentious flow of Rembrandts entering the country would slow to a trickle.[3] As the availability of pictures on the art market slowed and scholars increasingly scrutinized overly ambitious Rembrandt attributions, both private collectors and museums were provided far fewer opportunities to acquire his paintings. The intriguing and often controversial story of the collecting and connoisseurship linked to Rembrandt paintings in America serves as the basis of this exhibition and its accompanying catalogue. By revisiting many of the issues and controversies set forth by Valentiner in *Rembrandt Paintings in America*, the organizers of the current exhibition thought it appropriate to adopt a similar title.

An exhibition is not a book, so while Valentiner had the luxury of illustrating and briefly discussing all the "Rembrandts" then in the United States and Canada, a highly selective approach grounded in reality had to be adopted for potential loans to an exhibition. As with any exhibition, and for a variety of well-justified reasons—loan restrictions, condition problems, theft, and conflicts with other exhibitions—not all loan requests could be approved, or approved for all of the venues.[4] Nevertheless, every effort was made to assemble a remarkably diverse yet representative group of pictures reflecting the issues associated with the collecting and connoisseurship of Rembrandt paintings in America. To achieve the organizers' goals, considering autograph paintings by Rembrandt alongside examples previously but no longer assigned to him was crucial. In doing so, we hope the public will better understand this important chapter in American art collecting and the ongoing controversies linked to "Rembrandt" versus "not Rembrandt."[5]

Many of the questions posed here focus on the who, how much, and when of Rembrandt collecting in America. Fortunately, these issues are answered with a large degree of confidence in the following pages, in particular George Keyes's thoughtful essay "Rembrandt Paintings and America." As a stellar cast of collectors—among them J. Pierpont Morgan, Benjamin Altman, Henry Clay Frick, Isabella Stewart Gardner, Henry O. Havemeyer, Peter A. B. Widener, and Andrew Mellon—flexed their financial muscles (and admittedly their considerable egos), an impressive number of Rembrandt's paintings and their non-Rembrandt counterparts entered the country's private collections beginning in the late nineteenth century.[6]

FIG. 1
W. R. Valentiner (far left) before *The Feast of Esther*, c. 1957. Reprinted by permission of the North Carolina Division of Archives and History and the *News and Observer*, Raleigh

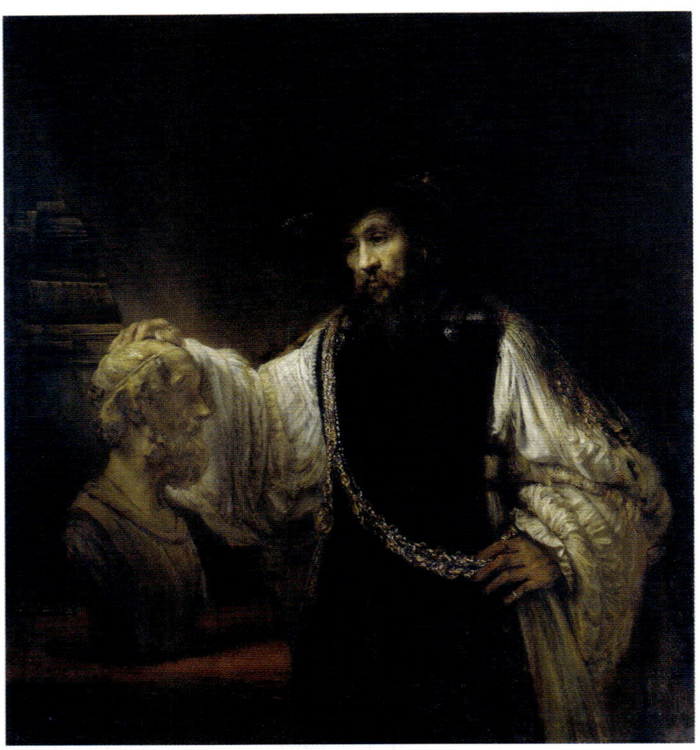

FIG. 2

Over time, and reflecting the generosity and civic spirit of such collectors, the majority of these pictures were bestowed to American art museums. For example, all but one of the Rembrandts at the Metropolitan Museum of Art in New York and the National Gallery of Art in Washington, the two largest collections of the master's paintings in America, came via gift rather than purchase. The only exception was the purchase of *Aristotle with a Bust of Homer* (FIG. 2) now in New York.

In their pursuit of Rembrandt, many of these collectors were willing to pay exorbitant prices for his pictures. While their efforts ultimately represent a story of opportunities taken, it must be stressed that many "mistakes" were made in the overheated and highly competitive market for Rembrandt paintings as it took root in the late nineteenth century. This situation brings us to the exhibition's key questions, which have haunted scholars and collectors for generations: What is a genuine Rembrandt painting and what is not? As experts passed judgments on the authenticity of his works, what issues did they consider?

In making their Rembrandt purchases, collectors had long been dependent on the word of old master art dealers, as well as the opinions of scholars and museum professionals such as William Valentiner. As the twentieth century dawned, Rembrandt oeuvre catalogues were clearly coming into vogue, with their authors competing among themselves in having the "final" say on whether or not a work was painted by Rembrandt. Between the 1880s and the 1920s, for example, catalogues by Wilhelm von Bode, Cornelius Hofstede de Groot, and Valentiner nearly doubled the number of Rembrandt paintings accepted as autograph. Each new discovery seemed to carry a story, as the work in question might represent a previously overlooked example from the painter's misunderstood juvenilia, a forgotten masterpiece rediscovered in an English country house or an eastern European castle, or a painting whose authorship was revealed only after careful examination with the assistance of scientists working in conservation labs, then a discipline still in its infancy.

For example, *The Polish Rider* (FIG. 3) in the Frick Collection was rediscovered by Bode in 1883 and seen by Abraham Bredius a decade later.[7] The painting was wrestled at considerable cost from the collection of Count Tarnowski and his wife, Valérie Stroynowski, of Dzików, in Galicia. It was Roger Fry, the English critic, artist, and at the time curator of paintings at the Metropolitan Museum of Art, who negotiated for its purchase by Henry Frick in 1910.

In hindsight, it has become clear that collectors were regularly ill-served by expansive catalogues now known to be populated with later copies, outright forgeries, and scores of misat-

FIG. 2
Rembrandt van Rijn, *Aristotle with a Bust of Homer*, 1653, oil on canvas, 143.5 x 136.5 cm (56 ½ x 53 ¾ in.). The Metropolitan Museum of Art, New York; Purchase, special contributions and funds given or bequeathed by friends of the Museum, 1961; 61.198

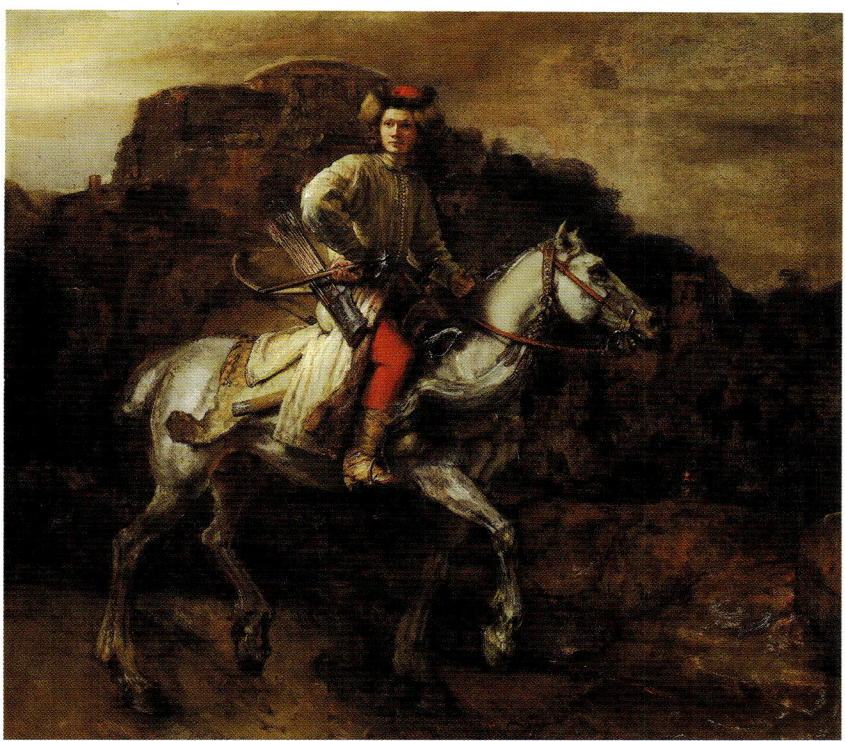

FIG. 3

tributions dating to the seventeenth century. Equally culpable were some of the art dealers who were understandably motivated by financial gain.[8] Building on a largely discredited nineteenth-century Romantic notion of Rembrandt as an isolated, misunderstood genius, late nineteenth- and early twentieth-century cataloguers increasingly loosened the boundaries applied to Rembrandt's range of subject matter and his remarkably complex painting style. As the cult of Rembrandt intensified, collectors were especially drawn to his self-portraits and portraits of his wife and other purported family members.[9]

One such example of Valentiner's penchant for championing images thought to show either the artist or one of his relatives is the *Bust of a Young Man* (see PLATE 22, p. 98), now at the Fogg Art Museum. Serving as the first catalogue entry for his 1930 Detroit Rembrandt exhibition, Valentiner identified the painting as an autograph self-portrait. Today, the picture is considered to have been executed in the style/imitation of Rembrandt, and not a portrait of the painter. In addition, his nuanced and expressive later pictures were highly valued, as many saw in them reminders associated with the artist's increasingly troubled life and waning popularity. Consequently, a century later scholars are still immersed in undoing the misattributions, misinformation, and myth surrounding Rembrandt and his art.

The task of determining the validity of an attribution falls under the inexact science of connoisseurship. A connoisseur is defined as "a person with informed and astute discrimination, especially concerning the arts or matters of taste"; the word comes from the Latin *cognoscere,* to get acquainted with, to know thoroughly.[10] Connoisseurship has long been an essential part of the study of Rembrandt's painted oeuvre, perhaps reaching an early plateau with Abraham Bredius and those experts cited above, continuing with Kurt Bauch and Horst Gerson in the 1960s, the founding of the Rembrandt Research Project (RRP) in 1969, and today with opinions expressed by Ernst van de Wetering and others.

Now, as then, the task has not been easy. Not only does a connoisseur need to recognize Rembrandt's individual stylistic traits, but also the mind-set he brought to his chosen subject matter. Rembrandt was an artist whose stylistic parameters were exceedingly broad, with his paint application typically moving from smooth to thick as his career progressed. In addition, the penetrating psychological insights he brought to both his portrait sitters and narrative subjects, enhanced by his remarkable mastery of light and shadow, while difficult to define, clearly mark his genius. Thus, Rembrandt connoisseurs have been tasked with the nearly

FIG. 3
Rembrandt van Rijn, *The Polish Rider,* c. 1655, oil on canvas, 101 x 151.4 cm (39 3/4 x 59 5/8 in.). The Frick Collection, New York; Henry Clay Frick Bequest; 1910.1.98

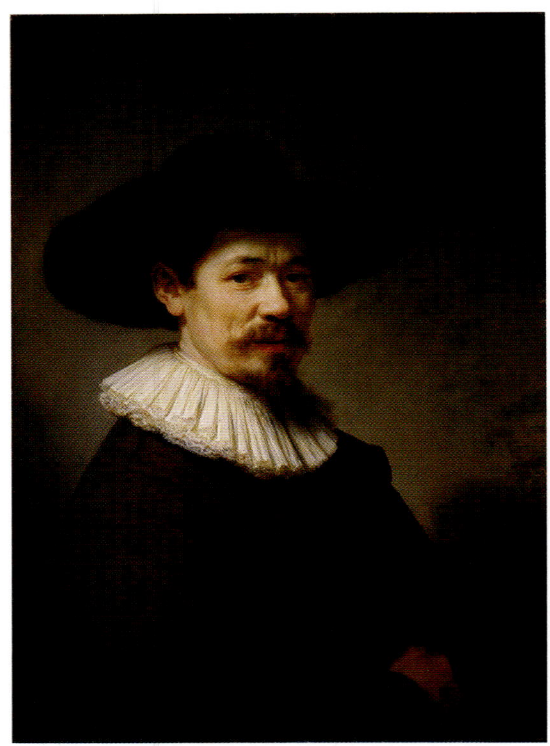

FIG. 4

impossible job of sorting out the master's autograph pictures from those examples produced by members of his workshop and circle, as well as by imitators and forgers.[11] In addition, the condition of a painting can greatly confuse the issue, thus making some Rembrandt attributions nearly impossible to confirm.

Interestingly, questions linked with Rembrandt attributions were not unknown during the painter's lifetime. It was during his activity in Amsterdam, first in the employ of Hendrick Uylenburgh (1584 or 1589–c. 1660) between 1631 and 1635, and then as the master of a large workshop with many pupils, that a Rembrandt brand became established in Holland.[12] Imitations followed, and by 1637, for example, copies of his paintings had already been documented.

Before proceeding with an overview of Rembrandt and his reception in America, the journey begins with a discussion of relevant events in the artist's life that continue to have repercussions today. They include his training, aspirations and fame, workshop practices, and the trials and tribulations of his later years, including the impact of mounting debt. These fascinating topics are among those addressed in Tom Rassieur's two essays in this volume, "Rembrandt in the Seventeenth Century," a biography of the artist, and "Rembrandt's Leiden Years: Mastering His Craft and Defining His Genius," which discusses paintings in this exhibition executed during Rembrandt's activity in his hometown of Leiden.

After the death of Rembrandt in 1669, his reputation briefly suffered as a consequence of the popularity of classicism, a style largely anathema to the doggedly expressive and painterly manner explored by the artist during his last years. Rembrandt's fame did not, however, wane for long. In spite of the best efforts of some early critics, among them Arnold Houbraken (1660–1719) and Gerard de Lairesse (1641–1711), collectors ratcheted up their efforts to acquire Rembrandt pictures in the decades and then centuries that followed.[13] As his paintings left the Dutch republic for their new homes in Russia, France, Germany, and especially England (no noble family could be without a painting by Rembrandt) during the eighteenth and nineteenth centuries, a clear precedent was set for an emerging group of American collectors about to enter the fray just before the turn of the twentieth century.[14] Once these individuals caught the Rembrandt fever, they continued to battle their competitors for decades.

Scores of pictures appeared on the art market, including an impressive array of masterpieces from France, where, to use the words of Alison McQueen, a "cult of Rembrandt" had arisen in the nineteenth century and where a number of factors collided in a perfect storm for

FIG. 4
Rembrandt van Rijn, *Portrait of Herman Doomer*, 1640, oil on panel, 75.2 x 55.2 cm (29 5/8 x 21 3/4 in.). The Metropolitan Museum of Art, New York; H. O. Havemeyer Collection, Bequest of Mrs. H. O. Havemeyer, 1929; 29.100.1. Photo: The Metropolitan Museum of Art/Art Resource, NY

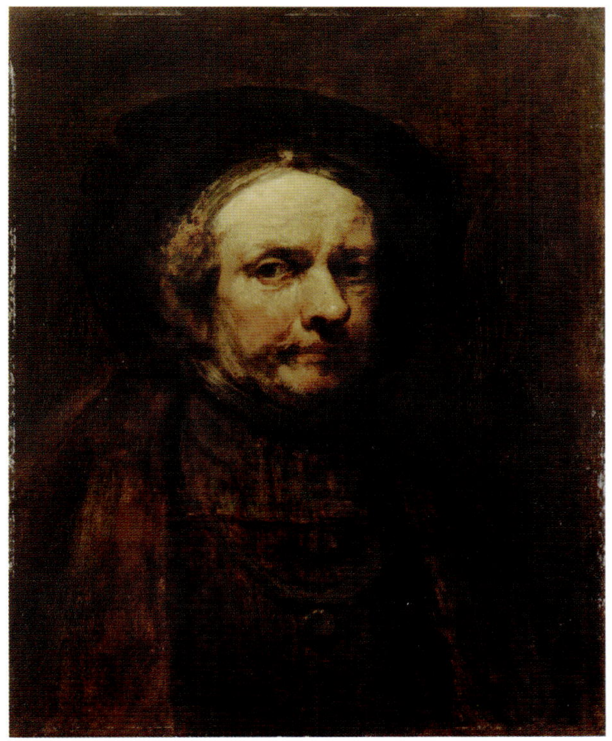

FIG. 5

American collectors.[15] It began with the financial hardships suffered by Europeans following periods of warfare and economic decline. With European collectors in need of cash to continue their lifestyles, wealthy American businessmen were only too happy to trade their Gilded Age dollars for Rembrandt paintings. Once the floodgates opened, American collectors' appetites grew almost exponentially. Newspapers in New York, Chicago, Boston, and even small towns such as Asheville, North Carolina, announced recent Rembrandt purchases in their headlines. At the same time, strong criticism was beginning to come from the Europeans who realized their treasures were crossing the Atlantic at an accelerating rate. The Dutch press, in particular, warned its readers about losing the country's culture.[16]

Rembrandt paintings found new homes with some of the era's greatest American collectors. Many of these individuals will be discussed in the following essays. Esmée Quodbach, who has focused her research on the early Rembrandt arrivals in America, has discovered much new information on the topic.[17] After a number of false starts with incorrectly attributed pictures, she has determined that the *Portrait of Herman Doomer* (FIG. 4) now in New York was the first Rembrandt to come to America. The New York dealer William Schaus purchased the portrait of the Amsterdam frame maker for roughly $42,000 in 1884 (in today's buying power approximately $950,000). Other works by Rembrandt quickly followed, including a handful of significant acquisitions by Henry O. Havemeyer (see PLATES 10, 11, pp. 64, 65).[18] The first autograph history painting by Rembrandt came a number of years later, when Charles T. Yerkes bought *Philemon and Baucis*, now at the National Gallery of Art (see PLATE 41, pp. 150).

Interestingly, the efforts of these and other collectors followed some years after a handful of American painters had already turned to Rembrandt as a source of inspiration for their own art. Asher Brown Durand (1796–1886), for example, while traveling in Europe in 1840, painted on commission a copy (FIG. 5) of Rembrandt's *Self-portrait* at the Uffizi Gallery in Florence. This flurry of copying and collecting eventually coincided with exhibitions devoted to Rembrandt and his paintings, and the previously cited Rembrandt oeuvre catalogues. It should come as no surprise that many of these undertakings were supported by collectors and their dealers, who, in spite of clear conflict of interest, made every effort to have their works included in catalogues and exhibitions.[19]

The uncertainty and controversy surrounding Rembrandt attributions over much of the last century can be directly linked to these initiatives. An exhibition mounted in Amsterdam

FIG. 5
Asher Brown Durand, *Self-portrait* (after Rembrandt), 1840, oil on composition board, 54.9 x 45.7 cm (21 ⅝ x 18 in.). Wadsworth Atheneum Museum of Art, Hartford; Gift of Mr. and Mrs. Frederick Sturges III; 1979.170

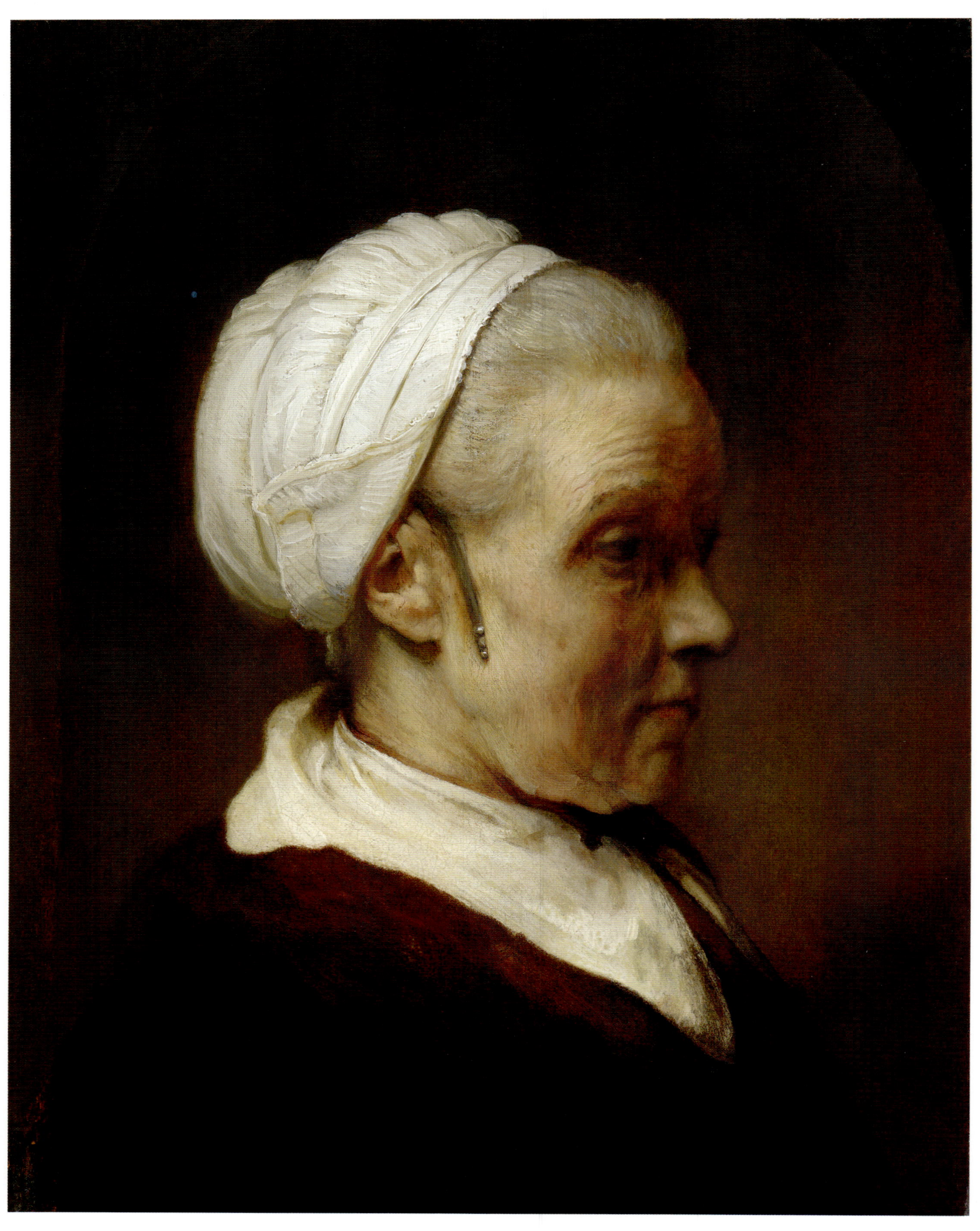

PLATE I [CAT. 26]
Rembrandt van Rijn
Study of an Elderly Woman in a White Cap, c. 1640
Oil on panel, 53.3 x 36.5 cm (21 x 14⅜ in.)
Private collection, New York

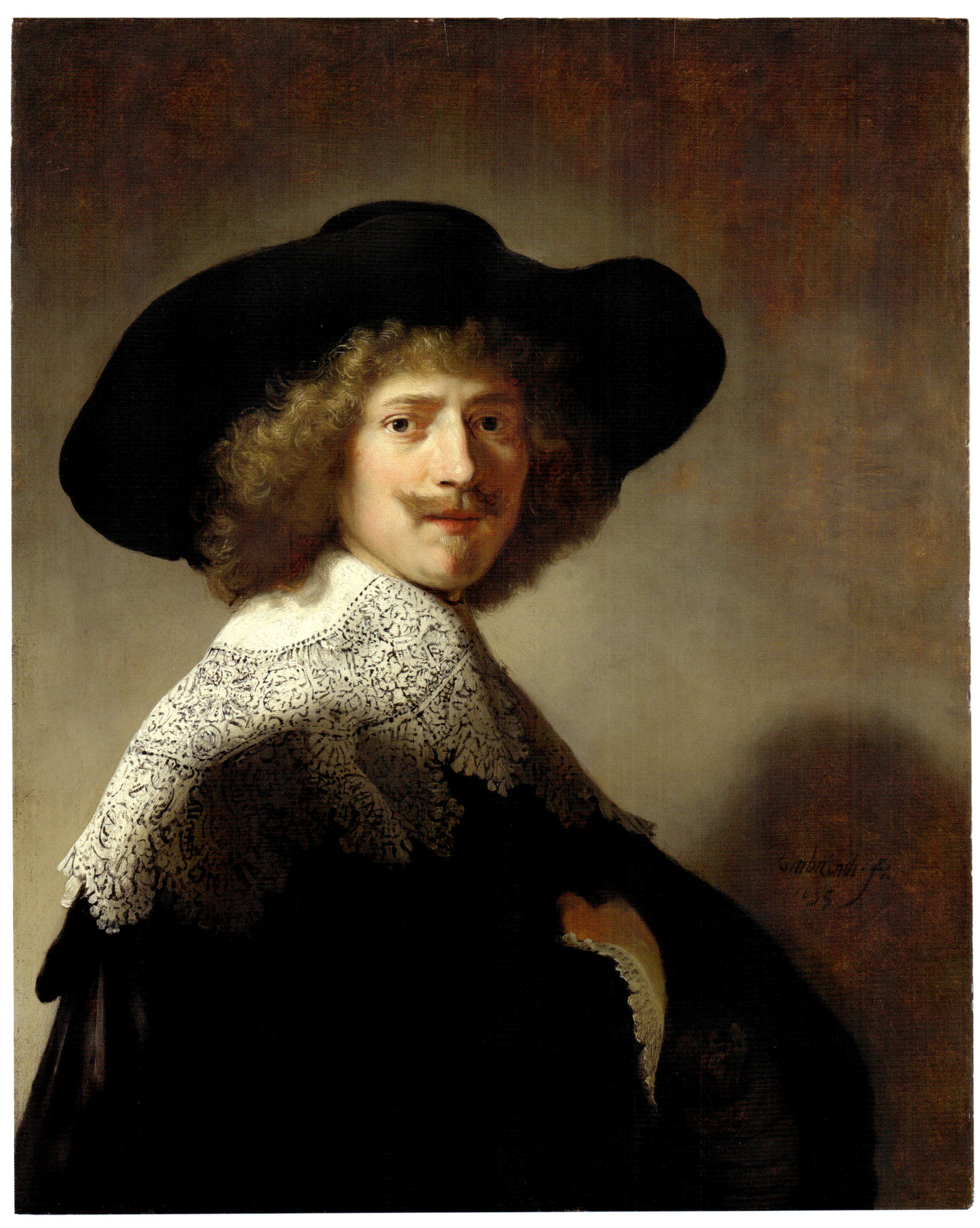

PLATE 2 [CAT. 20]
Rembrandt van Rijn
Portrait of Anthonie Coopal, 1635
Oil on mahogany panel, 83.7 x 67 cm (32 7/8 x 26 3/8 in.)
Private collection, New York

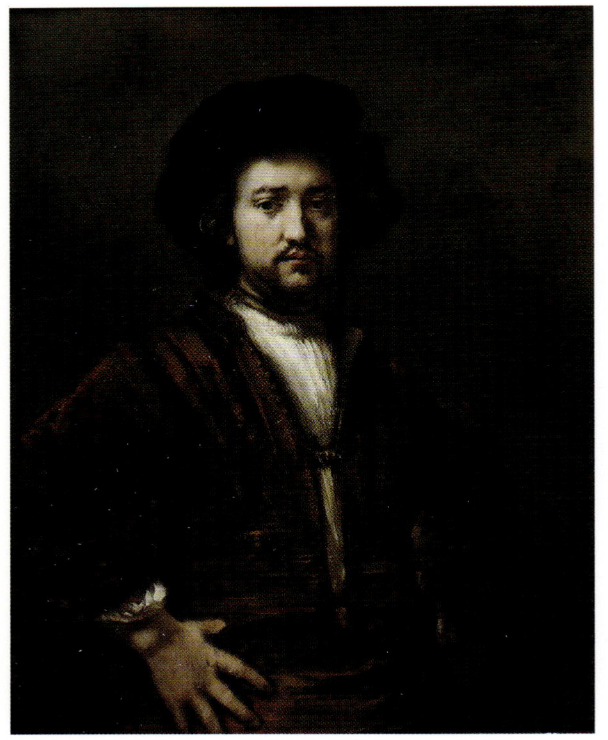

FIG. 6

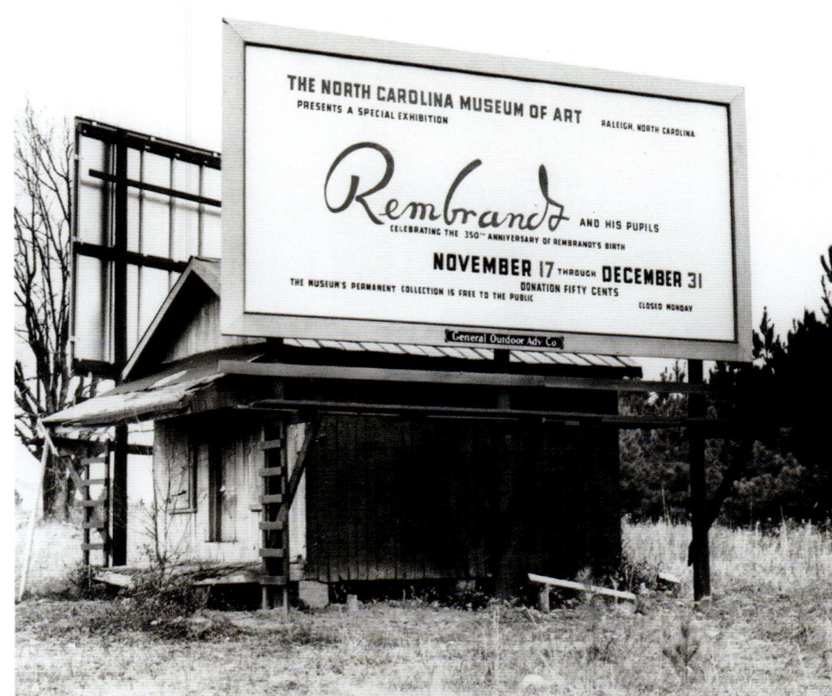

FIG. 7

in 1898, for example, served as an early gauge to the popularity and pollution associated with Rembrandt and his oeuvre during the period. While "never before had so many paintings and drawings by the 'King of Art' been brought together from all over Europe," the show was regrettably filled with more misattributions than masterpieces.[20] The same could be said for an exhibition with a large group of "Rembrandts," *Paintings by Old Dutch Masters,* shown a decade later in New York as part of the city's Hudson-Fulton Celebration.[21] The driving force of arguably the first blockbuster show in America—attendance topped 288,000 between 20 September and 30 November 1909—was none other than William Valentiner, then decorative arts curator at the Metropolitan Museum of Art. Of the thirty-six Rembrandts he included, only fourteen can today reasonably be considered works by the master. Nevertheless, the checklist represents a telling snapshot of the incredibly high aspirations of American collectors up to that time.

During his long and distinguished career, Valentiner would have few equals within the museum and scholarly worlds on this side of the Atlantic. As a curator, connoisseur, consultant, editor, and administrator, he brought an enormous amount of expertise to American collectors and the country's fledgling art institutions. Trained as an art historian in his native Germany, he was groomed by many of the most esteemed connoisseurs of his day there and in the Netherlands. Writing his doctoral thesis on Rembrandt, he returned his focus to the artist often throughout his lifetime.[22] For good and bad, Valentiner eventually became the expert most associated with the expansion of Rembrandt's oeuvre during the first half of the twentieth century. In his defense, however, Valentiner's flawed opinions were largely in line with those of his European colleagues.

Attribution questions, many arising from Valentiner's scholarship, are central to this exhibition and its accompanying catalogue. While the essays treat this issue to varying degrees, George Keyes tackles this controversial and intriguing topic in greater depth in "The Elusive Nature of Portraiture: Rembrandt as a Portraitist in Amsterdam."

Interestingly, ongoing attribution controversies have played a much smaller role in discussions of Rembrandt's history paintings in America, a subject covered in my catalogue essay in this volume. Collectors have understandably shown a far greater interest in his portraits than his biblical and mythological scenes over the decades, in part because of availability on the art market, but also as a consequence of many owners who seemed to have disdained such subject matter. Still, a number of successes can be noted in this area. Specifically, American collectors

FIG. 6
Rembrandt van Rijn, *Portrait of a Man with Arms Akimbo*, 1658, oil on canvas, 107.4 x 87 cm (42 ¼ x 34 ¼ in.) Art market, United States

FIG. 7
Billboard advertising the exhibition *Rembrandt and His Pupils.* Courtesy North Carolina Museum of Art, Raleigh

have shown a marked affinity for Rembrandt's single-figure history compositions, chief among them male saints and female mythological and historical figures.

During the more than one hundred years of acquisitions by American collectors and museums, the Rembrandt landscape has changed significantly with regard to his accepted oeuvre. In other respects, however, the dial has moved very little. Concerned parties are still at the mercy of experts, as pronouncements from a new generation of art historians continue to make headlines. Today, however, researchers are increasingly dependent on the findings of conservators and scientists. As a clearer understanding of the painting methods and materials used by Rembrandt and some of his closest pupils and followers has emerged in recent decades, scholars have dramatically reduced the number of paintings they accept as autograph Rembrandts. Following a period of severe cuts to the painter's oeuvre, a pruning often accompanied by howls of criticism, it seems the pendulum has now started to move in the opposite direction once again.[23]

Among the paintings in the exhibition that have been resuscitated in recent years is the *Self-portrait with Shaded Eyes* (see PLATE 7, p. 44), a work that had been drastically overpainted early in its history and assigned to Govaert Flinck (1615–1660). *Study of an Elderly Woman in a White Cap* (PLATE 1), an informal oil study by Rembrandt, had suffered a similar fate, although the program of overpaint was far less intrusive to Rembrandt's original intent.[24] By contrast, a more traditional connoisseurship question has surrounded another picture from the same collection, *Portrait of Anthonie Coopal* (PLATE 2). Painted on an expensive mahogany panel and displaying stylistic elements typical of Rembrandt's paintings from the mid-1630s, one wonders why some scholars have opted to exclude it from his oeuvre.

Art magazines, newspapers, and now the Internet continue to tout sales of Rembrandt's works, as the record auction price for one of his paintings (FIG. 6) recently reached more than $33 million.[25] Exhibitions of Rembrandt's paintings also continue at a pace even greater than in previous eras. In this arena American museums have made significant contributions, beginning with the 1909 New York exhibition. In the following decades, Rembrandt shows marked each generation's changing view of the artist and his art (see Appendix).

Valentiner retained his position as the unchallenged Rembrandt scholar in America until the years just before his death in 1958. In addition to serving as curator of the Dutch exhibition at the Metropolitan Museum of Art in 1909 and writing *Rembrandt Paintings in America* in 1931, he also organized groundbreaking exhibitions devoted to Rembrandt at museums where he served as director, including one at his last posting in Raleigh (FIG. 7).[26] With his death, the torch was passed to a younger generation of Rembrandt connoisseurs, with Dutch scholars leading the way.

Still, American museums and the scholarly community have continued to make noteworthy contributions to Rembrandt studies in recent decades. Two exhibitions, *Rembrandt after Three Hundred Years* (Chicago, Minneapolis, Detroit) and *Rembrandt and His Pupils* (Montreal and Toronto), distinguished themselves among the worldwide celebrations devoted to Rembrandt during the tercentenary of the artist's death in 1969.[27] One can argue that these shows were surpassed only by an exhibition held at the Rijksmuseum during the same year. The introduction to the catalogue that accompanied the Amsterdam show provides a glimpse of how Rembrandt was viewed on both sides of the Atlantic three hundred years after his passing.

> There is a lot of activity around and about Rembrandt these days. Newspapers talk of iconoclastic attitudes towards his work and of a new, sober appreciation of his personal life. He did not paint quite as much as we had thought, he was neither quite so poor nor so misunderstood; he did not behave all that well towards his housekeeper. And with all this and because of it, he has become one of the topics of the hour. For which other historical figure, artist or no, gets such headlines in the papers or unleashes such controversy as he does? He is in the public eye, the focus of discussion, the object of critical investigation. All the excitement around him goes to show how much of a presence he still is in the world and how much he still means to us today.[28]

As we fast-forward from 1969 to 2006, the date of the four hundredth anniversary of the painter's birth, another celebration of Rembrandt and his vast accomplishments again captured the attention of the public through scores of articles, books, exhibitions, and compact disks showing his works. The tenor of the quote cited above still held true, but much, in fact, had changed. Expert opinions offered by Valentiner and the early cataloguers of Rembrandt's oeuvre were becoming an art historical distant memory. More important, the significant percentage of misattributed Rembrandts embedded in the exhibitions of 1969 fell dramatically by 2006, a reality owing largely to the opinions of the Rembrandt Research Project.[29]

With the afterglow of these most recent celebrations now fading, and many decades before the next anniversary year comes around in 2069, one wonders how Rembrandt and his art will be viewed decades from now. Will the shifting sands of connoisseurship remain a contentious issue, or will most of the long-simmering controversies finally be laid to rest, perhaps owing to new breakthroughs in conservation science? Will a single voice exert his or her authority on the issue as Valentiner did a century ago?

Equally intriguing is whether future generations, in hearing the name Rembrandt, will think first of a toothpaste or art supplies, rather than the painter and his remarkable paintings, prints, and drawings. Will there be private collectors of Rembrandt paintings in fifty years or one hundred years, or are we to assume that most if not all his accepted works will have found homes in public museums? Finally, are there any undiscovered Rembrandt paintings still lurking in the attics of manor houses, in museum storage bins, or under layers of overpaint? Interesting questions all, but well beyond the snapshot of the past and present provided in *Rembrandt in America*.

NOTES

1 Valentiner 1931. While the vast majority of the following discussions regarding collecting in America focus on the United States, collections in Canada also play a role in this topic. Valentiner (1931), for example, cites three Canadian private collections with Rembrandts, one in Montreal and two in Toronto. Since then a small number of autograph works by Rembrandt have entered some of Canada's museums.

2 For example, between 1883 and 1923, eight catalogues devoted to Rembrandt's paintings appeared in print. The number of pictures included in them ranged from 377 by Bode (1883) to Valentiner's (1923) count of 714. For a graphic listing of these catalogues and their numerical contents, see Schwartz 2006, pp. 14–15.

3 Some readers may find it surprising that not all the Rembrandt paintings crossing the Atlantic between the late 1880s and the present remained in America. One such example is included in the exhibition, a loan from Rotterdam (see plate 42); others are discussed elsewhere in this volume.

4 For example, there are loan restrictions for paintings from the Frick Collection in New York and the Benjamin Altman Collection at the Metropolitan Museum of Art. In addition, most readers are well aware of the theft of Mrs. Gardner's pictures from the Isabella Stewart Gardner Museum in 1990.

5 Many of these same issues, but limited to the Rembrandt holdings at the Metropolitan Museum of Art, prompted the excellent exhibition, with accompanying catalogues by Hubert von Sonnenburg and Walter Liedtke, *Rembrandt/Not Rembrandt* (1995).

6 These collectors and their often insatiable appetites for Rembrandts have been the topic of a number of studies. Among them is the discussion by Nancy T. Minty (2008). Also see Liedtke in The Hague and San Francisco 1990, esp. pp. 31–54.

7 Catherine Scallen (2004, pp. 130–32) traces the story of Bode and Bredius's thrilling rediscovery of the painting. Considered a major new addition to Rembrandt's oeuvre at the time, it was brought to the attention of a larger audience when included in the 1898 exhibition of his works in Amsterdam. The attribution to Rembrandt is now rejected by many Rembrandt scholars.

8 Perhaps the most despicable of the dealers was Leo Nardus, who sold scores of "copies, fakes, or comparatively minor works incorrectly attributed" to Rembrandt and others to Peter A. B. Widener. Jonathan Lopez recently wrote of the misdeeds perpetrated by Nardus (Lopez 2007; quote p. 76).

9 As his many publications on Rembrandt's portraits suggest, Valentiner seems to have been particularly adept in "identifying" Rembrandt family members.

10 *The American Heritage Dictionary of the English Language*, ed. William Morris (Boston, 1981), pp. 282–83.

11 The enormity of the task is demonstrated by the vast number of pictures that fall into all these categories. Headway in sorting out some of the "hands" has occurred in the previous years and decades. Werner Sumowski (1983) attempted the broadest overview of this material in the six volumes he published on the paintings of the Rembrandt School.

12 For an excellent discussion of the business connections between Rembrandt and Uylenburgh, see London and Amsterdam 2006, esp. pp. 126–60.

13 Houbraken 1718–21 (2nd ed. 1753); De Lairesse 1707 (2nd ed. 1740).

14 For an overview of Rembrandt in England during the eighteenth century, see New Haven 1983.

15 McQueen 2003.

16 See Edwin Buijsen, "The Battle against the Dollar: The Dutch Reaction to American Collecting in the Period from 1900 to 1914," pp. 60–78, in The Hague and San Francisco 1990.

17 Quodbach 2004–5.

18 In fact, the Doomer portrait may have lost the race to America. A year earlier, in 1883, the New Yorker Henry Marquand had acquired *Portrait of a Man* (now at the Metropolitan Museum of Art), a damaged work whose attribution to Rembrandt has not been universally accepted. Liedtke (2007, 2: no. 155, pp. 676) acknowledges the picture's shortcomings but does accept it as Rembrandt.

19 For example, Wilhelm von Bode's eight-volume catalogue of Rembrandt's paintings (Bode 1897–1906) was partially underwritten by the Paris dealer Jacques Sedelmeyer, who during the course of his career had seen approximately one hundred "Rembrandts" pass through his gallery.

20 Taken from Thiel 1992 (p. 123), summarizing his study on the Amsterdam exhibition of 1898 (Amsterdam 1898).

21 New York 1909.

22 His thesis was entitled *Rembrandt und seine Umgebung* [Rembrandt and his environment]. For a biography of Valentiner, see Sterne 1980.

23 The original members of the Rembrandt Research Project had projected a Rembrandt oeuvre of roughly 250 paintings. Ernst van de Wetering, the only original member still working on the project, has expanded the corpus by accepting some works that previously had been rejected. For a discussion of his working methods, see Corpus 2005 and Wetering 1997. The RRP will end with the forthcoming publication of a summary volume reproducing all 320 paintings that in the opinion of Ernst van de Wetering are by Rembrandt.

24 For illustrations of the various stages of the removal of the overpaint in each of the paintings, see Wetering 2008, pp. 211–13. See also the discussion in Rassieur's essay "Rembrandt in the Seventeenth Century" in this volume, p. 43, fig. 14.

25 Sale, Christie's, London, 8 December 2009, lot 12. The painting sold to an American private collector, having been in another American private collection for four decades before the sale. It first came to New York in 1931, and between 1958 and 1974 resided at Columbia University, New York, a gift from George Huntington Hartford II.

26 Detroit 1930; Los Angeles 1947; and Raleigh 1956.

27 Chicago 1969; Montreal and Toronto 1969. See also Chicago 1973, a published record of a symposium that took place in Chicago, 22–24 October 1969, on the occasion of *Rembrandt after Three Hundred Years*.

28 P. J. J. van Thiel (p. 9) in Amsterdam 1969.

29 See Corpus 1982–89, Corpus 2005, and Corpus 2010. In addition, but on a smaller scale, the approach taken by Hubert von Sonnenburg and Walter Liedtke in *Rembrandt/Not Rembrandt* (New York 1995) provided a remarkably instructive examination of attribution issues attached to Rembrandt paintings at the Metropolitan Museum of Art.

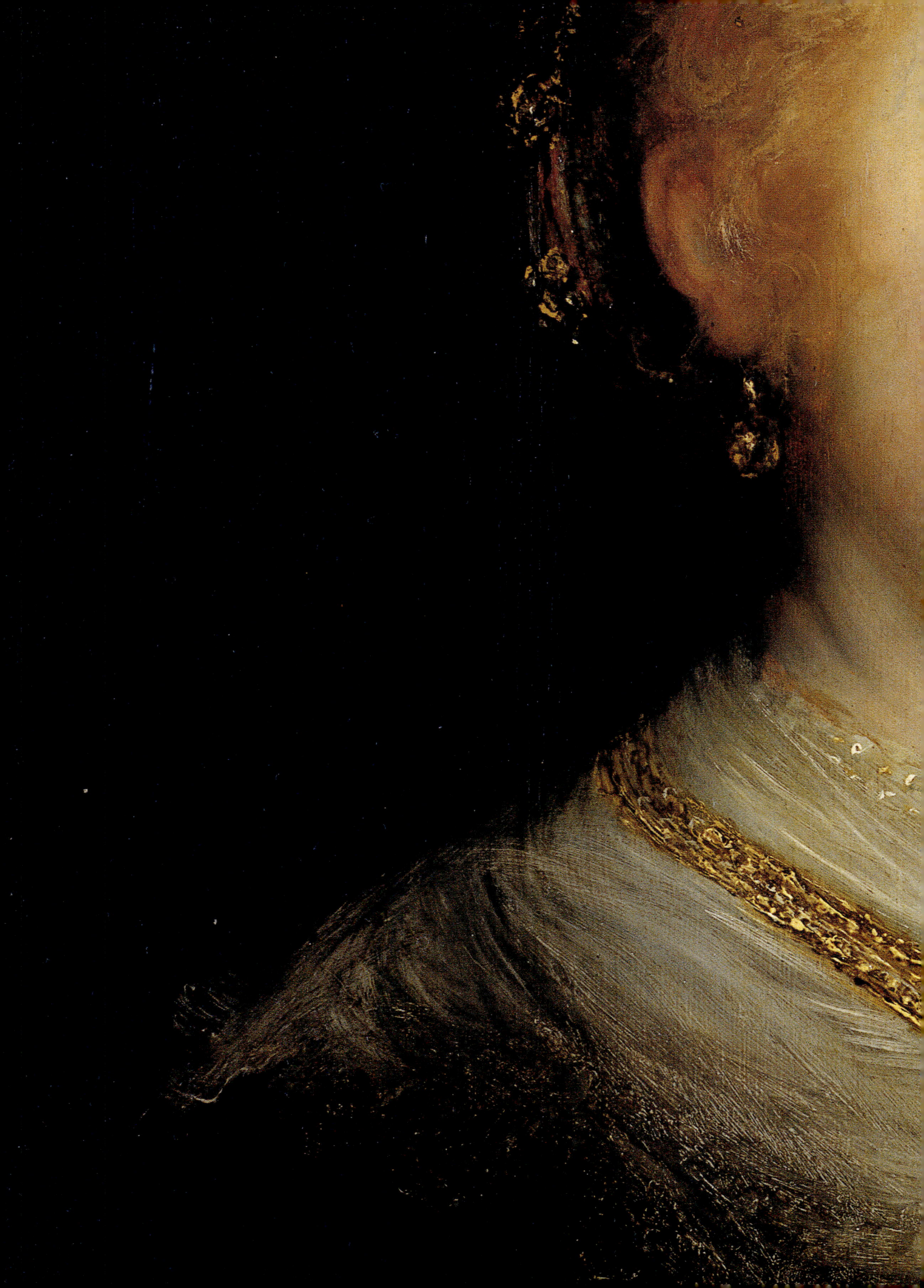

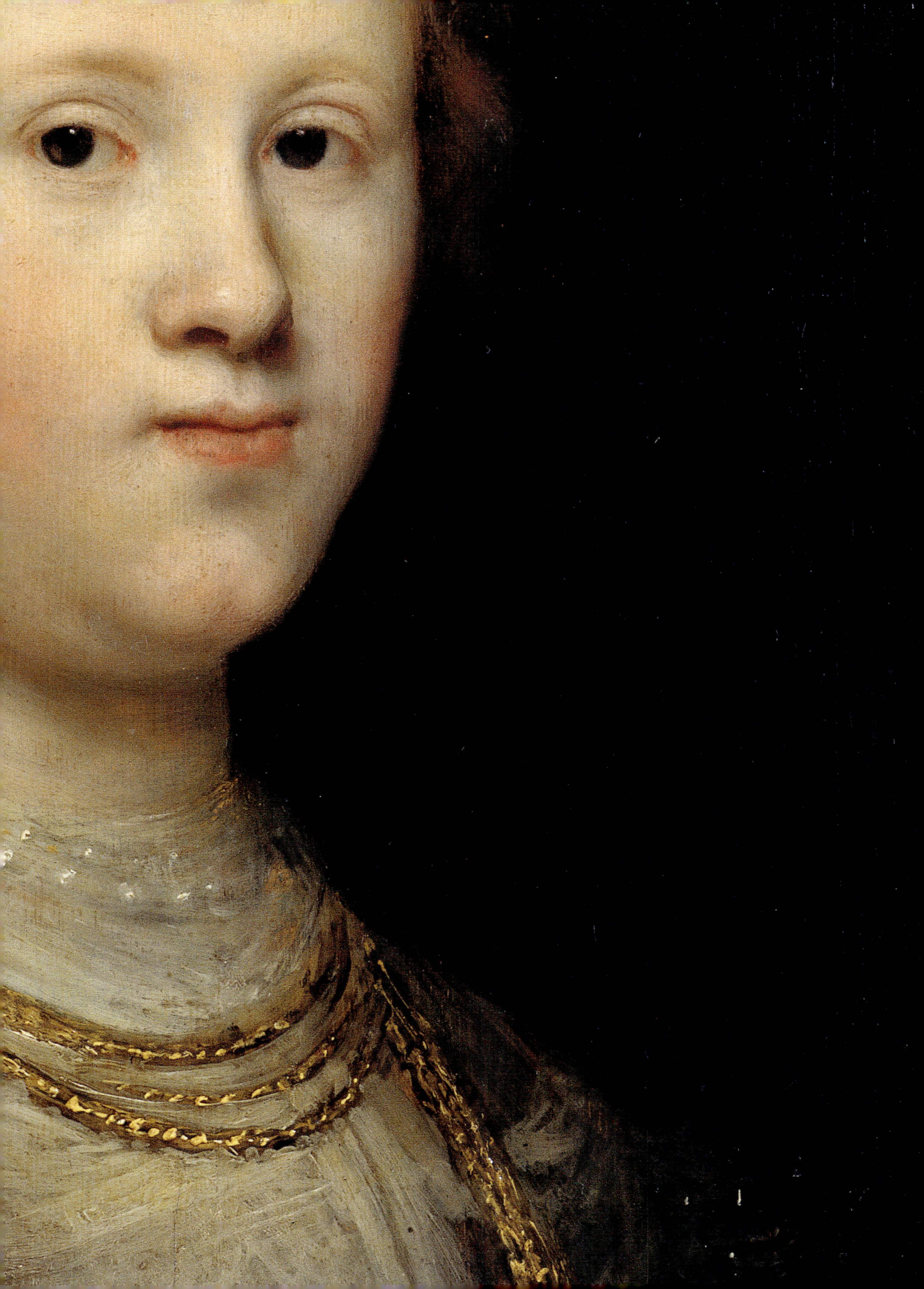

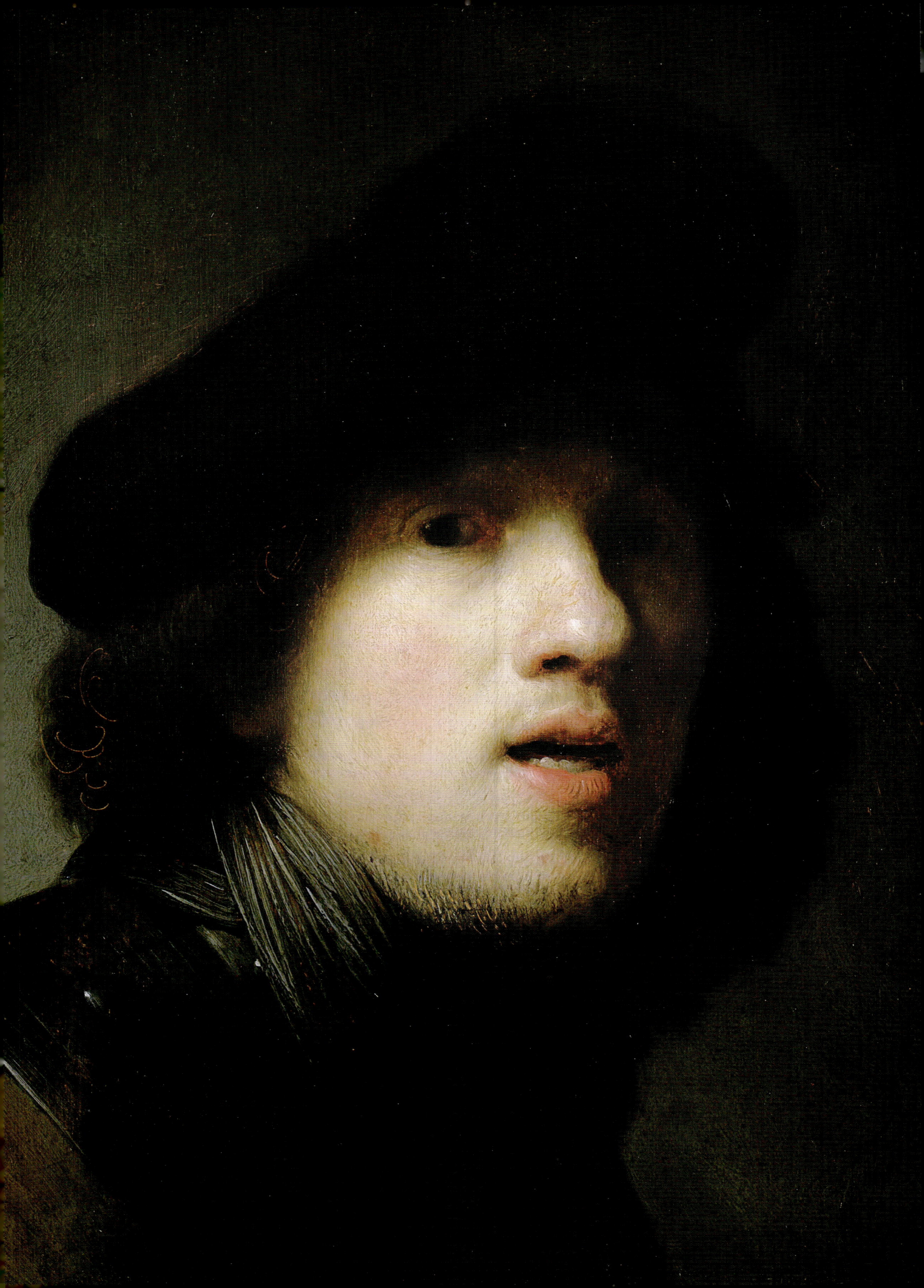

Rembrandt in the Seventeenth Century

TOM RASSIEUR

For a seventeenth-century artist, Rembrandt's life is unusually well documented, yet defining the boundaries of his painted output has proven quite difficult. Rembrandt has come to hold almost mythical status in American culture. His name has become a synonym for excellence, and American collectors, both individual and institutional, have eagerly sought to acquire his works. The results have been checkered. Dozens of paintings once believed to be by his hand have been reassigned to other artists or simply placed in the limbo of unidentified authorship. The situation can be a source of contention, embarrassment, anxiety, and occasionally opportunity.

This biography is intended to address the simple question, "If Rembrandt was such a genius, why is it so hard to tell which paintings are his?" That challenge is valid and prompts an exploration of fundamental aspects of Rembrandt's life that continue to have repercussions today: his training, his aspirations, his teaching, his fame, his bankruptcy, and the trials of his later years.[1] At each stage of his working life, new complications planted the seeds of confusion. While many aspects of Rembrandt's life were not unusual for his time, his enormous talent created exceptional incentives to imitate his work as well as unusually wide-ranging opportunities to do so.

Rembrandt was born in the town of Leiden on 15 July 1606. His father, Harmen, owned a windmill on the opposite bank of the Rhine River, hence the boy's full name Rembrandt Harmenszoon van Rijn. He attended Latin school until he was about thirteen years old. In 1620, he matriculated at the University of Leiden, but he appears not to have pursued his studies. Instead, he served a three-year apprenticeship with local artist Jacob Isaacsz. van Swanenburgh (c. 1571–1638), who, had he not been Rembrandt's first teacher, would probably now be a largely forgotten painter of dramatically illuminated hell scenes, townscapes, and portraits. Though a few of his hell scenes remain, none of Van Swanenburgh's townscapes and portraits have been identified.[2]

As Van Swanenburgh's pupil, Rembrandt would have learned the many disciplines required to move from raw materials to finished painting. In broad terms, the tutelage included the preparation of materials, the establishment of a composition, and the application of paint, with each of these procedures encompassing countless details. What may have been remarkable about Rembrandt's encounter with Van Swanenburgh is the training that he would have received in the expressive use of light and dark. Though Rembrandt would far surpass the sophistication of his teacher's efforts in this realm, the painter of hell scenes may have provided the underpinnings of his student's later achievements.

As part of his training, Rembrandt may have been called on to make copies or variants of Van Swanenburgh's paintings. He may even have participated in the painting of some pictures that were marketed as his teacher's work, as such practices were common at the time. Unfortunately, none of these possible "collaborations" have been identified. Certainly Rembrandt went on to assign such duties to his own students in his role as a teacher.

Among the earliest identifiable paintings by Rembrandt is *The Operation (Touch)* (see PLATE 19, p. 91), an allegory of the sense of touch from a series devoted to the five senses. This candlelit scene features not only sharp contrasts between light and dark but also the effect of light on translucent material such as wax and skin, glancing highlights on metallic surfaces, and the variability of light on soft materials such as cloth and fur. From this early exercise, we might surmise that Van Swanenburgh planted in Rembrandt seeds of interest that would flourish beyond all expectation in the coming years.

A less obvious influence the older artist may have had on his young apprentice was his attitude toward art and his avenues of inspiration. Van Swanenburgh, it should be noted, had spent twenty-four years in Italy. He probably told Rembrandt of the artistic wonders he had seen there and may also have shown him Italian paintings, sculptures, drawings, and especially prints. Throughout his maturity Rembrandt continually borrowed ideas from Italian art, usually refashioning what he found into his own unique creations.[3]

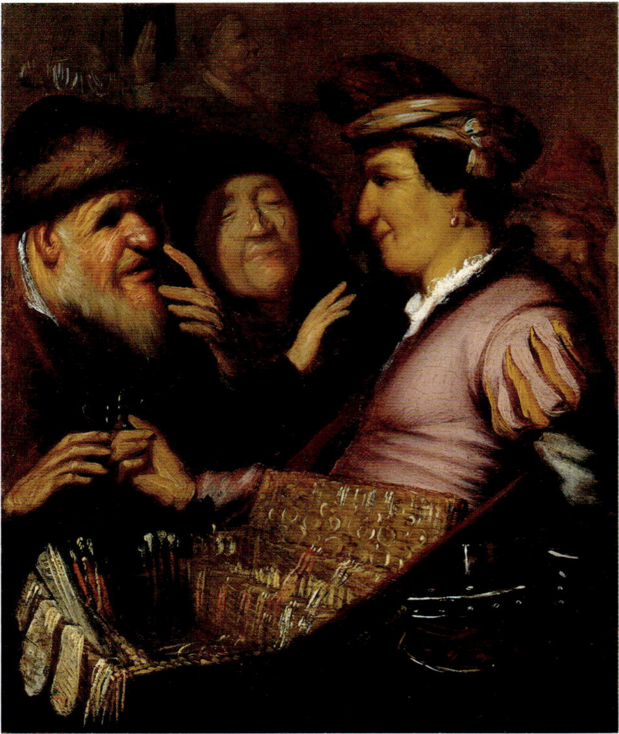

FIG. 8

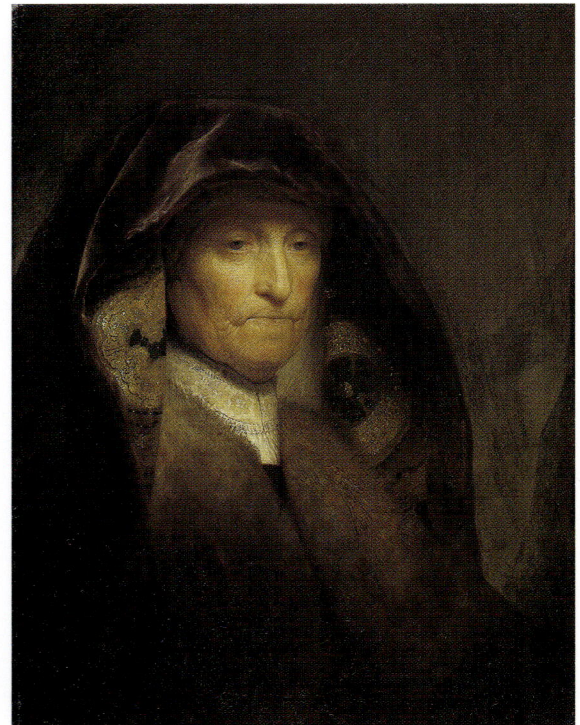

FIG. 9

Jan Lievens (1607–1674), also from Leiden, was another major figure in Rembrandt's early life.[4] Though younger than Rembrandt, he began painting earlier and developed his talents sooner. He began his apprenticeship with a local painter at the age of eight and two years later moved to Amsterdam for further training in the studio of the renowned Pieter Lastman (1583–1633). Lastman specialized in the prestigious field of history painting—meaning that he produced complex, multifigural scenes derived from historical, biblical, and mythological tales. Lievens stayed with Lastman for about two years before returning to Leiden, where he established himself as an independent master in 1621.

What was Rembrandt to make of this? The younger Lievens had set himself up as a master when Rembrandt had only one year of apprenticeship under his belt. We know Rembrandt had his eye on Lievens, for at least one painting in Rembrandt's series The Five Senses (FIG. 8) contains direct borrowings from a much more accomplished painting by Lievens.[5] Moreover, as soon as Rembrandt had served his time with Van Swanenburgh, he too went to Amsterdam to study with Lastman.

Pieter Lastman has long been portrayed as the primary formative influence on Rembrandt. The relationship has recently been called into question, for Rembrandt stayed in Amsterdam only six months and the paintings that he produced shortly thereafter can be interpreted as direct critiques of both Lastman's technique and his compositions. Yet, it would be wrong to say that Rembrandt got nothing from Lastman. Like Van Swanenburgh, Lastman had been to Italy and could convey to his young pupil what he had absorbed there. His compositions, though ultimately unsatisfactory to Rembrandt, had narrative and visual coherency far beyond the productions of Van Swanenburgh. Such works proved to be an enormous stimulus to Rembrandt.[6] The paintings that Rembrandt produced shortly after having been with Lastman were vastly superior to the few believed to have been created before.

Interestingly, no painting made by Rembrandt while working in Lastman's shop has come to light. Could Rembrandt imitate his master so well that we cannot detect the hand of the student? For many years, Rembrandt would return to Lastman's paintings for use as points of departure in his own work.

By about 1625, Rembrandt was back in Leiden, at last an independent master. We do not know why he cut short his time with Lastman. Had he learned all he could from him? Were there family matters that drew him home? Did he want to pull even with Lievens, who had taken

FIG. 8
Rembrandt van Rijn, *The Spectacles Peddler (Sight)*, c. 1624–25, oil on panel, 21 x 17.8 cm (8¼ x 7 in.). Private collection

FIG. 9
Jan Lievens or Rembrandt van Rijn, *Portrait of an Old Woman (Rembrandt's Mother)*, c. 1630–31, oil on panel, 61 x 47.4 cm (24 x 18⅝ in.). English Royal Collection, Windsor Castle; RCIN 405000

such a prodigious lead? In any case, Rembrandt and Lievens developed what appears to have been a friendly rivalry. Because they depicted one another and often shared models, it is possible that they also shared studio space. And here the great confusion begins. Though hindsight tells us that Rembrandt was the genius, Lievens was the more experienced of the two artists. They shared the experience of Lastman's example, and they could look over one another's shoulders to share and steal ideas. The subjects of their paintings were often the same. Their materials were the same.

In time, the two young painters attracted attention. Chief among them was Constantijn Huygens, the polymathic secretary to Prince Frederik Hendrik, who paid them a visit. Not only did this connection later lead to important commissions for Rembrandt, but it also resulted in a lengthy account in which Huygens took the measure of the two artists.[7] He noted their industry—even worrying that their unstinting labors would ruin their health. He saw in Lievens a greater degree of bravura showmanship, a desire to make large, elaborate paintings. In Rembrandt he saw a streak of intense perfectionism that sought and achieved in small works a degree of expressiveness that exceeded that found even in vastly larger paintings. Huygens urged them to go to Italy to study the wonders of ancient and Renaissance art, but they replied that they had too little time and could in any case see all that Italy had to offer right there in Holland.

To a degree they were right, for their teachers had shown the two that they could learn a great deal from prints, drawings, and paintings (all of which Rembrandt went on to collect), and since Amsterdam was the hub of the European art market, they could see major paintings that came up for auction. Years later, for instance, Rembrandt witnessed the sale of an exquisite portrait by Raphael. On that occasion, he sketched its appearance and noted—perhaps with a touch of envy—its enormous price and then proceeded to make two self-portraits modeled on the Renaissance masterpiece.[8]

Paintings by Rembrandt and Lievens were so close in style and substance that their authorship quickly became confused. A 1632 inventory of Frederik Hendrik's collection lists two paintings that had been executed just a year or two earlier as being the work of Lievens; yet, they are now believed to be by Rembrandt. Conversely, a painting of an old woman traditionally identified as Rembrandt's mother was made about 1630 or 1631 and soon entered the English royal collection (FIG. 9). In a 1639 inventory it was identified as a Rembrandt, but scholarly opinion of the last thirty years has moved the painting into the Lievens column—with some dissenting voices.

The Feast of Esther (see PLATE 47, p. 160) is so bold and sumptuous that it came to be known as a Rembrandt. As late as the 1970s, sharp disagreements over its authorship continued. Lievens's artistic identity came into focus only when a 1979 exhibition brought together and gave order to a large number of his works.[9] Fortunately, there are now enough firmly attributed paintings by both Rembrandt and Lievens to permit sufficient comparisons needed to sort out their works. While not conclusive, the results provide a much clearer understanding of the parameters of their respective oeuvres. The case of Lievens and Rembrandt is somewhat simplified by the fact that as independent masters each was allowed to sign his own work. Though their output became confused, each produced works derived from his own impulses.

The case of Rembrandt's students is more complex, for the students were meant to paint in the style of the master and were prohibited from signing their works. Even as a young man, Rembrandt took on students. We do not know how many he had, but two that are documented illustrate the fact that his students could be extremely talented or merely competent. His earliest recorded student in Leiden was Gerard Dou (1613–1675), who was with him from 1628 to 1631. Dou's later pictures are considered seminal for the minutely detailed, highly polished style of painting known as Leiden fine painting (*fijnschilderij*, in Dutch), which flourished for decades. His earliest dated picture is 1636; what he painted earlier largely remains a matter of speculation.[10]

What did Dou do in Rembrandt's shop? Could he have participated in painting the brilliantly rendered still-life elements sometimes found in the foreground of Rembrandt's pictures? Certainly the notion of Rembrandt and Dou working together on a painting has received serious consideration in recent literature and could prove to be a productive area of inquiry. Could he have painted small Rembrandtesque compositions that show less sophistication than his master's most

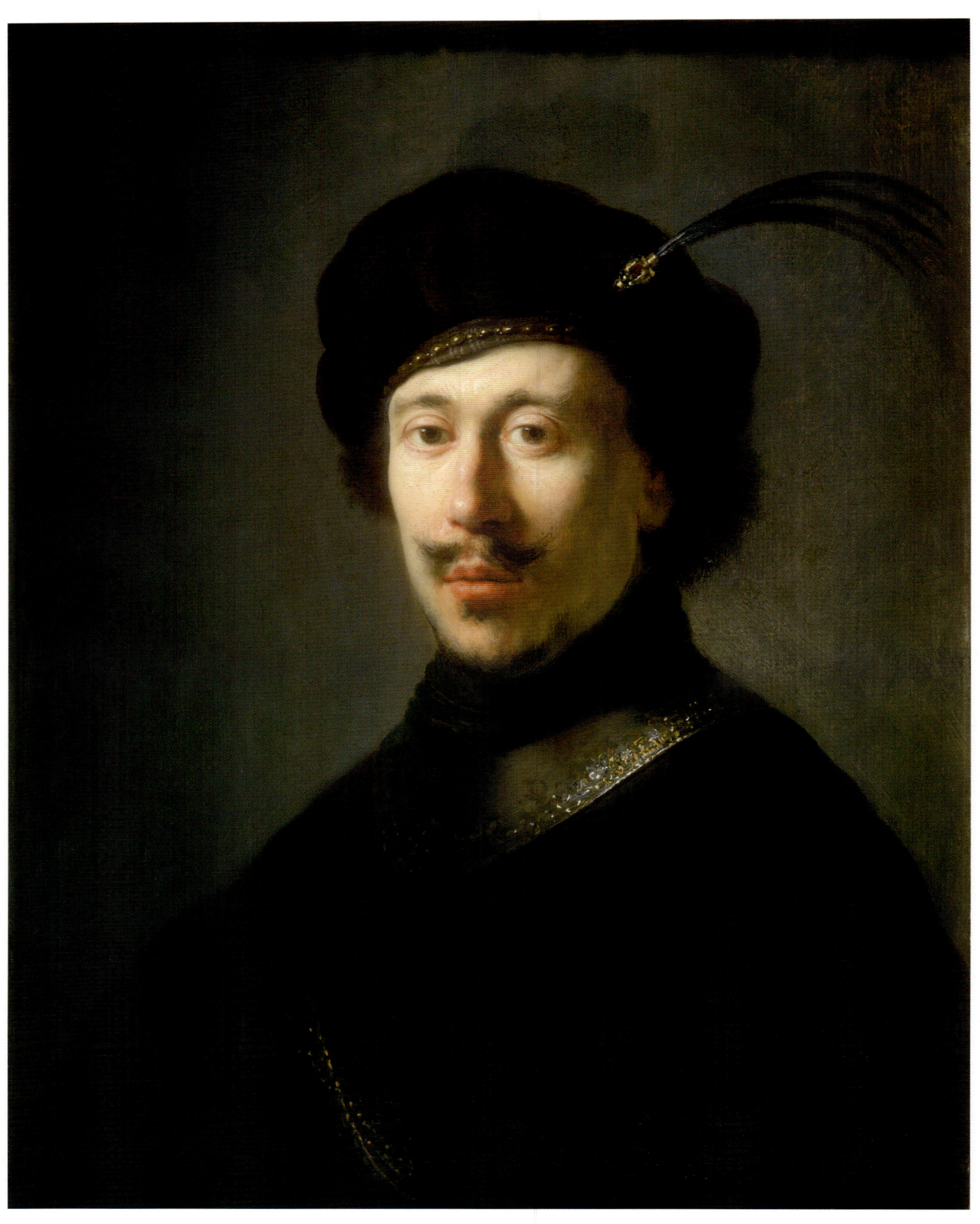

PLATE 3 [CAT. 8]
Rembrandt van Rijn (workshop of; Isaac de Joudreville?)
Bust of a Young Man in a Gorget and Plumed Cap, c. 1631/32
Oil on oak panel, 57.7 x 46 cm (22 3/4 x 18 1/8 in.)
The San Diego Museum of Art

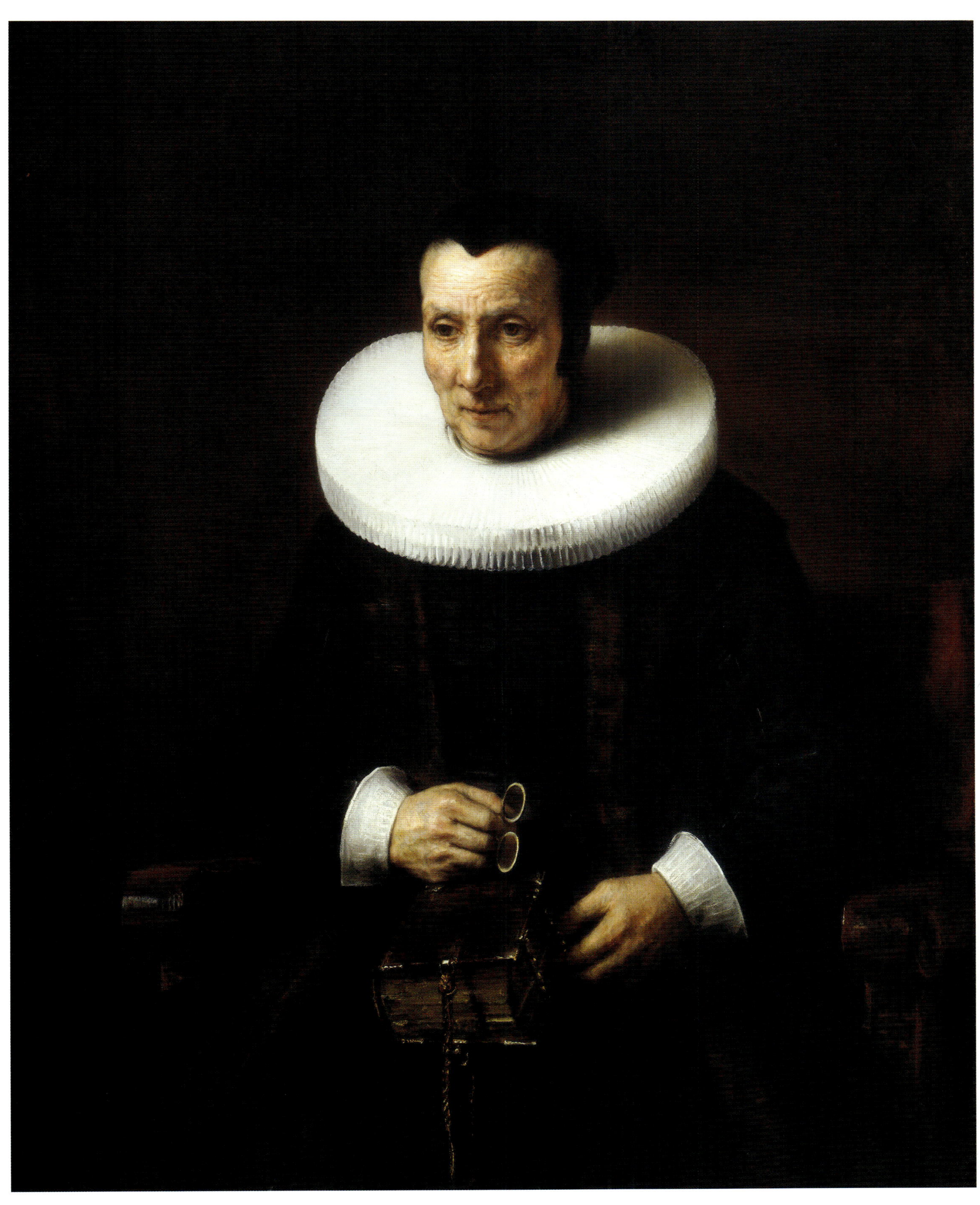

PLATE 4 [CAT. 23]
Rembrandt van Rijn and workshop
An Old Lady with a Book, 1637
Oil on canvas, 109.7 x 91.5 cm (43 ¼ x 36 in.)
National Gallery of Art, Washington

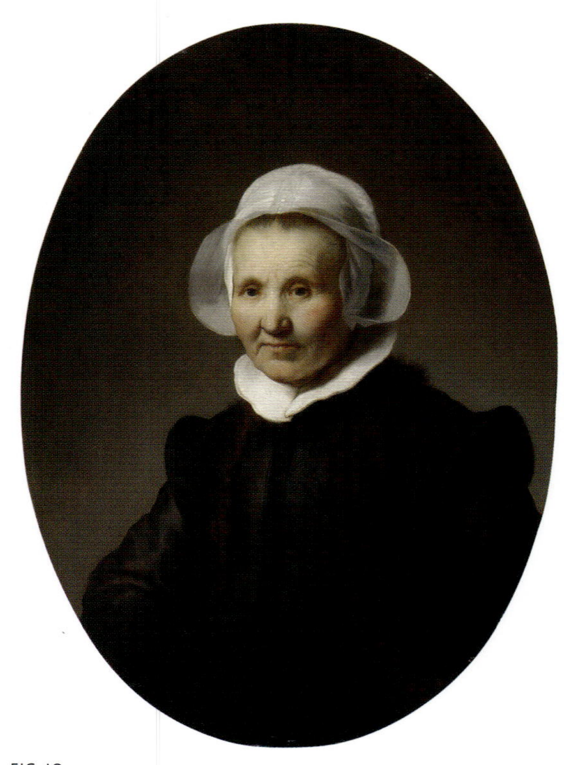

FIG. 10

accomplished works of the period? Here one thinks of works such as *A Scholar by Candlelight* (see PLATE 20, p. 94). Some researchers have rejected an attribution to Dou on stylistic grounds, but since Dou was in Rembrandt's studio to learn to paint like the master, it could well be that to some extent he succeeded. He may even have painted in multiple styles, just as Rembrandt did—sometimes infinitely fine, sometimes rough. Perhaps he only later channeled his energies toward the fine manner.

Not all Rembrandt's students possessed such great talent, with Isaac de Joudreville (1613–1648) a clear case in point. Joudreville landed in Rembrandt's studio from 1629 to 1631. Here, he seems to have taken to heart Rembrandt's advice to paint self-portraits while making faces in the mirror—learning to become actor and audience at the same time—a method that Rembrandt himself employed as a means to improve his depiction of emotion. In Joudreville's hands the results were sometimes so comical that he has become a laughingstock among Dutch art historians. Whether Joudreville was capable of contributing to the studio's Rembrandt-brand production is an open question. Yet, beyond doubt is that he contributed significantly to Rembrandt's income. Joudreville was an orphan, and surviving accounts show that his guardians paid the master one hundred guilders per year for his tutelage.

By about 1631, Rembrandt seems to have felt ready to move on to the greater opportunities offered by the thriving art market of Amsterdam. *Old Man with a Gold Chain* (see PLATE 24, p. 102) may be seen as Rembrandt's demonstration piece advertising his ability as a portrait painter. Rather than being an actual portrait, the painting is more likely an unusually large and highly finished character study, a *tronie*, meant to evoke in this case the noble character of an aging military man. With this painting as his calling card, it comes as no surprise that Rembrandt quickly found work in Amsterdam.

Rembrandt entered the workshop of Hendrick Uylenburgh (1584 or 1589–c. 1660), the owner of a major art dealership that among other services maintained a painting studio that provided portraits. Although Rembrandt's earlier choice of Lastman as a teacher and the content of many of his early prints and paintings indicate his desire to be a history painter, making portraits for Uylenburgh's shop represented a foot in Amsterdam's lucrative door. Portraits provided him with an income, and they brought him into contact with many potential patrons. With the ability to deliver stunningly handsome likenesses such the *Portrait of a Sixty-two-year-old Woman* (FIG. 10), Rembrandt quickly made a name for himself. In fact, at this time he started

FIG. 10
Rembrandt van Rijn, *Portrait of a Sixty-two-year-old Woman (Portrait of Aeltje Uylenburgh)*, 1632, oil on panel, 73.7 x 55.8 cm (29 x 22 in.). Collection of Eijk and Rose-Marie de Mol van Otterloo

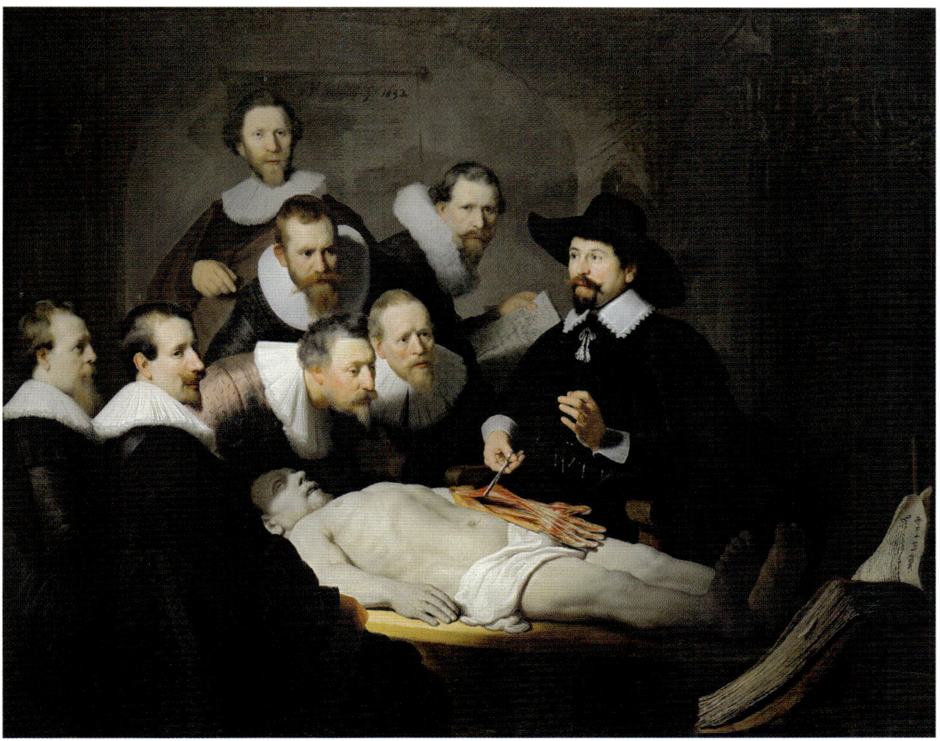

FIG. 11

signing his work "Rembrandt" rather than with the monogram that he had used in Leiden.

The relationship with Uylenburgh would prove so successful that Rembrandt invested in the business and eventually married Uylenburgh's cousin Saskia. He also seems to have maintained some degree of autonomy, for he continued to be involved with a printmaking business in Leiden in collaboration with Johannes van Vliet (c. 1610–1637).

Uylenburgh's workshop probably gave Rembrandt the means to establish relationships with other artists in his studio. The as yet unidentified previous chief of the studio may well have become his assistant, and Joudreville may also have followed his teacher to Amsterdam. In any event, Rembrandt and his team began to turn out portraits at a prodigious rate. Some are still considered to be entirely the work of Rembrandt, and others are extremely skillful imitations of his style. Some paintings no longer believed to be by Rembrandt have been tentatively assigned to other artists, such as Joudreville (PLATE 3), and many others still await specific attribution. Still others are sometimes believed to be collaborations (PLATE 4), but considerable argument on this subject continues.

What one may say with greater confidence is that Rembrandt's style became the Uylenburgh style, and Rembrandt's signature—or a facsimile—was appended to the paintings that emerged from the studio. All these paintings would have been sold as "Rembrandts," as the master defined the style and exerted quality control on the products of his studio. It is difficult to say the degree to which the patrons understood the difference between paintings by Rembrandt's hand and those painted under his supervision. Even if they did know exactly what they were getting, those who sat for assistants could have become complicit in the confusion when they invited friends and family to admire their "Rembrandts."

While in Uylenburgh's studio, Rembrandt received all types of portrait commissions: busts, half-lengths, three-quarter-lengths, and occasionally full-lengths and groups. Only three pairs of his full-length portraits are known to survive. Among them is the seated pair depicting Johannes Elison and his wife, Maria Bockenolle (see PLATES 28, 29, pp. 118, 119), the largest of Rembrandt's portraits in America. His group portraits have not come into American hands, for they generally had civic significance and remained in institutional collections. One such major commission was *The Anatomy Lesson of Dr. Nicolaes Tulp* (FIG. 11), a painting that demonstrated Rembrandt's ability to produce portraits of exceptional vitality—a characteristic made all the more evident by the presence of a rather convincing cadaver.

FIG. 11
Rembrandt van Rijn, *The Anatomy Lesson of Dr. Nicolaes Tulp*, 1632, oil on canvas, 169.5 x 216.5 cm (66 3/4 x 85 1/4 in.). Royal Cabinet of Paintings Mauritshuis, The Hague; inv. 146

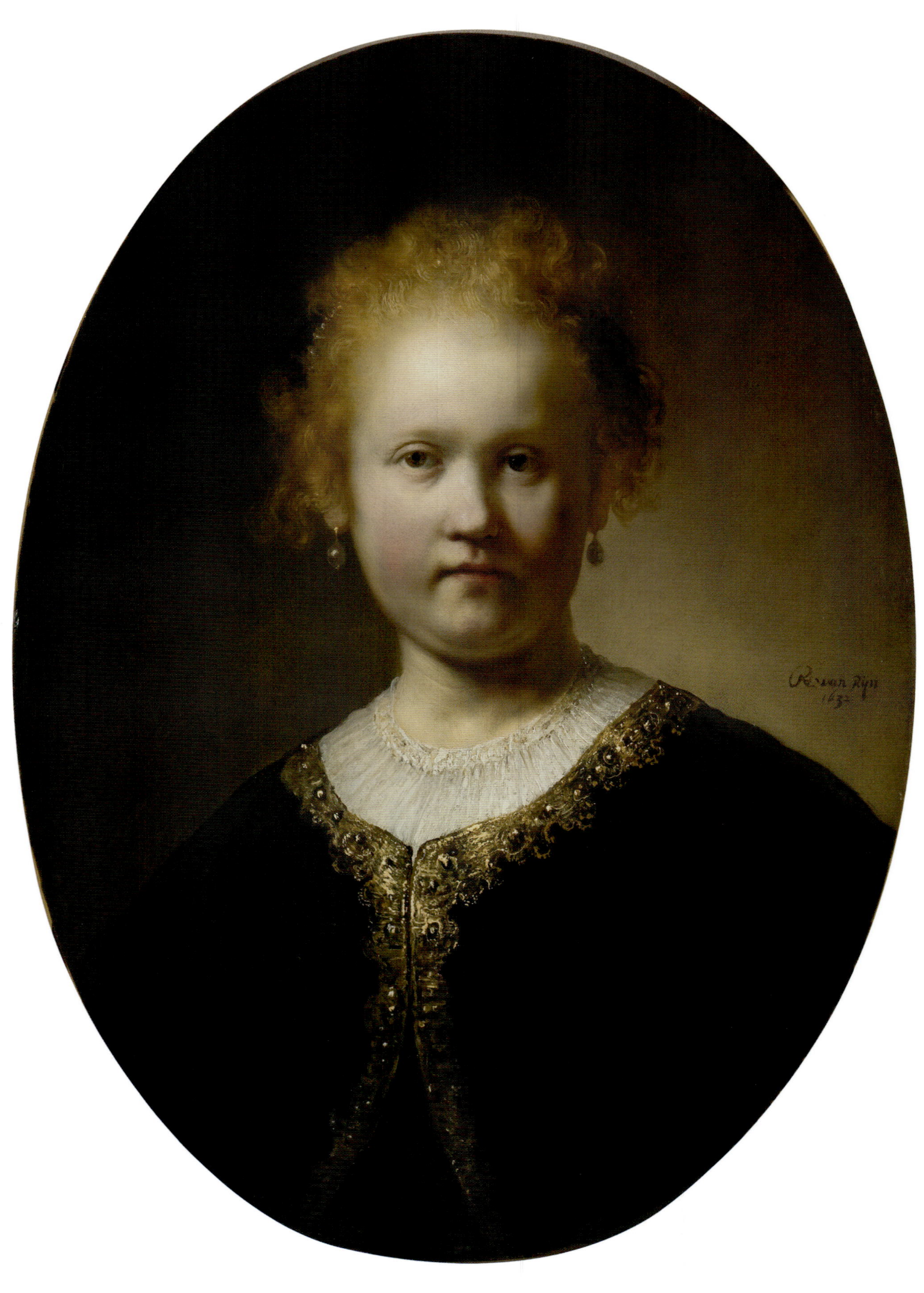

PLATE 5 [CAT. 12]
Rembrandt van Rijn
Portrait of a Girl Wearing a Gold-trimmed Cloak, 1632
Oil on oval panel, 59 x 44 cm (23¾ x 16⅞ in.)
Private collection, New York

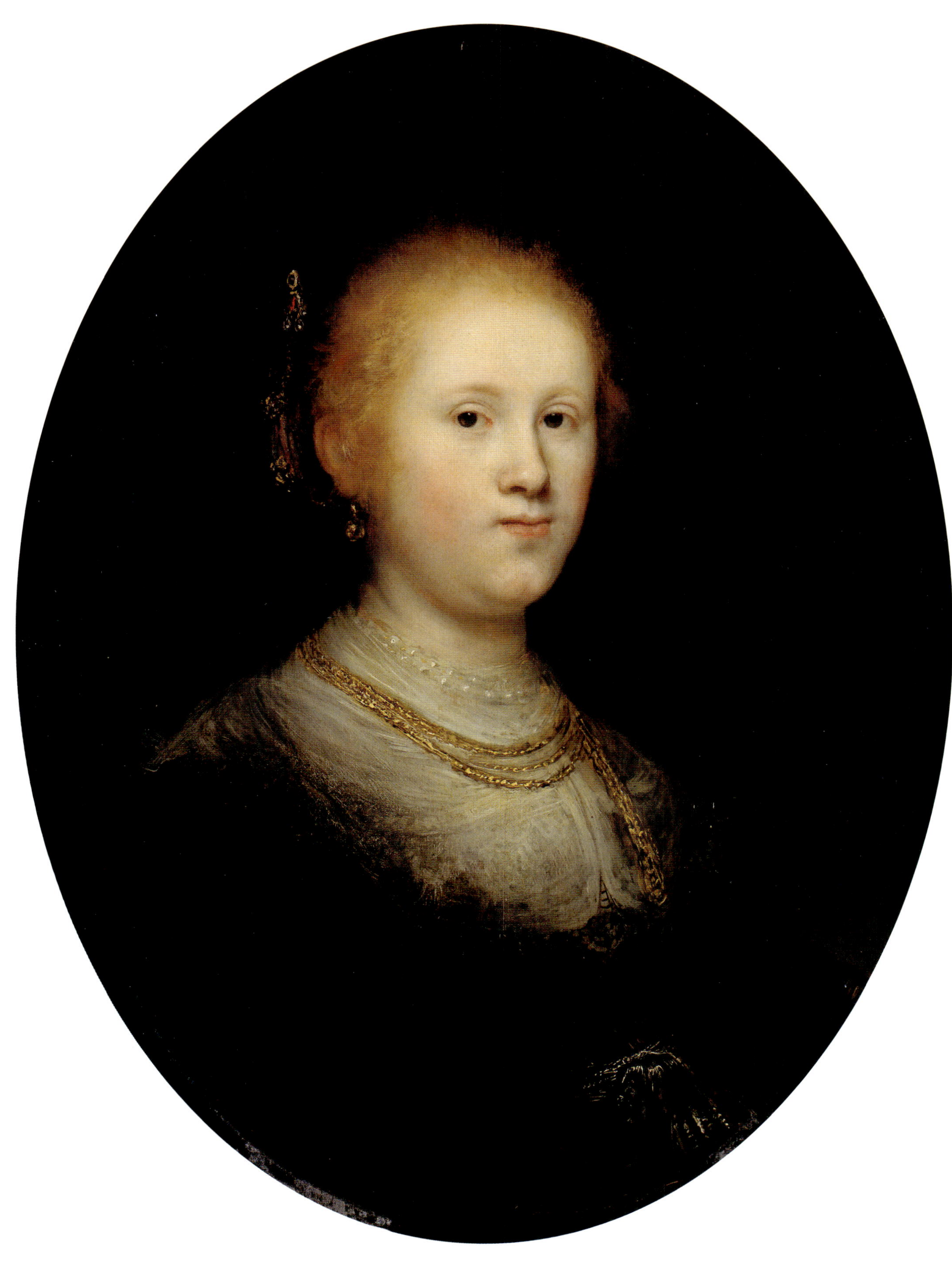

PLATE 6 [CAT. 13]
Rembrandt van Rijn (workshop of)
Portrait of a Young Woman, 1632
Oil on oval panel, 63.8 x 49.2 cm (25 1/8 x 19 3/8 in.)
Allentown Art Museum, Pennsylvania

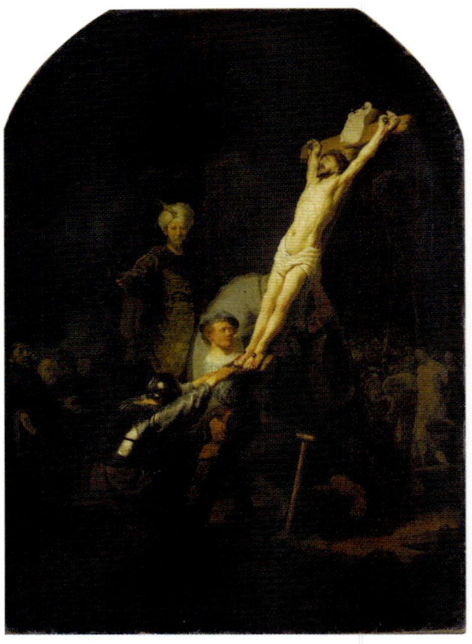

FIG. 12

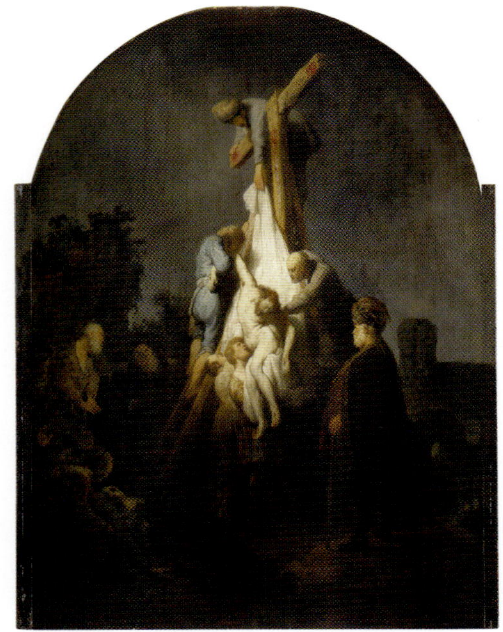

FIG. 13

A class of paintings akin to portraiture is known in Dutch as the *tronie*, a term often translated as "character head," although simply head or face might be better. Paintings now called tronies are thought to be imaginary portraits of generic character types. Seventeenth-century inventories sometimes, however, use the word to describe portraits of identifiable sitters. Numerous paintings by Rembrandt and his assistants are now considered to be tronies.

It appears that Rembrandt would sometimes produce a painting that assistants then used as a model for further variants. Rembrandt's *Portrait of a Girl Wearing a Gold-trimmed Cloak* (PLATE 5) led to a group of pictures, such as one of a young woman wearing gold necklaces (PLATE 6). Although traditionally identified as Rembrandt's sister, one wonders if Rembrandt's prototype might have been a slightly fanciful portrait of a member of the Uylenburgh household, which served to aid his assistants in the production of highly Rembrandtesque "portraits" of other young women. Whether they were fictional tronies or actual portraits, the pictures that emerged from the studio were, nevertheless, marketed as "Rembrandts."

Rembrandt's growing reputation as well as his earlier acquaintance with Constantijn Huygens may have led to Rembrandt's first royal commission, two biblical scenes, *The Raising of the Cross* (FIG. 12) and *The Descent from the Cross* (FIG. 13). Having established a busy studio and garnered both civic and royal commissions, the young artist had proven both his ambition and his ability. He had become a man of substance and was ready to marry. In 1634 he wed Saskia Uylenburgh, his employer's first cousin and daughter of the mayor of the town of Leeuwarden. At first the newlyweds lived in Hendrick Uylenburgh's house, but anticipating the arrival of their first child and fueled by Rembrandt's desire to become an independent master, the couple moved to a rented house less than a year later. Their son Rombartus died in infancy, but Rembrandt's new studio proved a success.[11]

Once he had his own studio in Amsterdam, Rembrandt took on students. One wonders if any came with him from Uylenburgh's studio. At this juncture the names of many of his students are documented. Nearly all came to him as journeymen. It appears that if he took on beginners, they were more likely to be amateurs who paid him for instruction but not room and board, as was more typical. Several of his students went on to become very successful artists after their departure from his studio. Rembrandt seems to have been so popular an instructor that he could be choosy about whom he took on. This situation allowed him to maximize his income, for the journeyman already knew how to paint and could quickly learn to imitate his style to create "Rembrandts" for sale.

Rembrandt produced painted, drawn, and etched self-portraits throughout his career. They may have started as vehicles for the investigation of emotion, but eventually they became part of

FIG. 12
Rembrandt van Rijn, *The Raising of the Cross*, c. 1633, oil on canvas, 96.2 x 42.5 cm (37 ⅞ x 16 ¾ in.). Bayerische Staatsgemäldesammlungen, Alte Pinakothek, Munich

FIG. 13
Rembrandt van Rijn, *The Descent from the Cross*, c. 1634, oil on cedar panel, 89.4 x 65.2 cm (35 ⅛ x 25 ⅝ in.). Bayerische Staatsgemäldesammlungen, Alte Pinakothek, Munich

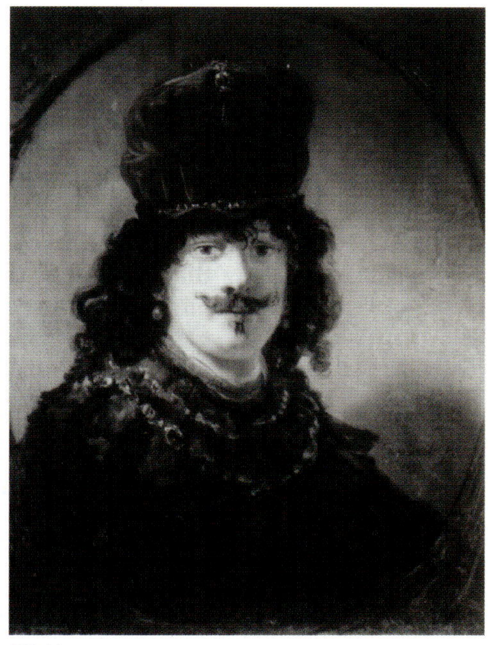

FIG. 14

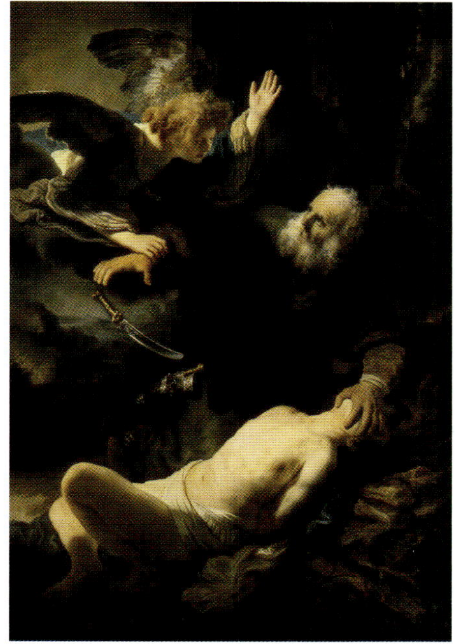

FIG. 15

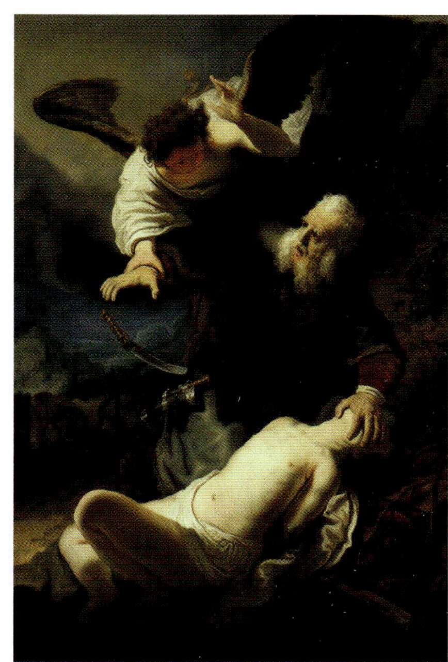

FIG. 16

his effort to market himself and his art. It is now believed that a number of paintings that seemed to be self-portraits were actually produced by studio assistants. Much like the tronies discussed above, such "self-portraits" stemmed from prototypes that Rembrandt made and kept in the studio. Sometimes it is difficult to determine the exact genesis of a given self-portrait. *Self-portrait with Shaded Eyes* (PLATE 7) may have started as an autograph Rembrandt but was then completed or overpainted by an assistant. Later, perhaps because the painting had grown stale in the studio inventory, the picture was transformed into a tronie of laughable absurdity (FIG. 14). Rembrandt seems to have geared his studio to respond to market demands for his likeness, but he also seems to have overestimated demand from time to time. Recent study of his self-portraits has involved both weeding out studio versions and uncovering autograph productions.[12]

The works of students or studio assistants were not limited to small portrait-format pictures; sometimes they were large, ambitious, multifigured extravaganzas. In 1635 Rembrandt completed a large painting depicting an angel arresting Abraham as he was about to sacrifice Isaac (FIG. 15). Another version dated 1636 also bears Rembrandt's signature (FIG. 16), and when it first appeared in documentary records in 1760, it was attributed to him. Within twenty years, however, it was reattributed to Ferdinand Bol (1616–1680), one of Rembrandt's most talented students. That attribution lasted more than a century. Today most scholars believe the Munich version to be the work of Govaert Flinck (1615–1660).

The eighteenth-century writer Arnold Houbraken, who had direct contact with some of Rembrandt's students, recorded that Flinck arrived in Amsterdam about 1634. There he may have joined Uylenburgh's studio, working under Rembrandt's supervision and then following him when he went off on his own. Houbraken noted that various pictures Flinck painted were mistaken for and sold as Rembrandts—quite possibly including the Munich version of Abraham's sacrifice.[13] Though this second version was executed with less attention to detail and nuance than Rembrandt's own, it demonstrates the ability of his students to produce magnificent paintings through extensive recycling of compositional elements coupled with variation of specific features—here, notably, the angel. Such an accomplishment may have signaled to Flinck that he was ready to strike out on his own. Soon after leaving Rembrandt's studio, he developed a style independent of his master's and went on to a highly successful career, winning commissions for large-scale public works.

One reason Bol is no longer thought to be the author of the Munich version of Abraham's sacrifice is that he could not have joined Rembrandt's studio until 1636 and may not have arrived until 1637. Even if he arrived in 1636, it is unlikely that he would have developed his mastery of Rembrandt's style sufficiently to make—or to be trusted to make—such a large and convincing

FIG. 14
Rembrandt van Rijn and workshop, *Self-portrait with Shaded Eyes* [cat. 17], before removal of overpaint

FIG. 15
Rembrandt van Rijn, *The Sacrifice of Isaac*, 1635, oil on canvas, 193 x 132 cm (76 x 52 in.). The State Hermitage Museum, St. Petersburg; inv. GE-727

FIG. 16
Rembrandt van Rijn (workshop of; probably Govaert Flinck), *The Sacrifice of Isaac*, 1636, oil on canvas, 195 x 132.3 cm (76¾ x 52⅛ in). Alte Pinakothek, Munich

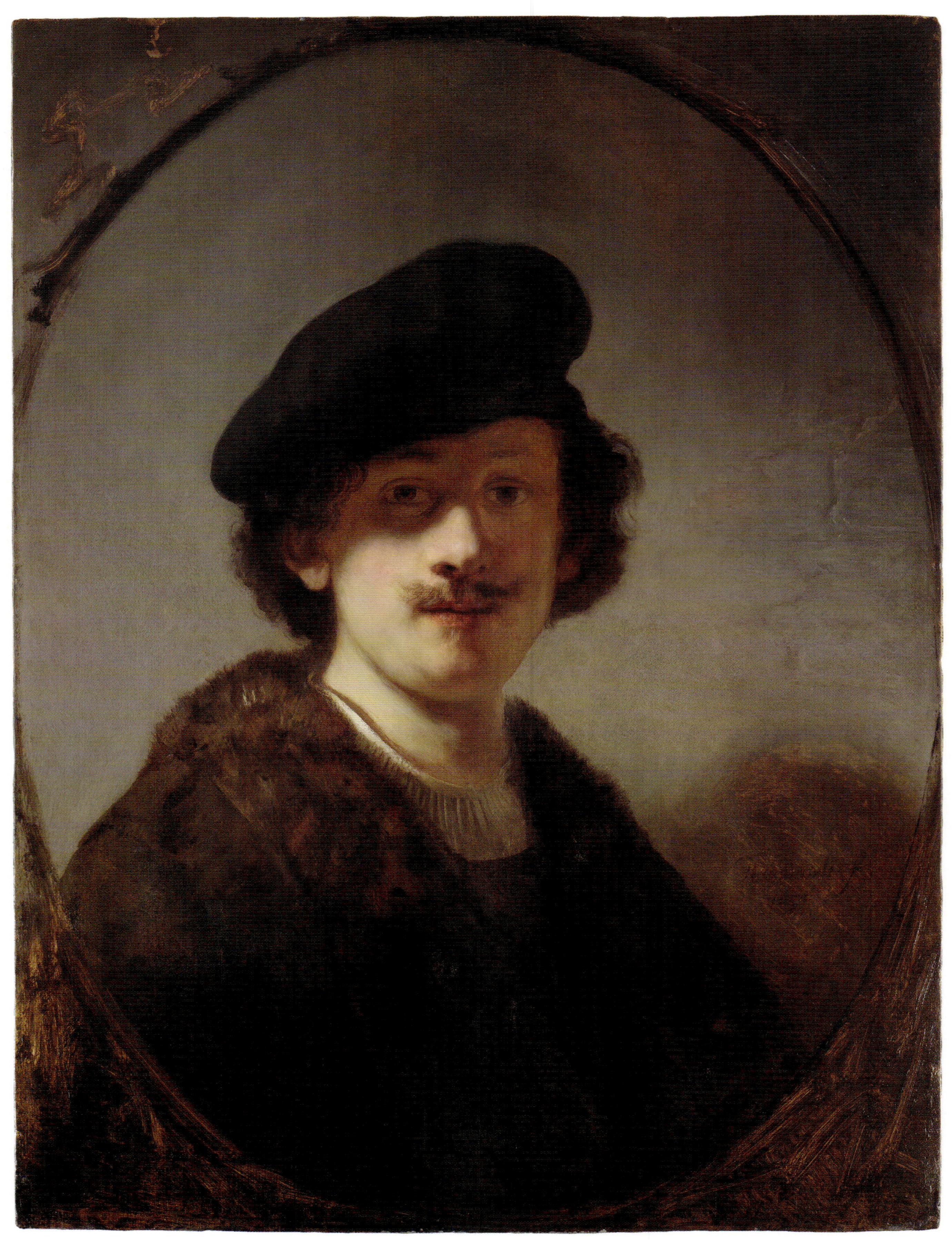

PLATE 7 [CAT. 17]
Rembrandt van Rijn
Self-portrait with Shaded Eyes, 1634
Oil on panel, 70.8 x 55.2 cm (27 ⅞ x 21 ¾ in.)
Private collection, New York

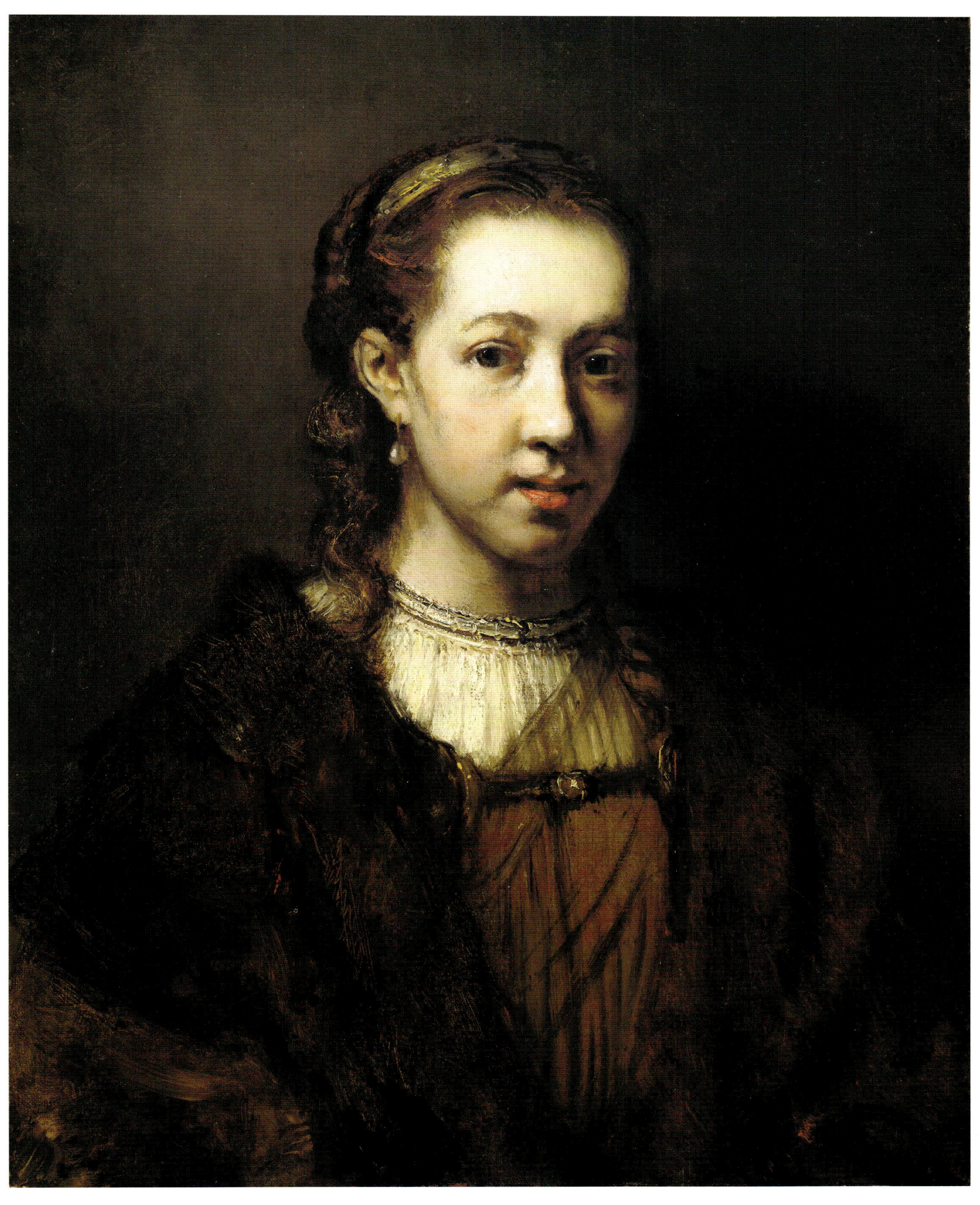

PLATE 8 [CAT. 31]
Rembrandt van Rijn (follower of)
Portrait of a Woman (Hendrickje Stoffels?), c. 1653
Oil on canvas, 65.5 x 54 cm (25 ¾ x 21 ¾ in.)
Collection of Isabel and Alfred Bader, Milwaukee

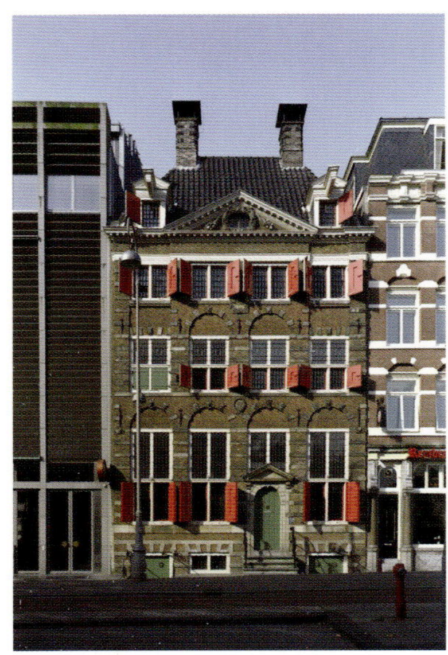

FIG. 17

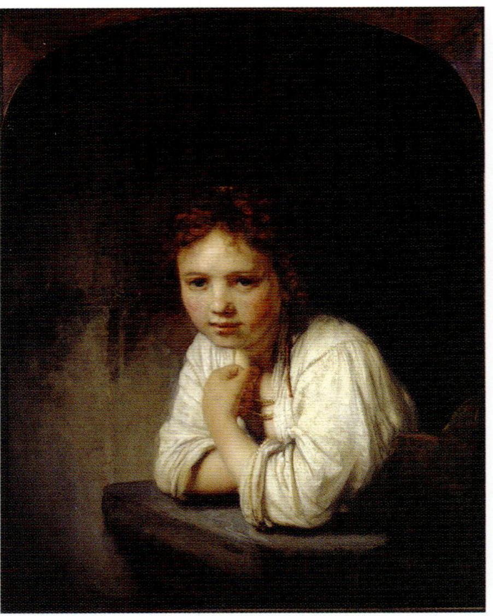

FIG. 18

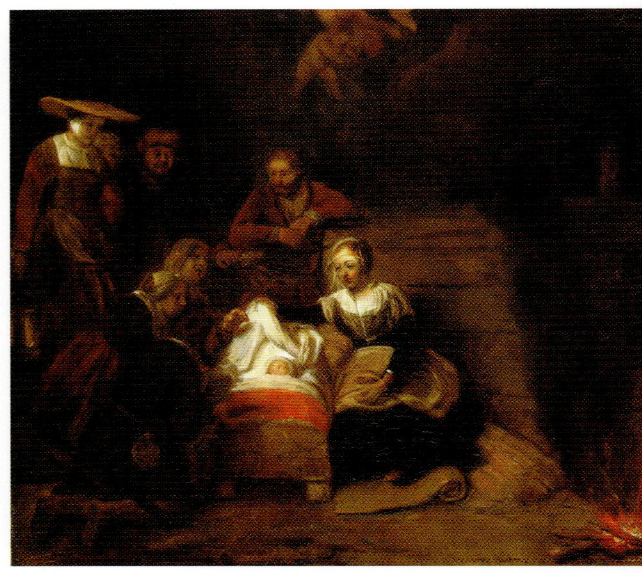

FIG. 19

"Rembrandt." Bol stayed with Rembrandt until 1641 and in that time developed a strong command of Rembrandt's style. His signed work as an independent master remained Rembrandtesque for nearly a decade, until he joined Flinck in catering to the growing taste for the theatrical elegance characteristic of Flemish painting in the wake of Peter Paul Rubens (1577–1640) and Anthony Van Dyck (1599–1641).

Whereas Bol and Flinck's participation in Rembrandt's studio during the 1630s is documented, the presence of other young artists is known but less well defined. Everything about examples by Gerbrandt van den Eeckhout (1621–1674) confirms Houbraken's report that Eeckhout was Rembrandt's student.[14] Though like his master, Eeckhout traversed a wide range of subject matter, he was primarily a painter of religious subjects. He proved to be a productive artist and probably contributed significantly to Rembrandt's studio output while he was there, especially in light of Houbraken's report that he and Rembrandt were "great friends."

Another artist who almost certainly worked with Rembrandt in the second half of the 1630s is Jan Victors (1619/20–after 1676). Though he tended to paint on a considerably larger scale than Van den Eeckhout, he too looked back to Rembrandt's lessons for the compositions and style of his works as an independent master.

By 1639, Rembrandt had risen to the top echelon of artists in Amsterdam. He had won another round of royal commissions—the *stadtholder* wanted further images from the Passion of Christ to complement the ones Rembrandt had already delivered. In order to house his family and growing studio as well as present himself as a gentleman, Rembrandt decided to purchase a large house (FIG. 17) next door to that of Hendrick Uylenburgh. The house is now a museum, and though it is heavily restored, one can still sense the elegance of the reception rooms where Rembrandt showed paintings and his ever-growing collections of art and curiosities from the far reaches of the world. He had two large studios—one where he painted and another for his assistants. In addition, a smaller room seems to have housed a printing press for his etchings. One gets the sense of a house brimming with creativity, productivity, and commerce.

Rembrandt had also become a favorite son of Leiden by that time. In a 1641 address before artists there, the painter Philips Angel (c. 1618–after 11 July 1664) lauded the "keen and deep reflection of his works" and their emotional content.[15] That same year Jan Jansz. Orlers, chronicler and sometime mayor of Leiden, published the first printed biography of Rembrandt, calling him one of the most celebrated painters of the century.[16] Clearly he had moved to the first rank of painters, and his was the style to emulate. His student body was also growing. In addition to Bol, who seems to have joined Rembrandt in his new household, soon coming to work with him were Samuel van Hoogstraten (1627–1678), Abraham Funerius (c. 1628–1654), and Carel Fabritius (1622–1654).

Regrettably, the last two artists died young. Fabritius left behind a small body of signed

FIG. 17
Façade of the Rembrandt House, Amsterdam. The Rembrandt House Museum, Amsterdam

FIG. 18
Rembrandt van Rijn, *A Girl at a Window*, 1645, oil on canvas, 81.6 x 66 cm (32 1/8 x 26 in.). Dulwich Picture Gallery, London; DPG163

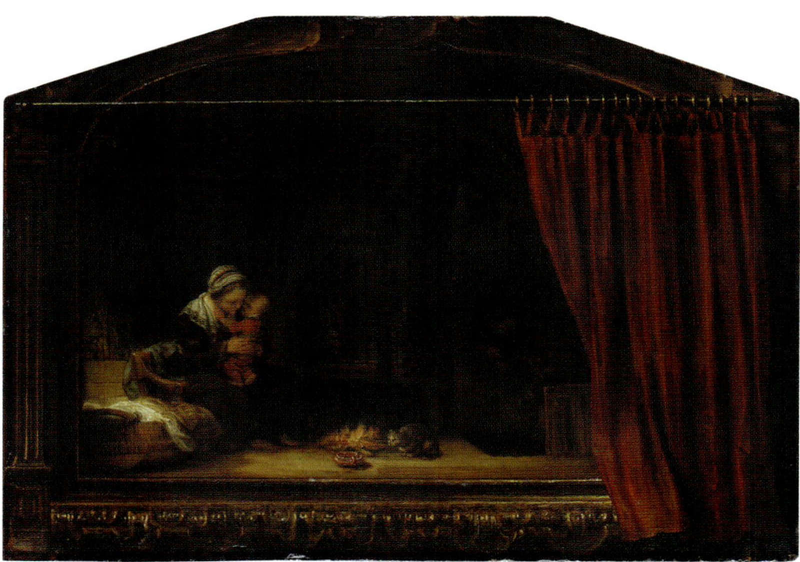

FIG. 20

paintings that reveal him to have been a very talented artist who would have been a skilled contributor to the studio's output. By contrast, none of Funerius's paintings have been identified; he is known only as a draftsman of landscapes.[17]

Van Hoogstraten is a different case, as he built a productive, successful, and well-documented career. He appears to have worked with Rembrandt from the early to mid-1640s, a period during which Rembrandt experimented with trompe l'oeil, a type of painting meant to be so convincing that the viewer momentarily believes the depicted subject is in fact present. Rembrandt's arresting picture of a young woman leaning out a window of 1645 (FIG. 18) is one of several signed paintings of girls and young women at windows. Another showing a young woman at a half-height door is sometimes ascribed to Van Hoogstraten (see FIG. 29, p. 63).

In the 1640s, Rembrandt and his studio produced several paintings depicting the Holy Family in indoor settings. These works seem to have held strong appeal for Van Hoogstraten, as is made clear by a very Rembrandtesque *Adoration of the Shepherds* signed by the newly independent twenty-year-old artist and dated 1647 (FIG. 19). That painting raises the strong possibility that some of the workshop versions of the Holy Family are very likely to have been painted by Van Hoogstraten. One painting that combined trompe l'oeil elements with the Holy Family theme was signed and dated by Rembrandt in 1646 (FIG. 20). If Van Hoogstraten did not participate in the painting (though this author has long suspected that he did), he must have been fascinated by its trompe l'oeil frame and the painted faux curtain that seems to cover almost a third of the image.

Van Hoogstraten returned to his home town of Dordrecht by early 1648 and worked there in a Rembrandtesque style until 1651. That year he moved to Vienna and commenced five years' service in the imperial court of Ferdinand III. There, he impressed his patron with his extremely refined—sometimes trompe l'oeil—manner. Two Van Hoogstraten paintings still in Vienna (Kunsthistorisches Museum) bear the stamp of lessons learned in Rembrandt's studio, even though Rembrandt's is far from the first name to pop into a viewer's mind upon seeing them.

One shows a bearded man peering out a window, certainly stemming from the series of young women. The other is a view of the Burgplatz, a vast courtyard of the imperial palace.[18] Few reproductions show the entire painting, for even today viewers are fooled by the painted trompe l'oeil frame. Further blurring the boundary between truth and illusion, Van Hoogstraten originally provided an aperture for insertion of a small clock rather than painting the clock on the tower at the far side of the court. Once again, it appears that a Rembrandt student took off at a tangent from the ever-changing arc of Rembrandt's artistic development.

In 1642, Rembrandt completed a major commission, a group portrait for a militia company. The painting, now in Amsterdam's Rijksmuseum, is officially known as *The Company of Frans Banning Cocq*, but it is far more widely known as *The Night Watch*. The painting is so large that

FIG. 19
Samuel van Hoogstraten, *The Adoration of the Shepherds*, 1647, oil on canvas, 58.2 x 70.8 cm (22 7/8 x 27 7/8 in.). Dordrechts Museum

FIG. 20
Rembrandt van Rijn (and workshop?), *The Holy Family*, 1646, oil on panel, 46.5 x 68.8 cm (18 1/4 x 27 1/8 in.). Staatliche Museen Kassel, Gemäldegalerie Alte Meister

Rembrandt probably had to find someplace other than his studio in which to paint it. Some have guessed that he might have used a nearby church, others that he built a temporary shelter in the rear court of his home. Group portraiture already had a grand tradition in Holland: militia portraits could be large, with each of the figures being flattered, extra attention of course being paid to the officers. Rembrandt's painting stands apart from all others in its exceptional degree of animation, the intense illusion of space and tactility, the near obscuring of the faces of lesser members of the company, and the inclusion of allegorical figures, who play such active roles that we practically hear gunfire when we observe the picture. When placed in the large hall where it was surrounded by other militia portraits, the painting would have screamed the name of Frans Banning Cocq, but even louder it would have called the name of Rembrandt.

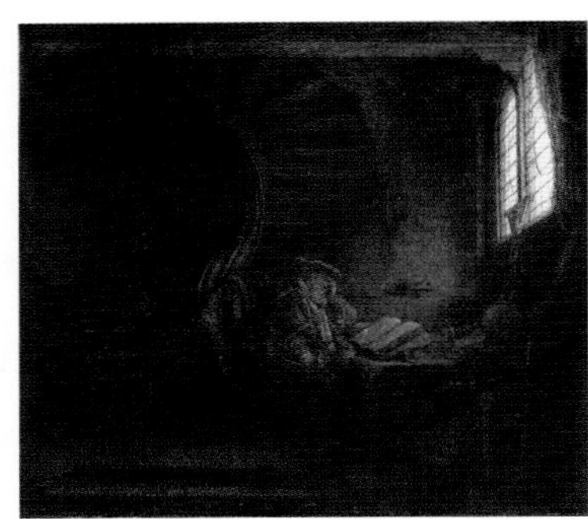

FIG. 21

The exceptional nature of the picture and the fact that Rembrandt never painted another one like it have given rise to speculation about whether the work was considered so out of place and so unsatisfactory to some of the sitters—who would have paid good money to be in it—that the painting caused Rembrandt to fall from favor. Equally plausible is that Rembrandt felt he had better things to do with his time. The truth is probably more complicated.

Rembrandt's personal life in his new home seems to have started off happily, but soon met with tragedy. Titus, his first child to survive infancy—Rembrandt and Saskia had lost three children earlier in their marriage—was born there in 1641. The following summer Saskia died. Her death obviously affected Rembrandt and his art. While paintings usually had to meet the requirements of patrons or at least be suitable for decor, etchings could be more personal. Shortly after he lost Saskia, Rembrandt produced some remarkably melancholic etchings, most notably *St. Jerome in His Study* (FIG. 21). He also turned to landscape etching, giving rise to the theory that he sought comfort in walks through the outskirts of Amsterdam.

Saskia's will gave Rembrandt the use of her estate until such time as he remarried, which would trigger an obligation to pay it in full to their infant son Titus. Such a provision was not uncommon, for it protected the child from getting short shrift within a reconfigured family. Typically, clauses of this type were strongly enforced, for in a time when life expectancies were short, the relatives of the deceased kept a watchful eye out for money that might revert back to them. Because Rembrandt's spending habits always kept him short of cash, the likelihood of his remarrying was small. This situation led to major problems for him as the years passed.

In order to care for Titus, Rembrandt hired a childless widow as a nurse. Her name was Geertje Dircx, and she soon became Rembrandt's mistress. In 1649 they had an acrimonious breakup, probably over Rembrandt's attentions to a new housekeeper, the young Hendrickje Stoffels. Rembrandt offered Geertje a sixty-guilder annual pension, but she decided to file a breach-of-promise suit. Rembrandt was ordered to pay her two hundred guilders per year. When it came time to sign the agreement, Geertje created a scene and would not cooperate. With the aid of her brother, Rembrandt succeeded in having Geertje confined to a *spinhuis*—a workhouse for deranged women—for a term of twelve years. After five years Geertje was released on grounds of ill health, and she died a year later.

Against this troubling backdrop, Rembrandt began an enduring love affair with Hendrickje Stoffels (PLATE 8). Twenty years his junior, she became his muse and mistress. Rembrandt painted her in various guises (see FIG. 85, p. 154), some perhaps pointedly chosen in response to the societal pressures brought to bear on their relationship. By summer of 1654, Hendrickje was obviously pregnant. The church council repeatedly summoned her, but only after the fourth request did she appear. She was made to confess that she was living with Rembrandt as a whore and was excommunicated. This was a serious punishment, for in addition to spiritual exile,

FIG. 21
Rembrandt van Rijn, *St. Jerome in His Study*, 1642, etching (B 105), 15 x 17 cm (5 7/8 x 6 3/4 in.). Minneapolis Institute of Arts; Gift of Mrs. Ridgley Hunt, 1940; P.11,655

it meant that she could not count on the church for help if she should fall into poverty. The incident also meant that for many, Rembrandt became a social pariah, a difficult situation for an artist relying on the patronage of thriving members of a highly organized society.

Regardless of his personal situation, Rembrandt managed to keep bringing talented students and assistants into his studio. Nicolaes Maes (1634–1693) probably arrived in the late 1640s and remained for about four years. Maes learned much about lighting and brushwork from Rembrandt, and then went on to develop his own breed of genre scene, usually of women in domestic interiors. Nevertheless, Maes certainly had the skill to produce "Rembrandts," and one looks for his hand in some of the images of alluring young women as well as stolid elderly figures such as those in *Hannah and Samuel in the Temple* (on loan to the National Gallery of Scotland, Edinburgh).

While his time with Rembrandt is not well documented, Willem Drost (1633–1659) produced work that points to such a relationship. Before entering Rembrandt's studio, Drost also may have studied with Samuel van Hoogstraten. His term in the studio probably overlapped with Maes's. The small but varied group of paintings ascribed to him display emotional depth, convincing form, as well as very Rembrandtesque gestures and lighting.[19] He lived for just under a decade after leaving Rembrandt's workshop, and half of that time was spent in Italy. Could there be an unidentified Italian corpus of paintings? In any case, he too was capable of producing history paintings, portraits, and tronies under Rembrandt's name.

In the early 1650s, Rembrandt's painting took on a new breadth, as he seems to have become increasingly interested in the later works of the Venetian Renaissance master Titian. In 1654 he painted the *Portrait of Jan Six,* which remains a treasure of the Six family in Amsterdam (see FIG. 71, p. 135). Its daring application of paint and the informality of the pose so animated the sitter that the painting became the standard by which those connoisseurs with somewhat adventurous artistic taste would judge other portraits.

Another portrait, this one of an unidentified man in a fur-lined coat (see PLATE 34, p. 130) painted the same year, cannot be said to be so dashing, but its seeming casualness coupled with its broad handling give the sitter an immediate presence. Though some sitters still required precision in their portraits, a large portion of Rembrandt's later works were executed in his loose, impressionistic style. The restricted palette of colors that he chose in this period—and for most of the paintings he executed for the remainder of his career—also suggests that he identified himself not only with Renaissance masters but also with Apelles, the legendary painter of Greek antiquity who used only black, white, yellow, and red pigments. Apelles stood for the apogee of painting, for in the absence of any surviving paintings, his superiority was inarguable. Certainly the most widely admired of Rembrandt's later Titianesque works are his *portraits historiés* of Hendrickje and, above all, his unflinching self-portraits.

During the 1650s the reality of insurmountable debt began to close in around Rembrandt. In 1639 he had agreed to pay too much for his stately house and was far behind on his mortgage payments. He also had continued to collect art in quantity. In addition, the artist's personal affairs had alienated him from potential patrons, and his persistent interest in deep shadows, dark colors, rough textures, blocky forms, and introspection left him at odds with changes in taste that favored bright colors, smooth surfaces, and often, melodramatic action.[20] He could be off-putting even to patrons who wanted his work. Documents relating to his sale of two paintings to a prominent Sicilian collector demonstrate that Rembrandt's arrogance or uncompromising artistic integrity—call it what you will—turned what should have been a glorious moment of international recognition into a dispute with a patron who may have had a legitimate complaint about unsightly defects in the materials used in the paintings that the artist delivered.[21]

Rembrandt was quickly heading toward bankruptcy. He began to borrow from Peter to pay

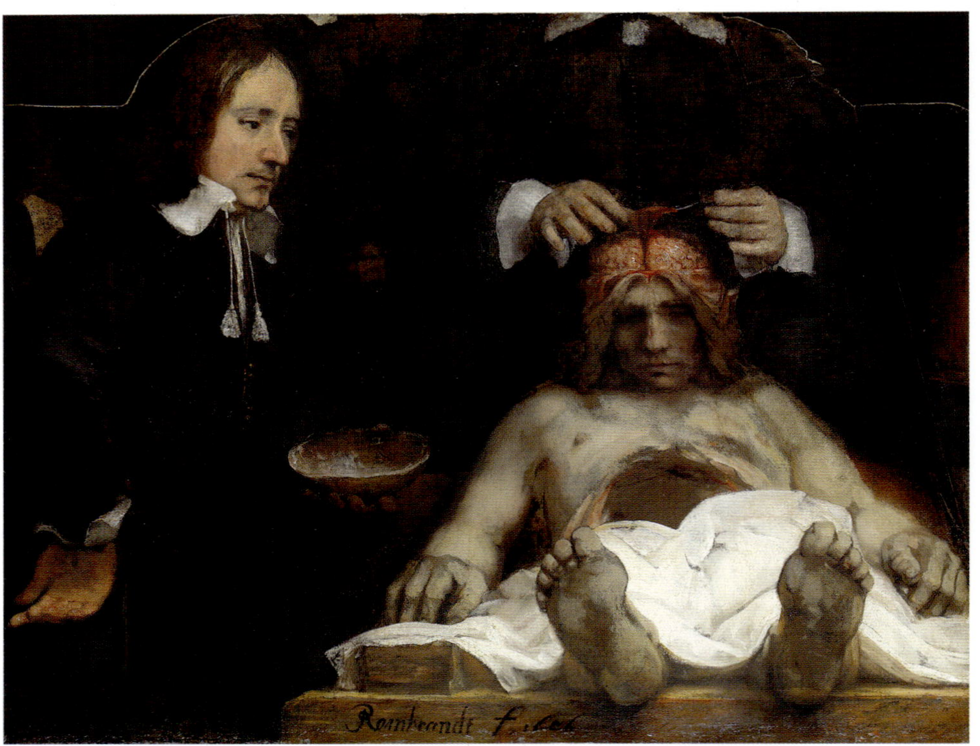

FIG. 22

Paul. His circumstances remind one of modern-day mortgage woes and transferred balances on credit cards. He held a series of auctions in an attempt to raise money to pay off his creditors. These sales are only partially documented, but what we do know suggests that the prices were low. In 1655, Rembrandt's creditors had had enough of him and of his financial maneuvering; a loan was called that forced him to attempt selling his house. The sale fell through, and it took him three years to unload the place.[22] Just a few years ago this tale seemed odd to modern ears, yet how familiar the story sounds now.

Scholars have made much of the inventory taken of Rembrandt's possessions in 1656 in conjunction with his voluntary declaration of bankruptcy. The document does indeed tell us a great deal about the contents of his home.[23] There were dozens of paintings listed as being by Rembrandt, only one of which was specifically itemized as being unfinished. About eight paintings were listed as being touched up by Rembrandt, and a few others were listed as being copies of his work. The inventory cited dozens of paintings by Dutch, Flemish, and Italian masters; it is nearly impossible to determine which ones Rembrandt considered part of his collection and which ones were stock-in-trade, for he, like many other painters of the time, also dealt in pictures.

How odd it is that an inventory of so many pictures in an active studio would list only one as being unfinished. Were there more unfinished than indicated? Had others been spirited away? Why were so few paintings listed as copies of Rembrandt when we know that many such copies—or at least variants—were produced in the studio? Did "by Rembrandt" mean truly autograph or simply a product of his studio? Such open questions only begin to suggest what we don't know about what the inventory notary saw that day.

An even bigger question concerns what was in the auctions for which we have no catalogues. Did Rembrandt sell off his assistants' work and other stock, keeping more personal paintings just in case he could satisfy his creditors before having to give them up? Had he already sold off unfinished pictures? If so, did other painters purchase them with the intent to finish them? Could overpainting—such as happened to the recently restored *Self-portrait with Shaded Eyes* (see PLATE 7, p. 44)—have occurred outside Rembrandt's studio? Rembrandt lost control of his studio in the mid-1650s, which may account for the relatively large number of Rembrandtesque pictures from that time—pictures for which no Rembrandt students have been identified as likely authors.

By the time his finances wound down, Rembrandt found himself in different circum-

FIG. 22
Rembrandt van Rijn, *The Anatomy Lesson of Dr. Joan Deyman*, 1656, oil on canvas, 100 x 134 cm (39 3/8 x 52 3/4 in.). Amsterdams Historisch Museum; SA 7394

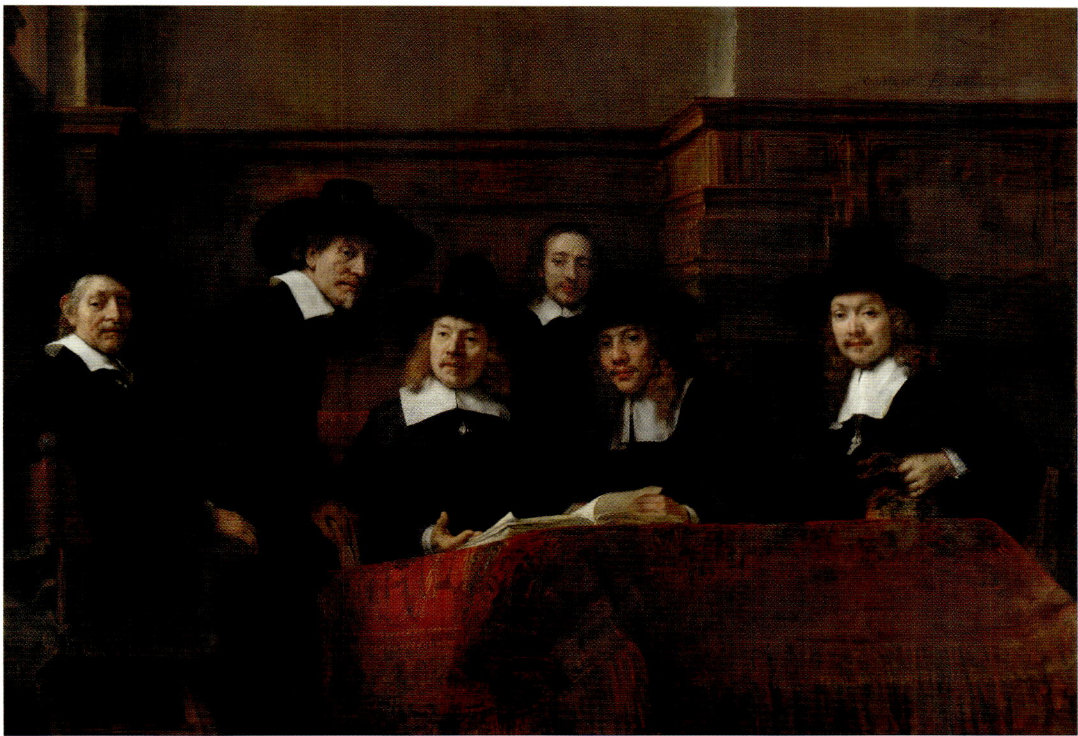

FIG. 23

stances. He and his family had moved to much smaller quarters in a working-class section of Amsterdam. In order to shelter any income from further claims, Hendrickje and Titus had formed a company in which Rembrandt was an employee. He was no longer surrounded by his collections, and he no longer had studio space—if indeed he still had need—for large numbers of assistants. One wonders if such downsizing may have served to give Rembrandt more freedom to paint as he wished. His overhead was lower, and he was no longer obligated to manage a large operation. In a sense he became more than ever his own patron, and when potential patrons came calling, they certainly did not choose him because he was fashionable.

Despite his bankruptcy, however, Rembrandt continued to receive substantial commissions. In 1656, well before the financial dust had settled, he was called upon to paint a group portrait staged as an anatomy class—a subject that had helped boost his profile back when he was working in Uylenburgh's studio. This time the principal sitter was Dr. Joan Deyman (FIG. 22). For the focal point of the composition, Rembrandt combined careful observation of an actual dissection with images from Andreas Vesalius's seminal 1543 treatise on anatomy and from Italian art, particularly Orazio Borgianni's (c. 1575–1616) and Andrea Mantegna's (c. 1431–1506) versions of the Lamentation of Christ (San Salvatore in Lauro, Rome, and the Brera, Milan, respectively). Though most of the painting was destroyed by fire in 1723, the surviving fragment and Rembrandt's sketch of the finished work suggest that the picture was originally about 2.5 x 3 meters (8 x 10 feet).[24]

In 1661 the city of Amsterdam commissioned a large history painting, *The Oath of Claudius Civilis* (Nationalmuseum, Stockholm), as part of the extensive decorative scheme for its palatial new town hall. Rembrandt's participation was an afterthought, for he was called in only as a substitute after the death of Govaert Flinck to paint one picture in a large cycle that had been ordered from his fashion-conscious former student. Measuring about 5 meters (16 feet) square, the canvas was the largest that Rembrandt is known to have painted.

The story by Tacitus of the one-eyed Claudius [Julius] Civilis leading the Batavians in their rebellion against Rome held deep resonance in Dutch society, for it provided ancient precedent for the modern nation's resistance to Catholic domination. Rembrandt's nocturne shows men gathered around a banquet table touching swords, clearly preparing for a fight to the finish. Unfortunately, the painting's raw, dark, barbarian mystery seems not to have suited the refined modishness of the city fathers. Rembrandt was called upon to make changes, but he was not one

FIG. 23
Rembrandt van Rijn, *The Sampling Officials of the Cloth Drapers' Guild*, 1662, oil on canvas, 190.5 x 279.4 cm (75 x 110 in.). Rijksmuseum, Amsterdam

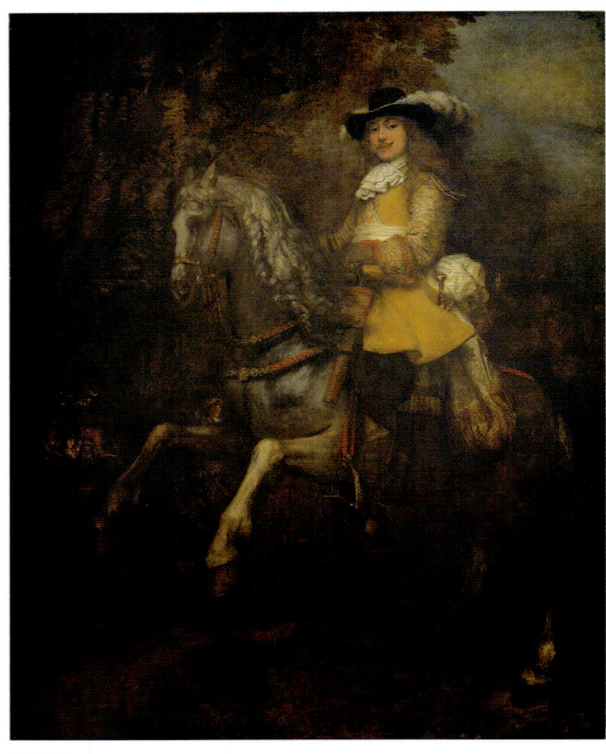

FIG. 24

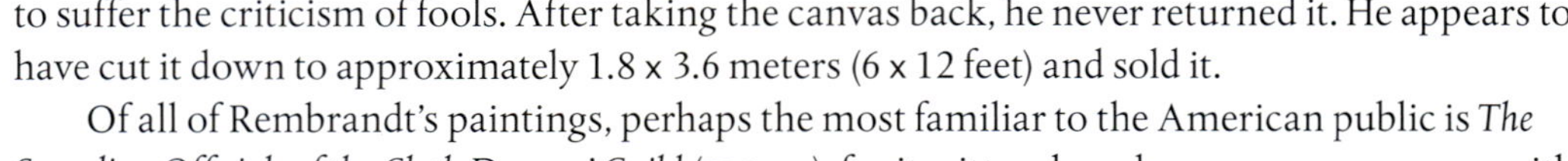

to suffer the criticism of fools. After taking the canvas back, he never returned it. He appears to have cut it down to approximately 1.8 x 3.6 meters (6 x 12 feet) and sold it.

Of all of Rembrandt's paintings, perhaps the most familiar to the American public is *The Sampling Officials of the Cloth Drapers' Guild* (FIG. 23), for its sitters have become synonymous with the words "Dutch Masters." The syndics were charged with sampling textiles to ensure that guild members produced high-quality products. The exquisite proto-impressionist tablecloth and the sharp-eyed gazes of the soberly attired syndics make their role immediately apparent.

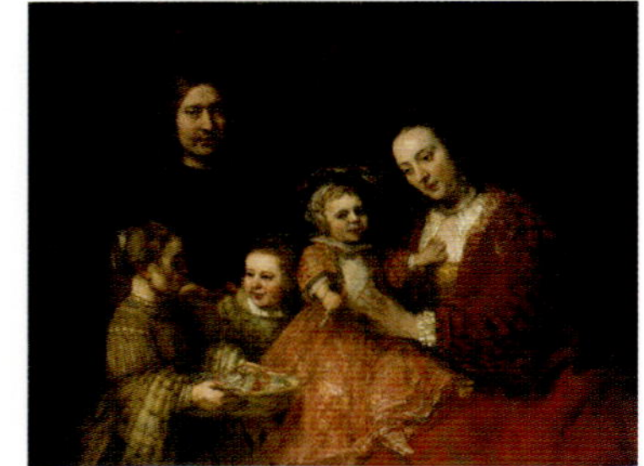

FIG. 25

In addition to such public commissions, Rembrandt received what appear to be major private commissions. Frederik Rihel, a prominent Amsterdam merchant, was an official of the civic guard that greeted the prince of Orange in 1661. He seems to have commemorated his role by ordering a ten-foot-tall equestrian portrait from Rembrandt (FIG. 24). The massive painting is Rembrandt's only known equestrian portrait, and one might say that if Rihel wanted such a picture, he would have been better off with an acolyte of Van Dyck. The horse is so unconvincing that some have questioned Rembrandt's authorship. Proponents argue, however, that Rembrandt rarely painted horses and that Rihel's inventory states that it is by Rembrandt. Could this have been a workshop collaboration?

Much more successful are two undated late paintings. One is *The Return of the Prodigal Son* (see FIG. 78, p. 147), which is nearly as large as the Rihel portrait and moving in every way that its counterpart is not. Many who see this somber painting say that it was their most memorable experience of a work of art. Rembrandt's experience of failure and rejection may have enabled him to pour unequaled empathy into this study of forgiveness. The other is what was probably Rembrandt's last group portrait, which depicts an unknown family, a couple with three young children (FIG. 25). Though probably never finished and badly damaged from heavy-handed restoration, the delightfully animated picture conveys the joys and concerns of parenthood. Rembrandt never lost his power to pull our heartstrings in any way he chose.

These large, late commissions tell us that even if Rembrandt lost much of his stature, he was never fully an outcast; moreover, he must have retained ardent admirers. Yet, a number of questions remain about Rembrandt's late career. After he moved into a smaller home, where did he paint such large pictures as Rihel's equestrian portrait, *The Return of the Prodigal Son,* and especially *The Oath of Claudius Civilis*. Did the parties commissioning large paintings provide him with work space? Also, how many students and assistants did he now have? While we don't

FIG. 24
Rembrandt van Rijn, *Portrait of Frederik Rihel on Horseback*, 1663(?), oil on canvas, 294.5 x 241 cm (116 x 94 7/8 in.). National Gallery, London

FIG. 25
Rembrandt van Rijn, *Family Portrait*, c. 1668, oil on canvas, 126 x 167 cm (49 5/8 x 65 3/4 in.). Herzog Anton Ulrich-Museum, Braunschweig; inv. GG 238

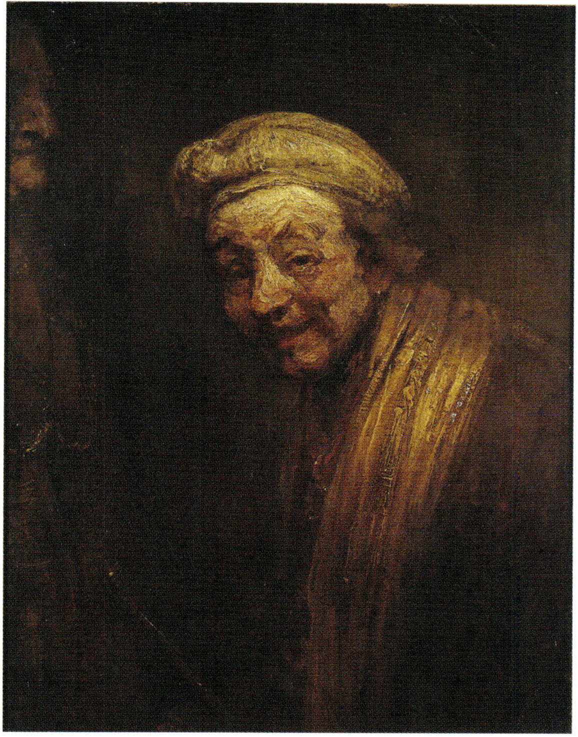

FIG. 27

know the full answer to these questions, we do know that he continued to attract followers in his later days.

The best known of Rembrandt's late students or assistants are Aert de Gelder (1645–1727), Johannes Raven (1634–1662), and perhaps Rembrandt's son, Titus (1641–1668). Of the latter's artistic achievements, almost no evidence exists. By contrast, De Gelder and Raven were both active in the studio, as each of them participated in what appear to have been drawing classes during which Rembrandt and the others drew from nude female models. Sometimes Rembrandt worked on a copper etching plate while the students drew on paper.

Raven's painting style remains unknown, but about a hundred works have been plausibly assigned to De Gelder. Having received his early training from Samuel van Hoogstraten, De Gelder entered Rembrandt's studio in the late 1650s or early 1660s. He lived until 1727 and—unlike most of the other students—remained Rembrandt's devoted follower. In a likely self-portrait of about 1710 (FIG. 26), a collector holds one of Rembrandt's most famous etchings, *The Hundred Guilder Print*. His work borrowed its palette, brushwork, and subject matter from Rembrandt. He often made direct compositional quotations as well.[25]

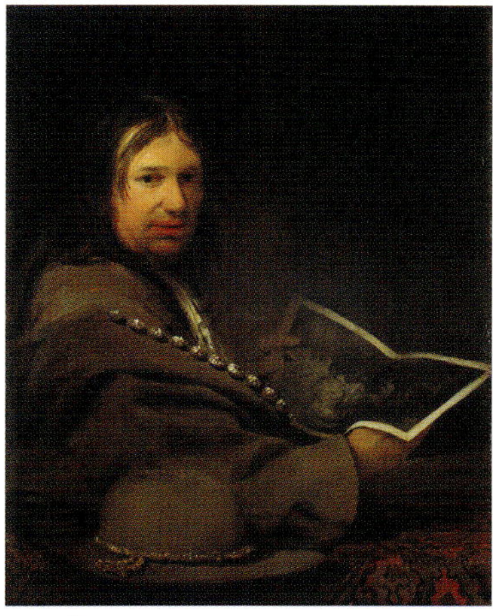

FIG. 26

Some have cited De Gelder's financial independence as the reason that he could continue to paint in such a notably Rembrandtesque style into the eighteenth century. Having no need to sell his work, he could paint in an unfashionable manner. That could be, but it may be that he catered to the same segment of art lovers that Rembrandt did during the last decade of his life. It may also be that in De Gelder's native town of Dordrecht, where he returned after spending a couple of years with Rembrandt, the demand for the latest fashion in art was not so urgent as in Amsterdam. The large quantity of De Gelder's mature paintings reduces the likelihood that many are still misidentified as "Rembrandts," but some of the marginal work that still goes under the master's name and some of the history paintings in search of an author may have stemmed from De Gelder's efforts in Rembrandt's studio or shortly thereafter.

Many paintings from Rembrandt's later years have a personal tenor. He took up the task of painting individual "portraits" of Christ's apostles, a loosely defined project that extended over several years. The seemingly mismatched group is highly unlikely to have resulted from a commission. Several of these paintings have entered American collections (see PLATES 43, 48, FIG. 84) and are discussed in Dennis Weller's essay "Rembrandt's History Paintings in America." Even closer to Rembrandt's heart must have been his posthumous portraits of Hendrickje—

FIG. 26
Aert de Gelder, *Portrait of a Collector* (Self-portrait with etching by Rembrandt?), c. 1685, oil on canvas, 79 x 64 cm (31 ⅛ x 25 ¼ in.). The State Hermitage Museum, St. Petersburg; inv. GE-790

FIG. 27
Rembrandt van Rijn, *Self-portrait as Zeuxis Laughing*, c. late 1660s, oil on canvas, 86 x 65 cm (33 ⅞ x 25 ⅝ in.). Wallraf-Richartz-Museum, Cologne

who died in 1663—sometimes simply as herself and sometimes cast in roles. Among the most moving of these is *Lucretia* (see PLATE 40, p. 145), dated 1666, and one of Rembrandt's last great paintings of any sitter other than himself.

Some of the most remarkable works of the master's later years were his self-portraits. He imagined himself in a rich costume with a gold scepter (see FIG. 35, p. 73)—a potentate and the prince of painters. He cast himself in the role of the apostle Paul within a series of paintings of saints and apostles (Rijksmuseum, Amsterdam). He painted himself as Zeuxis, a painter of Greek antiquity who was held up as a paragon of art surpassing the beauty of nature, but who also died choking with laughter as he painted a wrinkled old woman (FIG. 27). But perhaps most compelling of all are those studies in which he simply portrays himself as a man, confident, aged but unbent, unencumbered by worldly ambition (PLATE 9).

Of course in all his self-portraits any role-playing reveals only what he wanted us to see; yet, these direct gazes in the mirror are absolutely convincing as penetrating self-examinations that reveal within a single image a complex range of human emotion. In the case of the Washington picture mentioned above (see PLATE 9), one may sense regret but not despair, a world of memories and self-knowledge, compulsion to communicate, and Rembrandt's ever-present combination of impulsiveness and perfectionism. Perhaps these pictures are so engaging because they allow us to read into them our entire knowledge of Rembrandt's remarkable life and imagination. Once he has caught our eye, he stares us down in full knowledge that no one could paint like he did.

Outliving Titus by about a year, Rembrandt died on 4 October 1669. He was buried a few days later in the Westerkerk in Amsterdam.

NOTES

1 Much of the information contained in this biography of Rembrandt has been gleaned from the many studies devoted to the artist. Rather than citing them individually within the essay, see the works cited at the end of this volume. For a time line of events linked to Rembrandt's life, see Schwartz 2006, pp. 40–41. For Rembrandt's activity prior to his permanent relocation to Amsterdam, see especially Amsterdam 2002.

2 For an example of a Van Swanenburgh hell scene, see one that recently sold in London (Christie's, 30 April 2010, lot 8).

3 A number of studies devoted to this topic have been undertaken, perhaps chief among them Kenneth Clark's *Rembrandt and the Italian Renaissance* (Clark 1966).

4 For a discussion of the artist, see Washington 2008.

5 Rembrandt seems to have used Lievens's nearly contemporary *Tric Trac Players* (Spier Collection, Cape Town) for compositional inspiration. For an image of this painting, see ibid., fig. 2, p. 862.

6 The relationship between Lastman and Rembrandt was explored in the exhibition *Pieter Lastman: The Man Who Taught Rembrandt* (Amsterdam 1991).

7 For a translation of Huygens's comments regarding the two artists, see Leiden 1991, pp. 132–34. Also see the discussion in Weller's essay "Rembrandt's History Paintings in America" in this volume, p. 164.

8 For an illustration of Rembrandt's sketch of the Raphael, and a discussion of his use of the composition, see Clark 1966, pp. 124–27.

9 Braunschweig 1979.

10 Dou's career was the focus of an exhibition organized by the National Gallery of Art and the Dulwich Picture Gallery; see Washington 2000.

11 It was about this time the artist shifted his main focus from portraits to history painting; sometimes he combined the two. Rembrandt's portrait of Saskia in the role of the goddess Flora is a classic example of a *portrait historié*, a portrait in which the sitter assumes another persona (see fig. 87, p. 156). Although he wanted to concentrate on history painting, portraiture remained a reliable source of income. His uncanny ability to create stunningly effective likenesses at this stage of his career is seen in the 1637-dated *An Old Lady with a Book* (see plate 4, p. 37).

12 Corpus 2005.

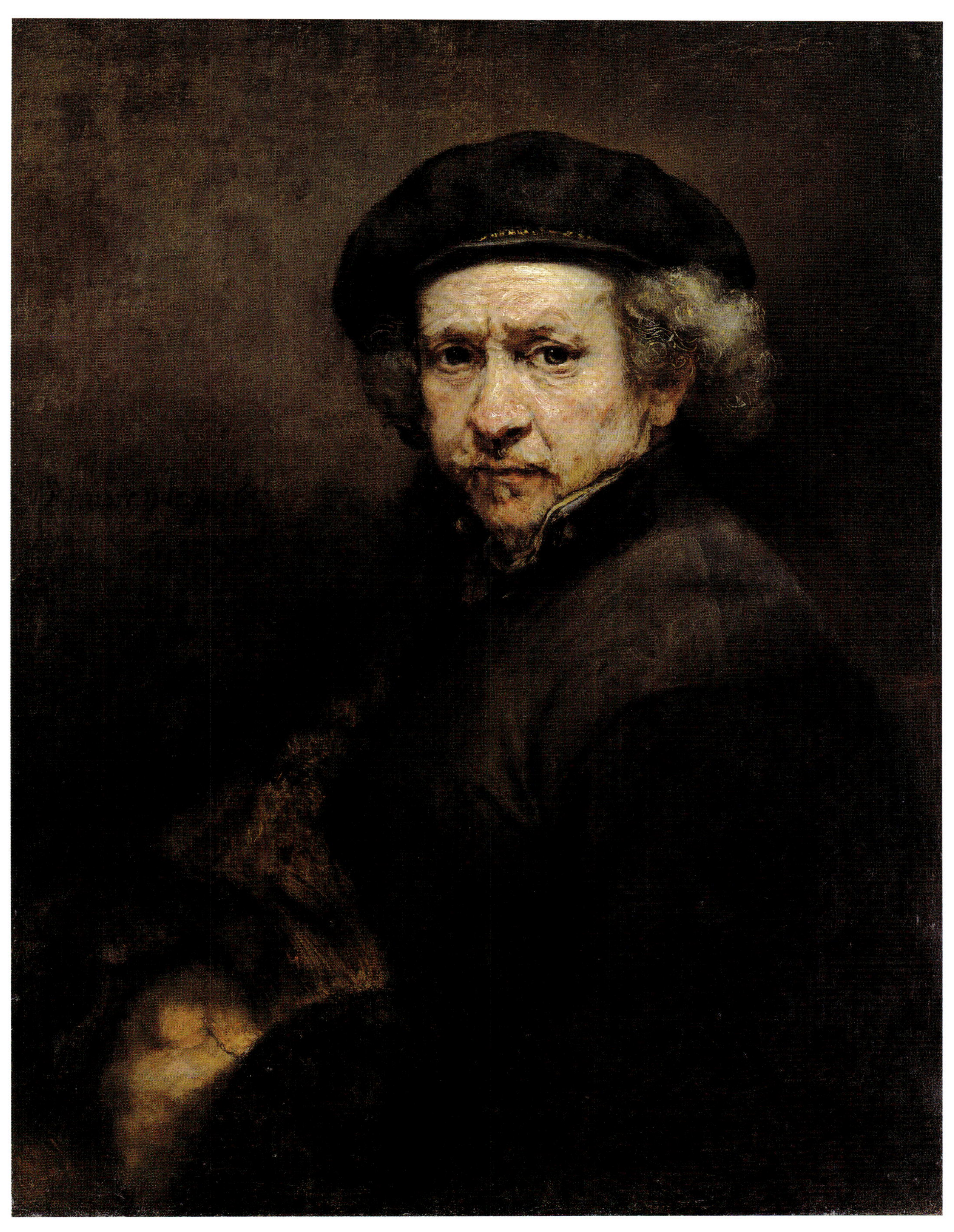

PLATE 9 [CAT. 34]
Rembrandt van Rijn
Self-portrait, 1659
Oil on canvas, 84.5 x 66 cm (33 ¼ x 26 in.)
National Gallery of Art, Washington

13 Houbraken 1753, 2: p. 21.

14 Ibid., p. 100.

15 His address was published the following year (Angel 1642).

16 Orlers 1641, p. 375.

17 The difficulty of reconstructing studio production is underscored by the fact that we have no solid starting point for identifying the paintings of an artist whose work is known only through drawings or verbal accounts. The difficulty of dealing with artists whose names remain unknown is even greater.

18 The two paintings are illustrated in Sumowski 1983, 2: nos. 880 and 886, respectively.

19 Bikker 2005.

20 Unlike Rembrandt, his former pupil Govaert Flinck did adopt his style to reflect popular tastes in Amsterdam and elsewhere. As a consequence it was Flinck and not Rembrandt who received the commission for the painted decorations of Amsterdam's new town hall in 1660. Flinck died that year and the commission was divided among a number of artists, including Rembrandt (see below).

21 The collector in question was Don Antonio Ruffo (1610/11–1678) from Messina. For a discussion of his commission from Rembrandt and the paintings in question, see Schwartz 2006, pp. 218–22.

22 For a full account of Rembrandt's financial problems, see Crenshaw 2006.

23 The inventory of Rembrandt's possessions, as well as other documents related to the artist's dismal financial picture during the 1650s, is included in *The Rembrandt Documents* (Strauss and Van der Meulen 1979).

24 The Mantegna and Borgianni pictures and their relationship to the Rembrandt painting are illustrated and discussed in Schwartz 2006, pp. 167–69.

25 Aert de Gelder was the subject of an exhibition in his native Dordrecht in the late 1990s (Dordrecht 1998). In translation it carried the fitting title *Arent de Gelder: Rembrandt's Last Pupil.*

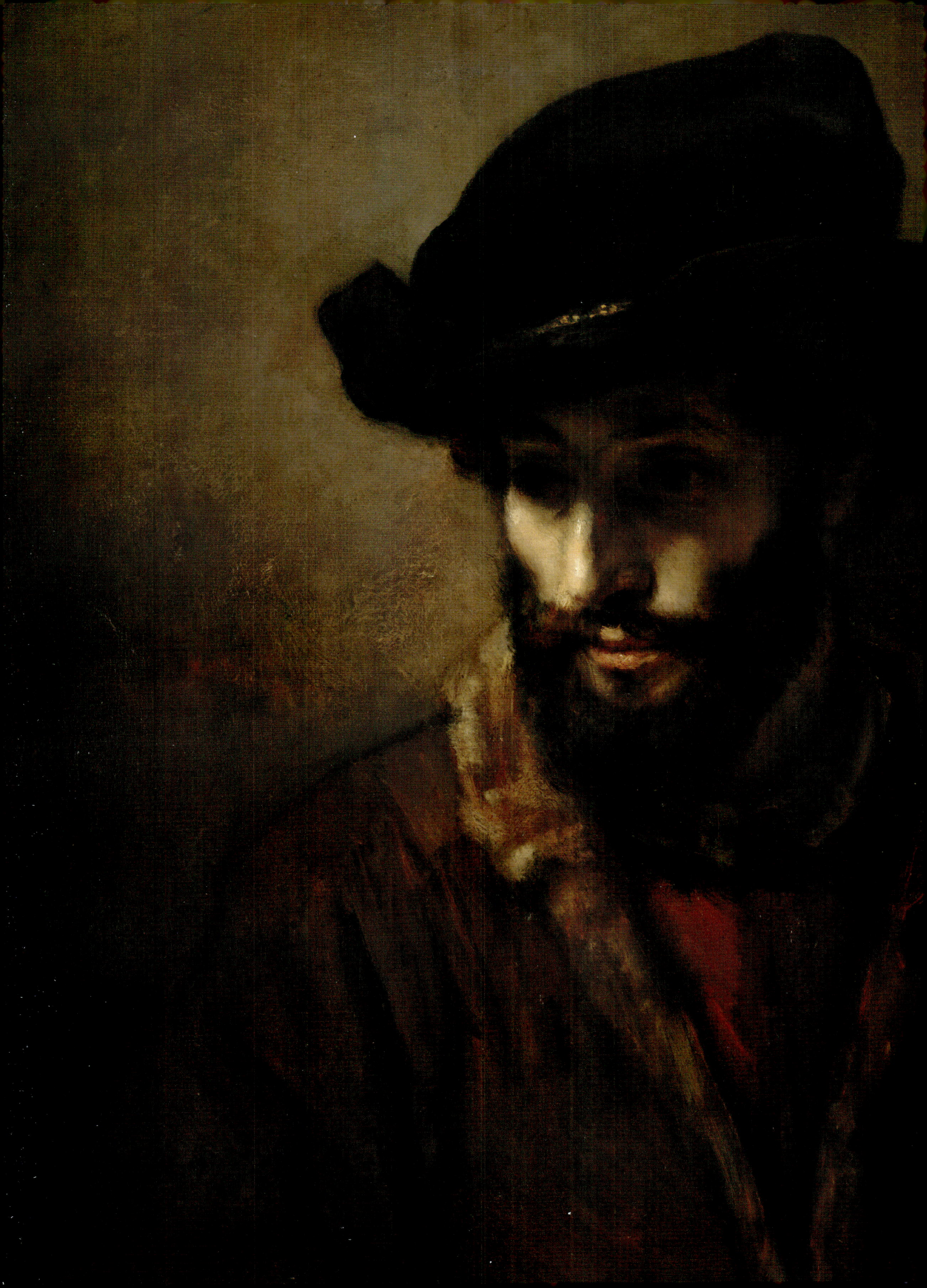

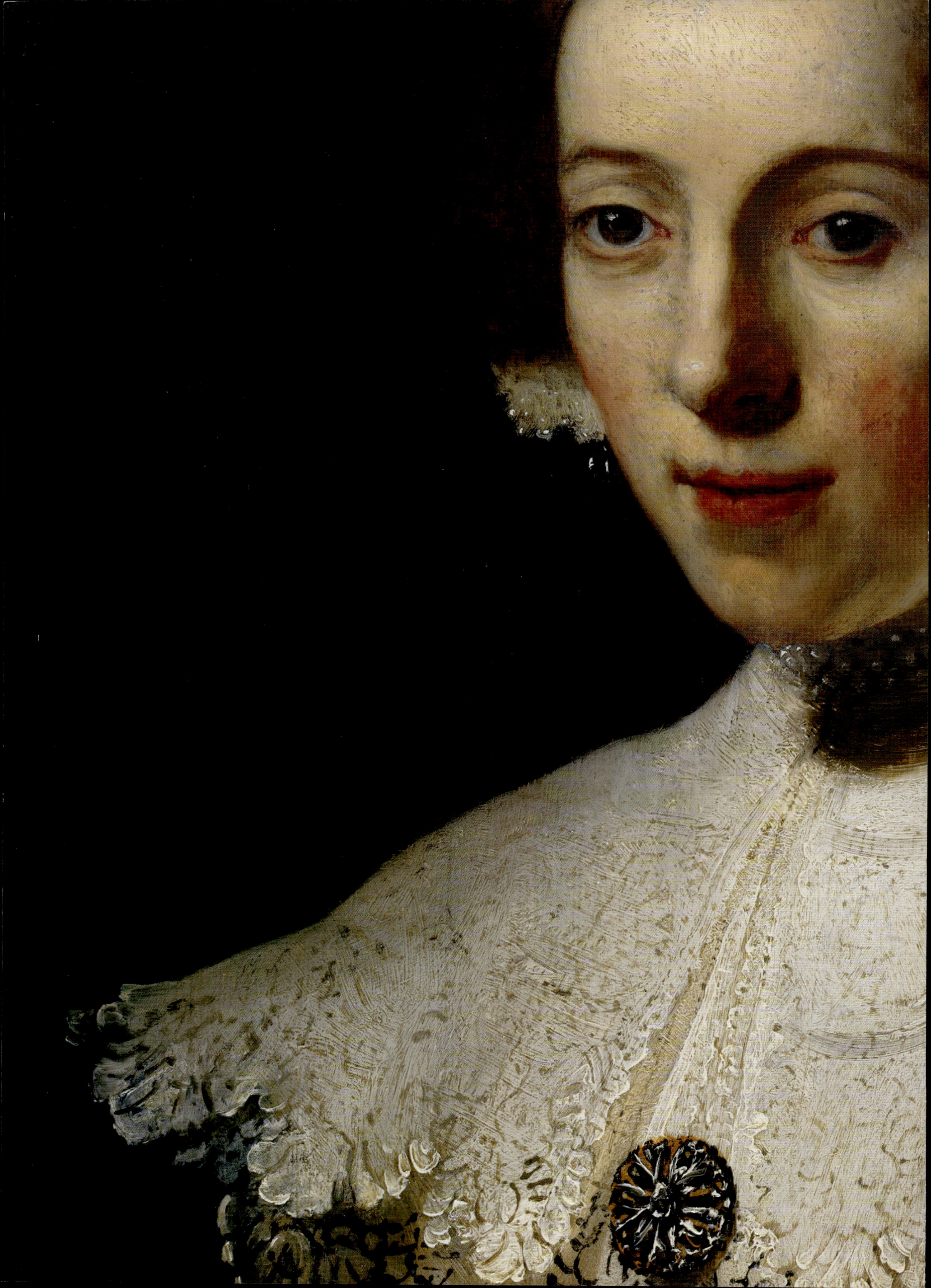

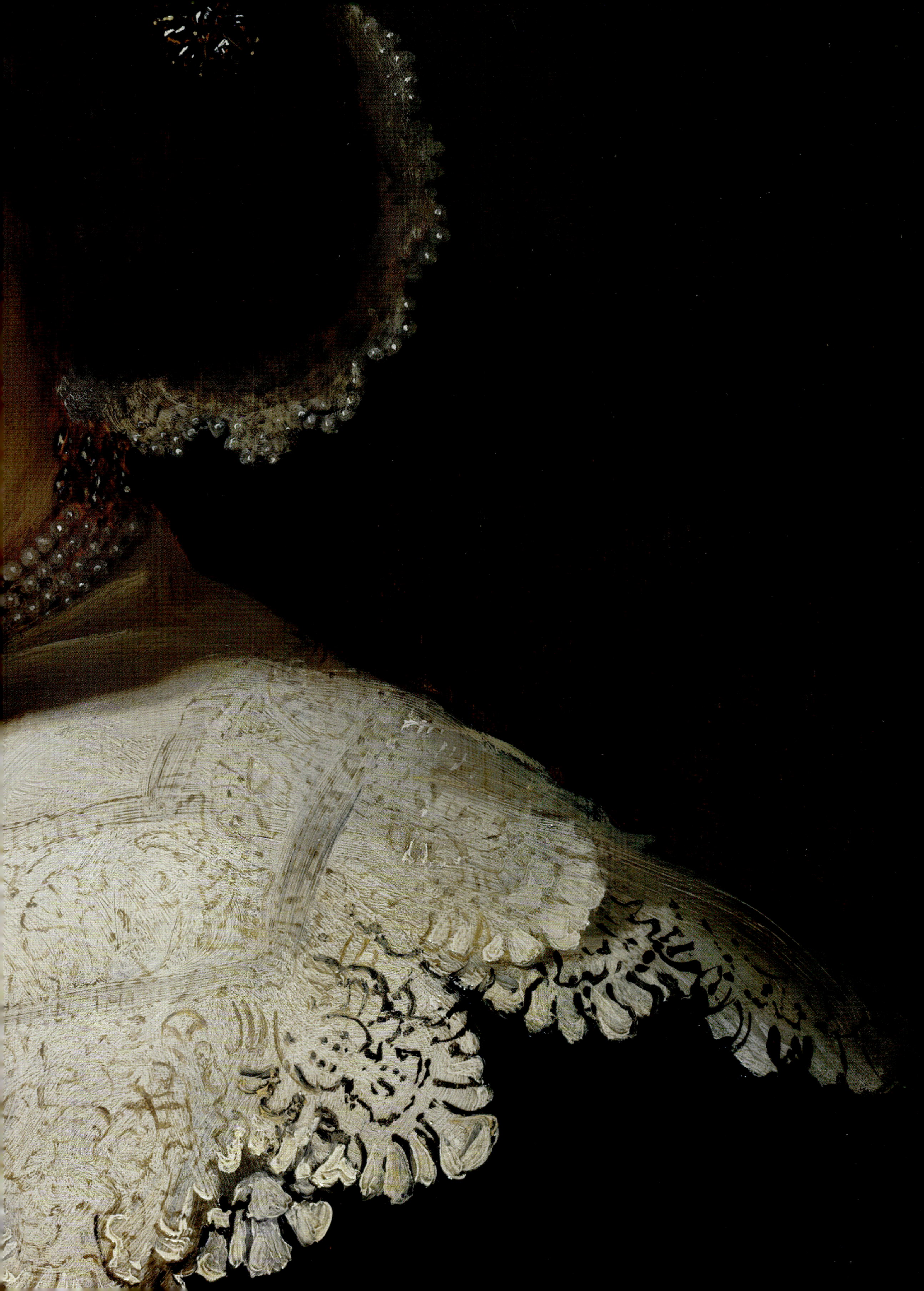

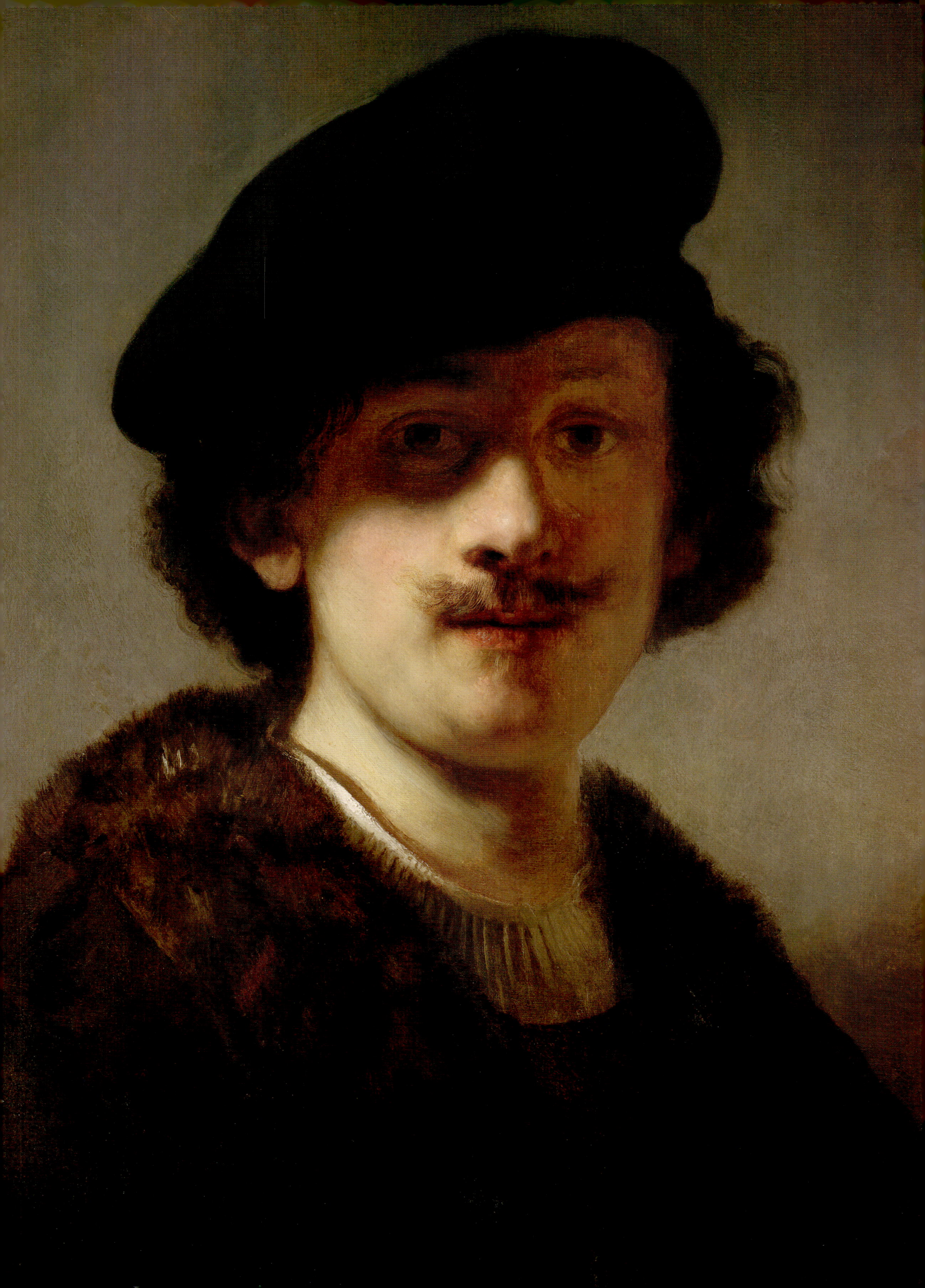

Rembrandt Paintings and America

GEORGE S. KEYES

Within the constellation of the most celebrated old master artists no name has attracted more attention or interest than that of Rembrandt Harmensz. van Rijn.[1] The unique character of his art, the seemingly unexpected direction of his stylistic development, and the circumstances of his personal life—all melded in the wider imagination of his critics—endow the name "Rembrandt" with an almost mythical character. His rank is equal to that of the greatest masters of the High Renaissance—Leonardo (1452–1519), Raphael (1483–1520), Titian (1485/90–1576), and Michelangelo (1475–1564). And like this quartet, Rembrandt is also perceived within the world of artistic adulation on a first-name basis.

Even at the beginning of his career in Leiden, Rembrandt boldly signed his paintings, first in monogram. As his career gathered apace and as his reputation expanded following his move to Amsterdam, Rembrandt tended more and more to sign his works solely with his first name. Moreover, his output of prints substantially reinforces this form of self-accreditation. Printmaking was in itself a formidable means of expanding one's reputation, as multiple impressions could reach a substantially wider audience or clientele. Rembrandt's unique contribution to the realm of printmaking lies beyond the scope of this project, but its high repute would ensure that he came to be recognized as one of the supreme geniuses of the graphic medium. His very uniqueness has attracted the attention of discerning collectors through the ages.

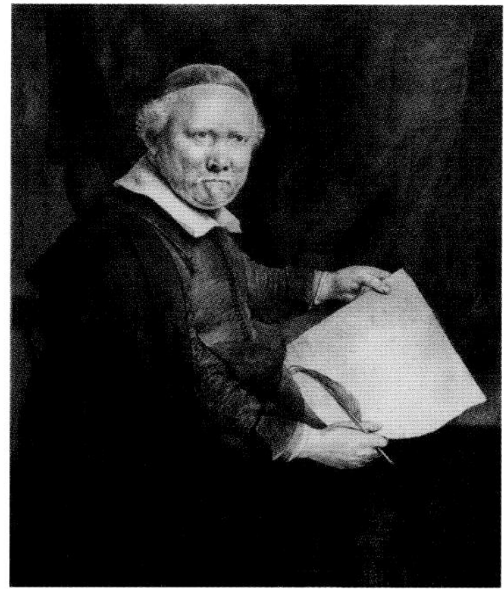

FIG. 28

It was in the realm of the graphic arts that certain aspiring American collectors began to acquire works by Rembrandt. Among the first was Francis Calley Gray, who bequeathed his collection of about four thousand prints to Harvard University, which received the gift in 1857. Among these were seventy-two impressions of Rembrandt prints, certain of which are of the highest quality (FIG. 28).[2] This collection was supplemented by the bequest of John Witt Randall of another twenty thousand or more prints, including forty more by Rembrandt.

Other American collectors of the late nineteenth century assembled important collections of Rembrandt prints. They included Henry F. Sewall of New York City, whose prints were acquired en bloc by the Museum of Fine Arts, Boston, through funding from Harvey D. Parker, in 1897.[3] They still form the core of that museum's large and distinguished print collection. Theodore Irwin of Oswego, New York, and George W. Vanderbilt assembled especially fine holdings of Rembrandt prints. J. Pierpont Morgan acquired both collections, to this day the *clou* (focal point) of the outstanding holdings at the Morgan Library & Museum, which is indeed universally recognized as one of the ranking collections of Rembrandt prints in the world.

Morgan's interest in Rembrandt has come to typify the driving link between the cachet of a celebrated old master artist and the phenomenal wealth of a new class of American plutocrats whose vast fortunes reflected the rise of post–Civil War America as an industrial powerhouse. Expansion of the railroads and the rapid urbanization of the United States fostered a number of industries—particularly steel, centered in what is now termed the "rust belt" of the Midwest. Efficiently feeding the rapidly expanding population required producing, packing, and shipping foodstuffs including enormous quantities of meat, with families such as the Armours and the Swifts joining the ranks of the superrich. With unprecedented impact the advent of the automobile heralded yet another new component of the economic mix, resulting in other great fortunes including that of John D. Rockefeller, whose Standard Oil Company would slake the thirst of the nascent auto industry. The glue holding much of this together was the system of railroads, whose expanding and competing operations generated fortunes for the Harrimans, Huntingtons, Stanfords, Vanderbilts, and other prominent families such as the Hills in Saint Paul, Minnesota, and Sir William van Horne in Montreal.[4] Not surprisingly, these industrialists were mutually attracted to one another and congregated in New York City during the season, in Newport, Bar Harbor, the Berkshires, and other socially appealing watering places in the summer, and at their preferred winter escape, the Jekyll Island Club in Georgia.

FIG. 28
Rembrandt van Rijn, *Lieven Willemsz. Van Coppenol (The Large Coppenol)*, c. 1658, etching (B 282), state iii, 34 x 29 cm (13 3/8 x 11 3/8 in.). Fogg Art Museum, Harvard University, Cambridge, Mass.; Bequest of Francis Calley Gray; G3283

The great families who dominated American industry and finance from the period extending roughly from 1880 until the outbreak of World War I came to personify what is generally referred to as the Gilded Age. This term carries with it the implication of America's coming of age as a rapidly rising and progressively more assertive world power. As such, the country and its most powerful citizens came into ever closer contact with Europe, whose class distinctions appealed to the fabulously rich new class of American plutocrats. Many fashioned elements of what they admired on the Continent into their own patterns of social behavior back home.

If the building of palatial residences was one manifestation of this limitless new wealth, the contents of these domiciles became another of no mean importance—at least to certain of their owners. For some, the domestic trappings of wealth found expression in opulent furnishings throughout in which contemporary or near-contemporary paintings agreeable in subject were interspersed along with mostly Renaissance tapestries. Much of the artifice of the expression of wealth was emulative in nature—the French Renaissance and eighteenth-century styles being particularly appealing prototypes. Serious competition developed from the English Tudor style—often of the Cotswold variety. All across America, the yearning to convey fulfillment through the expression of seemingly unfathomable wealth burst forth in domestic architecture on a scale that can only be described as awesome.

A handful of American plutocrats chose to seek further trappings of wealth inspired by European antecedents. Among those pursuits was the desire to assemble important collections of art of a type encountered in the palatial country houses and corresponding London residences of the English nobility, the châteaux of France, the palazzos of Italy, or more rarely the Schlösser of the German-speaking world. The English country house appears to have had the greatest appeal to the American imagination. Moreover, circumstances rooted more deeply in the past would prove to have enduring consequences in establishing the English as role models for the wealthier Americans of the Gilded Age.[5] The sheer quantity of art available in England was in no small measure due to fortuitous historical circumstances. The tumultuous disruptions on the European Continent precipitated by the French Revolution and followed by the constant military campaigns of Napoleon led to a significant dispersal of valued Continental European collections, many of which came to England. Likewise, in the later nineteenth century Paris lost its monopolistic position as the undisputed center of the international art trade. London came to be significant as well, especially for British grand-manner portraits of the eighteenth and early nineteenth centuries.

Those Americans who turned their attention to collecting European paintings tended initially to acquire subjects strongly realistic in tenor, with much focus on the French school of Barbizon and kindred French—indeed wider European—paintings of a more sentimental character along with the realist pictures of The Hague school. Collectors such as Peter Arrell Brown Widener of Philadelphia and Henry Clay Frick of New York City assembled large holdings of Barbizon material that, in the course of time, were superseded in importance by their growing interest in the old masters. In this pursuit Widener and Frick were anticipated by Charles T. Yerkes, who, before 1900, had assembled a large picture collection balanced equally between the European old masters and an equally wide-ranging collection of nineteenth-century European painters.[6] The various catalogues of the Yerkes collection indicate that he acquired notable Barbizon painting(s) from the I. Seney collection of New York City in 1891. He also acquired a number of British pictures from Thomas Agnew & Sons in London. British grand manner portraits and European old masters primarily of the seventeenth century and principally of the Dutch school was a combination that began to emerge as a pattern among the more distinguished collectors of the Gilded Age. It was already evident in the first catalogue of the collection of Peter A. B. Widener and would also come to characterize those of Frick, the Charles Phelps Tafts in Cincinnati, John Long Severance in Cleveland, and George Eastman in Rochester, New York. Other collectors such as Matthias Arnot in Elmira, New York, and William L. Elkins in Philadelphia focused primarily on their continuing acquisition of nineteenth-century European art.[7] Still others, like James J. Hill of Saint Paul, Minnesota, never entered the arena of old master collecting.

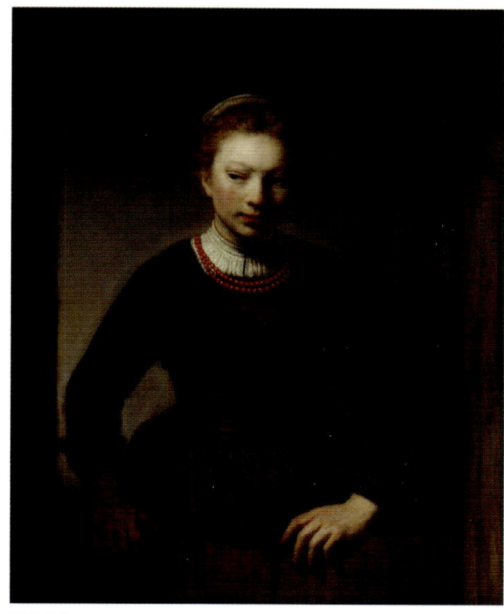

FIG. 29

The Yerkes collection was notable on several fronts not least because as early as 1893 it professed to contain no fewer than four Rembrandts. It also included paintings ascribed to Peter Paul Rubens (1577–1640) and Anthony Van Dyck (1599–1641). Its roster of Dutch masters included all the celebrated names with the exception of Vermeer, who would feature prominently in the great collections of Benjamin Altman, Frick, the Wideners, and Andrew Mellon. These artists included Frans Hals (1581/85–1666), Meindert Hobbema (1638–1709), Pieter de Hooch (1629–1684), Gabriel Metsu (1629–1667), Adriaen (1610–1685) and Isack (1621–1649) van Ostade, Paulus Potter (1625–1654), Gerard Terborch (1617–1681), and many others, not to mention as many as six works ascribed to David Teniers the Younger (1610–1690).[8]

The Detroit collector James E. Scripps, a local newspaper magnate, acquired roughly a hundred European paintings, mostly during a prolonged visit to Europe in 1887–88 ostensibly intended as a health cure. In fact, Scripps spent much time in contact with art dealers who were bidding at auction on his behalf. Scripps was particularly successful at the Corbett-Winder sale, where he acquired many of his finest Dutch pictures.[9] His greatest purchase was the large Rubens painting *David and Abigail*, acquired from the Secrétan collection. As a counterpart to this large-scale canvas Scripps bought a work then ascribed to Rembrandt, *The Death of Lucretia*(?) (see PLATE 39, pp. 144). This ambitious yet curious picture has long since been dismissed as a Rembrandt, but its attribution remains undetermined despite its distinctive painting technique characterized by much broad incising of the still-wet paint by the butt end of the brush. By presenting a sizable group of European old master paintings (roughly seventy in all) to the fledgling Detroit Museum of Art (the immediate precursor of the Detroit Institute of Arts), Scripps hoped to encourage others to follow suit. Ironically this initiative largely failed until William Valentiner arrived in Detroit in the early 1920s, first as advisor and then as director (1924–44) of the DIA.

A somewhat analogous situation evolved in Chicago in the mid-1890s, but with a different outcome. First, Charles Yerkes moved to the city, bringing his already sizable collection of European paintings. Charles L. Hutchinson, president of the Art Institute of Chicago (founded in 1879), traveled with his wife and his close friends the Martin Antoine Ryersons to Europe in 1890. While in Italy they saw the collection of the princes Anatole and Paul Demidoff, initially housed at Villa di San Donato in Florence. The two couples acquired more than a dozen excellent old master paintings from this source, works almost exclusively of the Dutch school that included fine, representative examples by Hobbema, Adriaen van Ostade, Adriaen van de Velde (1636–1672), and Reinier Nooms "Zeeman" (1623–1664). They then persuaded other wealthy Chicagoans to purchase pictures from the Demidoff collection with the express intention of presenting them to the new museum. Included in the group—in fact, the painting purchased by Ryerson and presented by him to the Art Institute—is the picture long attributed to Rembrandt, *Young Woman at an Open Half-door* (FIG. 29).[10] In 1891, as part of this campaign, Charles Yerkes

FIG. 29
Attributed to Rembrandt van Rijn, *Young Woman at an Open Half-door*, 1645, oil on canvas, 102.5 x 85.1 cm (40 3/8 x 33 1/2 in.). The Art Institute of Chicago; Mr. and Mrs. Martin A. Ryerson Collection; 1894.1022

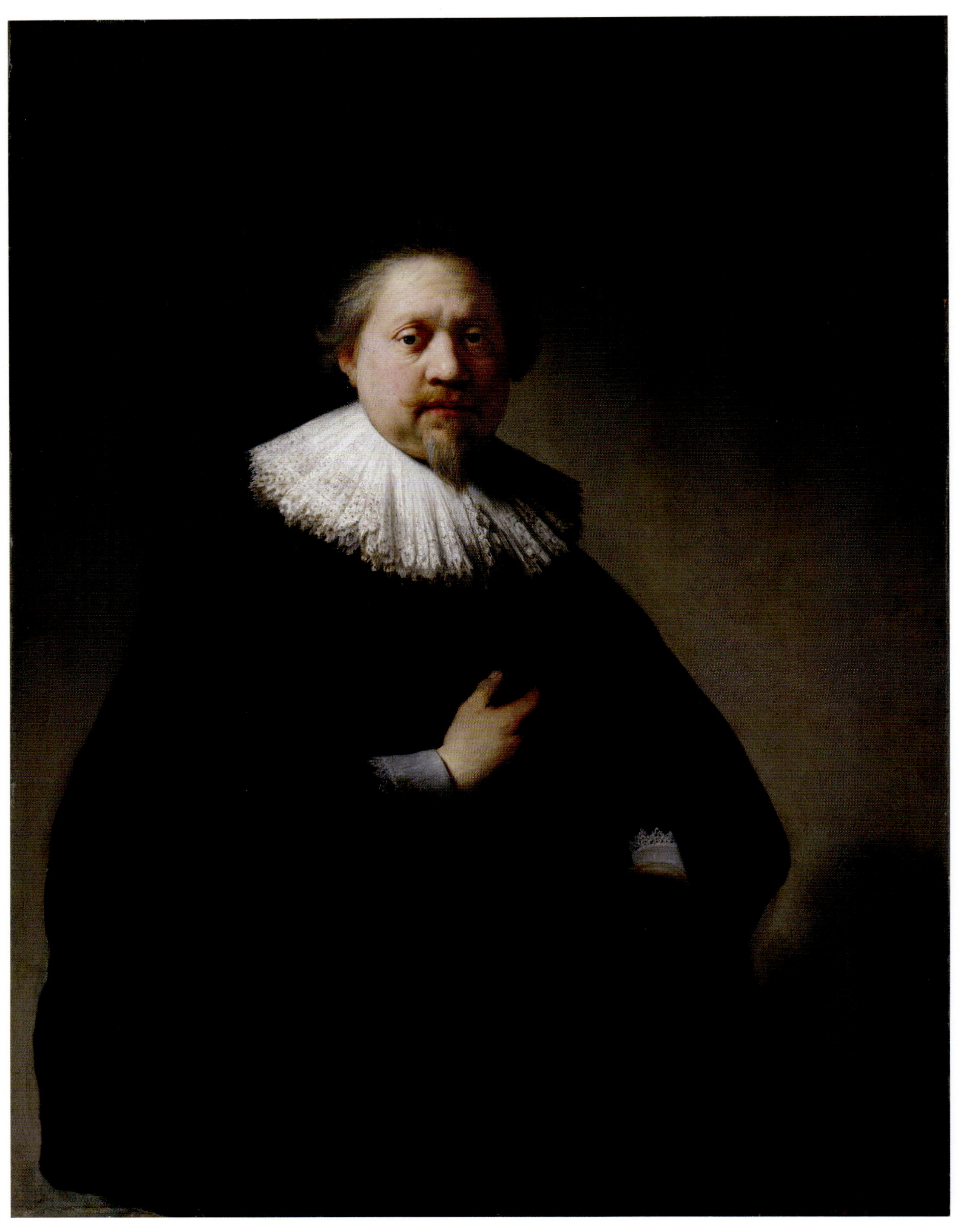

PLATE 10 [CAT. 9]
Rembrandt van Rijn
Portrait of a Man, Probably a Member of the Van Beresteyn Family, 1632
Oil on canvas, 111.8 x 88.9 cm (44 x 35 in.)
The Metropolitan Museum of Art, New York

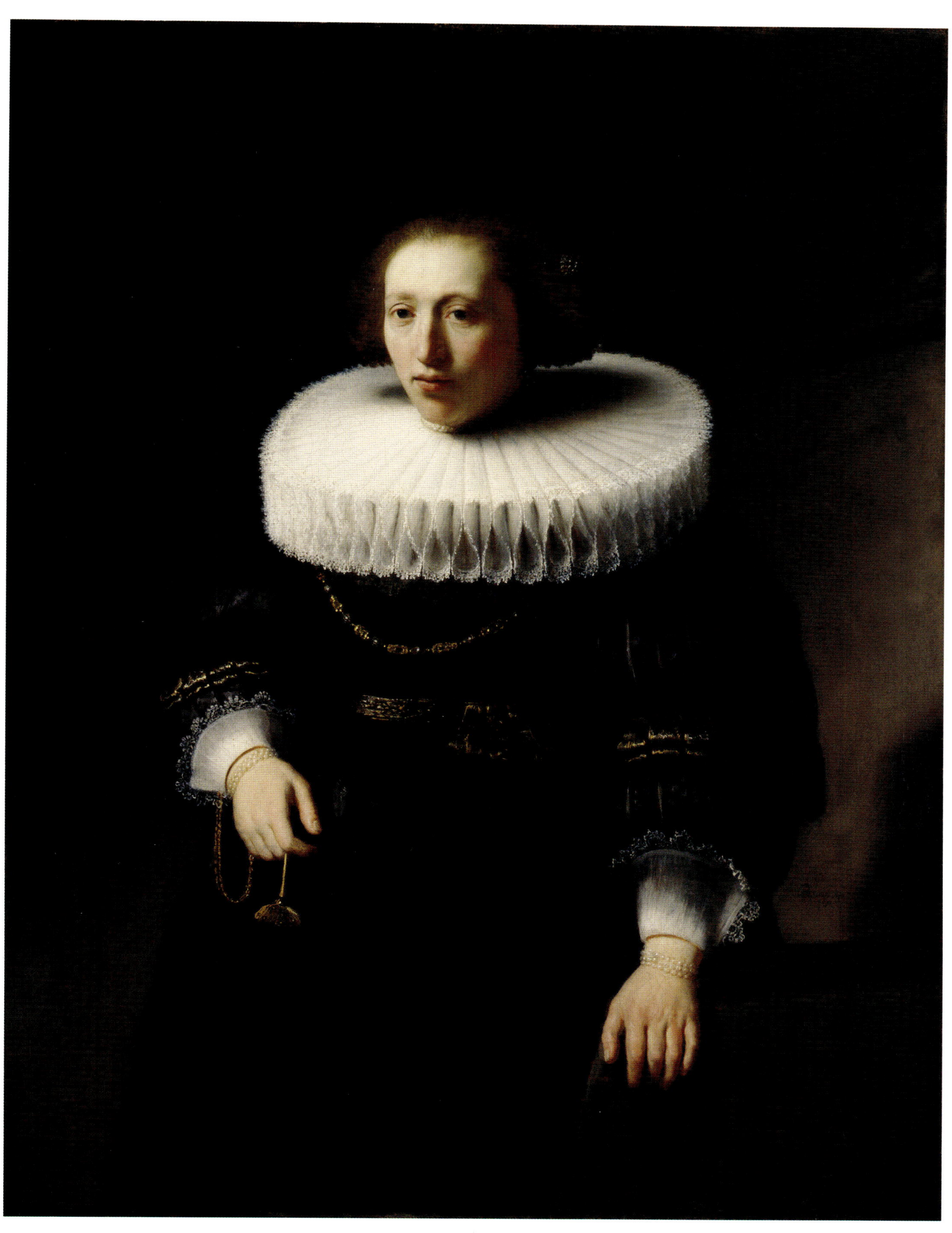

PLATE II [CAT. 10]
Rembrandt van Rijn
Portrait of a Woman, Probably a Member of the Van Beresteyn Family, 1632
Oil on canvas, 111.8 x 88.9 cm (44 x 35 in.)
The Metropolitan Museum of Art, New York

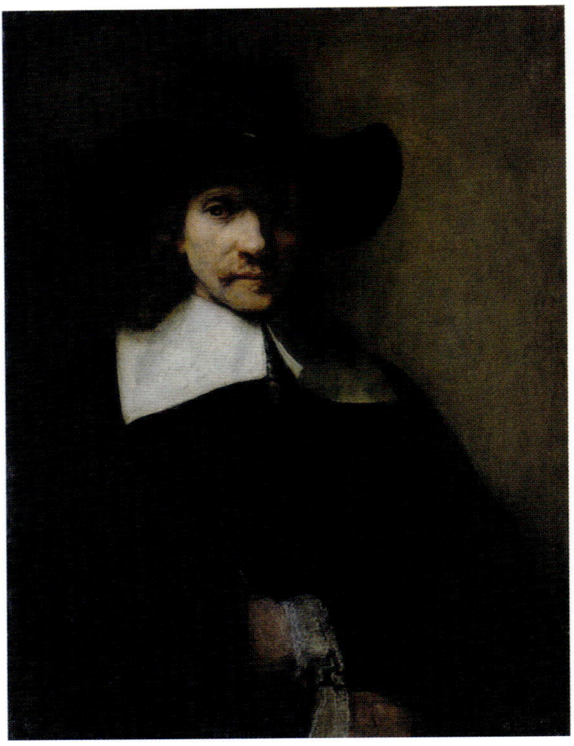

FIG. 30

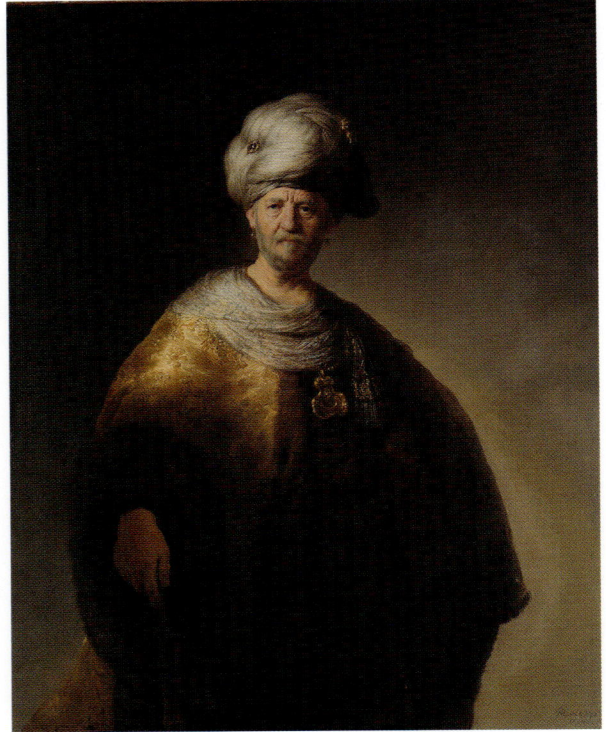

FIG. 31

presented to the Art Institute *The Music Lesson* by Terborch, also from the Demidoff collection.[11] Although the bulk of the Ryerson collection was not bequeathed to the Art Institute of Chicago until 1933, Ryerson had begun actively collecting decades earlier. His taste was broad-ranging, but he showed a strong predilection for the Italian Renaissance, the early Netherlandish school, and Dutch and Flemish masters of the seventeenth century. He also acquired rare early French artists such as the Master of Amiens (active 1515–1525) and the Master of Moulins (now identified as Jean Hey, active 1494–1504). Ryerson also bought contemporary and near-contemporary works by French and American artists, from Gustave Courbet (1819–1877) through the Nabis and painters such as Winslow Homer (1836–1910), John Singer Sargent (1856–1925), and John Twachtman (1853–1902).

If the Yerkes collection was the first available in print (his deluxe catalogue was published in 1893), he could not claim the distinction of being the first American collector to have acquired a major, indisputable picture by Rembrandt.[12] That honor lay elsewhere with the New York art dealer William Schaus, who bought the *Portrait of Herman Doomer* (see FIG. 4, p. 22), then simply known as *The Gilder,* from the French duke Charles-Auguste de Morny in 1884. Its high price—210,000 French francs ($42,000 at the time)—generated widespread interest. It certainly commanded sustained interest in the New York press, which stressed the great quality of this portrait in its campaign to find a lasting home in the United States.[13] Schaus was unable to find a buyer for *The Gilder* for more than four years, but in March 1889, Henry Havemeyer purchased the painting, purportedly for $80,000.[14]

By the late 1880s, the allure of Rembrandt's paintings attracted a handful of American collectors. Henry Marquand, who incidentally acquired the first Vermeer to enter an American collection, bought *Portrait of a Man* (FIG. 30) from Thomas Agnew & Sons in 1883 as his example of Rembrandt.[15] Although this picture in its substantially damaged state can count only as a poor reflection of Rembrandt's power as a portraitist, its place in Marquand's collection indicates the importance assigned to it by its owner, who, as trustee of the Metropolitan Museum of Art, wished to provide the museum with a distinguished roster of European old master paintings. Marquand acquired a second portrait, *Man with a Beard* (Metropolitan Museum of Art, New York). Its attribution to Rembrandt has long been challenged, considered by some to be an English pastiche of the eighteenth century. Most recently Walter Liedtke convincingly lists it as an early Dutch imitation of Rembrandt produced between 1680 and 1710.[16]

FIG. 30
Rembrandt van Rijn, *Portrait of a Man*, c. 1655–60, oil on canvas, 83.5 x 64.5 cm (32 7/8 x 25 3/8 in.). The Metropolitan Museum of Art, New York; Marquand Collection, Gift of Henry G. Marquand; 890; 91.26.7

FIG. 31
Rembrandt van Rijn, *Man in an Oriental Costume ("The Noble Slav")*, 1632, oil on canvas, 152.7 x 111.1 cm (60 1/8 x 43 3/4 in.). The Metropolitan Museum of Art, New York; Bequest of William K. Vanderbilt, 1920; 20.155.2

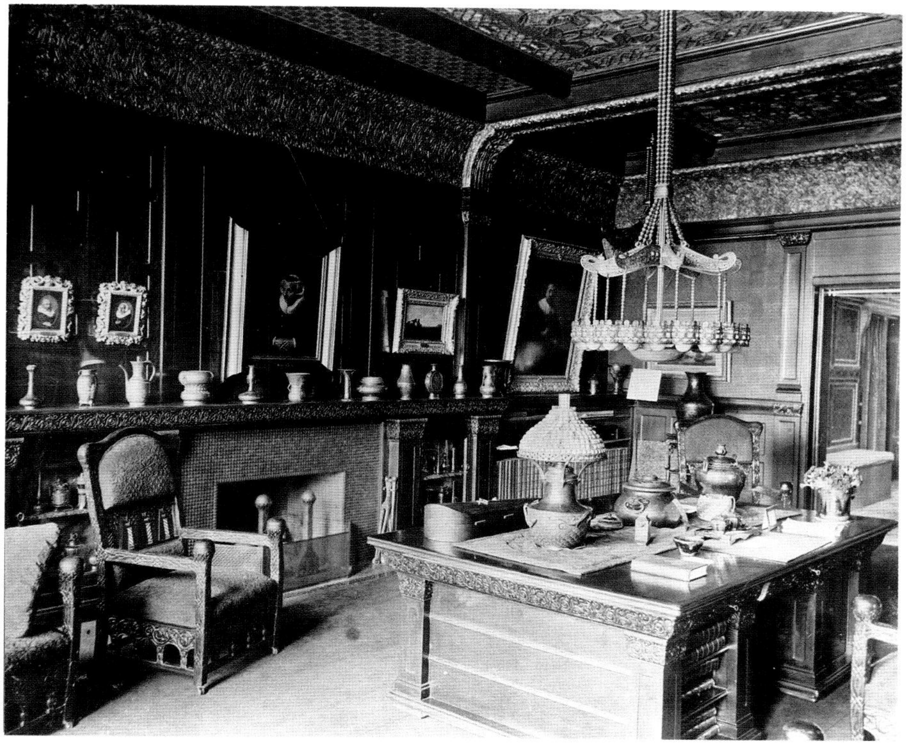

FIG. 32

As W. G. Constable pointed out, the character of the Marquand collection was a harbinger of what would soon follow. Marquand shifted his collecting focus from contemporary painting to the old masters, not to mention non-European cultures—namely the art of East Asia and the Islamic world.[17] One such collection essentially assembled by 1900 was that of William L. Elkins of Philadelphia. A friend of John G. Johnson and partner of Peter Widener, Elkins, like Widener and Yerkes, consolidated his fortune in public transit with city trolley systems. His initial fortune derived from developing the oil fields of western Pennsylvania for John D. Rockefeller's Standard Oil Company. His old master paintings were virtually all Dutch from the "Golden Age" of the seventeenth century and included capital pictures by Terborch, Hobbema, van Ostade, and Potter. In fact, the Terborch and Potter, like two of Isabella Gardner's Rembrandts, came from the Pelham-Clinton-Hope collection.[18] Despite these highlights the collection's median level of quality is uneven, and Elkins's "Rembrandt," *An Old Man in Fanciful Costume* (Philadelphia Museum of Art), has proven to be no more than an old copy of Rembrandt's original now in the Calouste Gulbenkian Museum in Lisbon.[19]

Relative to Marquand, other New York collectors of the period such as William K. Vanderbilt and Henry Havemeyer fared better in their Rembrandt acquisitions. Vanderbilt's *Man in an Oriental Costume ("The Noble Slav")* (FIG. 31), purchased by Mrs. Vanderbilt from Wertheimer at some point between 1882 and 1885 and subsequently bequeathed to the Metropolitan Museum of Art in 1920, remains one of the most popular and compelling early works by Rembrandt in the United States.[20]

Henry Havemeyer became interested in Rembrandt early on and was soon the proud owner of eight pictures by or attributed to the master, which he displayed together in his library—the so-called Rembrandt Room (FIG. 32). His first purchase was the pair of Van Beresteyn family portraits, acquired late in 1888 for $60,000 (PLATES 10, 11).[21] He subsequently acquired a second pair of portraits (Metropolitan Museum of Art, New York), now considered to be by a follower of Rembrandt painted in the mid-1640s.[22] This pair, plus two other portraits, came from the Parisian collection of Achille de Seillière—sold by his daughter the Princesse de Sagan (Jeanne Marguérite de Seillière) who inherited the collection assembled by her father.[23] Between 1888 and 1892 Havemeyer had purchased all eight of the Rembrandts that adorned his library. That he was able to acquire in such numbers within such a short time span was due in large measure to the uncertainty of the art market in Paris at the time.

FIG. 32
Interior of Rembrandt Room at the home of Henry Havemeyer, c. 1890s

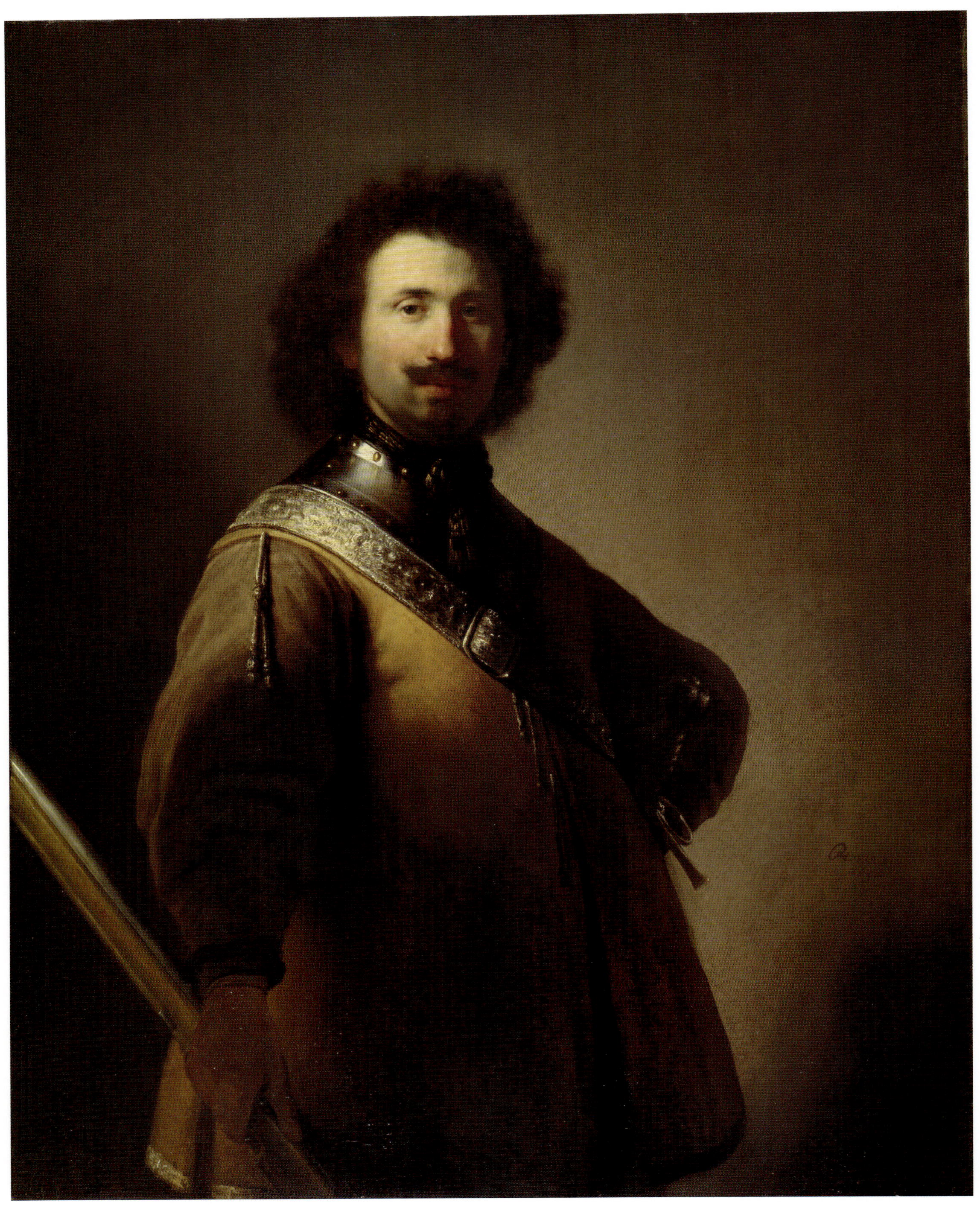

PLATE 12 [CAT. 11]
Rembrandt van Rijn
Joris de Caulerij, 1632
Oil on canvas, transferred to panel, 102.9 x 84.3 cm (40 ½ x 33 ¼ in.)
Fine Arts Museums of San Francisco, Legion of Honor

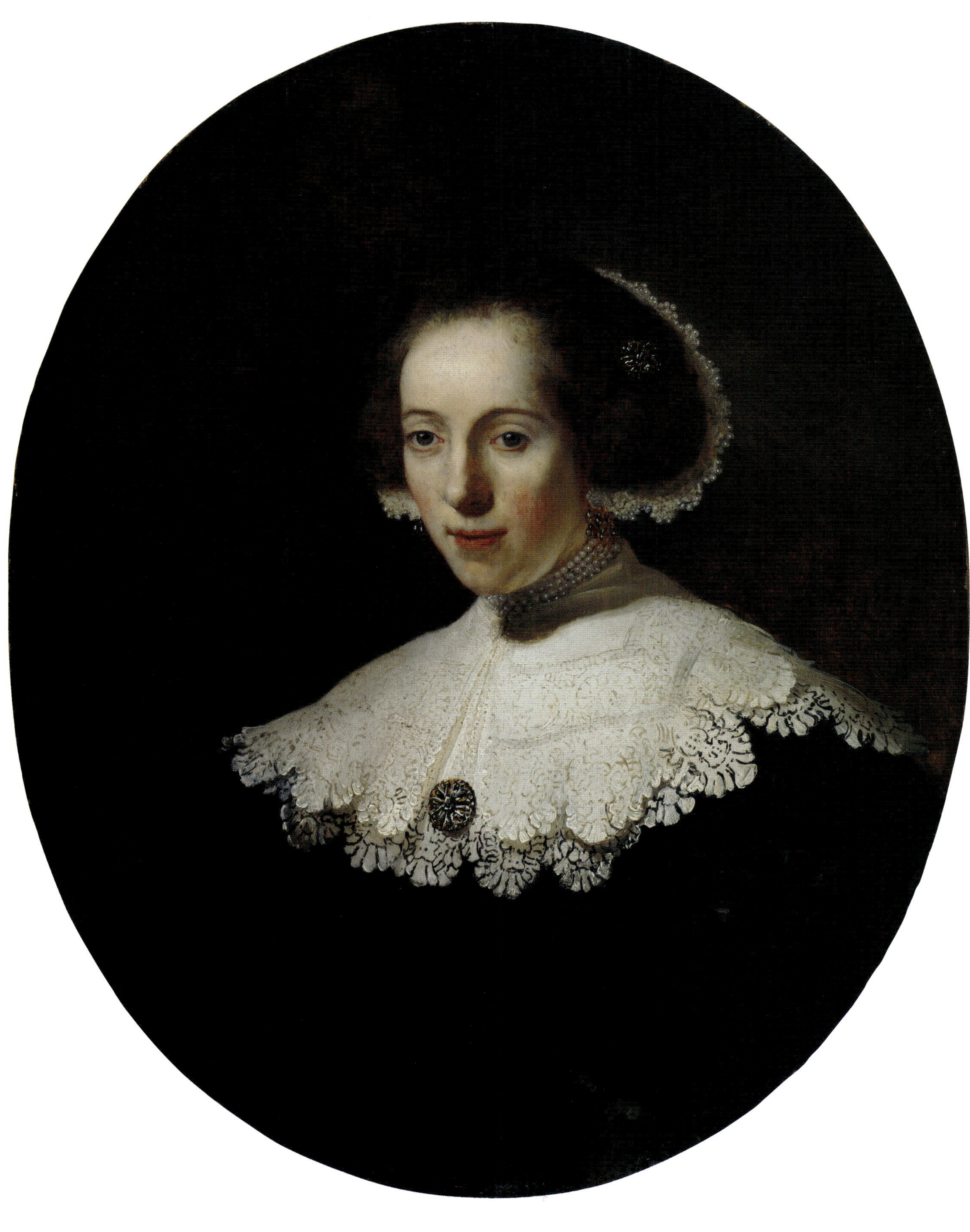

PLATE 13 [CAT. 21]
Rembrandt van Rijn and workshop
Portrait of a Woman, 1635 or earlier
Oil on oak panel, 77.5 x 64.8 cm (30½ x 25½ in.)
The Cleveland Museum of Art

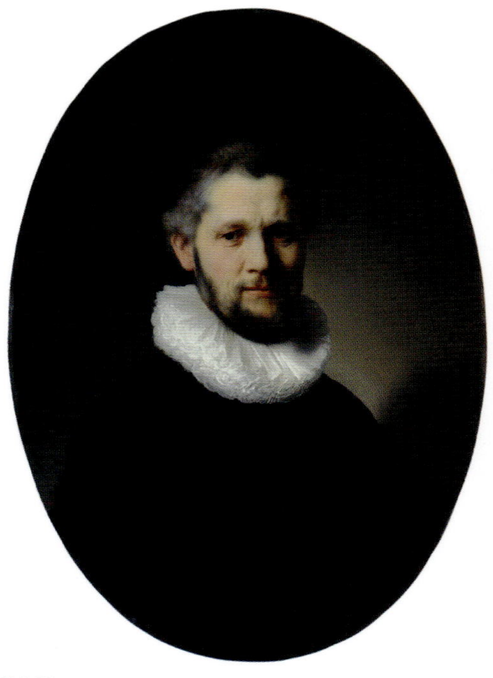

FIG. 33

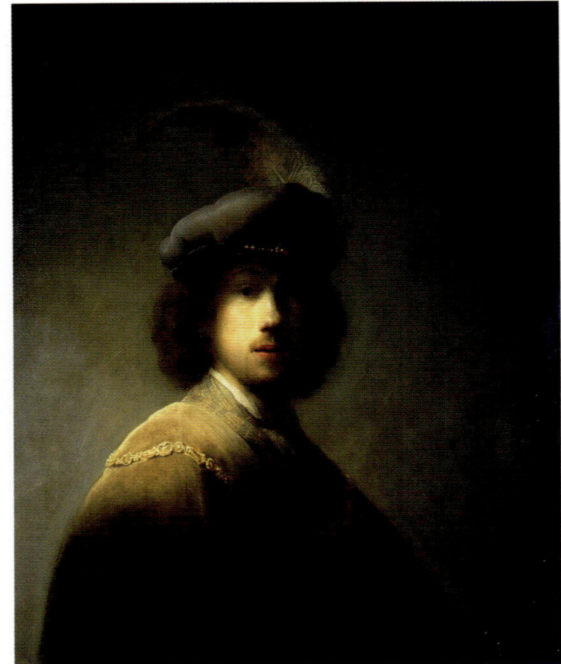

FIG. 34

Havemeyer was not alone in benefiting from the riches in the Seillière-Sagan collection. In or before 1889 James W. Ellsworth of Chicago and New York acquired the *Portrait of a Man,* signed and dated 1632 (FIG. 33), now in the collection of the Metropolitan Museum of Art.[24] Like the *Portrait of Herman Doomer,* this likeness is magnificently preserved. Shortly thereafter, in 1891, a Bostonian, Frederick L. Ames, acquired another pair of Rembrandt portraits from the Seillière-Sagan collection. His widow presented these oval panel paintings to the Museum of Fine Arts, Boston, in 1893, shortly after Ames's death.

The vast majority of Rembrandt paintings available to American collectors during the earlier years of the Gilded Age were portraits. This is not altogether surprising. Rembrandt's celebrated history pieces, whether drawn from the Bible or simply as civic commissions, had long entered the European public domain. Many had been prized possessions of the royal and princely collections forming the core of many of the greatest public picture galleries throughout Europe. As American collectors acquired European old master paintings in ever larger numbers, the quietly dignified portraits, primarily by seventeenth-century Dutch masters, were a fitting complement to the landscape and genre scenes that were such important components of these newly assembled collections.

At this point it is worth revisiting the collection of Charles T. Yerkes. His four Rembrandts—all of which were in his collection by 1893—are surprisingly diverse in subject. They included the glorious portrait *Joris de Caulerij* (PLATE 12), one of Rembrandt's most distinctive early Amsterdam period portraits—notable for its warm, glowing background. This painting, now in the Fine Arts Museums of San Francisco, is what might be deemed the most conventional of Yerkes's Rembrandts. *The Raising of Lazarus,* now in the collection of the Art Institute of Chicago, turned out to be a copy of Rembrandt's original panel painting now in the Los Angeles County Museum of Art, and *Philemon and Baucis* of 1658 (see PLATE 41, p. 150), now in the National Gallery of Art,[25] certainly represent a departure from the norm. Likewise the *Portrait of a Rabbi* (private collection, previously on loan to the Brooklyn Museum of Art) would prove to be one of the first of many examples in the indeterminate realm between portraiture and imaginary likeness that would haunt American collecting instincts throughout much of the following century.[26] Yerkes, like so many early American collectors of the Gilded Age, sincerely wanted his collection to enter the public domain—namely as a museum in New York City. However, the huge encumbrances on his estate resulted, instead, in the dispersal of his art collection at auction in 1910.

The diversity of Rembrandts in the Yerkes collection finds a counterpart in the four Rembrandts acquired by Isabella Stewart Gardner in Boston. Curiously, in 1866, roughly ten

FIG. 33
Rembrandt van Rijn, *Portrait of a Man,* 1632, oil on canvas, 75.6 x 52.1 cm (29¾ x 20½ in.). The Metropolitan Museum of Art, New York; Gift of Mrs. Lincoln Ellsworth, in memory of Lincoln Ellsworth, 1964; 64.126

FIG. 34
Rembrandt van Rijn, *Self-portrait,* 1629, oil on panel, 89.5 x 73.5 cm (35½ x 29 in.). The Isabella Stewart Gardner Museum, Boston

years before Gardner bought her Rembrandt, a Frenchman, Émile Durand-Gréville, traveled across much of the East Coast of the United States. When in Boston he described a picture he saw in the collection of Frances Brooks as the only alleged Rembrandt painting he knew of in America. This canvas, *Mercury and Aglauros* (see FIG. 81, p. 148), long in the collection of the Museum of Fine Arts, Boston, was only relatively recently recognized by Frits Duparc as a characteristic early work by Carel Fabritius (1622–1654). In the monographic exhibition devoted to this artist held in 2004–5, it was further discovered that this picture bears Fabritius's original signature.[27] This type of painting is perhaps symptomatic of the collecting aspirations of the trustees who founded the Museum of Fine Arts, Boston, and the Metropolitan Museum of Art in New York, both in 1870. To quote Joseph H. Choate, one of the founding trustees of the Met: "though the great masterpieces of painting and sculpture . . . could never be within their reach, yet it might be possible in the progress of time to gather together a collection of works of merit, which should impart some knowledge of art and its history to people who were yet to take almost their first steps in that department of knowledge."[28] Or to quote Martin Brimmer, founding trustee of the Museum of Fine Arts: "None the less, however, are the best pictures and marbles their prizes. The master's hand, expressing the master's mind, gives that which fills the eye and touches the imagination as nothing else can, and no opportunity should be neglected to procure for our museums works of this original and permanent value. The fact that such works of the older painters and sculptors are daily becoming more rare and costly, as they are gradually being gathered into the public collections of Europe, should be rather a stimulus than a discouragement; for at the rate which they are now being absorbed, they will, in another generation, be almost unobtainable."[29] Circumstances would soon demonstrate how wide off the mark these fears and concerns would prove to be.

In 1898, one of the most famous and distinguished British collections of Dutch pictures—that of Francis Pelham-Clinton-Hope—was dispersed in London. Among the masterpieces were two Rembrandts, *Christ in the Storm on the Sea of Galilee,* signed and dated 1633 (see FIG. 83, p. 149), and *A Lady and a Gentleman in Black* (see FIG. 60, p. 122). Isabella Stewart Gardner, on the recommendation of her trusted advisor Bernard Berenson, purchased both. Two years earlier, she had acquired Rembrandt's *Self-portrait* of 1629 (FIG. 34). The fourth of her quartet of Rembrandts, *The Landscape with an Obelisk,* entered the collection in 1900. Fairly recently this last picture was correctly identified as being by Govaert Flinck (1615–1660), even bearing the remains of his characteristic signature.[30] Three of these paintings were stolen in 1990, with only the *Self-portrait* remaining at Fenway Court to this day. Gardner's Rembrandts represent an unusual lot relative to the preponderance of single-figure portraits assembled by Henry Havemeyer, a circumstance that would also predominate in the collections of Benjamin Altman and the Wideners. Her *Christ in the Storm on the Sea of Galilee* is arguably the most distinguished of all Rembrandt's earlier history subjects to have found its way to America.

What began in the 1890s as a slowly increasing stream of indisputable and alleged Rembrandt paintings became a strong current after 1900. From the later 1880s onward, when American collectors began acquiring European old master and nineteenth-century paintings in ever larger numbers, a certain number of Parisian and London-based art dealers came to dominate the market. Names such as Charles Sedelmeyer, Durand-Ruel, Gimpel & Wildenstein, Kleinberger Co., and Charles Seligmann in Paris, and Thomas Agnew & Sons, Colnaghi, Duveen, and Arthur J. Sulley & Co. in London became purveyors of the most expensive and fashionable paintings and objets d'art that were so sought after by the hyperrich. Many of these concerns had offices or galleries in more than one city, including New York, which grew rapidly in importance as a center for the art trade. Firms like Knoedler & Company and Duveen had branches in all three cities. The most celebrated dealer of this period was undoubtedly Joseph Duveen whose ambitions led him to expand beyond London. He established sumptuous galleries in the Place Vendôme in Paris and on Fifth Avenue in New York City. Among his most distinguished clients Duveen would come to count Benjamin Altman, Arabella and Henry E. Huntington, Jules Bache, Henry Clay Frick (admittedly mostly for British grand manner portraits),[31] Peter and Joseph Widener, and Andrew Mellon. Certain American collectors such as Peter Widener showed a greater predilection for Arthur J. Sulley & Co. in London, whereas the Charles Phelps Tafts bought almost exclusively from Scott & Fowles—largely because of their trusted relationship with Charles F. Fowles, who tragically drowned in the sinking of the *Lusitania* in 1915. For collectors like the Tafts, having the convenience of purchasing largely in New York City helps explain why dealers like Knoedler, Duveen, Scott & Fowles, and Durand-Ruel set up branches in the New World.

As their taste became more refined certain American collectors came to feel a greater comfort level acquiring pictures that came from distinguished British aristocratic collections.[32] Partly because of this inclination they also tended to work more closely with English art dealers. The commonality of language, matched with the desire for British grand-manner portraits that fit nicely into the baronial homes being built for these collectors cum captains of industry, enabled them to include in their assemblage of old masters innumerable "fictive ancestor portraits."[33] This focus is especially evident in the case of Peter Widener and his son Joseph, Henry Clay Frick, and the Charles Phelps Tafts. It would find an echo in the far more modest collecting activities of major museum benefactors such as George Eastman in Rochester, New York; John Severance and his sister, Elisabeth Severance Prentiss, in Cleveland; Edward Drummond Libbey in Toledo; and Edsel and Eleanor Ford and members of the Fisher family in Detroit.

The collecting activities of Peter Widener constitute a singular instance that was to radically change the phenomenon of art collecting in the United States. Widener made his fortune in public transportation, in cable cars and subsequently electric trolleys. He increased his already enormous wealth through substantial investments in companies such as the U.S. Steel Corporation, the American Tobacco Company, the Standard Oil Company, and the Pennsylvania Railroad, among others.[34]

Peter Widener was a voracious collector whose first serious pictures were representative examples of the school of Barbizon—Corot (1796–1875), Daubigny (1817–1878), Diaz de la Peña (1807–1876), Jacque (1813–1894), Millet (1814–1875), Rousseau (1812–1867), and Troyon (1810–1865)—the usual roster. Partly inspired by his close friend and business associate John G. Johnson, Widener became interested in the old masters as well. Unfortunately both collectors came under the spell of the dubious—indeed often unscrupulous—activities of the picture dealer Leo (Leonardus) Nardus. Nardus fobbed off works by minor masters and outright forgeries masquerading as characteristic works by major old master painters, especially of the Dutch and Italian schools. Widener acquired ninety-three pictures from Nardus during the 1880s and 1890s. By 1907, Widener had come to question the supposed authenticity of many of those purchases and soon thereafter realized that, for all practical purposes, he had been badly swindled.[35]

Widener's friend Johnson deeply regretted having introduced Widener to Nardus. In forming his own collection Johnson first chose not to compete with his far wealthier friends for the most sought-after, big-name artists; instead he set out to acquire fine and interesting works by lesser-known masters. Second, he devoted much time to researching potential acquisitions and perusing auction catalogues and scholarly publications. Third, he sought the advice of experts. His candid self-assessment is salutary:

> Buying on my own sadly uninformed and misinformed knowledge, I have put my foot in it at times, but I might have fared far worse in the hands of those besides whom base jackals are innocents—the Dealers in art. Some most lucky purchases at very low prices of works now almost priceless go far to make the final result good. I have been badly used of the hands of a rascal. . . . Despite of him, the percentage of fakes is light. In many cases where I took chances, either I could not have gotten advice in time, or advice would have been impossible.[36]

Because of this perceived fraud, in 1908 Widener invited the Dutch connoisseur and expert Cornelius Hofstede de Groot to his palatial home outside Philadelphia, Lynnewood Hall, to assess his paintings. Focusing on the Dutch and Flemish schools, Hofstede de Groot determined that a depressingly large number were suspect and certainly not of sufficient quality to remain

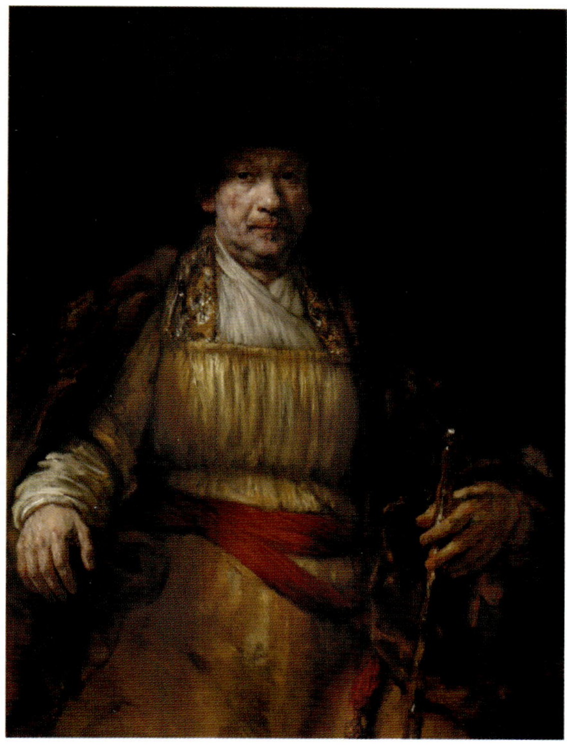

FIG. 35

in the collection. This led to a major purge of the collection in which roughly one hundred fifty paintings were disposed of. Hofstede de Groot, recognizing the scale of Nardus's deleterious impact on the collection, encouraged Widener to convene a group of experts to assess the collection. As a result Bernard Berenson examined the Italian paintings, Roger Fry the British, and Max J. Friedländer and Wilhelm von Bode the Netherlandish primitives. Hofstede de Groot also secured the assistance of William Valentiner. Several years later the two published their first volume—the Dutch and Flemish paintings in the Widener collection—in a set of three that represented the collection following its transformation in the wake of the radical cleansing that took place following Hofstede de Groot's momentous visit in 1908.[37]

From this point on Widener father and son consulted leading experts in making purchases. Their collection was soon emulated by other prominent American collectors.[38] Paintings dealers such as Joseph Duveen established close working relationships with many of the recognized experts. Duveen's most famous and provocative relationship of this order was with Bernard Berenson who, nonetheless, insisted on remaining free to advise whom he chose, including his initial patroness, Isabella Stewart Gardner.

The cleansing operation of the Wideners' paintings and their ensuing purchases transformed their collection into one of the most splendid of all American assemblages of old master paintings. They were not without rivals however. Several New York collectors also assembled fabulous collections in the years prior to and following World War I. The most notable and visible of them was Henry Clay Frick, whose purchases of two celebrated Rembrandts—*Self-portrait* of 1658 (FIG. 35) and *The Polish Rider* (see FIG. 3, p. 21)—assume pride of place among the galaxy of Frick's Dutch pictures.[39] In 1880 Frick, together with Andrew Mellon and two other young Pittsburghers, traveled to Europe and were able to see the Wallace Collection in London, at that time still maintained as a private collection. The visit left an indelible mark on Mellon and Frick. In establishing the Frick Collection in his mansion at Fifth Avenue and 70th Street, Frick clearly intended to create a magnificent American counterpart to the Wallace Collection. Interestingly, Mellon chose a different path in creating the National Gallery of Art, which closely resembles London's National Gallery.[40]

A second New Yorker, Benjamin Altman, assembled a magnificent group of Dutch and Italian old masters crowned with works by Rembrandt and Hals. At the time of his death in 1913 Altman had acquired, to his mind, no fewer than eleven paintings by Rembrandt. Although

FIG. 35
Rembrandt van Rijn, *Self-portrait*, 1658, oil on canvas, 133.7 x 103.8 cm (52 1/8 x 40 7/8 in.). The Frick Collection, New York; 1906.1.97

FIG. 36

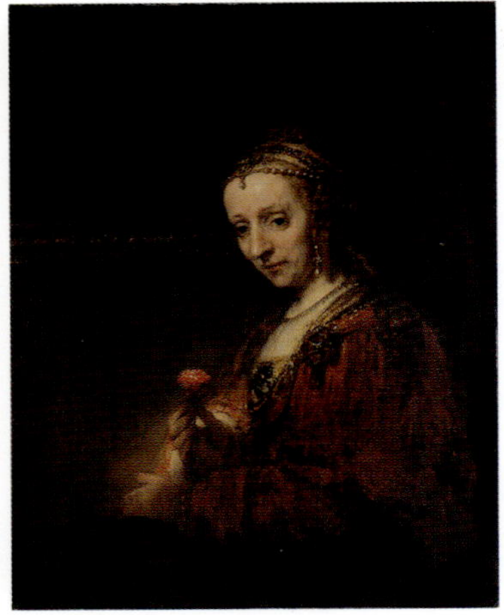

FIG. 37

recent connoisseurship has whittled this number down to six,[41] Altman's array of Rembrandt portraits contains such renowned masterpieces as *Self-portrait* of 1660 (Metropolitan Museum of Art, New York) and the haunting late pair, *Man with a Magnifying Glass* (FIG. 36) and *Woman with a Pink* (FIG. 37).[42] John G. Johnson, who informally monitored the collecting conquests of his wealthiest colleagues, expressed bemusement at the seemingly insatiable appetite Altman had for Rembrandt portraits. In 1909 he declared:

> The Wise Men of America know especially since Mr. Joseph Duveen has confirmed the fact, that Rembrandt is a great artist and they are insatiable in gluttony of his portraits. Mr. Altman feels very properly, that he cannot get too much of a good thing. He now has eight. Make it a dozen.[43]

Other collectors such as Mrs. Collis P. Huntington (later Mrs. Henry E. Huntington) and Alfred W. Erickson acquired major Rembrandt paintings. The Huntingtons owned *Flora* (see PLATE 44, p. 155), *Hendrickje Stoffels (as the Sorrowing Virgin)* (see FIG. 85, p. 154), and *Aristotle with a Bust of Homer* (see FIG. 2, p. 20). The latter was subsequently sold and purchased by Erickson.[44]

Almost without exception each of these major collectors of Rembrandt paintings came to the decision to present their collections, in one fashion or another, to institutions within the public domain.[45] In the case of Isabella Stewart Gardner, Henry Huntington, and Henry Clay Frick, the benefactors created their own storied public museums. The restrained and elegant patrician city residence of Frick is in complete contrast to Gardner's imaginative realm of a fictive Venetian gothic palace frozen in time. The Charles Phelps Tafts of Cincinnati also envisaged that their collection would enter the public domain but, like Frick, as a house museum.[46]

While there is no question that the great cities of the eastern seaboard of the United States were the center of the most ambitious collecting of European old master paintings, the example of the Tafts is, nonetheless, illuminating in the example they set within their community. Cincinnati, the queen city of the Ohio River, became an important hub by the mid-nineteenth century. It can claim the important distinction of being one of the very first cities west of the Appalachian Mountains to establish a civic art museum (founded in 1881).[47] As the city prospered, certain local collectors, inspired by the Tafts, wished to express their support for the city's municipal museum by acquiring small but choice selections of European old master paintings. Mary M. Emory acquired several fine pictures by artists such as Terborch, Joos van Cleve (?–1540/41), Lucas Cranach the Elder (1472–1553), Anthony Van Dyck, Hals, the Netherlandish Master of the Saint Lucy Legend (active 1475–1505), and a putative Rembrandt, *Young Girl Holding a Medal*. She acquired her pictures from the most reputed dealers of the period—Scott & Fowles (incidentally the primary source of the Taft paintings), Duveen, Kleinberger, and Seligmann. Her bequest dates from 1927. Emory did not restrict her interests to the Dutch school but acquired works by Italian and Spanish masters as well. They include some of the most important old master paintings in the museum's collection, ranging from Murillo (1618–1682) and Velázquez (1599–1660)

FIG. 36
Rembrandt van Rijn, *Man with a Magnifying Glass*, c. 1660–64, oil on canvas, 91.4 x 74.3 cm (36 x 29 ¼ in.). The Metropolitan Museum of Art, New York; Bequest of Benjamin Altman, 1913; 14.40.621

FIG. 37
Rembrandt van Rijn, *Woman with a Pink*, early 1660s, oil on canvas, 92.1 x 74.6 cm (36 ¼ x 29 ⅜ in.). The Metropolitan Museum of Art, New York; Bequest of Benjamin Altman, 1913; 14.40.622

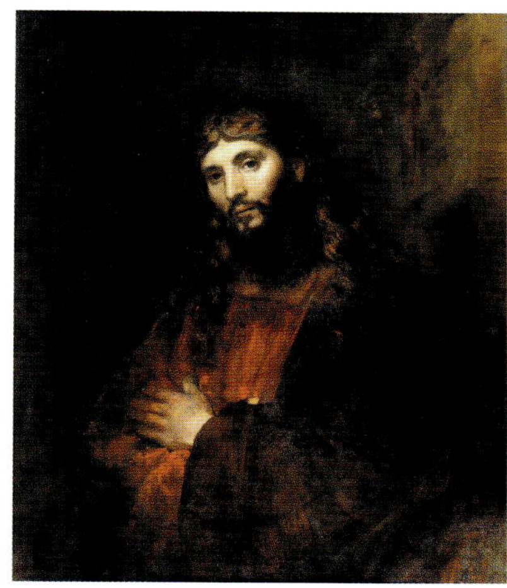

FIG. 38

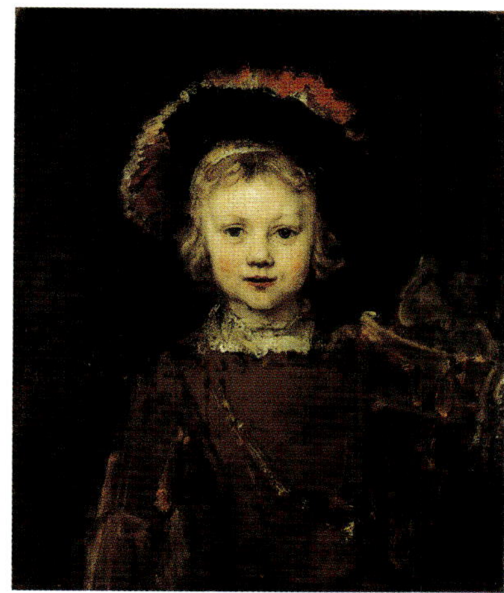

FIG. 39

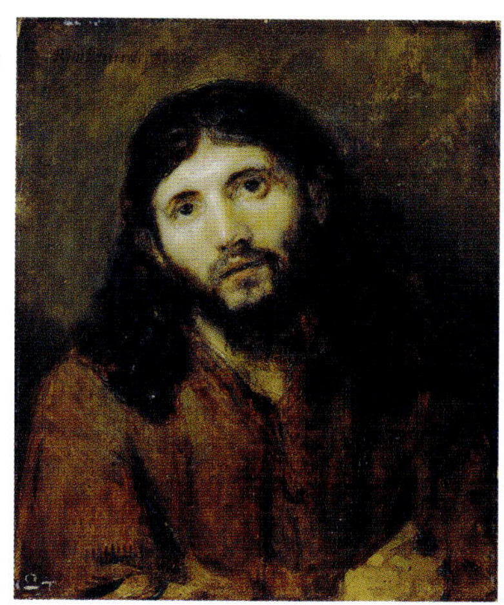

FIG. 40

to the *Portrait of Philip II* by Titian (c. ?1485/90–1576) and *A Sibyl and a Prophet* by Andrea Mantegna (1430/31–1506).

Mary Hanna also assembled a small collection (hardly more than a dozen paintings), most of which she gave to the Cincinnati Art Museum in 1946. These included a strong representation of Dutch masters including works by Terborch, Aelbert Cuyp (1620–1691), Jan van der Heyden (1637–1712), Hobbema, Metsu, and Jacob van Ruisdael (1628/9–1682). Like Mary Emory, Hanna bought from only the most prominent dealers—primarily Scott & Fowles and Knoedler & Company.[48] Among her purchases was *A Young Boy,* now classified as circle or follower of Rembrandt but which she bought as a *Portrait of Titus,* by Nicolaes Maes (1634–1693).

A somewhat parallel situation evolved in Cleveland with the collecting activities of John L. Severance and his sister, Elisabeth Severance Prentiss.[49] John Severance was a trustee of the Cleveland Museum of Art whose personal collection of European paintings attributed to old masters numbered little more than a dozen. His bequest in 1942 included pictures by Albrecht Bouts (1452/5–1549), Cima da Conegliano (1459/60–1517/18), Cuyp, Drouais (1699–1767), Gainsborough (1727–1788), Holbein (1460/65–1534), Lawrence (1769–1830), Nattier (1685–1766), Reynolds (1723–1792), and Turner's (1775–1851) celebrated *Burning of the Houses of Lords and Commons,* among others. Also included was his Rembrandt, *Bust of a Young Man with a Gold Chain* (see PLATE 23, p. 99), acquired from Knoedler & Company by 1921.[50] His small and eclectic grouping of old master paintings was evidently assembled partly with the museum in mind. His taste, like that of so many other American collectors of the period, reflects the ambitions of the great plutocrats of the Gilded Age, with a focus on the Dutch school, British grand-manner portraiture, and masters of the Italian Renaissance, along with the occasional Netherlandish master.

Elisabeth Prentiss was first married to Dudley P. Allen for whom the Allen Memorial Art Museum at Oberlin College is named. She bequeathed the majority of her paintings to the Cleveland Museum of Art. Her collection, like that of her brother, included British (Gainsborough), French (Lancret [1690–1743]), Italian Renaissance masters (Fra Angelico [1395/1400–1455], Granacci [1469–1543], Pinturicchio [1452–1513], and Andrea del Sarto [1486–1531]), but also works by Terborch and Rembrandt. Her *Portrait of a Woman* (PLATE 13, p. 69), a product of Rembrandt's early Amsterdam studio, conveys a gracious sense of bourgeois refinement despite its very damaged state. Mrs. Prentiss made the decision not to present her Hobbema, Turner, and Reynolds to the Cleveland Museum of Art but to Oberlin instead. She doubtless did so because her brother had already presented the Cleveland museum with important examples by the same artists. Like her brother she acquired the majority of her paintings from Knoedler & Company but also bought from Duveen and other prominent dealers.

We encounter a very similar situation in the case of George Eastman in Rochester, New York. Founder of the Kodak Camera Company, Eastman had the financial wherewithal to purchase works of the highest quality. His taste, like that of the Severance siblings, was essentially conservative with its focus on realist landscape painters of the nineteenth century

FIG. 38
Rembrandt van Rijn, *Bust of Christ,* c. 1657–61, oil on canvas, 109.2 x 90.2 cm (43 x 35 ½ in.). The Hyde Collection, Glens Falls, New York; 1971.37

FIG. 39
Rembrandt van Rijn, *Portrait of a Boy,* c. 1655–60, oil on canvas, 64.8 x 55.9 cm (25 ½ x 22 in.). The Norton Simon Foundation, Pasadena; F.1965.2.P

FIG. 40
Attributed to Rembrandt van Rijn, *Head of Christ,* c. 1648–50, oil on oak, 24.5 x 21.3 cm (9 ¾ x 8 ⅜ in.). The Detroit Institute of Arts; Founders Society Purchase; 30.370

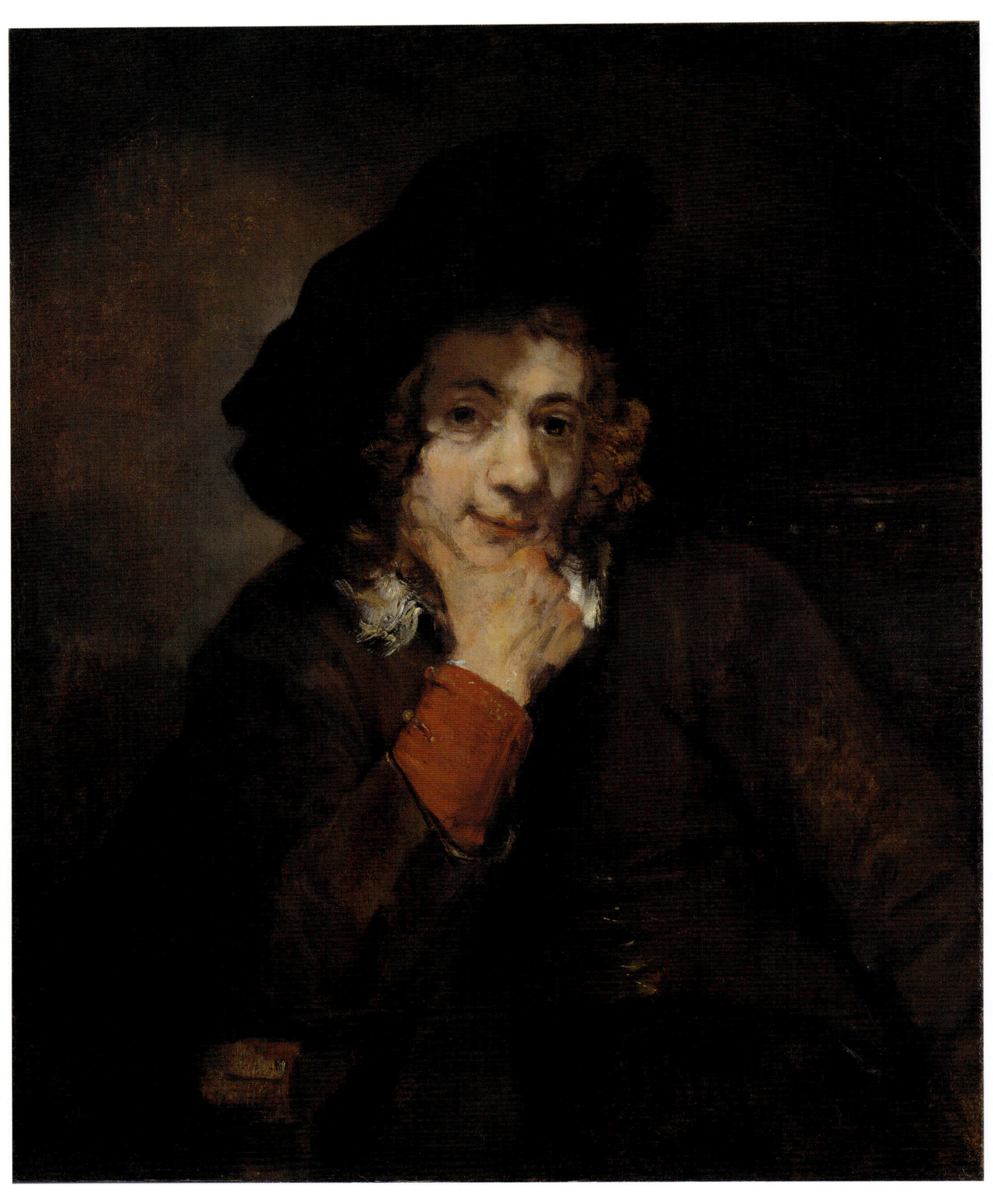

PLATE 14 [CAT. 35]
Rembrandt van Rijn
Titus, the Artist's Son, 1660
Oil on canvas, 81.3 x 68.7 cm (32 x 27 in.)
Baltimore Museum of Art

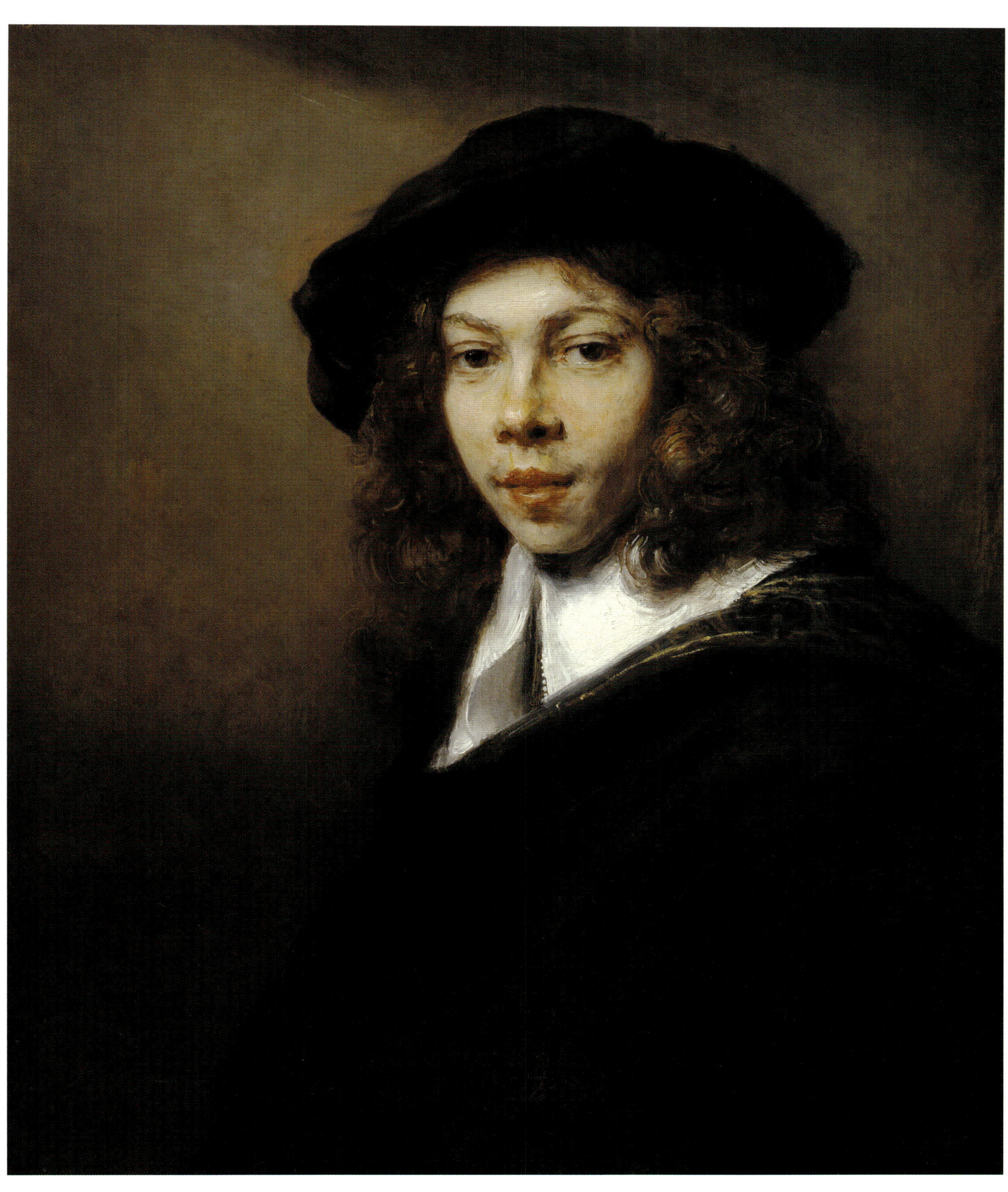

PLATE 15 [CAT. 38]
Rembrandt van Rijn
Portrait of Young Man, 1666
Oil on canvas, 71.6 x 62.8 cm (28 1/4 x 24 3/4 in.)
The Nelson-Atkins Museum of Art, Kansas City

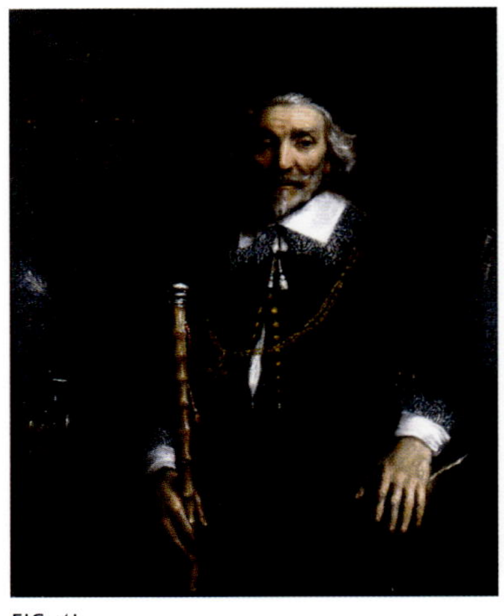

FIG. 41

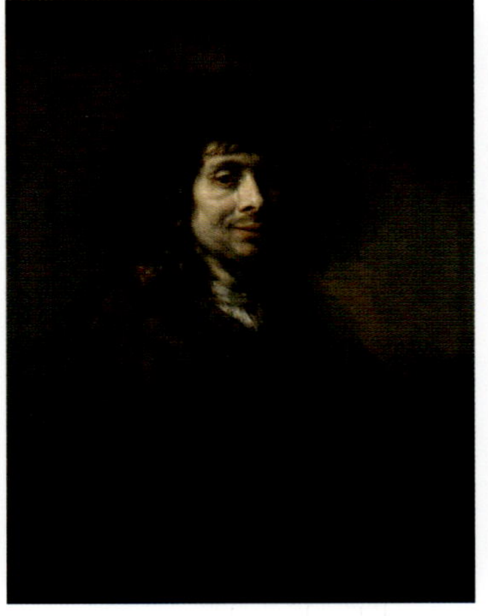

FIG. 42

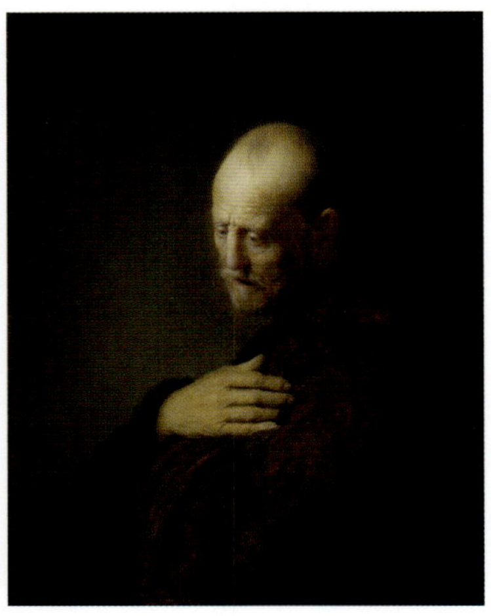

FIG. 43

(Daubigny, Jacob Maris [1837–1899], Millet, and Fritz Thaulow [1847–1906]), but also British grand-manner portraitists (Raeburn [1756–1823], Reynolds, and Romney [1734–1802]). Eastman also acquired portraits by Tintoretto, Van Dyck, Hals, and Rembrandt (see PLATE 36, p. 132), plus a masterpiece by Jan van de Cappelle (1626–1679). He bought his pictures exclusively from Knoedler and purchased the great majority between 1905 and 1914.[51]

Edward Drummond Libbey, who founded the Toledo Museum of Art in 1901 and whose fortune established the sustained international reputation of that insitution, bequeathed his collection to the museum in 1926. Included were not only old masters from various European schools, with a preponderance of British grand-manner portraiture and the Dutch masters of the seventeenth century, but Spanish painters as well. Highlights include portraits by Holbein and Joos van Cleve, a splendid Venetian view by Turner, and Rembrandt's *Young Man in a Plumed Hat* (see FIG. 54, p. 113).[52]

Like Mary Emory and Mary Hanna in Cincinnati or John L. Severance and Elisabeth Severance Prentiss in Cleveland, two collectors in Baltimore acquired small but fine collections of European old master painting with a strong focus on British and Dutch portraits.[53] Jacob Epstein and Mary Frick Jacobs acquired Rembrandt portraits from Joseph Duveen—Epstein *Old Man Wearing a Red Hat* (see PLATE 38, p. 137) in 1924 and Jacobs *Titus, the Artist's Son* (PLATE 14) in 1927.[54]

Other collectors active between the two world wars acquired paintings by or attributed to Rembrandt that would later enter and enrich public collections. One singular example is that of Herschel Jones, the newspaper magnate in Minneapolis whose unorthodox choice of Rembrandt's late *Lucretia* (see PLATE 40, p. 145), now in the Minneapolis Institute of Arts, arguably remains the greatest example of Rembrandt's late style in an American collection.[55]

John Ringling, the circus impresario whose enduring monument is the John and Mable Ringling Museum complex in Sarasota, Florida, also sought Rembrandts (see PLATE 46, p. 159) along with his cache of works by Rubens, wide-ranging collection of Venetian masters of the sixteenth century, and large-scale Italian baroque pictures. Whereas Herschel Jones landed himself a masterpiece, Ringling's foray into Rembrandt was less successful. Both pictures in the collection present complex attribution issues.[56] The same can be said for the "Rembrandts" in the collections of Senator William A. Clark, now part of the Corcoran Gallery of Art in Washington, D.C.,[57] and the more notorious collection of Thomas Barlow Walker of Minneapolis—now long dispersed and probably better forgotten.

Robert Sterling Clark—no relation to Senator William A.—also acquired two putative Rembrandt paintings. In 1923 he purchased from Knoedler *Portrait of a Man Reading* (see PLATE 33, p. 125), which had only recently been rediscovered and published by Abraham Bredius, who waxed eloquently about its great quality.[58] The Clark painting would appear to be the original that inspired many copies and reproductive prints.[59] Clark's other painting, *The Crucifixion,* is a most perplexing composition inspired perhaps by Rembrandt's late religious prints and drawings—but no specific source is demonstrably evident.

FIG. 41
Rembrandt van Rijn (studio of; Jürgen Ovens?), *Portrait of Dirck van Os*, 1662, oil on canvas, 101 x 85 cm (40¾ x 34½ in.). Joslyn Art Museum, Omaha; Museum Purchase; 1942.30

FIG. 42
Rembrandt van Rijn (studio of), *Portrait of a Young Man (perhaps an artist)*, 1661–62, oil on canvas, 89.9 x 70.8 cm (35⅜ x 27⅞ in.). Saint Louis Art Museum; Museum Purchase and funds given anonymously; 90:1950

FIG. 43
Rembrandt van Rijn (studio of), *An Old Man in Prayer*, c. 1628–30, oil on panel, 75.3 x 59.7 cm (29⅝ x 23½ in.). Museum of Fine Arts, Boston; Arthur Rotch Fund; 03.1080

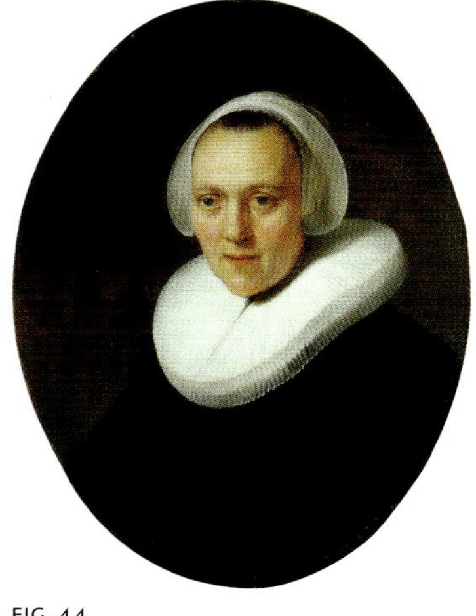

FIG. 44

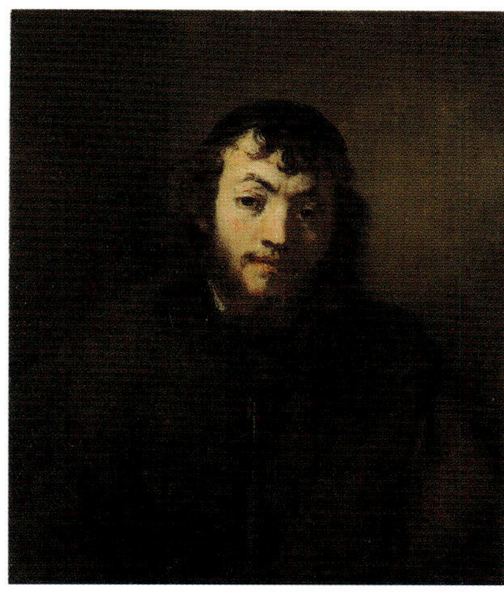

FIG. 45

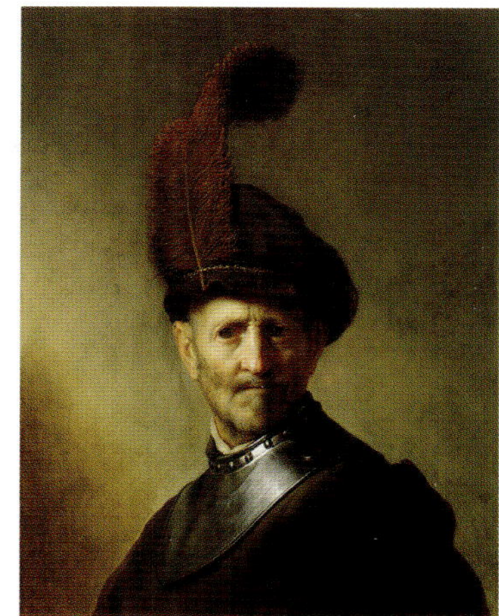

FIG. 46

Other American collectors were also attracted to the allure of Rembrandt. For example, the Hydes in Glens Falls, New York, acquired the monumental *Bust of Christ* (FIG. 38), sold by the Soviet government from the Orloff-Davidoff collection in 1933. Alvan T. Fuller of Boston purchased the magnificent late *Portrait of a Man in a Fur-lined Coat* (see PLATE 34, p. 130) now in Toledo.[60]

The three largest cities in California have all secured important Rembrandt paintings from private benefactions. Through the generosity of Mr. and Mrs. Roscoe Oakes, the Fine Arts Museums of San Francisco is now the fortunate possessor of the portrait *Joris de Caulerij* (see PLATE 12, p. 68), formerly in the Yerkes collection. The Timken Museum of Art in San Diego possesses the great *St. Bartholomew* of 1657 (see PLATE 43, p. 153), presented by the Putnam Foundation. In Los Angeles, J. Paul Getty gave one of his Rembrandts, *Portrait of Marten Looten* of 1632 (see PLATE 26, p. 114), to the Los Angeles County Museum of Art in 1953, whereas his namesake museum received the late *St. Bartholomew* of 1661 (see PLATE 48, p. 161). Norton Simon acquired several Rembrandt paintings including the celebrated *Portrait of a Boy* (FIG. 39), traditionally but erroneously identified as Titus van Rijn, the artist's son. Armand Hammer also secured Rembrandt paintings, including the well-known late work *Juno* (see FIG. 93, p. 166), the heart of his collection and the core of the European paintings collection at UCLA.

The interwar years also saw the rise of another aspect of American collecting—the role of the museum professional, usually the museum director, in determining and selecting acquisitions. The most conspicuous example of this phenomenon is William Valentiner, who, as director of the Detroit Institute of Arts from 1924 until 1944, purchased Rembrandts for his museum. He first acquired *The Visitation* of 1640 (see FIG. 88, p. 156) in 1927 and then *Head of Christ* (FIG. 40) in 1930, sold by the Soviet government from the imperial Palace of Pavlovsk. Valentiner also advised collectors in the United States during this period, including the Hydes. Unfortunately, because of his excessively expansionist notion of Rembrandt as a painter, many, indeed most, of his recommendations have not withstood the test of time. Even after he left Detroit, Valentiner continued to pursue Rembrandt in his successive positions, as the collection of the North Carolina Museum of Art can attest.

As the newer museums, primarily in the Midwest, continued to grow, they secured, among other things, substantial restricted funds for art acquisitions. While none could ever hope to assemble the range and depth of the holdings of the Metropolitan Museum of Art or the National Gallery of Art, each community deemed it eminently desirable to have Rembrandt represented by at least one excellent example of his brilliance as a painter. Thus began a sustained roll call of notable purchases beginning in 1931 with the newly founded Nelson-Atkins Museum of Art in Kansas City, which purchased the *Portrait of a Young Man* of 1666 (PLATE 15). This acquisition was followed in Omaha by the Joslyn Art Museum's 1942 purchase of the *Portrait of Dirck van Os* (FIG. 41), a painting now attributed to the school of Rembrandt with a tentative proposal that its actual author may be Jürgen Ovens (1623–1678).[61]

World War II caused something of a hiatus in museum purchasing until about 1950. Even at that date the expansionist tendency in Rembrandt connoisseurship continued to have its

FIG. 44
Rembrandt van Rijn, *Portrait of a Forty-year-old Woman*, 1634, oil on panel, 66 x 52.5 cm (27 x 21 ¾ in.). J. B. Speed Art Museum, Louisville; Museum Purchase; inv. 77.16

FIG. 45
Rembrandt van Rijn, *Portrait of a Young Jew*, 1663, oil on canvas, 65.8 x 57.5 cm (25 ⅞ x 22 ⅝ in.). Kimbell Art Museum, Fort Worth; AP 1977.04

FIG. 46
Rembrandt van Rijn, *An Old Man in Military Costume*, c. 1630–31, oil on panel, 66 x 50.8 cm (26 x 20 in.). The J. Paul Getty Museum, Los Angeles; inv. 78.PB.246

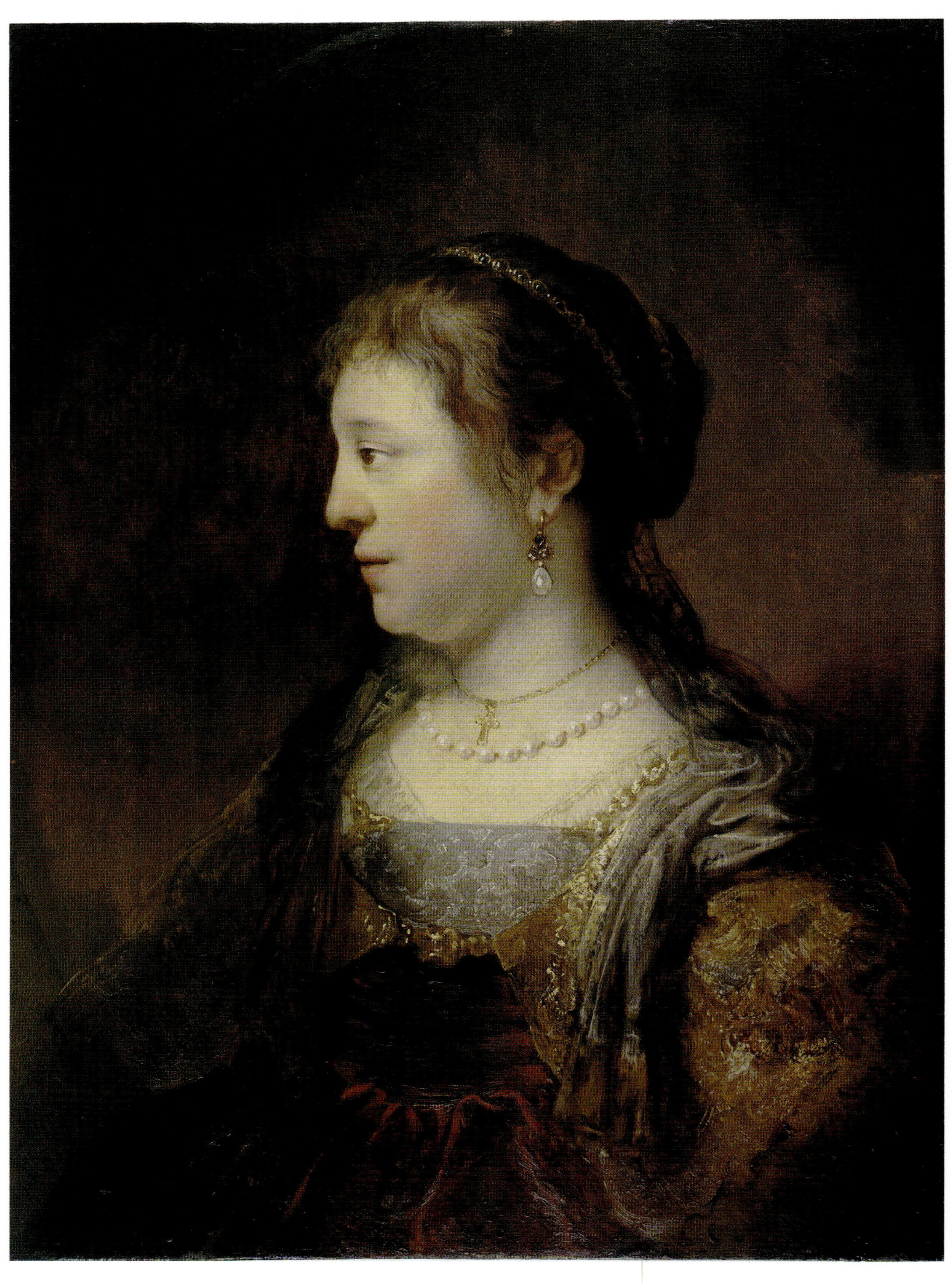

PLATE 16 [CAT. 22]
Govaert Flinck (attributed to)
Portrait of a Woman in Profile (Saskia?), 1636
Oil on panel, 68.6 x 52.7 cm (27 x 20¾ in.)
Wadsworth Atheneum Museum of Art, Hartford

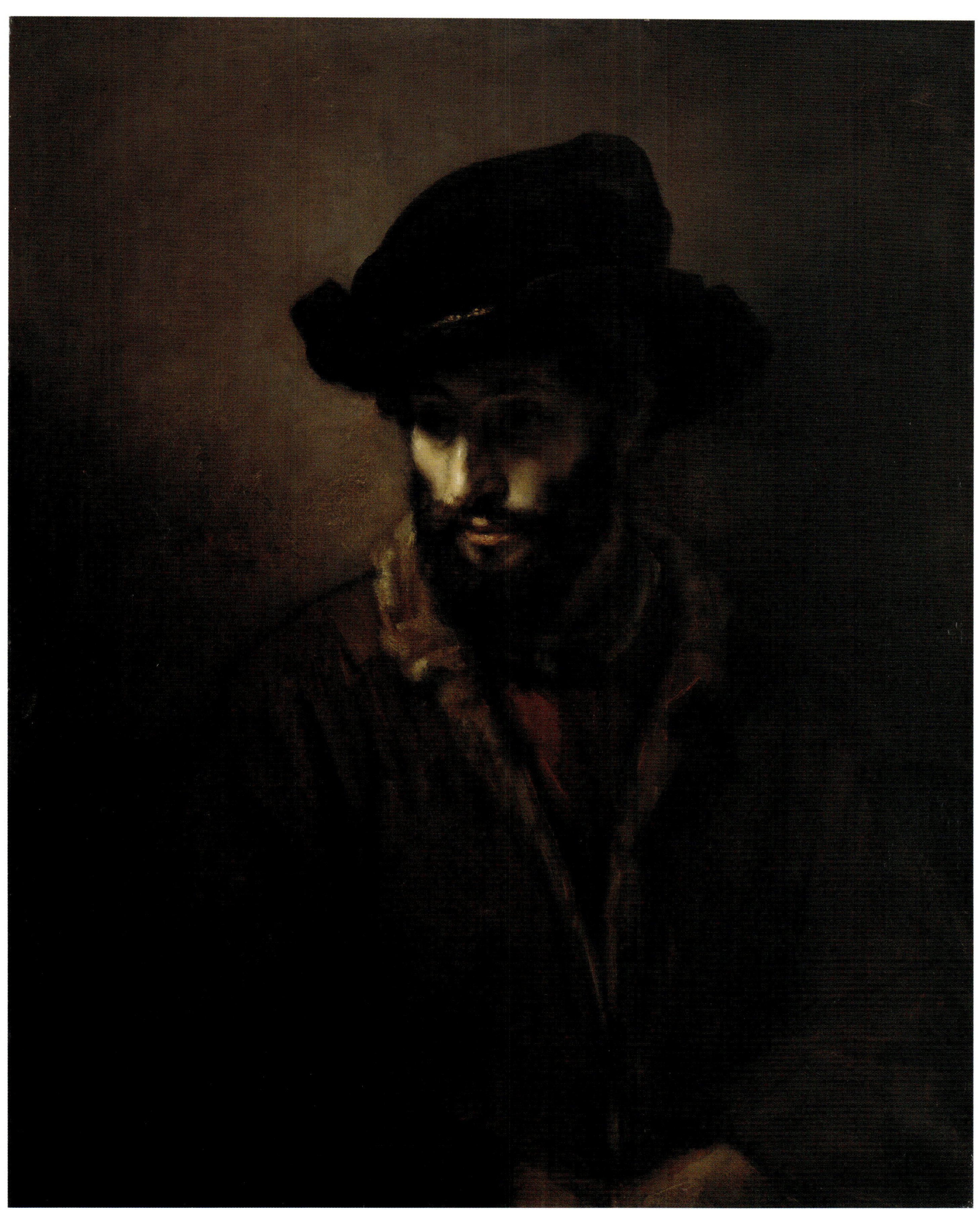

PLATE 17 [CAT. 33]
Rembrandt van Rijn (workshop of)
Portrait of a Man, ca. 1655–60
Oil on canvas, 84.5 x 69.2 cm (33 ¼ x 27 ¼ in.)
The Cleveland Museum of Art

impact—sometimes, as it turned out, not for the best. The Saint Louis Art Museum purchased its *Portrait of a Young Man*, putatively signed and dated 1662 (FIG. 42). That work is now no longer accepted as by the master. The same is true for the *Portrait of a Young Man* (possibly Titus van Rijn) bought by the Wadsworth Atheneum Museum of Art with the Sumner funds in 1954. This canvas is now listed as by an imitator of Rembrandt.[62] Its other would-be Rembrandt, a gift to the museum in 1961, is now ascribed to Govaert Flinck (PLATE 16). In 1950 the Cleveland Museum of Art purchased *Portrait of a Man* (PLATE 17) and in 1967 *Old Man Praying* (see PLATE 49, p. 162). Today neither is accepted as an original. The Worcester Art Museum made its attempt in 1958 purchasing a *St. Bartholomew*, which no longer passes muster.

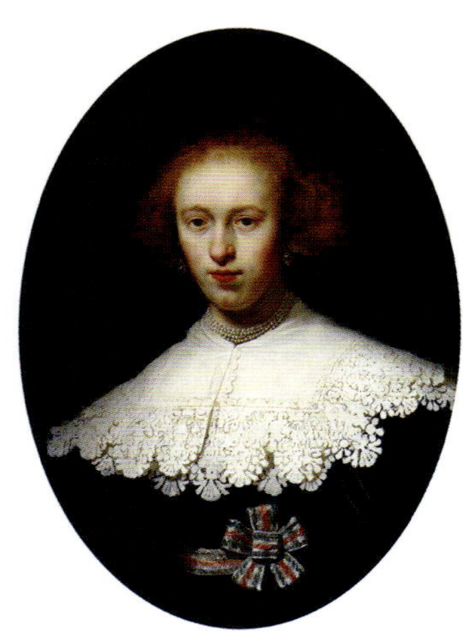

FIG. 47

The Museum of Fine Arts, Boston, was fortunate in receiving certain Rembrandt paintings as gifts. It also purchased a number of works by or ascribed to the master. For example, in 1903 it acquired *An Old Man in Prayer* (FIG. 43), now considered a studio work from the artist's Leiden years. In 1939 it acquired *An Evangelist Writing*, a picture so damaged as to make it hard to assess.[63] In continuing its quest for more Rembrandt paintings, in the mid-1950s the museum purchased its two imposing, life-size companion portraits of the Dutch Reformed preacher Johannes Elison and his wife, Maria Bockenolle (see PLATES 28, 29, pp. 118, 119).

In the wake of Gerson's revised edition of Bredius's *Rembrandt Paintings* (1969) and the published volumes of the Rembrandt Research Project, American museums have shown great care when making the commitment to purchase Rembrandt paintings. The Toledo Museum of Art under the directorship of Roger Mandle purchased *Man in a Fur-lined Coat* (see PLATE 34, p. 130), formerly owned by Alvan T. Fuller.[64] Likewise, the Speed Art Museum in Louisville acquired its beautifully preserved *Portrait of a Forty-year-old Woman* of 1634 (FIG. 44) in 1977.[65] The Kimbell Art Museum acquired from the collection of Sir William van Horne *Portrait of a Young Jew* (FIG. 45), one of Rembrandt's most luminous late portraits. The J. Paul Getty Museum in Los Angeles has acquired three Rembrandt paintings—*An Old Man in Military Costume* (FIG. 46) and two history subjects, *The Abduction of Europa* (see FIG. 82, p. 149) and *Daniel and Cyrus before the Idol Bel* (see FIG. 91, p. 165). Most recently the Museum of Fine Arts, Houston, acquired its first Rembrandt, *Portrait of a Woman* (FIG. 47).

By a set of unique circumstances the only university art museum equipped to collect Rembrandt paintings, and drawings and prints as well, was the Fogg Art Museum (now Harvard University Art Museums) of Harvard University. Paul Sachs, the great museum-oriented art history professor and mentor, was also a great collector of drawings and prints. The Harvard art history department also attracted two preeminent Dutch specialists, Jakob Rosenberg and Seymour Slive, both of whom have published widely on Rembrandt. With the financial help of Edward Forbes, the Harvard museum has purchased and attracted as gifts a number of pictures by or associated with Rembrandt. On a far more modest scale other college and university art museums have purchased prints or the occasional drawing by Rembrandt. Perhaps the most notable example that comes to mind is Wolfgang Stechow's recommendation to the Allen Memorial Art Museum at Oberlin College to acquire its outstandingly beautiful impression of *St. Jerome Praying under a Tree* (Bartsch 1797, no. 107), a stunning, cleanly wiped impression in the second state, particularly rich in burr.[66] Knowing that Oberlin could never hope to acquire a Rembrandt painting, nor even his prints in quantity, the purchase of such an important print has enabled students to fathom Rembrandt's unique genius.

FIG. 47
Rembrandt van Rijn, *Portrait of a Woman*, 1633, oil on panel, 65.3 x 48.8 cm (25¾ x 19⅛ in.). The Museum of Fine Arts, Houston; Gift of Isabel B. and Wallace S. Wilson, Caroline Weiss Law, Fayez Sarofim, the Blanton and Wareing familes in honor of Laura Lee Blanton, the Fondren Foundation, Houston Endowment Inc., Mr. and Mrs. George P. Mitchell, Ethel G. Carruth, Mr. and Mrs. Charles W. Duncan, Jr., Marjorie G. Horning, Mr. and Mrs. E. J. Hudson, Jr., Mrs. William S. Kilroy, Mr. and Mrs. Charles W. Tate, and Nina and Michael Zilkha; with additional gifts from the Linda and Ronny Finger Foundation, Ann Trammell, and Mr. and Mrs. Temple Webber in memory of Caroline Weiss Law; and additional funding from the Alice Pratt Brown Museum Fund and the Agnes Cullen Arnold Endowment Fund; inv. 2004.3

NOTES

1 My task in preparing this essay has been made infinitely easier and far more pleasurable because of my huge indebtedness to the immensely scholarly contributions of Walter Liedtke and Esmée Quodbach—Liedtke 1990; Quodbach 2002 and Quodbach 2004–5. Their investigations into the earlier American collecting of Dutch and Flemish old master paintings are fundamental to our understanding of this fascinating subject. Likewise Sutton 1986 provides invaluable shorter overviews of the many collections featuring Dutch art in the United States. The respective contributions of these three authors form much of the basis for this essay.

2 Slive 1978, pp. 453–63, esp. p. 453; Cohn 1986, pp. 224, 229.

3 The entire collection is catalogued under the credit line "Harvey D. Parker Collection."

4 As pointed out by Liedtke, in Antwerp 1992, pp. 11–28, esp. p. 21.

5 As Behrman points out, the American millionaire collectors of the "Duveen Era" could buy the family portraits and other works of art owned by European lords and ladies, thereby strengthening their sense of identification and equality with the British aristocracy and other great European rulers and princely families; Behrman 1972, p. 82.

6 Yerkes 1893; Yerkes 1904, vol. 1.

7 Sutton 1990, pp. ix–x.

8 As Liedtke points out, Teniers was almost considered an honorary member of the Dutch school in the eyes of American collectors of this period; Liedtke, in Antwerp 1992, pp. 11–28, especially p. 13. Sutton 1986 itemizes the number of paintings by each artist in public collections in the United States. Hardly more than a dozen names are substantially represented. Not surprisingly, they are the artists of greatest repute, headed by Rembrandt and Frans Hals but also including Aelbert Cuyp, Jan van Goyen, Meindert Hobbema, Pieter de Hooch, Nicolaes Maes, Aert van der Neer, Adriaen van Ostade, Jacob van Ruisdael, Salomon van Ruisdael, Jan Steen, Gerard Terborch, and Philips Wouwerman. Although with numerically fewer paintings, Vermeer is also well represented in the U.S.

9 These include characteristic works by Gerrit Berckheyde, Karel Dujardin, Jan Steen, and Emanuel de Witte, among others; see Keyes et al. 2004, nos. 5, 27, 94, 111 (repr.).

10 Burt 1977, pp. 175, 178–79.

11 This picture is a variant of a composition originating with Terborch, also known in a version in the Isabella Stewart Gardner Museum in Boston—see Gudlaugsson 1959–60, 2: no. 221.I.a (Gardner Museum workshop replica); no. 221.II (Art Institute of Chicago variant), pp. 203–5.

12 Based on current scholarly opinion, Henry Marquand's *Portrait of a Man* is technically the first authentic picture by Rembrandt to enter an American collection. The painting's ruinous condition makes it difficult to assess and precludes defining it as a major work by the artist; see Liedtke 2007, 2: no. 155 (repr.), pp. 676–78.

13 Quodbach 2004–5, pp. 90–107, esp. pp. 90, 98, 105–6.

14 Ibid., p. 107; Liedtke 2007, 2: no. 148 (repr.), pp. 604–12.

15 Liedtke 2007, 2:, no. 155 (repr.), pp. 676–78.

16 Ibid., no. 178 (repr.), pp. 782–85. For further discussion of Marquand, see Tomkins 1970, pp. 73–75, and Constable 1964, p. 105.

17 Constable 1964, p. 105.

18 Peter Widener also bought a number of notable paintings—ten in all, from the same source; see Widener 1885. Of them, only four were retained in the collection and are now in the National Gallery of Art—paintings by Aelbert Cuyp, Anthony van Dyck, Adriaen van Ostade, and Jan Steen. Likewise the Boston collector Stanton Blake also purchased from the same source paintings by Jan van Huysum, Gabriel Metsu, and Nicolaes Maes—works he placed on loan at the Museum of Fine Arts, Boston that were subsequently purchased by the museum in 1889; Whitehill 1970, pp. 77–78.

19 Sutton 1990, pp. ix–x, 246 (repr.); Liedtke 1990, p. 41.

20 Liedtke 2007, 2: no. 142 (repr.), no. 142 (repr.), pp. 554–67.

21 Quodbach 2004–5, p. 107; Liedtke, vol. 2, nos. 143–44 (repr.), pp. 568–84.

22 Liedtke, 2007, 2: nos. 164–65 (repr.), pp. 718–23.

23 Quodbach 2004–5, p. 99.

24 Ibid., p. 98; Liedtke, 2007, 2: no. 141 (repr.), pp. 550–54.

25 Wheelock 1995, inv. 1942.9.65, pp. 247–52.

26 This picture is now given to Govaert Flinck—see Liedtke 1990, p. 38 and n.115.

27 The Hague and Schwerin 2004, no. 6 (repr.), pp. 30–32; 106–10.

28 Quoted from Tomkins 1970, pp. 16–17. The 1871 purchase by the Metropolitan Museum of Art of 174 European old master and nineteenth-century pictures assembled by William T. Blodgett fit these collecting aspirations to a tee.

29 Quoted from Whitehill 1970, pp. 13–14.

30 Schneider 1985.

31 Frick's preferred dealer was Knoedler & Company, where he developed a close working relationship with Charles Carstairs; New York 1968, p. xxxii.

32 Quodbach 2002, pp. 43–44, 47, 49, 68.

33 Ibid., pp. 63, 64.

34 This and the following discussion of Widener is drawn from Quodbach 2002, pp. 42–95. For a more concise encapsulation of the Widener Collection, see Constable 1964, pp. 115–19.

35 For Nardus, see Lopez 2007, pp. 76–83.

36 Saarinen 1958, pp. 106–07.

37 Quodbach 2002, p. 80, indicates that Hofstede de Groot rejected a total of 150 works—a substantial percentage of the entire picture collection. Other victims of Nardus included John G. Johnson, Sir William van Horne, M. C. D. Borden, and even (albeit to a modest degree) J. Pierpont Morgan; Lopez 2007, p. 80.

38 Lopez 2007, pp. 81–83; Quodbach 2002, pp. 80–81; and E. Quodbach, "American Collections Rich in Dutch Art de eerste Amerikaanse Reis van Cornelis Hofstede de Groot in 1908," pp. 65–79, esp. pp. 74–75, in Ghent 2005.

39 The celebrated portrait of Nicolaes Ruts was acquired for the Frick Collection long after its founder's death.

40 See Constable 1964, pp. 119–25.

41 Liedtke 2007, vol. 2, classifies six of the eleven as autograph and the remaining five as "style of Rembrandt."

42 For Altman, see Tomkins 1970, pp. 169–74; Haskell 1970; Liedtke 1990.

43 Quoted from Saarinen 1958, p. 108. Incidentally, Johnson's efforts to secure paintings by Rembrandt were modest. He avoided the craze for portraits but secured for himself a head of Christ and *The Finding of Moses*. This latter picture currently lacks defenders as a Rembrandt even though it is included in Bredius. Johnson also acquired a ragtag group of other pictures associated with Rembrandt that are of dubious quality and little consequence.

44 For the Huntingtons, see Behrman 1952, pp. 143–57; Constable 1964, pp. 113–15; Tomkins 1970, pp. 190–91. Arabella Yarrington married Collis P. Huntington, the lead partner/owner of the Central Pacific Railroad. He died in 1900. Thirteen years later she remarried. Her new husband, Henry E. Huntington, was Collis's nephew. Henry created the Huntington Library in San Marino, California. However, Arabella's son, Archer, from her marriage to Collis, presented the Rembrandt paintings in the collection—namely the *Portrait of Hendrickje Stoffels* and *Flora*—to the Metropolitan Museum of Art in memory of his father.

45 This point is repeated by the various authors who have examined the subject of Gilded Age collecting; Constable 1964, pp. 9, 99, 122. He quotes Henry Clay Frick: "I want this collection to be my monument." John Walker, second director of the National Gallery of Art, stressed how important this sentiment was for Isabella Stewart Gardner, Andrew Mellon, and Armand Hammer as well. Walker quotes Hammer concerning the collecting of paintings: "You are connecting yourself with something that really is immortal, something that has survived all these centuries. You are preserving something for Posterity." Bernard Berenson's interpretation of this is somewhat more cynical. For him the "'squillionaires'" possession of art resulted in "a kind of ego-inflation, as though the collector had assisted in the creation of what he bought"; Walker 1974, pp. 78–79, 93, 132, 232.

46 For the Tafts, see Constable 1964, pp. 131–32. Constable notes that the Taft collection is unique for retaining its large grouping of Barbizon and Hague school pictures, which most of the other Gilded Age collectors had sold or pruned judiciously. For the pictures in the Taft Collection, see "European and American Paintings," in Taft Museum 1995.

47 Chicago was first, establishing the Art Institute of Chicago in 1879.

48 She, together with Mr. and Mrs. Charles Taft and Stevenson Scott (the partner of Charles F. Fowles), presented Zurbarán's *St. Peter Nolasco Recovering the Image of the Virgin* to the Cincinnati Art Museum in memory of Fowles, who perished on the *Lusitania*.

49 See Constable 1964, p. 129; Milliken 1936; Milliken 1944.

50 This painting was assigned to Rembrandt in Corpus 1982–89, 1: no. A23, but subsequently reassigned to his workshop, possibly Isaac de Joudreville, in the Corrigenda of Corpus 1982–89, 2: p. 838.

51 B. Brayer, "George Eastman Collector," in Rosenthal 1979, pp. 2–6; Peters 1988.

52 Libbey was also a great admirer of The Hague school artists. As a result Toledo is especially rich in this material as well.

53 Epstein and Jacobs were also the source of the two great Frans Hals portraits—*Portrait of a Woman* (acquired by Jacob Epstein from Duveen in 1924) and *Portrait of Dorothea Berck, Wife of Joseph Coymans* (acquired by Henry Barton Jacobs from Duveen in 1929; ex collections Rodolphe Kann, Mrs. Collis P. Huntington, and Henry E. Huntington); see Slive 1970–74, 3: nos. 96, 161, respectively, pp. 55, 82–83.

54 Jacob Epstein (1864–1945) immigrated to the United States from Lithuania and created a successful department store in Baltimore. He acquired most of his paintings in the later 1920s from Duveen and Knoedler. Mary Frick Jacobs (1851–1936), following the death of her first husband in 1896, married Dr. Henry Barton Jacobs. She was a prominent social hostess in Baltimore and Newport, Rhode Island. She bought most of her paintings from the Blakeslee Galleries of New York City between 1900 and 1916. She was a founding member of the Baltimore Museum of Art and offered her major paintings to this museum shortly before her death. For these two collectors see Baltimore 1984, pp. xii, xiv, 39–40, 42.

55 Jones acquired this picture in about 1927 from Henry Reinhardt and Company (c. 1926–27). It entered the collection of the Minneapolis Institute of Arts in 1934, apparently as a partial gift/partial purchase.

56 *Woman in a Fanciful Costume* and *The Lamentation* (plate 46, p. 159). Ringling Museum 1986, nos. 46, 47, as Reynier van Gherwen (entries by A. F. Janson), p. 112.

57 See Liedtke 1990, p. 46; Hartwell 2001; Washington 1978.

58 Bredius 1920: 208.

59 For further discussion of this picture see my other essay in this volume, "The Elusive Nature of Portraiture," pp. 113–39.

60 Fuller owned a small but fine collection primarily of old masters but also including pictures by Monet and Renoir. The Fuller Foundation presented most of them, excepting the Rembrandt, to the Museum of Fine Arts, Boston.

61 Day and Sturges 1987, no. 36 (repr.), pp. 52–54.

62 Hartford 2009, no. 9 (repr.), pp. 22–23.

63 Washington and Los Angeles 2005, fig. 8 (identified as St. John), p. 21.

64 This painting had long been on loan to the Museum of Fine Arts, Boston. Toledo's gain was certainly Boston's loss, and not the only one. Rembrandt's oval *Portrait of a Young Woman*, long on loan from the collection of Robert Treat Paine, was recently acquired by a private collector in New York City.

65 It is the companion painting to a *Portrait of a Man*, now in the Norton Simon Museum in Pasadena.

66 Boston and New York 1969, no. 105 (repr.), pp. 154, 159.

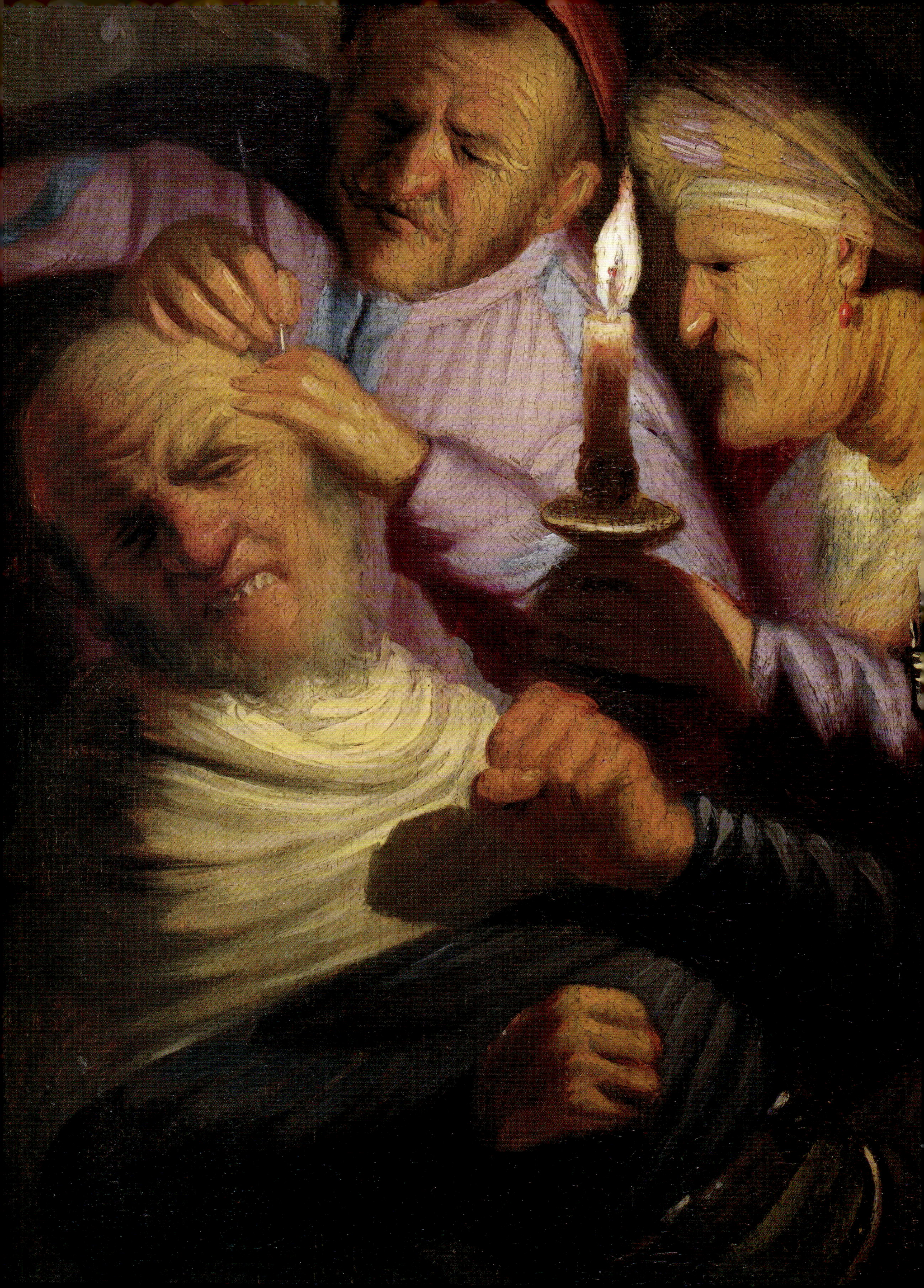

Rembrandt's Leiden Years: Mastering His Craft and Defining His Genius

TOM RASSIEUR

By surveying Rembrandt's early paintings in American collections, we can observe his astonishing development from awkward student to full-fledged master. This early period comprises four main phases: studies with his first teacher, a local Leiden master named Jacob van Swanenburgh (1571–1638); a relatively brief sojourn in the Amsterdam studio of Pieter Lastman (1583–1633); activity as an independent master back in Leiden; and, finally, a period of two or three years when he was splitting his time between the Amsterdam studio of Hendrick Uylenburgh (1584 or 1589–c. 1660) and his own endeavors back in his hometown.

Rembrandt's early years have been the subject of extensive scrutiny and rethinking in recent years. The Rembrandt Research Project (RRP) devoted some eight hundred pages to the subject in the first two volumes of its monumental series *A Corpus of Rembrandt Paintings,* published in 1982 and 1986.[1] In 2000 and 2001 separate exhibitions in America and Europe focused on Rembrandt's early years.[2] In 1996, an exhibition studying Rembrandt's collaborations with printmaker Johannes van Vliet (c. 1605–1668) brought into sharper focus the fact that Rembrandt retained strong ties with Leiden even after his 1631 relocation to Amsterdam.[3] As a result of this flood of scholarship, several paintings in American collections have seen their fortunes wax and wane as their attributions have swung back and forth between "Rembrandt" and "Not Rembrandt." No one has had the last word in this field.

The history of Rembrandt's paintings begins with one that he signed and dated 1625 (see FIG. 74, p. 143). But what about the prehistory? Is there anything earlier? Thirty years ago, scholars were loath to wade into such murky waters. The strongest candidates for the title "Earliest Known Rembrandt Paintings" are three small panels from what was probably a series of five allegories of the senses, two of which, *The Three Singers (Hearing)* and *The Operation (Touch),* have made their way into a private collection in New York (PLATES 18, 19). The other picture, *The Spectacles Peddler (Sight)* (see FIG. 8, p. 34), remains in a European collection. Due to the lack of any documented pre-1625 pictures, and taking into account the compromised condition of these paintings, the RRP authors decided not to make a pronouncement on their authenticity in 1982. Instead, they hedged their bets and said, in essence, if they are by Rembrandt, they must predate 1625.

Subsequent restoration has removed distracting alterations likely made to the pictures in the mid-eighteenth century. Also removed was nearly all doubt about their authenticity.[4] Though smaller and simpler than Rembrandt's extant paintings dated 1625 and 1626, *Hearing* and *Touch* share with them many stylistic characteristics such as brushwork, palette, character types, and lighting. The pair is now widely accepted as authentic and usually dated 1624–25. If these assumptions are correct, they were probably painted in Leiden, near the end of Rembrandt's apprenticeship with Jacob van Swanenburgh and prior to his departure for his journeyman's study with Pieter Lastman in Amsterdam.

Hearing is represented by a chorus of singers, and *Touch* by a surgery that none of us would care to undergo. In them, we can already see Rembrandt's sense of humor—light in *Hearing* and dark in *Touch.* Each picture includes three figures. The trio of singers in *Hearing* includes an old man wearing a fur-lined tabard (an old-fashioned garment by the 1620s), an old woman sporting a colorful turban wound from striped cloth, and a young man in a beret. The ages of these musicians and their perceived abilities as performers may suggest that we would prefer our hearing were less acute. In the young man's features, especially the long jaw line, one might recognize the features of the artist-prodigy Jan Lievens (1607–1674), of whom we shall hear more shortly. If so, he would have been about seventeen years old. An equally plausible scenario finds the figure representing a self-portrait, a conclusion prompted by the boy's round face and somewhat bulbous nose. Rembrandt often played cameo roles in both his paintings and his prints.*Touch* also includes a turbaned figure, this time an old man who assists the barber surgeon.

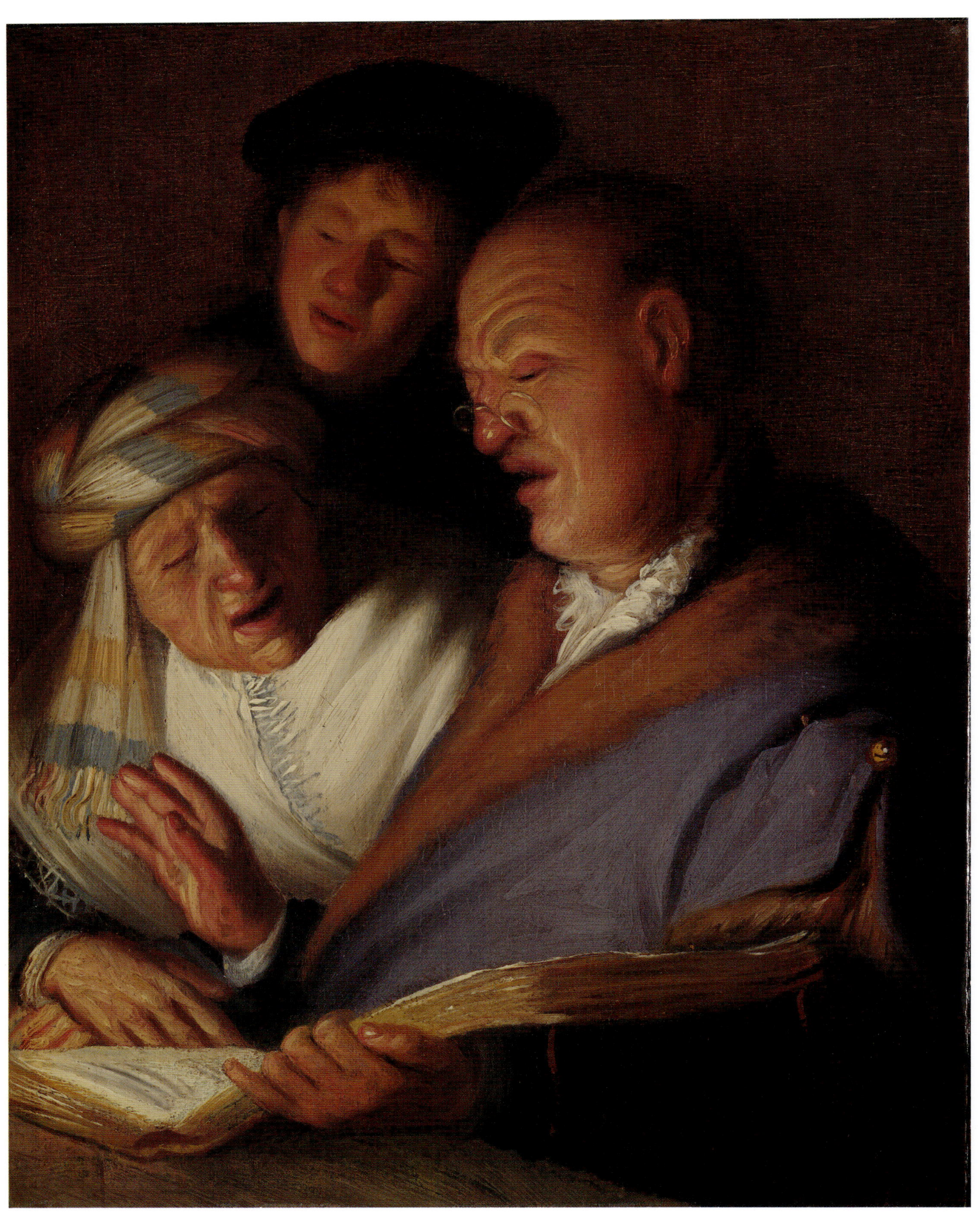

PLATE 18 [CAT. 1]
Rembrandt van Rijn
The Three Singers (Hearing), c. 1624/25
Oil on oak panel, 21.6 x 17.8 cm (8½ x 7 in.)
Private collection, New York

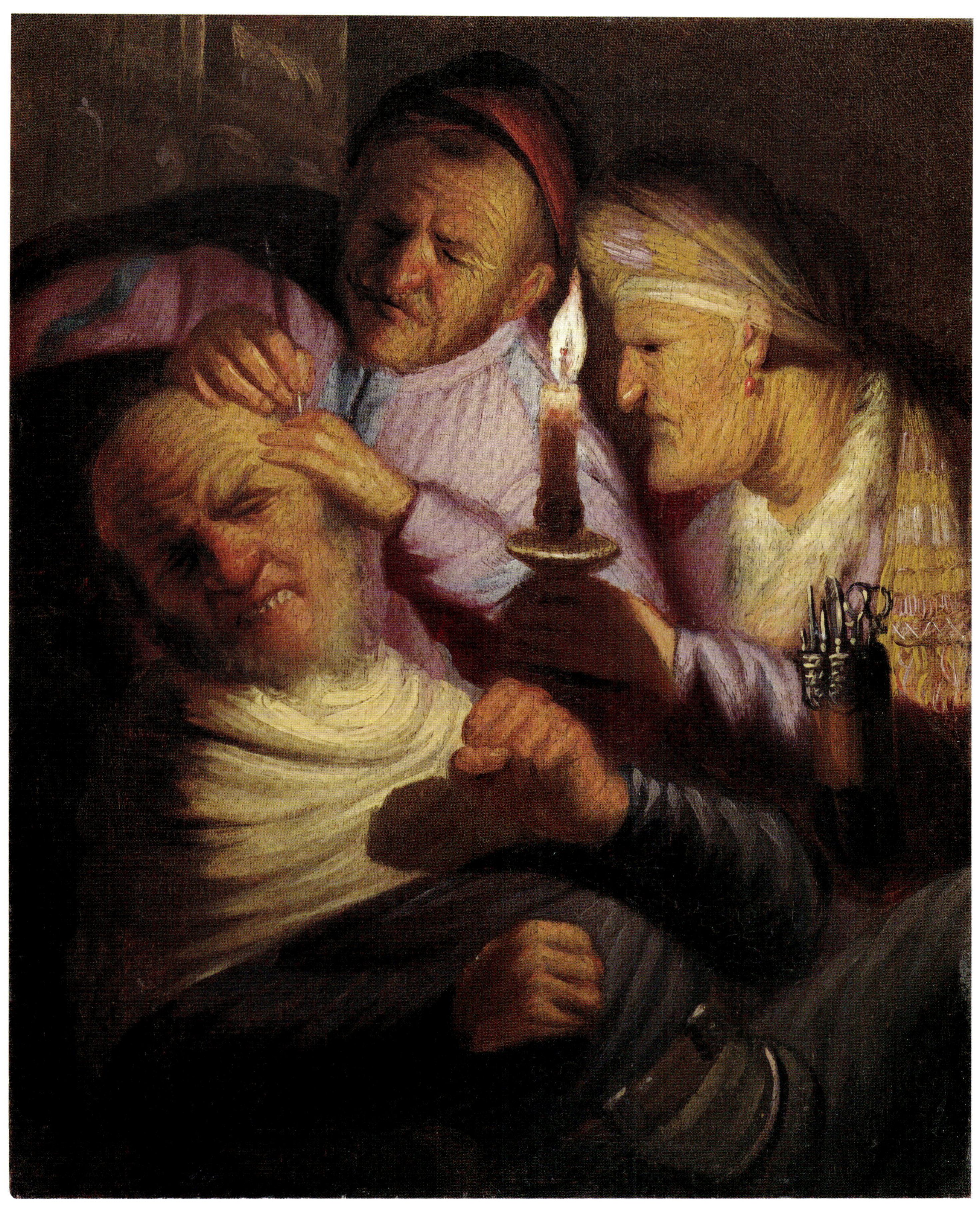

PLATE 19 [CAT. 2]
Rembrandt van Rijn
The Operation (Touch), c. 1624/25
Oil on oak panel, 21.5 x 17.7 cm (8 ½ x 7 in.)
Private collection, New York

He holds a candle and stands ready to hand over any required instruments as he stares intently at the ongoing procedure. The patient's crooked teeth bite hard on his lower lip as he clenches his fists and winces at the pain. The surgeon, who has thoughtfully supplied a cloth to protect the patient's clothing from the inevitable stream of blood, bears down on his victim with intense concentration. The theatrical attire of the surgeon and his assistant suggests they are charlatans and that the scene is rooted in the type of humorous social commentary embedded in the prints of the sixteenth-century Flemish artist Pieter Brueghel the Elder (c. 1525/30–1569) and his followers.[5]

Both *Hearing* and *Touch* reveal Rembrandt's interest in the artistic trends notable in the work of Caravaggio (1573–1610) and his followers in both Italy and the Netherlands, especially the city of Utrecht. Key elements of Caravaggism seen in Rembrandt's pictures are the concern for dramatic lighting and the intense physicality, even to the point of overstepping the bounds of decorum. The young artist's interest in such matters may have been stimulated by his first teacher, for Van Swanenburgh had spent many years in Italy and was himself a specialist in extravagantly lit scenes of Hell. Though Rembrandt is extremely unlikely ever to have seen an authentic painting by Caravaggio, he could learn much about his style from the works that poured out of Utrecht in the early 1620s.

Still, even as Rembrandt absorbed lessons from others, he was already testing his own ideas. The pictures executed by Utrecht artists such as Gerrit van Honthorst (1592–1656) and Hendrick ter Brugghen (1588–1629) tend to be evenly painted, while Rembrandt varied his application of paint to a greater degree. To heighten the physical presence of his pictures, he contrasted thicker paint and distinct brushstrokes in some areas with scant coverage in others. Light playing over the raised ridges of his sculpted brushstrokes added drama to the candlelit scenes.

The Feast of Esther (see PLATE 47, p. 160) in Raleigh, a large and impressive painting rediscovered in 1936, is often cited as an example of the transformation of Rembrandt connoisseurship in the twentieth century. Of equal importance are its lessons about Rembrandt's position as a young artist making the transition from apprentice to journeyman.

The subject comes from the Old Testament book of Esther, which drew Rembrandt's attention repeatedly during the first two decades of his career. This particular scene, Esther 7:1–7, shows the Jewish queen risking her life to expose the plan of her husband's closest advisor to commit genocide against all the Jews in Persia. The king, Ahasuerus, clenches his outstretched fists and trains his eye on the minister, Haman, who throws up his hand in astonishment as his true character is unmasked. The virtuous royal couple is bathed in light, while Haman is nearly silhouetted in shadow.

Knowing that Rembrandt was interested in the story of Esther, and seeing the psychological drama played out with gesture, dramatic allegorical illumination, and richly varied application of paint drawn from a familiar palette of colors, many connoisseurs attributed the painting to Rembrandt when it appeared on the art market. Given the desire of early twentieth-century scholars to discover Rembrandt paintings, it is not surprising that they held up *The Feast of Esther* as an ambitious work by the young genius. However, as this big, bold painting came to be seen as anomalous among Rembrandt's early works, especially in the scale of its figures and the showy but sometimes ineffectual brushwork, other suggestions came forward.

Could this be the work of Rembrandt's second teacher, Pieter Lastman, who is known for his interest in biblical subjects, animated figures, and bright palette? Could the canvas represent a collaboration between Rembrandt and another young painter from Leiden, Jan Lievens? Indeed, the well-positioned aesthete Constantijn Huygens, writing about 1630, had noted that Lievens was audacious and liked to work on a large scale.[6] Could the painting actually be by Lievens himself? His development as a painter was not well understood until it was studied in preparation for an exhibition staged in 1979, but the works gathered together at that time revealed that *The Feast of Esther* was entirely the work of the lesser-known artist, a conclusion that has met with consensus.[7]

What does a painting not by Rembrandt tell us about him? In this case we see what the young artist was up against. Lievens, though a year younger than Rembrandt, had much more experience. He had been painting since he was eight or nine years old, and had already completed a two-year journeyman's stint with the famous Pieter Lastman in Amsterdam. In

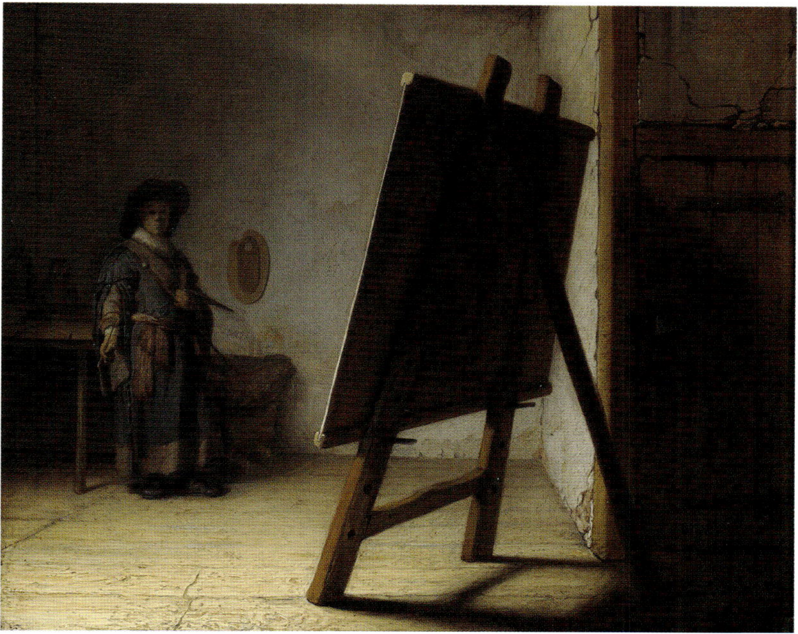

FIG. 48

1625, his paintings were far more sophisticated than those of Rembrandt. Lievens, too, was interested in the work of the Dutch Caravaggisti, but unlike Rembrandt's comparatively modest examples, his work could compete directly with pictures by the Utrecht masters. Rembrandt could not help but see that he had better hurry if he wanted to catch up.

Is it any wonder that Rembrandt sought out Pieter Lastman to further his artistic knowledge? After all, Lievens had shown him what a painter could learn under the Amsterdam artist's tutelage. Rembrandt went to work with Lastman for about six months. No paintings by Rembrandt from that period can be identified with any certainty. For many years, Lastman's impact on Rembrandt's figures, compositions, colors, subject matter, and narrative technique was considered profound. A decade ago, however, Ernst van de Wetering, the longest-running member of the original RRP and now considered the foremost scholar of Rembrandt's paintings, argued strenuously that Rembrandt found little to learn in Lastman's studio and positioned his own work as an ongoing critique of his master's.[8] Given the changes seen in Rembrandt's paintings after his brief stay with Lastman, as well as his ongoing references to his master's work, one can see that Rembrandt was an ardent practitioner of *aemulatio*—striving to equal or surpass another. Thus, he positioned himself as both indebted student and critic.

At some point in 1625 Rembrandt returned to Leiden from Amsterdam and set himself up as an independent master. He began to take on students and put his highly inventive imagination to work. At the same time, Rembrandt developed a friendly rivalry with Lievens and the two came to be seen as a pair, much as Braque and Picasso would be in their exploration of Cubism nearly three centuries later. Neither pair of artists is known to have shared studio space, but they certainly shared ideas and drew upon similar wells of inspiration. They were also discussed as pairs, often as a vehicle to compare and contrast the attributes of the individuals.

When Huygens wrote about Rembrandt and Lievens, he noted that "Rembrandt . . . devotes all his loving concentration to a small painting, achieving on that modest scale a result which one would seek in vain in the largest pieces of others."[9] Though Huygens referred directly to another painting, which showed Judas returning the thirty pieces of silver (see FIG. 75, p. 146), his comments are perfectly apt for a remarkable little gem of a painting belonging to the Museum of Fine Arts, Boston, but unfortunately out of the country during the course of the present exhibition. Painted about 1629, *The Artist in His Studio* (FIG. 48) captures our attention with its novel invention, subtlety, complexity, and convincing depiction of both matter and space. Though lacking inscriptions, every inch of the painting bears Rembrandt's signature.

This painting might be seen as a self-mocking psychological self-portrait. The artist, dwarfed by a large easel in the foreground, stands at the back of the space and wears an outdated

FIG. 48
Rembrandt van Rijn, *The Artist in His Studio*, c. 1629, oil on panel, 21.5 x 31.9 cm (8 1/2 x 12 1/2 in.). Museum of Fine Arts, Boston; acc. 38.1838

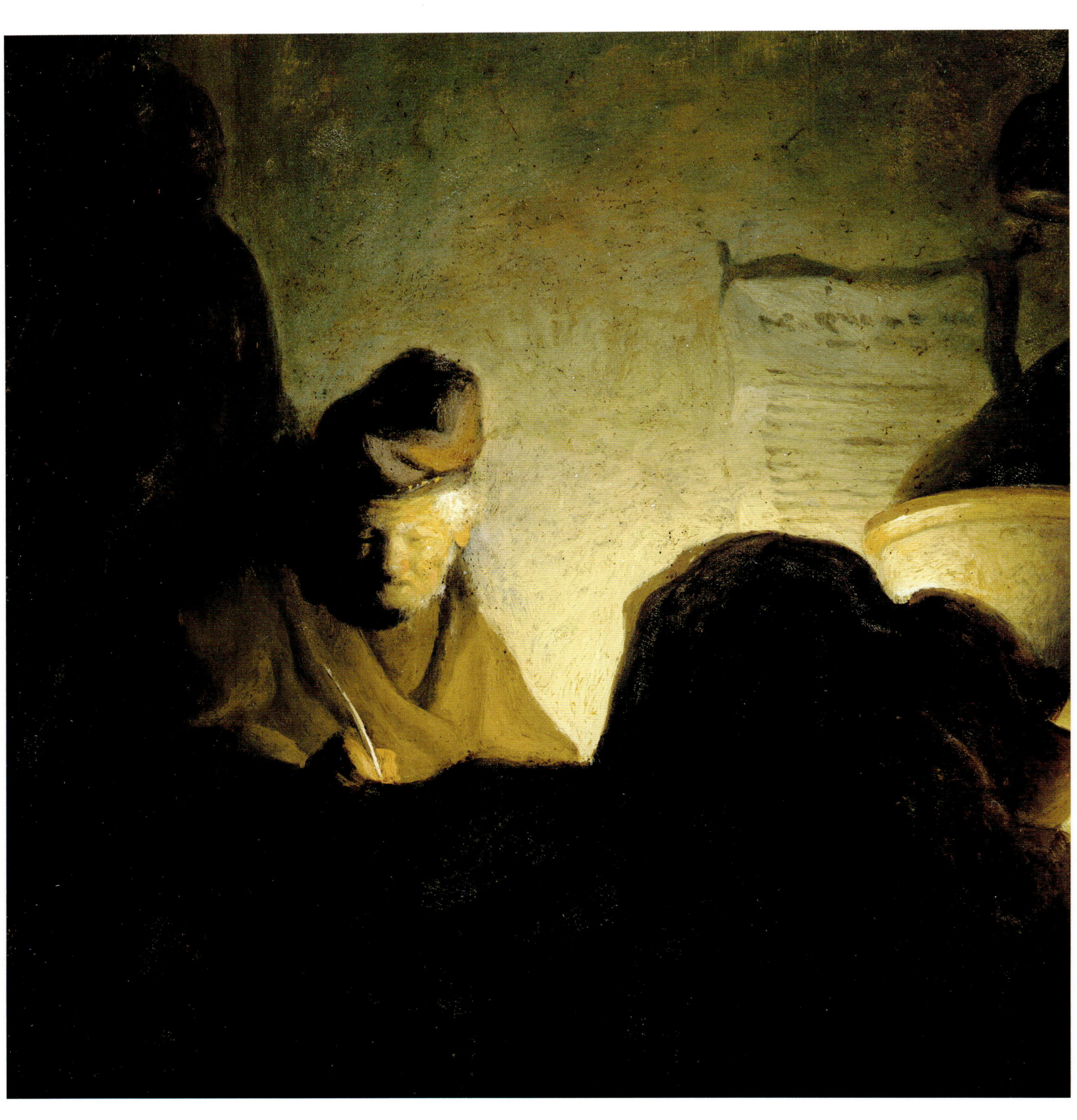

PLATE 20 [CAT. 3]
Rembrandt van Rijn (attributed to)
A Scholar by Candlelight, c. 1628/29
Oil on copper, 13.9 x 13.9 cm (5 ½ x 5 ½ in.)
Collection of Isabel and Alfred Bader, Milwaukee

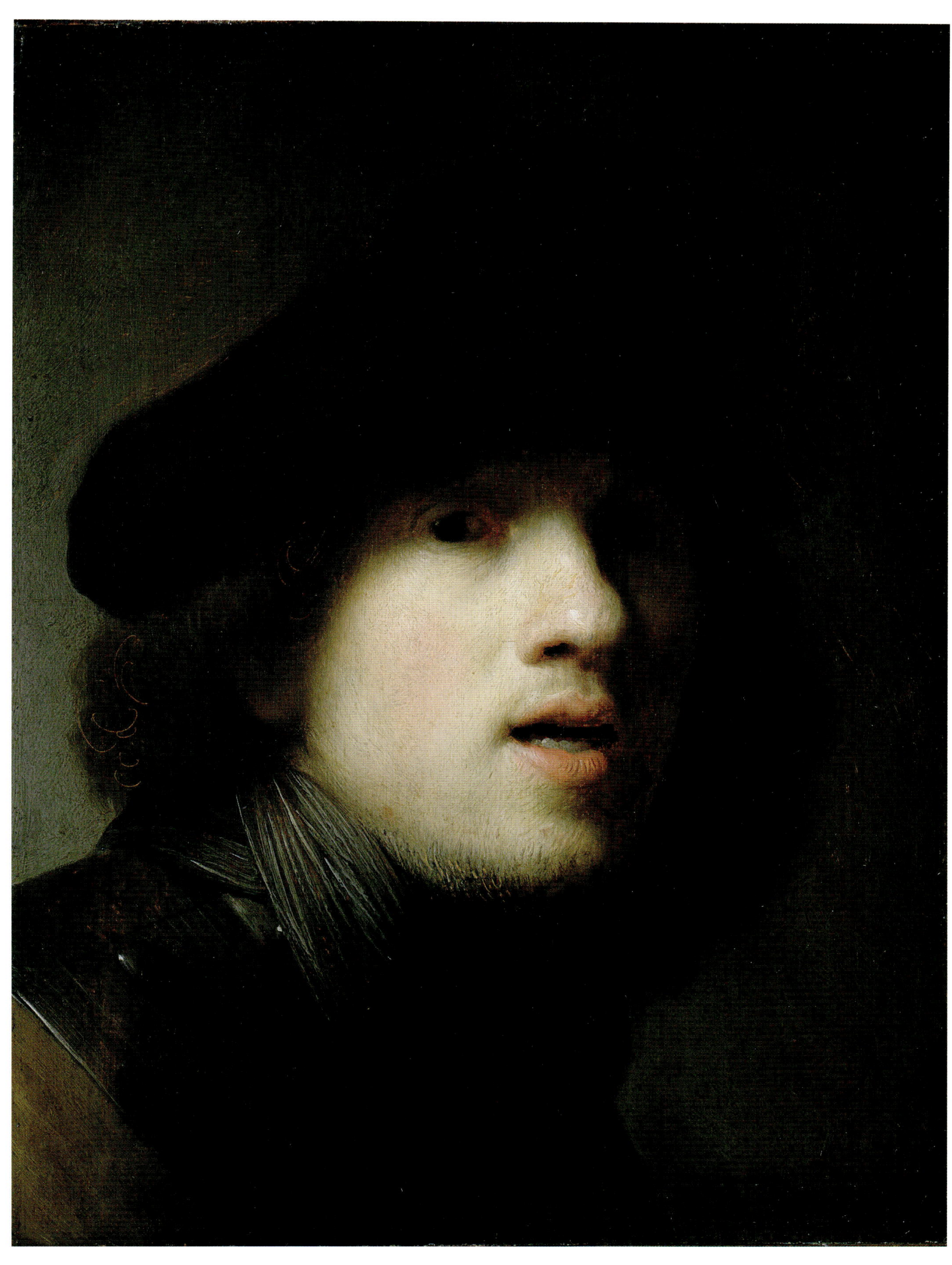

PLATE 21 [CAT. 4]
Rembrandt van Rijn
Self-portrait (Study in a Mirror), c. 1629
Oil on panel, 44.5 x 34.3 cm (17 ½ x 13 ½ in.)
Indianapolis Museum of Art

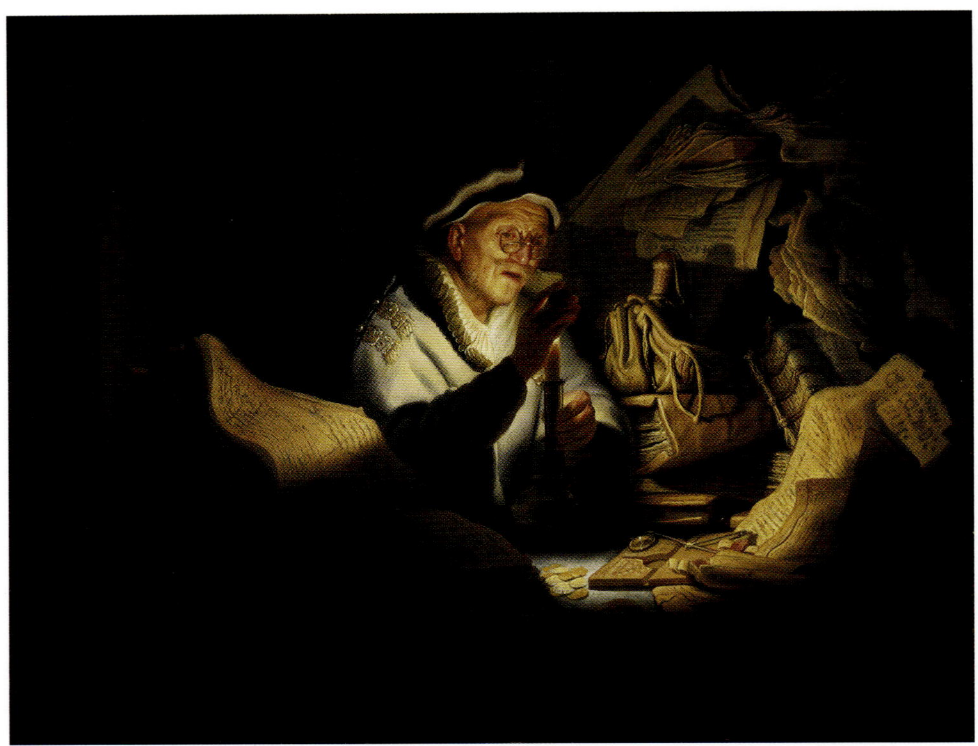

FIG. 49

and oversized tabard. He wears a comically floppy hat and has coals for eyes. This young artist knows that he needs to grow, and he is prepared to do so. He delicately holds a single brush in his right hand; his left grasps a fistful of brushes, with his palette supported by his thumb and his maulstick by his pinkie. He is surrounded by other tools of his trade: extra palettes, a massive and well-worn stone for grinding pigments, and containers for solvents and oil. The onlooker assumes this young artist has yet to find worldly success, as his walls are bare and rising damp has caused the plaster to spall. The door and floor are both rough hewn, with the rich textures of the wood modeled in thick paint. In addition, the large wooden panel on the easel faces away from us. We cannot see what, if anything, is painted on it, suggesting Rembrandt was already acquainted with the seductive power of concealment. The painter stands back—waiting, thinking, planning. There is no model striking a pose, nor do we see any preparatory drawings nearby.

This painting will not imitate nature; it will come from the artist's imagination. Light pours in from our left, producing a symphony of shadows and perhaps the glow of inspiration. It catches the edge of the easel, resulting in one sharp, linear highlight. This fine bright line recalls the ancient story of Apelles announcing himself to Protogenes by painting a single fine line across a panel. Rembrandt would go on to match himself against all the great painters of history, ultimately adopting Apelles's palette of black, white, red, and yellow as his own. This small painting, the size of a sheet of notebook paper, swallows up the large panel on the easel, literally embodying Rembrandt's ability to outstrip large works with ones of smaller scale.[10]

Reconstructing an artist's oeuvre is like assembling a jigsaw puzzle that has no cleanly cut edge pieces: the pieces need to fit together; gaps may be left; the boundaries remain unknown. *A Scholar by Candlelight* (PLATE 20) is a perfect example of a painting that represents a puzzle piece in search of a fit. It comes from the collection of Dr. and Mrs. Alfred Bader, long the premier collectors of Rembrandt and Rembrandtesque paintings in America.[11] Painted on copper, a support occasionally used by Rembrandt, the composition shows an old man working at night. His candle, which is hidden behind a large open book, illuminates the man, his quill pen, a globe, some kind of broadside, and a vessel hanging on the wall, which is also partly washed by light. This small work is certainly Rembrandtesque, but does it fit into "his" puzzle?

Rembrandt painted a number of nocturnal scenes following his return to Leiden, some of which can be compared to *A Scholar by Candlelight*. Dated 1627 and possibly an allegory of

FIG. 49
Rembrandt van Rijn, *The Money Changer (Parable of a Rich Man)*, 1627, oil on oak, 31.7 x 42.5 cm (12 ½ x 16 ¾ in.). Staatliche Museen Preussischer Kulturbesitz, Gemäldegalerie, Berlin; inv. 828 D

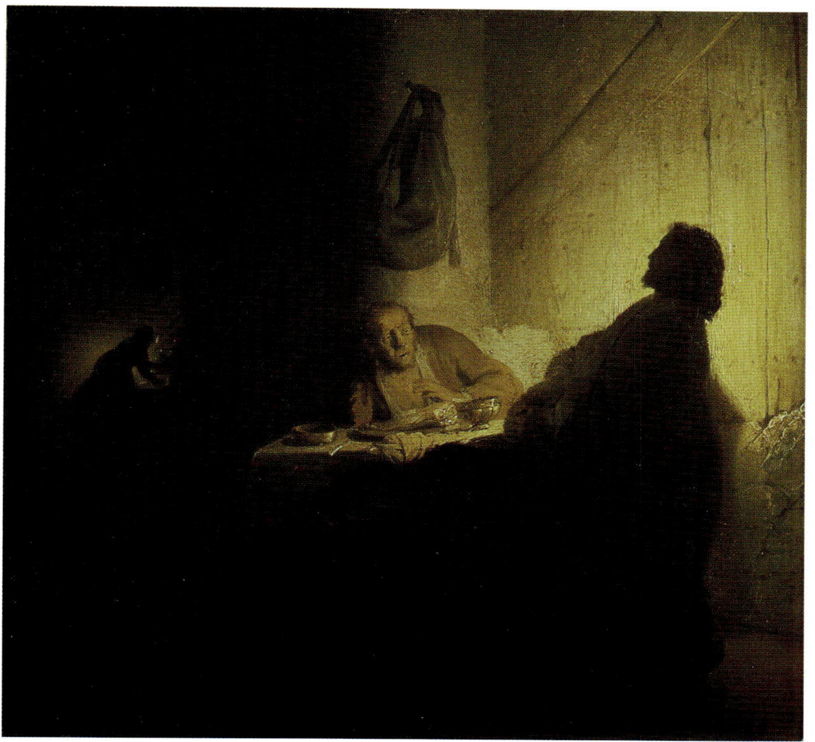

FIG. 50

greed, *The Money Changer (Parable of a Rich Man)* (FIG. 49), in Berlin, shows the extremes to which Rembrandt could take his lighting schemes—radiant illumination starkly contrasted with deep darkness. Strong silhouetting also appears in *Christ at Emmaus* (FIG. 50), a painting from the late 1620s in Paris. Both of these paintings have long garnered consensus as being absolutely authentic Rembrandts.[12]

Compared to the Berlin and Paris works, *A Scholar by Candlelight* bears some resemblance in subject matter and treatment to early paintings by Rembrandt. The inscription on an eighteenth-century etching of the painting states that it is by Rembrandt, as do other eighteenth-century opinions. The picture formerly bore the initials of Rembrandt's first student, Gerrit Dou (1613–1675), but confirmation of longstanding suspicions that the monogram was a later addition led to its removal in 1958.

A Scholar by Candlelight has long been doubted as a Rembrandt and was dismissed by the Research Committee in 1982, at which time it was likened to another rejected picture, *The Flight into Egypt* (FIG. 51) in Tours.[13] Ernst van de Wetering tentatively restored the Tours picture to Rembrandt's oeuvre in 2001; so, the case of *A Scholar by Candlelight* was reopened too.[14] In the same publication, Bob van den Boogert, curator of the Rembrandt House Museum but who professes not to be a Rembrandt expert, wrote a forceful argument against restoring *A Scholar by Candlelight* to Rembrandt.[15] He noted that the varied application of paint achieved none of the plasticity of form found in authentic Rembrandts. He further noted that the shadows, lighting, and sense of space lack the convincing subtlety seen in Rembrandt's work of the late 1620s.[16] What are we to make of a painting that shows clear knowledge of—but not full mastery of—the new types of paintings being produced in Leiden? Are we looking at the work of a student? Echoing the thoughts of whoever added the now-removed monogram, the name of Gerrit Dou has been forwarded, but there is still too little evidence to assign any secure attribution. Such are the tantalizing mysteries of Rembrandtesque paintings, as loose puzzle pieces still remain on the table. Still, *A Scholar by Candlelight* does tell us something about Rembrandt: his paintings were identifiably new in character, and students wanted to learn how to work in his style. Moreover, the style, while highly imitable, was difficult to master.

Working the puzzle is especially difficult when there are multiple versions of a painting, as is the case with the Indianapolis *Self-portrait (Study in a Mirror)* (PLATE 21).[17] The picture had come to America by 1951, when it was acquired by Dr. G. H. A. Clowes of Indianapolis.[18] On permanent

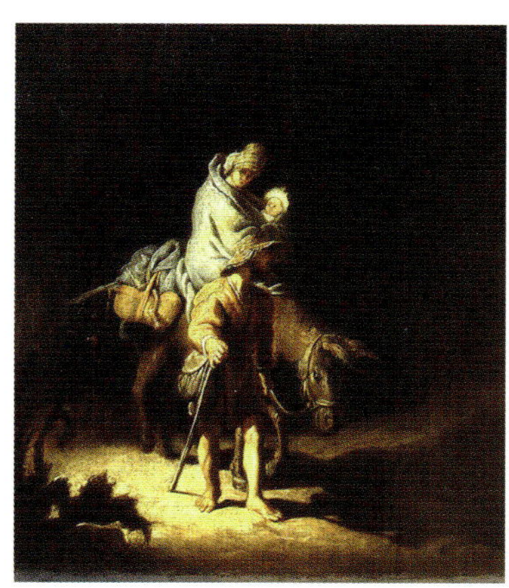

FIG. 51

FIG. 50
Rembrandt van Rijn, *Christ at Emmaus*, c. 1629, oil on canvas, 39 x 42 cm (15 3/8 x 16 1/2 in.). Museum Jacquemart-André, Paris; inv. 409

FIG. 51
Rembrandt van Rijn (?), *The Flight into Egypt*, 1627, oil on panel, 26.5 x 24 cm (10 1/2 x 9 1/2 in.). Musée des Beaux-Arts, Tours, 1950-13-1

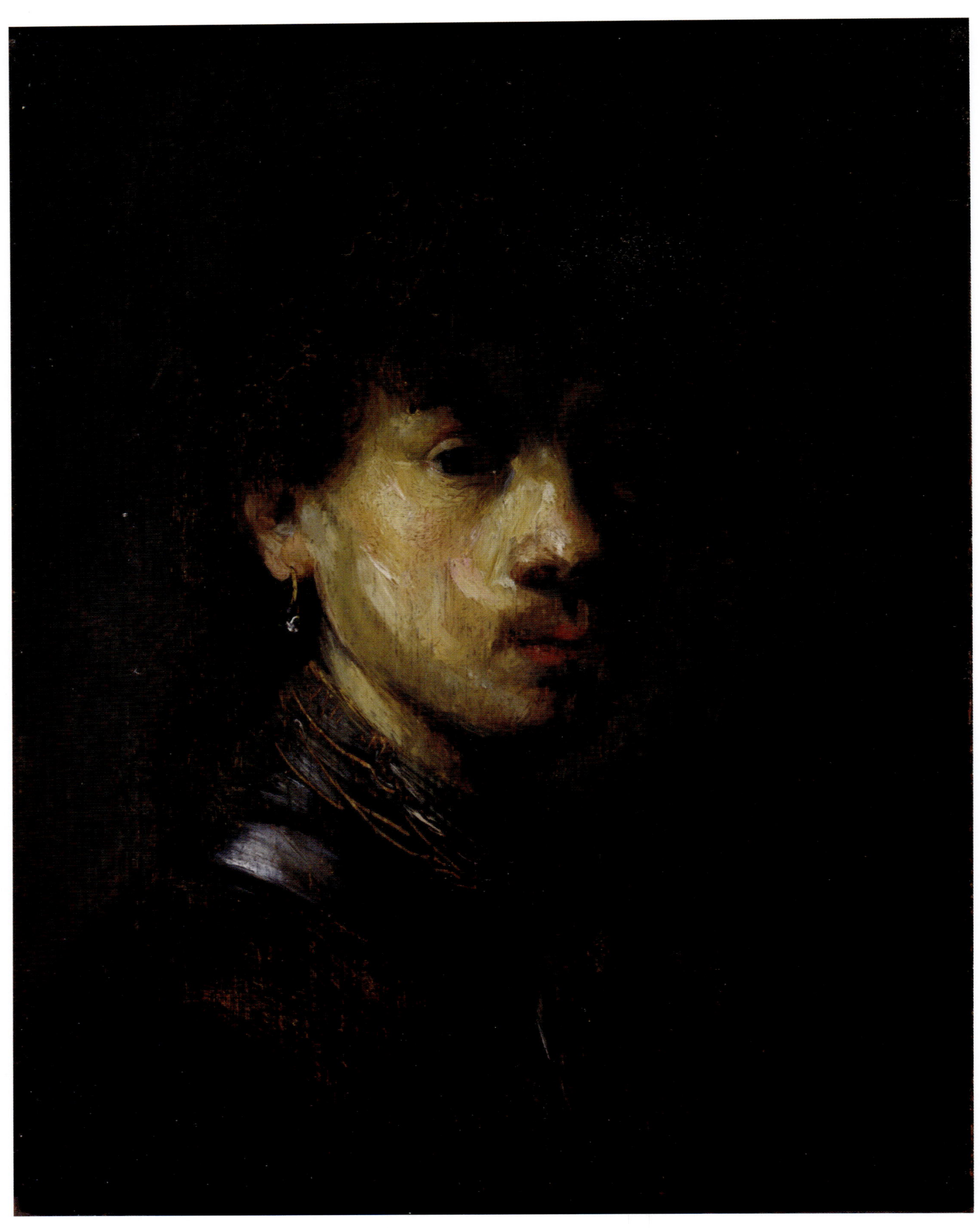

PLATE 22 [CAT. 5]
Rembrandt van Rijn (imitator of)
Bust of a Young Man, after 1629
Oil on oak panel, 22.9 x 18.3 cm (9 x 7 1/4 in.)
Fogg Museum of Art, Harvard University, Cambridge

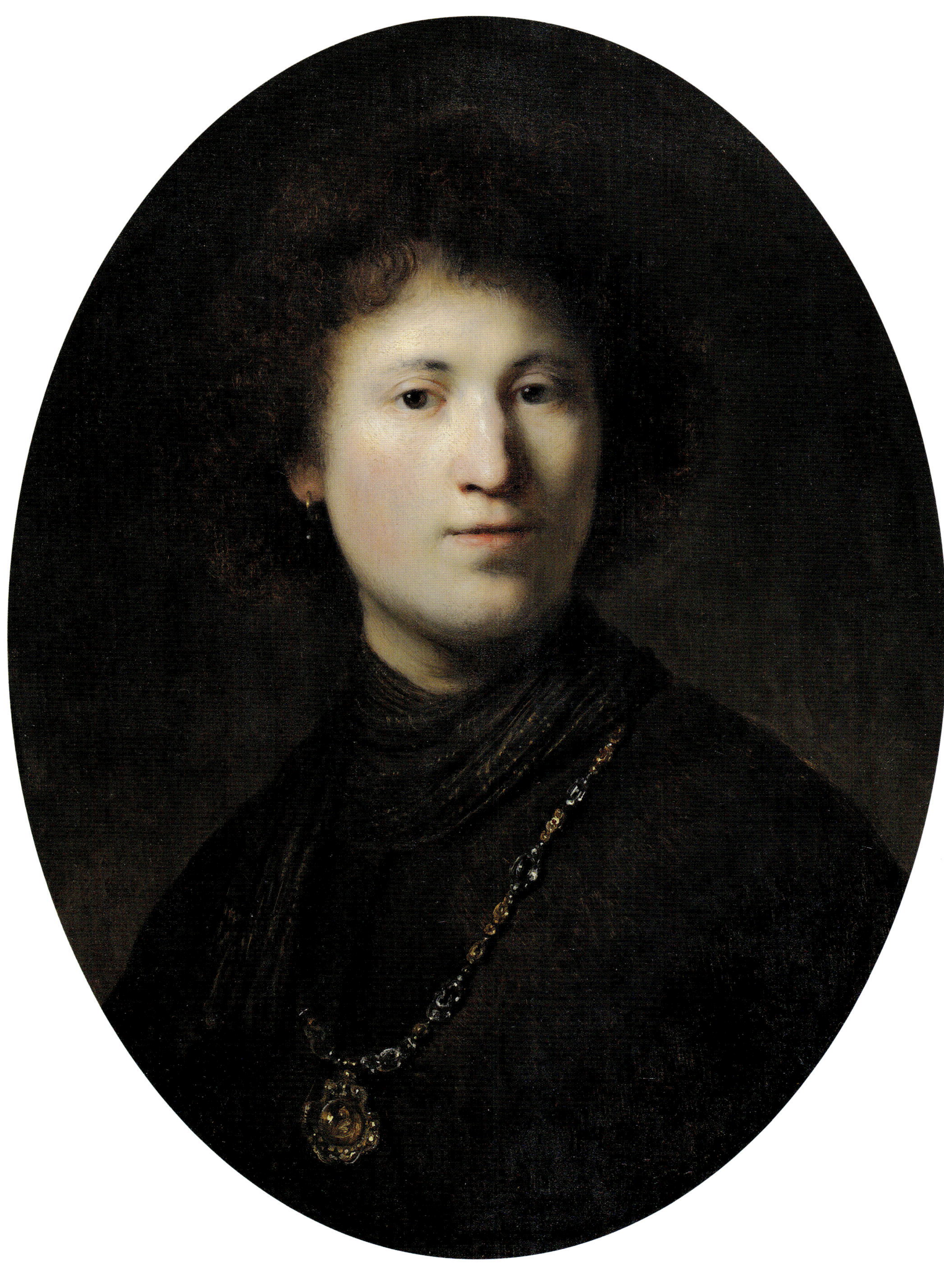

PLATE 23 [CAT. 6]
Rembrandt van Rijn and workshop
Bust of a Young Man with a Gold Chain, c. 1629 or 1632
Oil on oval panel, 57.7 x 43.9 cm (22 3/4 x 17 1/4 in.)
The Cleveland Museum of Art

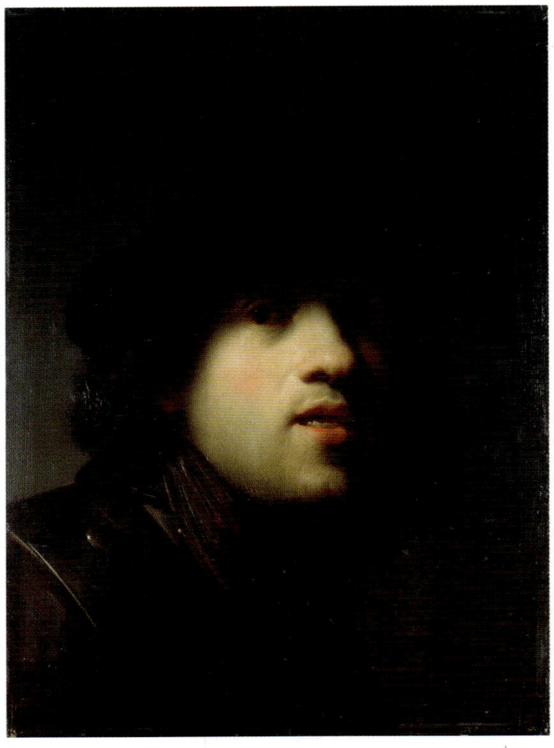

FIG. 52

display at the Indianapolis Museum of Art, the Clowes Fund Collection has retained ownership of the work since Dr. Clowes's death.

Self-portrait (Study in a Mirror) is known in at least seven versions, several of which are no longer locatable, thus posing serious challenges to the connoisseur. Two versions, the one in Indianapolis and another in the MOA Museum in Japan (FIG. 52), have generally been regarded as the best of the lot, but that may in part be because some have gone unseen in living memory.[19] In 1982 the Research Project—with dissent from Wetering—concluded that the MOA version was the original, despite the obvious evidence of changes to the composition in the Indianapolis version as revealed by X-ray. The committee came to the rather forced conclusion that the changes noted in the Indianapolis X-radiographs meant that the painting had started as a free copy but evolved into a close transcription. The reason for such strained argumentation was that most of the committee was attracted to the MOA version's similarity to a much-prized self-portrait of different composition in the Mauritshuis, a Dutch national collection in The Hague characterized as having the choicest examples of the master's paintings in its galleries.

The MOA and Mauritshuis panels share a smooth, highly refined—perhaps even precious—application of paint. A growing consensus of observers has noted, however, that they seem shallow, schematic, and less aggressively physical compared to other works.[20] Indeed, the MOA and Mauritshuis paintings are now regarded as the copies, and the Indianapolis *Self-portrait (Study in a Mirror)* is again regarded as the original (or prime) version. Some writers have suggested Rembrandt himself painted the copies, but the simplification of these images—especially notable in the overly regular facial features—mitigates against this hypothesis. One might also wonder if the slightly bug-eyed look of astonishment that is more pronounced in the MOA version could suggest that the copy was made in 1630 or later, thus showing awareness of Rembrandt's famously wide-eyed etched self-portrait of that year.[21] Sometimes puzzle pieces seem to fit, but then others are found that fit better.

Assuming that the Indianapolis version of *Self-portrait (Study in a Mirror)* is indeed the original, what can we learn from it? The work represents Rembrandt's earliest known painting of a life-size human face. Moreover, in it he has also attempted more complete modeling of the face. By comparison, in earlier paintings he had applied only enough highlights and tonal areas to suggest completeness. Here, he appears to be challenging himself to paint bigger and better,

FIG. 52
After Rembrandt van Rijn, *Self-portrait (Study in a Mirror)* (copy of cat. 4), c. 1629, oil on panel, 49.7 x 37.3 cm (19½ x 14⅝ in.). MOA Museum of Art, Atami

perhaps to pull even with his colleague Lievens and to prepare himself to seek portrait commissions from the most discriminating patrons. Rembrandt also engages in a bit of theatrical military role-playing by wearing an armor collar known as a gorget.

At the same time, the young painter already appears to render his own appearance with the unrelenting scrutiny so famous in the self-portraits from his final years. Here, for example, Rembrandt documented a few pimples along his jaw and chin. He shows himself with an open mouth, a motif that provided him the challenge of depicting extremely complicated facial terrain and the opportunity to extend the range of expression that he could then bring to his history paintings. He used the butt end of his brush to incise lines down to the underlayers of the paint as an efficient way to depict hair. The overall effect is one of startling immediacy, as his visage seems to invade the viewer's space. Rembrandt must have been pleased with the result, for he signed the painting while it was still wet, and then appears to have assigned several pupils or assistants the task of making copies.

While the Indianapolis self-portrait has gained substantial support as a Rembrandt, *Bust of a Young Man* (PLATE 22) has seen its fortunes fall. New York financier Paul M. Warburg bought the painting in 1926, and his son James P. Warburg bequeathed it to the Fogg Art Museum in 1969.[22] When the elder Warburg bought the painting, Valentiner published it as a Rembrandt self-portrait, estimating it as "a psychologically interesting self-revelation by the young master executed with a surprising freedom of technique and the finest feeling for tone values."[23] By 1969, the attribution was no longer convincing to Gerson, but he offered no suggestion about the circumstances of its making.[24] In 1982, the RRP declared the painting an imitation. What had been "surprising freedom" to Valentiner was "incoherent" to them. They sharply questioned the painter's familiarity with Rembrandt's early painting style as well as with the appearance of an actual gorget. They also dismissed the identification of the painting as a likeness of Rembrandt. With regard to the actual age of the painting, they withheld judgment.[25] Overall, the RRP ruled out "the possibility that the painting might have been done by one of his circle."

Though today's critic might see the Fogg *Bust of a Young Man* as an unconvincing imitation of Rembrandt's style made by an outsider with little affiliation to the master, other paintings not—or probably not—by Rembrandt raise interesting questions and lead us to try to understand the nature of his relationships with his followers. One such fascinating painting is *Bust of a Young Man with a Gold Chain* (PLATE 23). While it is certainly far closer to Rembrandt than the Fogg picture, it has not gained the support accorded to the Indianapolis self-portrait. Purchased by Cleveland industrialist John L. Severance, the work entered the Cleveland Museum of Art in 1942 from his bequest. While accepting it as an original in 1982, the RRP had to account for its weak execution by ignoring its inscribed date of 1632 and backdating it to 1629.[26] Even with this designation as a less mature work, the painting still rankled connoisseurs, for it lacks the imposing physical presence already evident in Rembrandt's work of the late 1620s. Its flatness is particularly noticeable in the rendering of the body. The smooth face and almond-shaped eyes seem to point directly to the work of Rembrandt's early student Isaac de Joudreville (1613–1648).

By 1632, Rembrandt had already begun to serve as the master of Hendrick Uylenburgh's Amsterdam studio. Some have claimed that documented payments for Joudreville's lodgings in Leiden preclude his having continued to work with Rembrandt, but Rembrandt's ongoing relationship with printmaker Johannes van Vliet in Leiden suggests that he may have traveled the short distance between the two cities with some frequency. Perhaps Joudreville worked as Rembrandt's "Man in Leiden," or perhaps he sometimes accompanied him to Amsterdam. Either way it is entirely plausible that Rembrandt provided him with employment and ongoing training. Joudreville could be expected to produce a passable "Rembrandt," and one can even conjecture that he applied the somewhat unsure "Rembrandt" signature to the Cleveland painting himself. After all, it was quite normal to apply the studio master's signature to the work of students and assistants, and the sale of such works was an expected part of a master's income.

Here, Joudreville shows the sitter—quite possibly Joudreville himself—wearing a gold chain, as Rembrandt often did in his own self-portraits. This was a bit of wishful thinking. Aristocratic patrons occasionally granted such chains to worthy artists, but Rembrandt is not known to have ever received one. Joudreville probably never realized his dream either. Would

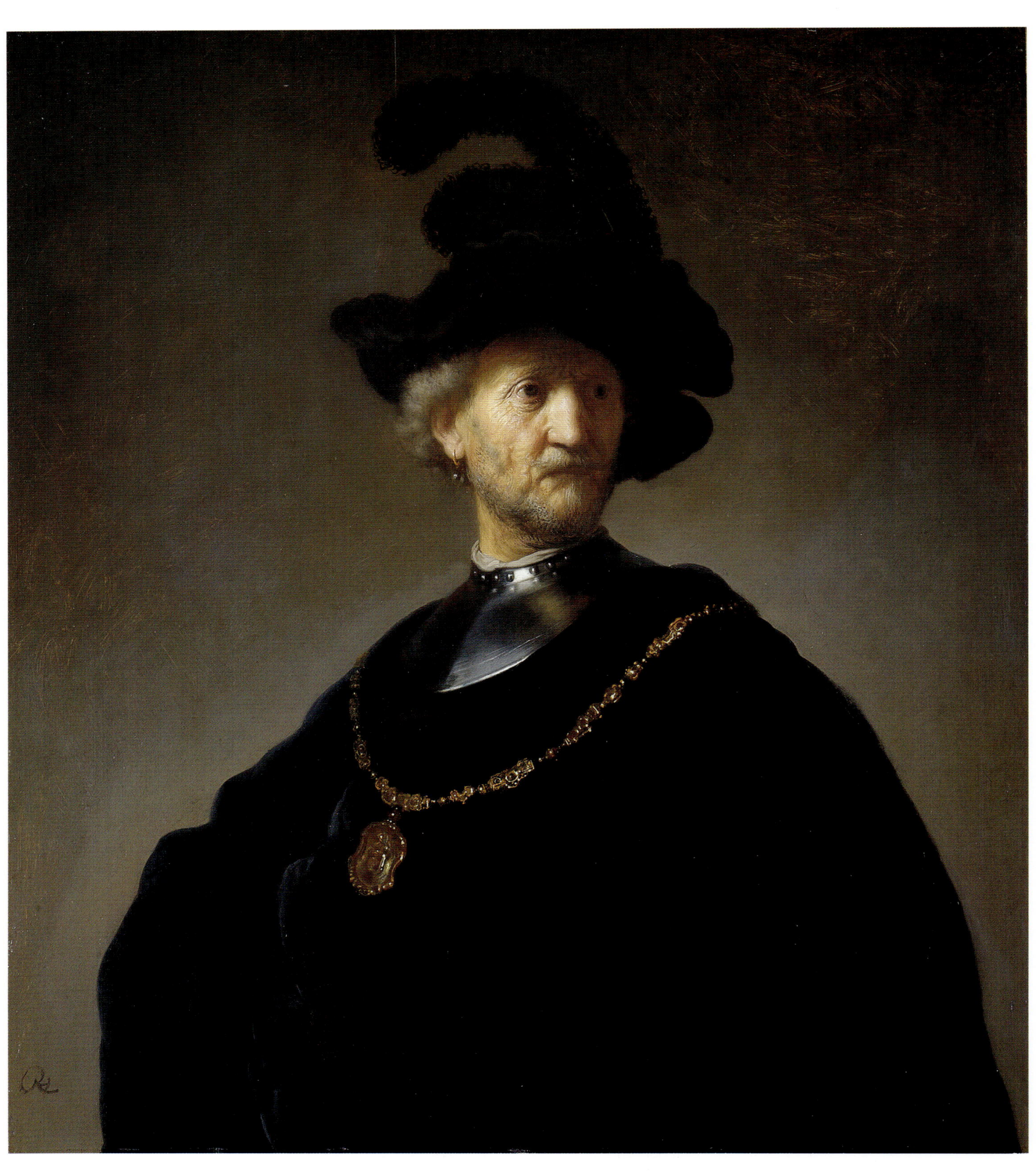

PLATE 24 [CAT. 7]
Rembrandt van Rijn
Old Man with a Gold Chain, c. 1631
Oil on panel, 83.1 x 75.7 cm (32 ¾ x 29 ¾ in.)
Mr. and Mrs. W. W. Kimball Collection, The Art Institute of Chicago

anyone have wanted a portrait of Joudreville? Perhaps not as a portrait per se, but in Holland there was a lively interest in *tronies*, painted heads or busts of characters not identified as specific individuals.

Another painting that may well be the work of Joudreville and that bears a tentatively applied Rembrandt signature and the date 1631 is in the San Diego Museum of Art (see PLATE 3, p. 36). This picture shows a man in a decorated gorget and a hat with a bejeweled plume. Again we are confronted with a Rembrandtesque subject executed without the convincing plasticity that we expect of Rembrandt. The attempt to create a dazzling effect on the gorget largely falls flat. One might entertain the possibility that the weaknesses result from an assistant in Amsterdam being unaccustomed to working for his new master, but Joudreville's authorship seems more likely, especially in light of the work's provincial feel compared to the standards of Amsterdam. The use of Rembrandt's RHL monogram also points to a Leiden origin, for after his arrival in Amsterdam, Rembrandt used more complete forms of his name in his signatures. The question of whether this is a tronie or a true portrait remains open to speculation.

To gain a sense of the vast disparity between the skill of Joudreville (or whoever made the paintings attributed to him) and Rembrandt, one may now turn to *Old Man with a Gold Chain* in the Art Institute of Chicago (PLATE 24). When, in 1913, this magnificent picture was put up for auction in Paris as a portrait of Rembrandt's father, it went unsold. The following year the widow of the piano and organ manufacturer William W. Kimball bought the painting and left it to the Art Institute when she died seven years later.

Old Man with a Gold Chain shows a balding old man with a beak nose who appears in several of Rembrandt's etchings and paintings of about 1630–31. He is traditionally identified as Rembrandt's father, Harmen, as was the case at the failed Paris auction of 1913, but evidence weighs against tradition. The present sitter appears in a Rembrandt etching dated 1631.[27] Harmen died in 1630, and a drawing of a different man is inscribed with his name in a contemporary hand.[28] The present painting appears to be an ambitious fantasy portrait—a tronie. Though past his prime, the sitter appears as a proud old warrior, alert and erect in posture. He wears a somber black cloak, but his accessories—a broad black velvet beret with two ostrich plumes, a large pearl earring, a lustrous steel gorget, an elaborately worked gold chain and medallion—speak to his dashing military past. Rembrandt seems to have relished collecting and deploying such evocative costume properties in his tronies and self-portraits. Rather than actually dressing his sitters in such gear, he may well have worked from draped dummies and elaborated them using his vivid imagination.

The grizzled hair and careworn terrain of the old soldier's face tell us his victories have been hard won; yet, Rembrandt's artistry leaves no doubt that the man before us retains a powerful spirit. The torsion of his spiral pose fills him with energy. The curvature of his chain reveals the broad mass of his upper body. The bright light entering from the left energizes the picture, catching the sitter's earring, reflecting off his gorget, and brightly illuminating the right side of his face, while leaving the left side in transparent shadow.

Rembrandt's infinitely varied brushwork further animates the surface: short strokes describe the texture of the face, while long, decisive strokes suggest the folds in the man's neck. His brush danced over the background to allow the warm brown underlayer to show through the gray paint. Around the outer contour of the man's body, Rembrandt overlapped layers of paint, partly to find the optimal outline and partly to create a halo of radiant light.

Why would Rembrandt put so much energy and labor into a large tronie at this juncture of his career? Perhaps he intended the imposing picture as an advertisement. Rembrandt may have taken the painting to Amsterdam to show potential patrons the astonishing skill that he could bring to bear in his portraiture. Anyone seeing this picture would know that the young newcomer was capable of producing an animated yet dignified likeness, somewhere on the cusp of truth and flattery. This painting is among the last he signed with his RHL monogram, for in his new surroundings he asserted himself as Rembrandt—a one-name artist in the tradition of Raphael (1483–1520), Michelangelo (1475–1564), and Titian (1485/90–1576). *Old Man with a Gold Chain* represents the culmination of Rembrandt's preparation to make his mark on Amsterdam and assume his role as one of the greatest painters of all time.

Traditionally, the story of Rembrandt's Leiden years ends here. Some twenty years ago, however, study of the watermarks found in the papers used to print his etchings led to the

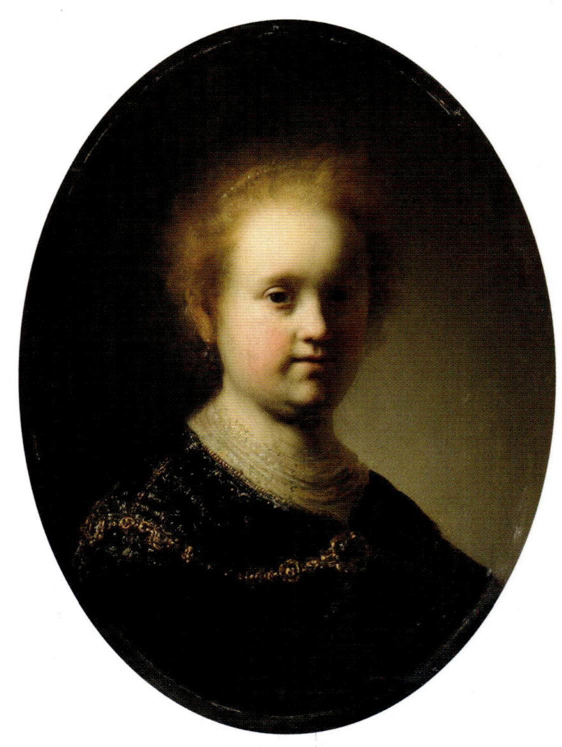

FIG. 53

realization that he maintained strong ties with Leiden even after his move to Amsterdam. The current perception is that Rembrandt shuttled back and forth between Leiden and Amsterdam for a few years. As a result, these years become somewhat hazy. Some pictures, such as the lovely *Portrait of a Girl Wearing a Gold-trimmed Cloak* (see PLATE 5, p. 40), signed and dated 1632 and now in a private collection in New York, could have been painted in either place. The picture was traditionally considered to be a portrait of Rembrandt's sister, but the absence of documentary basis for this identification and the sitter's fanciful, old-fashioned costume have led to its reassignment as a tronie, an anonymous character head. Nothing about the woman's countenance or her clothing suggests a specific historical or literary character, so it is unlikely to have been commissioned as a *portrait historié*—a portrait intended to associate the sitter with some specific historical, literary, or cultural reference. The mixture of a convincing, sober, lifelike face with an understatedly playful costume suggests that the image depicts one of Rembrandt's intimates, even though we cannot be so specific as to say she was his sister. Even if we could say with certainty that it depicts someone with whom he was familiar, we still could not say whether it was a very personal portrait or a tronie based on a handy model.

Portrait of a Girl Wearing a Gold-trimmed Cloak has a long association with another painting, *Bust of a Young Woman* (FIG. 53), in the Morehead Planetarium in Chapel Hill.[29] The two were sold as a pair as early as 1767, when they first appear in documentary records. Both panels appear to have originally been rectangular but were cut down to make them oval, which was already their state according to the 1767 description.[30] Both have traditionally been identified as "Rembrandt's sister." The Morehead painting, however, lacks the intense physical and psychological presence of the sitter that emanates from the New York picture. It also lacks the glowing sense of expansive space.

Many features of the Morehead painting, including the exuberant but weakly structured distribution of highlights in the sitter's garment, are strongly reminiscent of several paintings by Joudreville, Rembrandt's Leiden protégé. One could readily hypothesize that Rembrandt's *Bust of a Young Woman* was available to Joudreville in Leiden and that he painted variants of it. One significant difference between the two paintings—the types of wood on which they were painted—tempts speculation on their origin. The Morehead bust is painted on the customary oak. The *Portrait of a Girl Wearing a Gold-trimmed Cloak* is painted on the exotic mahogany. Perhaps Rembrandt encountered this tropical wood in the great port city of Amsterdam. It is typical

FIG. 53
Rembrandt (circle of; Isaac de Joudreville?), *Bust of a Young Woman*, c. 1632, oil on panel, 53.3 x 39.3 cm (21 x 15 1/2 in.). Morehead Planetarium, University of North Carolina, Chapel Hill

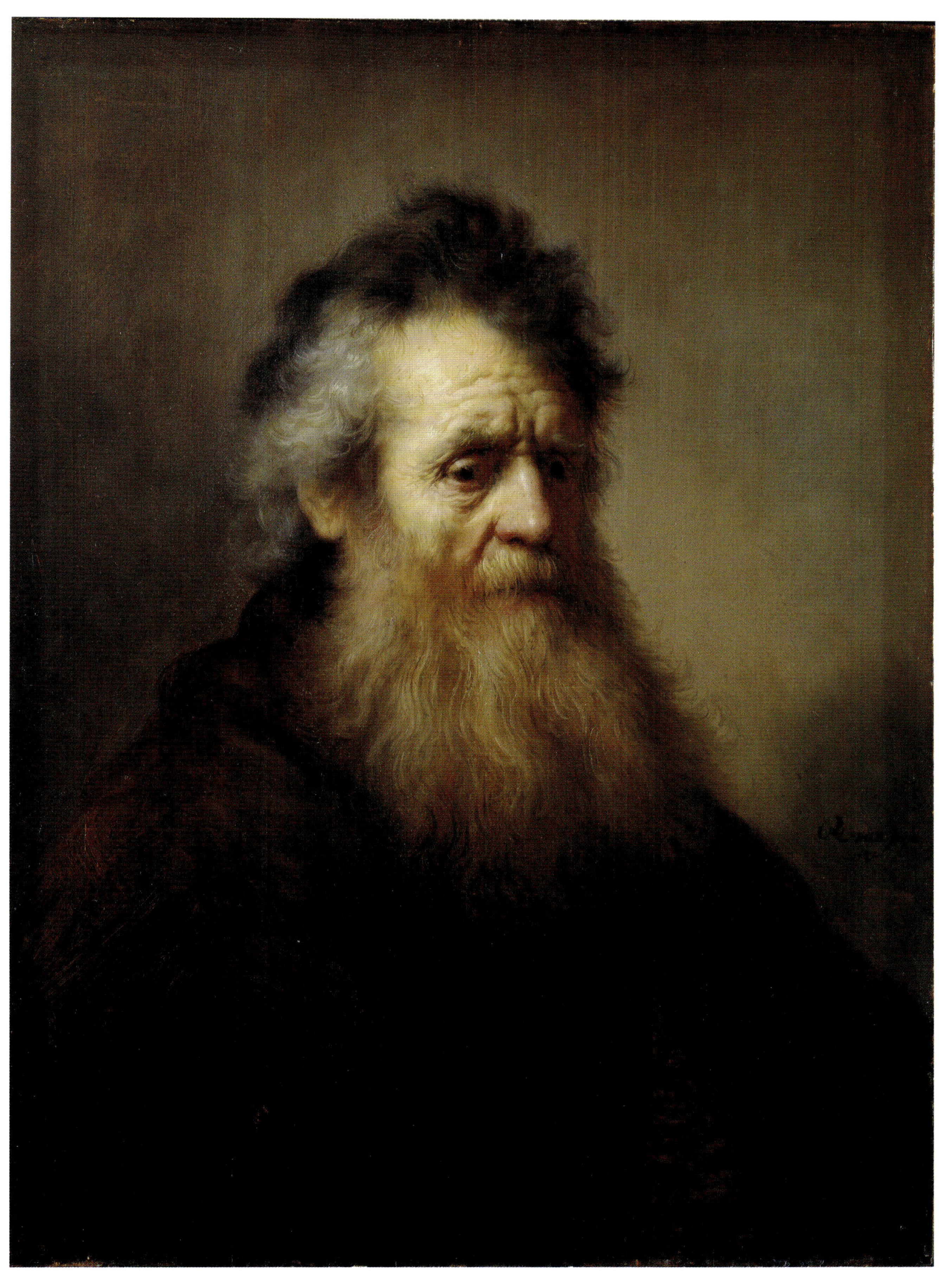

PLATE 25 [CAT. 14]
Rembrandt van Rijn
Portrait of an Old Man, 1632
Oil on cradled oak, 66.9 x 50.7 cm (26 3/8 x 20 in.)
Fogg Art Museum, Harvard University, Cambridge

of Rembrandt to seek out and test exotic materials, as is readily apparent in his use of Japanese papers to print his etchings.

Several other paintings may also be considered satellites of the autograph picture in New York, including one in the Samuel H. Kress Collection at the Allentown Art Museum in Pennsylvania (see PLATE 6, p. 41). In the early eighteenth century the painting was in the renowned collection of Philippe, duc d'Orléans, in whose family it descended until it was bought by George Kinnaird, 7th Lord Kinnaird, shortly after the French Revolution. By 1800, it was sold to George O'Brien Wyndham, 3rd Lord Egremont, whose family kept it at Petworth, a palatial country house famous for its spectacular collections. When the painting became available in the late 1920s, a period of economic stagnation in England, American dime-store magnate Samuel H. Kress must have found the provenance as attractive as the painting. The provenance, however, tells us more about the transfer of global wealth and power than it does about the quality of the picture.

Though Rembrandtesque in its subject, format, costume, and—superficially—brushwork, the Allentown picture lacks visual effect. Within a few years of its purchase, Kress hired Alan Burroughs, a pioneer in the scientific investigation of paintings, to examine his purchase.[31] Burroughs concluded that the painting displayed neither Rembrandt's technique nor his command of anatomy. Indeed, the painting appears flat and the features misplaced when compared to its counterpart in New York. The flatness is exacerbated by the Kress picture's frontal lighting, a feature highly unusual in Dutch portraits of the time. The tentatively inscribed signature is probably not authentic, but it may have been applied by the assistant producing a studio "Rembrandt" for sale by the master.

The changing understanding of Rembrandt's ongoing ties to Leiden have reopened some questions that earlier seemed to have been settled, among them the attribution of paintings made in the style shared by Rembrandt and Lievens. Since they shared many artistic ideas and were both extremely good painters, the line between them is difficult to define. A painting of a dramatically lit old man with a flowing beard, now in the Fogg Art Museum, Harvard University (PLATE 25), provides a challenging example of a painting whose critical fortunes continue to change. Until 1963, it was considered to be by Rembrandt even though the model had long been identified as one who sat for Lievens. Then, two distinguished Harvard scholars, Seymour Slive and Jakob Rosenberg, expressed doubts about Rembrandt's involvement while maintaining their belief in the authenticity of the "RHL van Rijn/1632" signature and date. They settled on Lievens as the author because of the picture's delicate, silvery touch. When Horst Gerson produced his critical catalogue of Rembrandt's paintings, he followed their lead. Other authors suggested that it might be by Jacob Adriaensz. Backer with retouches by Rembrandt or by Rembrandt and Lievens together. When volume two of the Rembrandt Research Committee Corpus, which covers the paintings dated 1632, appeared in 1986, the painting received no mention. In 1989, Werner Sumowski, the leading expert on the entire circle of artists around Rembrandt, called it the work of an anonymous student of Rembrandt.[32] That same year, Joshua Bruyn, writing in volume three of the corpus, concluded that it was a product of Rembrandt's workshop while bidding the painting farewell from the Rembrandt literature.[33] Well, it's back. The Fogg officially presents the painting as a Rembrandt and scholars are increasingly voicing that opinion. That a 1632 painting with such a Leiden flavor could be by Rembrandt invites further investigation of his ongoing attachment to his hometown despite his more fully understood ventures in Amsterdam. The present exhibition offers scholars a rare opportunity to compare the painting of the old man with many others by Rembrandt to see if the current swing of the pendulum is on course.

For now the exact nature of Rembrandt's activity and that of his assistants during his years of transition from Leiden to Amsterdam remains undefined, but it appears that he kept a Leiden studio going in some form—perhaps to maintain an established stream of income, perhaps to have a fallback position. Though he soon proved so successful in Amsterdam that he no longer needed his hometown base, Leiden had been the crucible in which he prepared himself for the intense competition of the great metropolis.

While Rembrandt was making the transition from Leiden to Amsterdam, he produced several magnificent portraits that helped to establish his position as the new artistic force in the big city, among them his portrait of Amsterdam merchant Marten Looten (see PLATE 26, p. 114).[34] Oil tycoon J. Paul Getty bought the painting from the estate of the prominent Amsterdam art auctioneer Anton W. M. Mensing in 1938 and donated it to the Los Angeles County Museum of Art in 1953.[35] This was probably the first genuine Rembrandt painting to take up long-term residence in California.

Apart from the artist's studies of his own likeness, Marten Looten is among Rembrandt's earliest portraits of an identified sitter.[36] Rembrandt made certain that Looten could be identified. He shows Looten holding a sheet of paper bearing his name in large cursive script. The sheet also bears a date, variously read as 11 or 12 January 1632. Rembrandt's monogram is also clearly visible farther down the sheet. No effort to decipher the text has proven convincing, and it may simply be Rembrandt's way of giving us the sense that we are seeing writing just as he presents us with the illusion of a nose or a hat. Looten appears to turn toward us at the instant we have interrupted his reading.

As with the other large portraits from this moment when Rembrandt was establishing his reputation, he took great care in his painting of Looten. He painted the face with a marvelous variety of confident strokes, some fluid, some halting, some broad, and some fine. He captures the wispiness of the beard, the firm shininess of the nose, the delicate musculature around the eyes, and the glistening wateriness within them. Yet, he does not overdo it. Some passages he leaves very thinly painted or only cursorily described. There is no detail in the ear to distract us from the face, especially the gaze. Rembrandt made adjustments to a number of sections in the painting. X-rays reveal that the index finger of the right hand was originally straighter, the hat was taller, and the outline of the mantle much bulkier. He took the unusual step of painting over the background a second time to ensure that his missteps would not be readily seen. His attitude about such matters would eventually change, especially in his practice as a printmaker. For the present, however, he was much more interested in proving he could produce a masterpiece than he was in revealing the path that he took toward his goal. Much of what has kept Rembrandt an interesting artist across the centuries is his combination of impulsiveness and perfectionism. Here he reigned in his spontaneity, sacrificing the markedly varied play of light that normally enlivens the background of his portraits in order to achieve the perfection that would appeal to the thriving Amsterdam businessmen and possibly even the royalty to whom he hoped to cater.

In Leiden, Rembrandt had served his first apprenticeship with Jacob van Swanenburgh, learning the basics of painting, discovering the wonders of Italy, and observing the expressive possibilities of darkness and light. There too, he saw in the work of Jan Lievens that he was in need of further training, and that Pieter Lastman's studio could be the ideal place to improve his skills. After a brief sojourn with the Amsterdam master, Rembrandt returned again to Leiden, intent on driving himself beyond even Lastman's achievements. He rapidly developed his mastery of texture, expression, space, light, and form. Rather than painting big, flashy pictures, he concentrated on perfecting his means of imaginative expression within the confines of intimate images. That concentrated effort rapidly propelled him to maturity. His skill and stylistic innovations attracted students and followers. He quickly developed into a teacher capable of training others to make such fine pictures that they could be confused with his own. Within five years, he found himself fully able to compete with the finest painters of Amsterdam, where he took over the leadership of the most productive studio in the city.

Looking back at the pictures that the brash young artist painted in Leiden, we see the rapid ascent of his learning curve. The earliest paintings such as the allegories *Hearing* and *Touch* are fascinating artifacts, the juvenilia of a great artist, perhaps exaggerated hack work in their own time and now prompting us to ask, "Is *that* really a *Rembrandt?*" Had he died immediately after making these pictures, we would not even recognize his name today. But soon we confront unusual yet truly arresting paintings, such as *Self-portrait (Study in a Mirror)* or *The Artist in His Studio*. These painstakingly executed, remarkably novel inventions—one startlingly in-your-face, the other an invitation to enter the imaginative world of the artist's mind—earned Rembrandt a place as an artist for his contemporaries to watch, and for subsequent generations to remember.

Finally, as he was stepping from Leiden to Amsterdam, with works such as *Old Man with a Gold Chain, Portrait of a Girl Wearing a Gold-trimmed Cloak,* and *Marten Looten*, he painted pictures that may have struck fear into the hearts of his competitors. Today, they touch our hearts with their enduring capacity to make us want to connect with individuals who have been gone for more than three hundred years. Rembrandt had arrived artistically; so, it was now time for him to depart his hometown.

NOTES

1 Corpus 1982–89, vols. 1–3. See also Corpus 2005 for a discussion of Rembrandt's self-portraits, including a number of examples from his Leiden years. In addition, a fifth volume, Corpus 2010, has just been published, one devoted to Rembrandt's small-scale history paintings. The RRP will end with the forthcoming publication of a summary volume reproducing all 320 paintings that in the opinion of Ernst van de Wetering are by Rembrandt.

2 See Boston 2000 and Kassel and Amsterdam 2001.

3 Amsterdam 1996.

4 Kassel and Amsterdam 2001, nos. 9, 10; and Corpus 2005, p. 627.

5 For a comprehensive overview of this material, see New York 2001. This exhibition focused on both the drawings and the prints linked to Pieter Brueghel the Elder, including many carrying comic overtones.

6 An English translation of Huygens's comments on Rembrandt and Lievens (taken from his autobiography) appears in Leiden 1991, pp. 132–34.

7 Braunschweig 1979. More recently, another exhibition (Washington 2008) has clarified some of the lingering questions regarding the character of Lievens's oeuvre.

8 Wetering, in Kassel and Amsterdam 2001, pp. 41–49.

9 Leiden 1991, p. 132.

10 When purchased by R. L. Douglas, the painting had strips of wood at top and bottom that gave it a vertical format. The strips were soon removed. Seymour Slive, "Rembrandt's 'Self-Portrait in a Studio,'" *Burlington Magazine* CVI, no. 740 (1964): 482–87, argues that the strip may have been added by Rembrandt. The Research Committee, Corpus 1982–89, 1: A18, argued against Slive's theory on the basis of the direction of the grain of the original panel, its beveled edges, and the discordant aging of the paint on the strips as seen in an old photograph.

11 The extent of the Bader collection, including scores of paintings linked to Rembrandt and his circle, a number of which have been donated to the Agnes Etherington Art Centre, Queen's University, Kingston, Canada, is seen in a recent catalogue of the collection (De Witt 2008).

12 See Corpus 1982–89, 1: A10 and A16, respectively.

13 Ibid., C18; for the RRP discussion of the Tours painting, see C5.

14 Wetering, in Kassel and Amsterdam 2001, fig. 23, p. 74, and pp. 76–77. The present author remains inclined to think it unlikely that Rembrandt painted the Tours picture.

15 Ibid., cat. 59, pp. 298–301.

16 One should note that of the handful of Rembrandt's paintings on copper, the majority show the application of gold leaf over the copper support. While this is not true of *A Scholar by Candlelight*, it should not necessarily be used as evidence to remove this painting from his oeuvre.

17 Corpus 1982–89, 1: A22, with several copies illustrated.

18 The painting was previously in the collection of Prince Jerzy Rafal Lubomirski, Geneva. Frederick Mont (formerly Mondschein) and Newhouse Galleries, New York, sold the painting to Dr. Clowes, who was for many years director of research at Eli Lilly and Co.

19 Corpus 1982–89, 1: Indianapolis version, A22 (copy 1), and the MOA version as autograph. See also Corpus 2005, pp. 162–64 and 598–601.
20 Corpus 2005, p. 164.
21 This approach is best seen in his *Self-portrait in a Cap, with Eyes Wide Open*, signed and dated "RHL 1630" (Bartsch 1797, no. 320).
22 Corpus 1982–89, 1: C35.
23 Valentiner 1926, 117–19.
24 Gerson/Bredius 1969, 4.
25 The RRP noted that an earlier dendrochronological study had been performed not on the panel on which the picture was painted, but had instead been performed on a one-piece wooden frame into which the painting had been set. Interestingly enough, the extra framing piece was made from a tree that could have been felled in 1629 at the earliest. Even if the 1629 date inscribed on the picture is correct, the framing piece would have to be a later addition.
26 Corpus 1982–89, 1: A23; and p. 838 (under A23) in Corrigenda et Addenda.
27 Bartsch 1797, no. 263.
28 Oxford, Ashmolean Museum. Benesch 1954–57, no. 56.
29 Corpus 1982–89, 2: C58.
30 Collection de Julienne auction catalogue (sale, Paris, 30 March–22 May 1797, lot 131).
31 In the early stages of his career, Burroughs worked at the Minneapolis Institute of Arts; he then moved to Harvard University, where he went on to take the lead in the use of X-rays to examine paintings.
32 Sumowski 1983, 4: no. 1919, p. 2943. Sumowski also provides a summation of earlier literature.
33 Bruyn, "Studio Practice and Studio Production," in Corpus 1982–89, 3: p. 24.
34 Corpus 1982–89, 2: A52.
35 Mensing died in 1937. Frederik Muller, a bookselling firm that Mensing had transformed into a major art auction house, sold his paintings, 15 November 1938. In addition to the Rembrandt, Getty bought other pictures that day.
36 Other early examples are *Nicolaes Ruts*, 1631 (see fig. 57, p. 116), *The Anatomy Lesson of Dr. Nicolaes Tulp*, 1632 (see fig. 11, p. 39), *Joris de Caulerij*, 1632 (see PLATE 12, p. 68), *Jacques de Gheyn III*, 1632 (Dulwich Picture Gallery, London), *Maurits Huygens*, 1632 (Hamburger Kunsthalle, Hamburg), and *Amalia van Marben*, 1632 (Musée Jacquemart-André, Paris). In all likelihood, only the Ruts portrait was completed before *Marten Looten*.

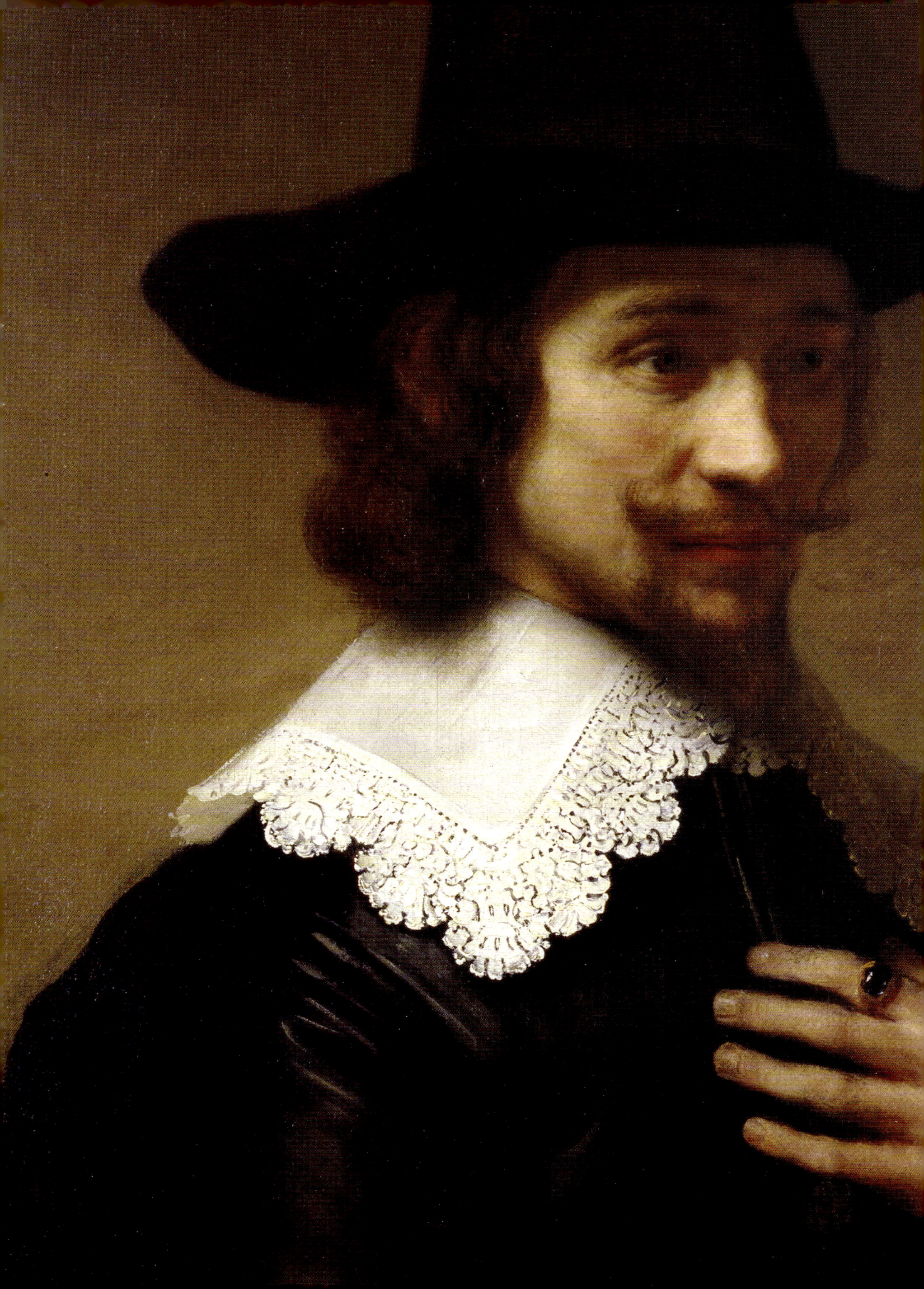

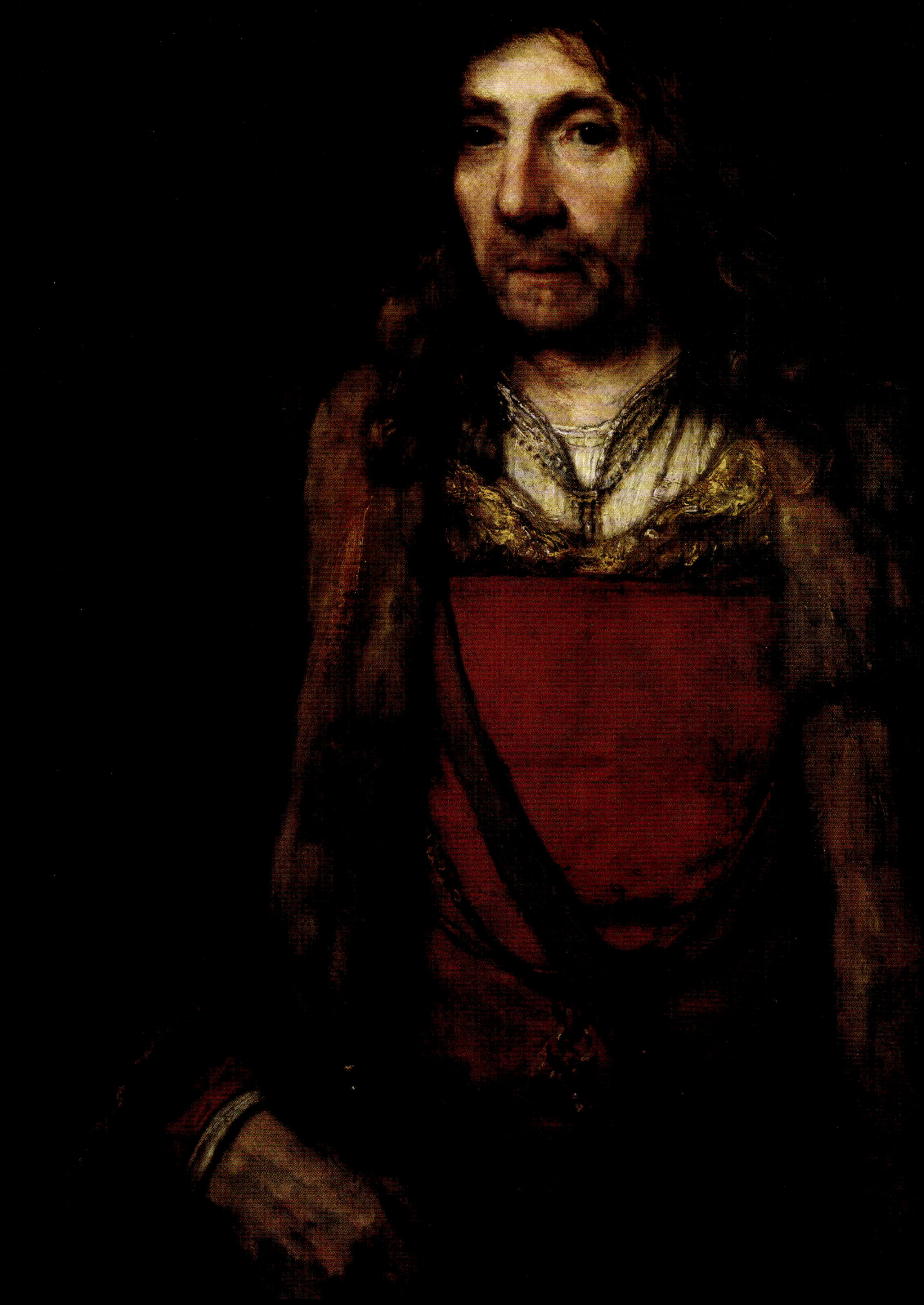

The Elusive Nature of Portraiture: Rembrandt as a Portraitist in Amsterdam

GEORGE S. KEYES

Rembrandt's move to Amsterdam was a protracted affair in that he appears to have maintained his studio in Leiden until late 1633 when he moved definitively to the great metropolis on the River Ij.[1] Thus paintings dated or datable to 1631 and 1632 are potentially transitional in nature. Examining certain pictures from this period is worthwhile in order to consider the degree to which they manifest the painter's awareness of the huge impact his permanent move to Amsterdam would have on his art and the new directions he would take.

By happenstance, two likenesses of young men have ended up in Ohio—the *Young Man in a Plumed Hat,* signed and dated 1631 (FIG. 54), in the Toledo Museum of Art and *Bust of a Young Man with a Gold Chain,* signed and dated 1632 (see PLATE 23, p. 99), in the Cleveland Museum of Art. Both raise interesting questions, as each youthful sitter wears a conspicuous chain of honor. These two pictures are, in all likelihood, not portraits but *tronies,* a Dutch term of the period in which models served as imagined character likenesses.[2] The term itself embraces a number of different aspects of characterization ranging from capturing expression to assuming an imaginary role and embodying recognizable accomplishments whether they are achievements of the mind or acts of physical prowess or heroism. Thus, the intent of tronies was wide-ranging.[3]

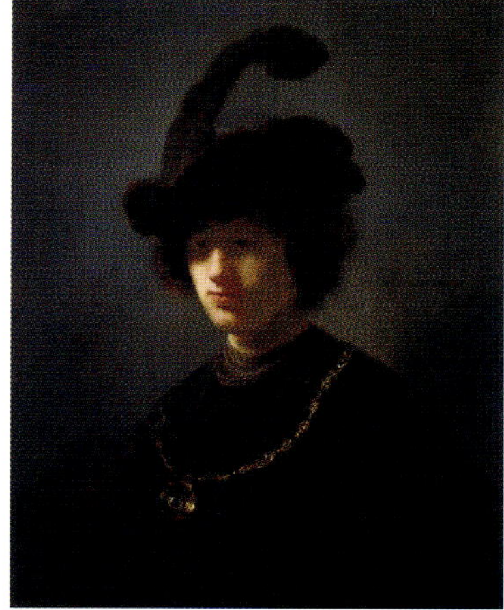

FIG. 54

The panel in Toledo is the more ambitious of the two—in size and deportment, and because it underwent a substantial transformation by the artist. The young man originally had slightly different features, a different, more modest chain of honor (still visible through the outermost paint layer), and a far simpler cap. Even the contours of the sitter's body were extended somewhat, as if the model had grown more bulky. In revising the composition Rembrandt painted the chain of honor vigorously with a juicy application of paint. He also energized the cap by emphasizing its scalloped contours with bold highlights. The large feather is also painted with great aplomb. The youth's countenance has a pensive quality, perhaps conveying inner thoughts about the recognition lavished on him as denoted by the golden chain.

The youth in the Cleveland painting seems even more adolescent and almost effeminate, yet he too wears a fine scarf, an earring, and an elaborate gold chain. This acclamation of youthful accomplishment appears to be the artist's primary intention, shifting the subject from the realm of portraiture to the realm of embodiment—the incarnation of youthful triumphs whether through activities of the mind or through physical prowess.

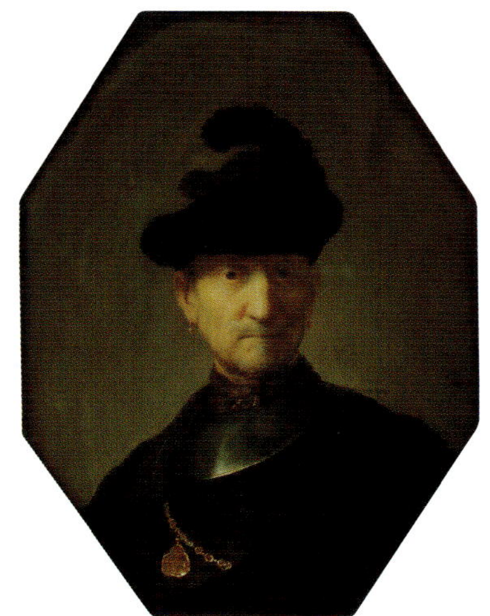

FIG. 55

Rembrandt also painted old men wearing gorgets, sometimes in combination with chains of honor. In pictures such as those in the Art Institute of Chicago (see PLATE 24, p. 102), the J. Paul Getty Museum (see FIG. 46, p. 79), and the Hermitage in St. Petersburg (FIG. 55), the men also wear conspicuous plumed hats, all markedly different as if each sitter was modeling one in a couturier's range of seasonal offerings. These demonstrably older, grizzled characters represent men of physical accomplishment honored in their older years. Their younger, more virile adult counterparts are curiously lacking in Rembrandt's repertory. Why this should be the case raises interesting psychological questions not to be dealt with here. Suffice it to say that when Rembrandt represented younger, adult men whose countenances do not yet betray the onset of middle age, these subjects were patrons who sought compelling and assuredly flattering likenesses. Such pictures belong to the domain of commissioned portraits.

Paintings such as the tronies of youths in Toledo and Cleveland find a significant parallel in Rembrandt's many self-portraits datable to his later Leiden years and extending into the mid-1630s after his move to Amsterdam. In many of the more ambitious examples—including those in the Isabella Stewart Gardner Museum in Boston (see FIG. 34, p. 70), the Walker Art Gallery in Liverpool (FIG. 56), the Musée du Louvre in Paris, the Uffizi Gallery in Florence, and the Mauritshuis in The Hague[4]—he, too, wears a conspicuous chain of honor. The painter, like his young men in Toledo and Cleveland, projects himself as worthy of public recognition—even

FIG. 54
Rembrandt van Rijn, *Young Man in a Plumed Hat*, 1631, oil on panel, 81.2 x 66 cm (32 x 26 in.). The Toledo Museum of Art; Gift of Edward Drummond Libbey; inv. 1926.64

FIG. 55
Rembrandt van Rijn (workshop), *Old Man in a Plumed Hat ("Rembrandt's Father")*, c. 1631, oil on panel, 36 x 26 cm (14 x 10⅜ in.). The State Hermitage Museum, St. Petersburg

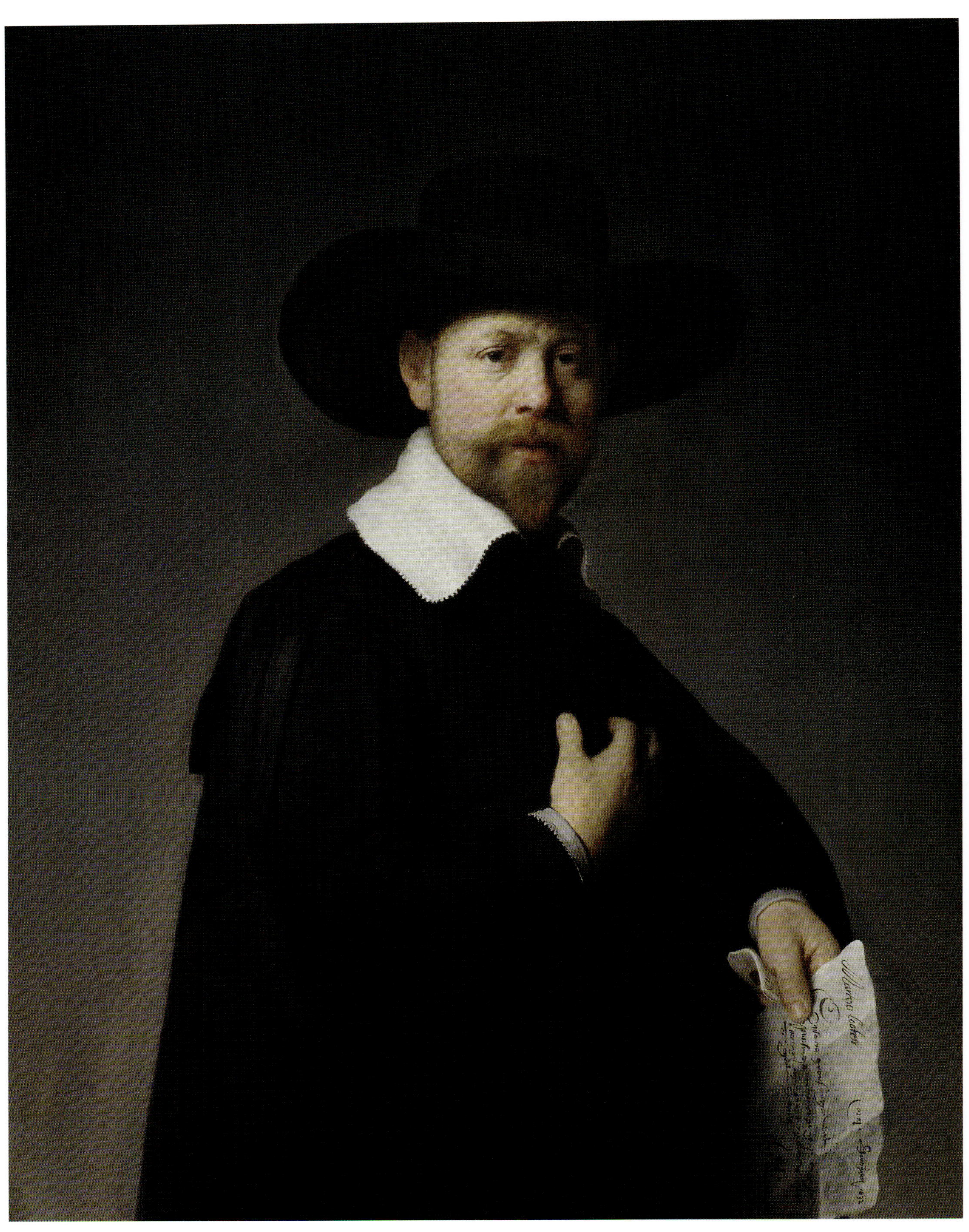

PLATE 26 [CAT. 15]
Rembrandt van Rijn
Portrait of Marten Looten, 1632
Oil on panel, 92.7 x 76.2 cm (36½ x 30 in.)
Los Angeles County Museum of Art

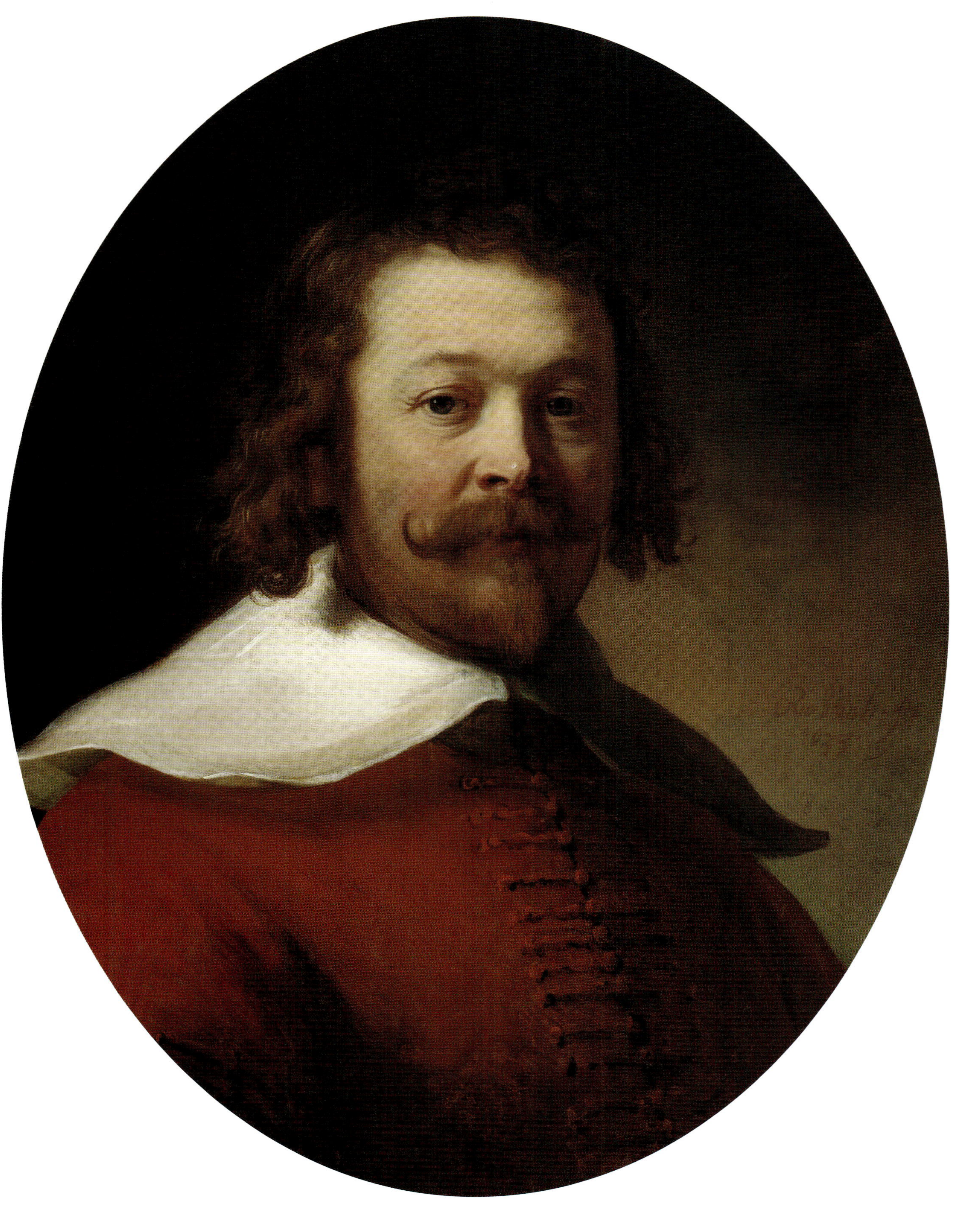

PLATE 27 [CAT. 16]
Rembrandt van Rijn
Portrait of a Man in a Red Doublet, 1633
Oil on panel, 63.5 x 50.8 cm (25 x 20 in.)
Private collection, New York

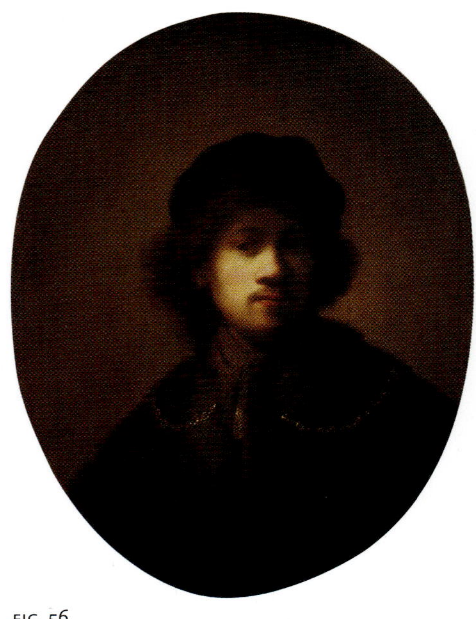

FIG. 56

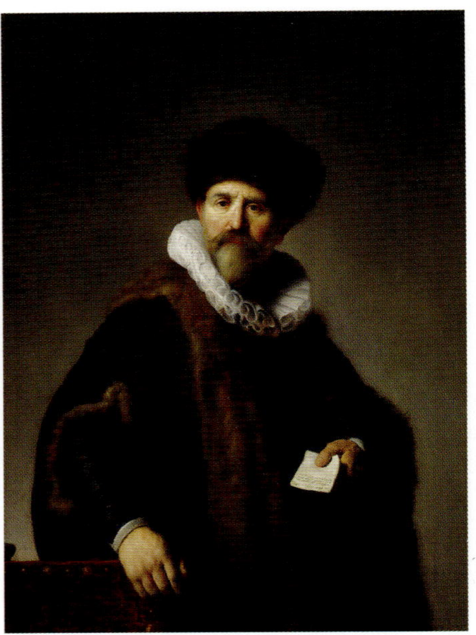

FIG. 57

admiration. And why not! For Rembrandt found himself to be the most sought-after portraitist in Amsterdam, heralded in no small measure by the brilliance of his first life-size group portrait, *The Anatomy Lesson of Doctor Nicolas Tulp* of 1632 (see FIG. 11, p. 39).

During this same year, 1632, Rembrandt began painting life-size portraits of dignified sitters, executed in roughly equal numbers on canvas or oak panel supports. Depending on the age and aspirations of the patron in question, these works range from reasonably conservative representations to others truly innovative in character. The pair of so-called Beresteyn family portraits now in the Metropolitan Museum of Art (see PLATES 10, 11, p. 64, 65) conform to the conservative strain yet are notable for their scale, fastidious attention to detail, and the projection of earnestly held probity.

Rembrandt's exposure to portraiture in Leiden, given its proximity to the stadtholder's court in The Hague, would have consisted primarily in confronting predictably formal yet somewhat formulaic portrait busts or three-quarter length portraits by Michiel Jansz. van Miereveld (1567–1641) and his studio or the analogous production of Jan Anthonisz. van Ravesteyn (c. 1572–1657). Conservative in mien, executed with a licked finish, and fixated on formal details of a status-defining nature, these formal likenesses were hardly infused with the animation Rembrandt had already exploited with such success in his tronies. By contrast, in Amsterdam he encountered a well-established, lively tradition dominated by painters such as Cornelis Pietersz. van der Voort (1576–1624), Werner Jacobsz. van den Valckert (c. 1580/85–1627?), and Nicolaes Eliasz. Pickenoy (1588–1650/56).[5] At this time the young Thomas de Keyser (1596/97–1667) was also establishing his reputation as a portraitist, particularly in the production of small panel paintings in which he represented two interacting figures. The most famous of those works is his *Portrait of Constantijn Huygens and His Secretary* of 1627 in the National Gallery in London.

Rudi Ekkart is entirely correct in recognizing that the tradition of portraiture in Amsterdam during the second and third decades of the seventeenth century was far more diverse, innovative, and even experimental than that found elsewhere in the Dutch Republic (with the possible exception of Haarlem), especially in The Hague. That this served as a stimulus to Rembrandt is also unquestionable; yet the roster of portraits he produced from 1631 to 1633—ranging from *Portrait of Nicolaes Ruts* (FIG. 57) in the Frick Collection and *Young Man at a Desk* of 1631 in St. Petersburg, to the *Portrait of Marten Looten* (PLATE 26) in Los Angeles[6] and *Joris de Caulerij* of 1632 (see PLATE 12, p. 68) in San Francisco, to the pair of 1633 now divided between the Taft Museum in Cincinnati and the Metropolitan Museum of Art in New York (FIGS. 58, 59)—indicate a degree of accomplishment that indelibly changed the character of portraiture in Amsterdam, not to mention the expectations of prospective clients at the time.

FIG. 56
Rembrandt van Rijn, *Self-portrait*, c. 1630, oil on panel, 69.7 x 57 cm (24¾ x 22 ¾ in.). Walker Art Gallery, Liverpool; WAG1011

FIG. 57
Rembrandt van Rijn, *Portrait of Nicolaes Ruts*, 1631, oil on panel, 116 x 87 cm (45⅝ x 34¼ in.). The Frick Collection, New York; 1943.1.150

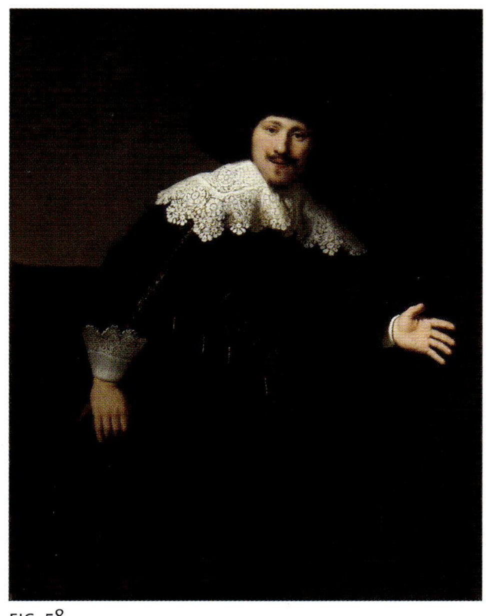

FIG. 58

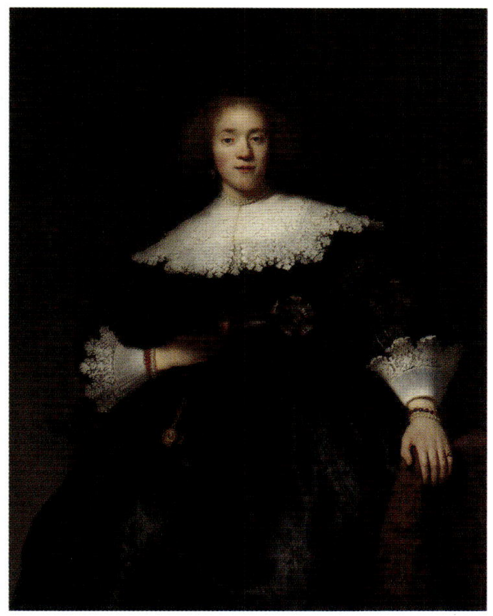

FIG. 59

What did Rembrandt infuse into his likenesses that distinguished his art from what preceded it? His interest in producing tronies seems to have had considerable bearing on this question. Those tronies, especially if we are prepared to include many self-portraits from his Leiden and early Amsterdam years, exhibit a phenomenal range that must have had, even as a by-product, great promotional value. Many of the qualities one associates with these images were attributes Rembrandt was able to incorporate into his portraits as well. Animation is certainly one of those traits, even though the element of appearance was, perforce, restrained. In fact, the animation conveyed by the face was often effectively calibrated with the act of gesturing. Hands and their actions define the creative activities of many of the sitters, and their facial expressions, such as slightly open mouths or penetrating gazes, underscore and perfectly complement their actions. Rembrandt introduces into his portraits a sense of intentionality that categorically individualizes his sitters even within their social strata. Like the more intentionally stereotyped images of painters such as Pickenoy and Van der Voort, Rembrandt's sitters also sport costly attire, magnificently starched lace collars and ruffs, and in the case of his female sitters, elaborately embroidered stomachers and gloves, and splendid jewelry—usually rendered with a degree of tactile finish that is often a marvel of painterly wizardry. Yet these badges indicating wealth and social standing are subservient to the painter's larger mission to animate his subjects—to render them truly believable, living presences. Their animation and gestures are a form of outreach that has considerable impact on the beholder. We feel that we know or could know these personages even though such a response is ultimately purely illusory. Still, the illusion is worth the gambit, and no doubt the sitters were happy with the results because the second illusion—that of a living likeness—was a remarkable, demonstrably successful investment in immortality.

During this period Rembrandt produced smaller-scale paired portraits, all on panel and often in an oval format. Their reduced scale restricted, often totally, the capacity for gesture. Therefore the focus on countenance to create a sense of animation was more discreet. Yet Rembrandt carefully calibrated the pairing of husband and wife to create a sense of marital bonding and dignity that simultaneously underscores a sense of social well-being. As is so often the case, husband and wife become separated and lose their identities as well—at least in terms of their painted depictions. One such instance involves the *Portrait of a Man in a Red Doublet* of 1633 (PLATE 27).[7] Rembrandt represents this portly figure in warm light concentrated on the man's face, ruff, and red garment. Despite the seemingly simple presentation of this sitter, the painter employs a number of pictorial devices that energize the subject. The man is turned slightly to the right yet turns his head to address the viewer. The light playing on his face suffuses it with the warm glow of a living countenance, which is echoed in the subdued yet glowing resonance of his red coat. By employing the intense white starched and falling collar as a bold

FIG. 58
Rembrandt van Rijn, *Portrait of a Man Rising from His Chair*, 1633, oil on canvas, 124 x 98.5 cm (48 7/8 x 38 3/4 in.). The Taft Collection, Bequest of Charles Phelps and Anna Sinton Taft; Taft Museum of Art, Cincinnati; 1931.409

FIG. 59
Rembrandt van Rijn, *Portrait of a Young Woman with a Fan*, 1633, oil on canvas, 125.7 x 101 cm (49 1/2 x 39 3/4 in.). The Metropolitan Museum of Art, New York; 43.125

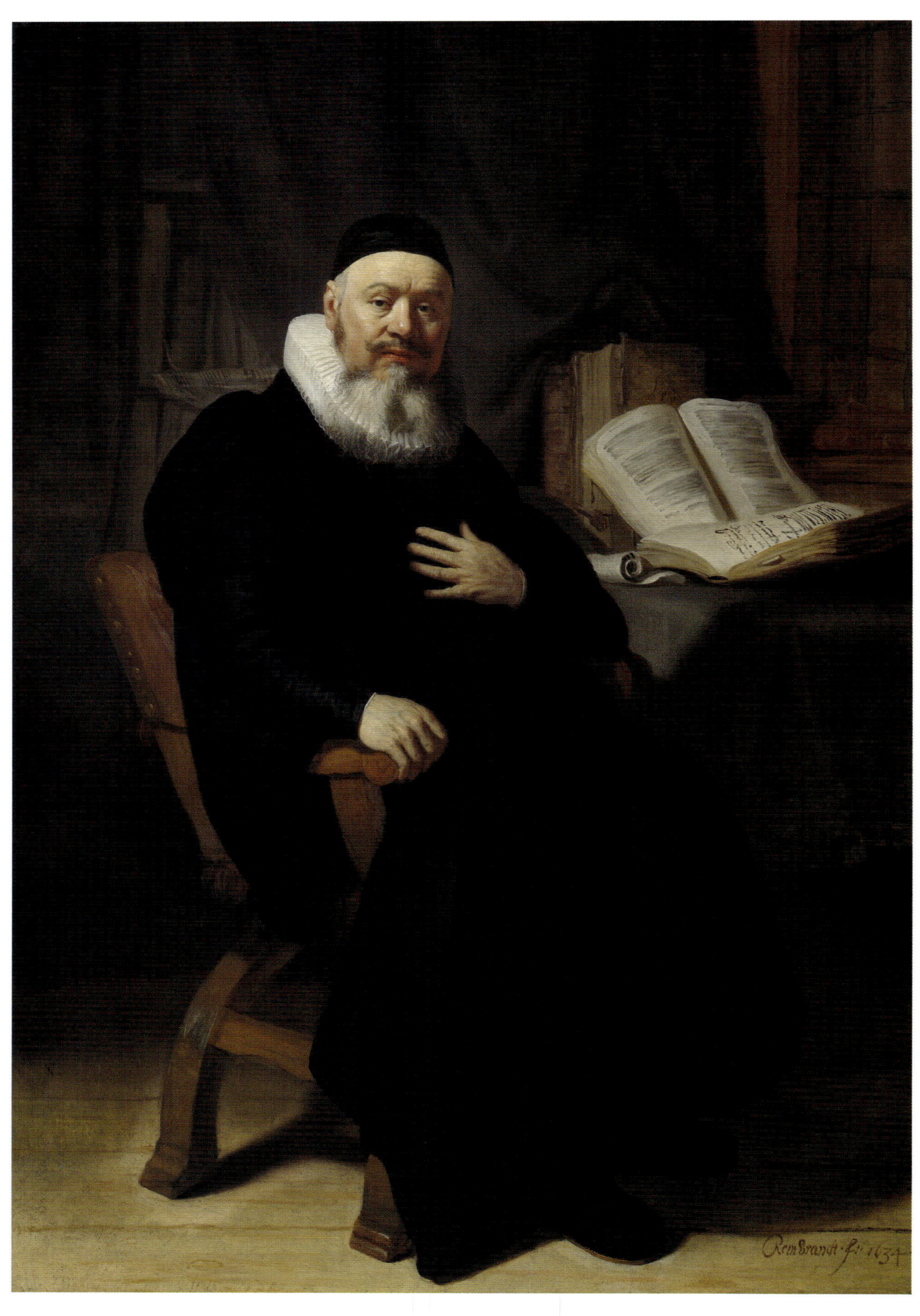

PLATE 28 [CAT. 18]
Rembrandt van Rijn
Portrait of the Reverend Johannes Elison, 1634
Oil on canvas, 174.1 x 124.5 cm (68½ x 49 in.)
Museum of Fine Arts, Boston

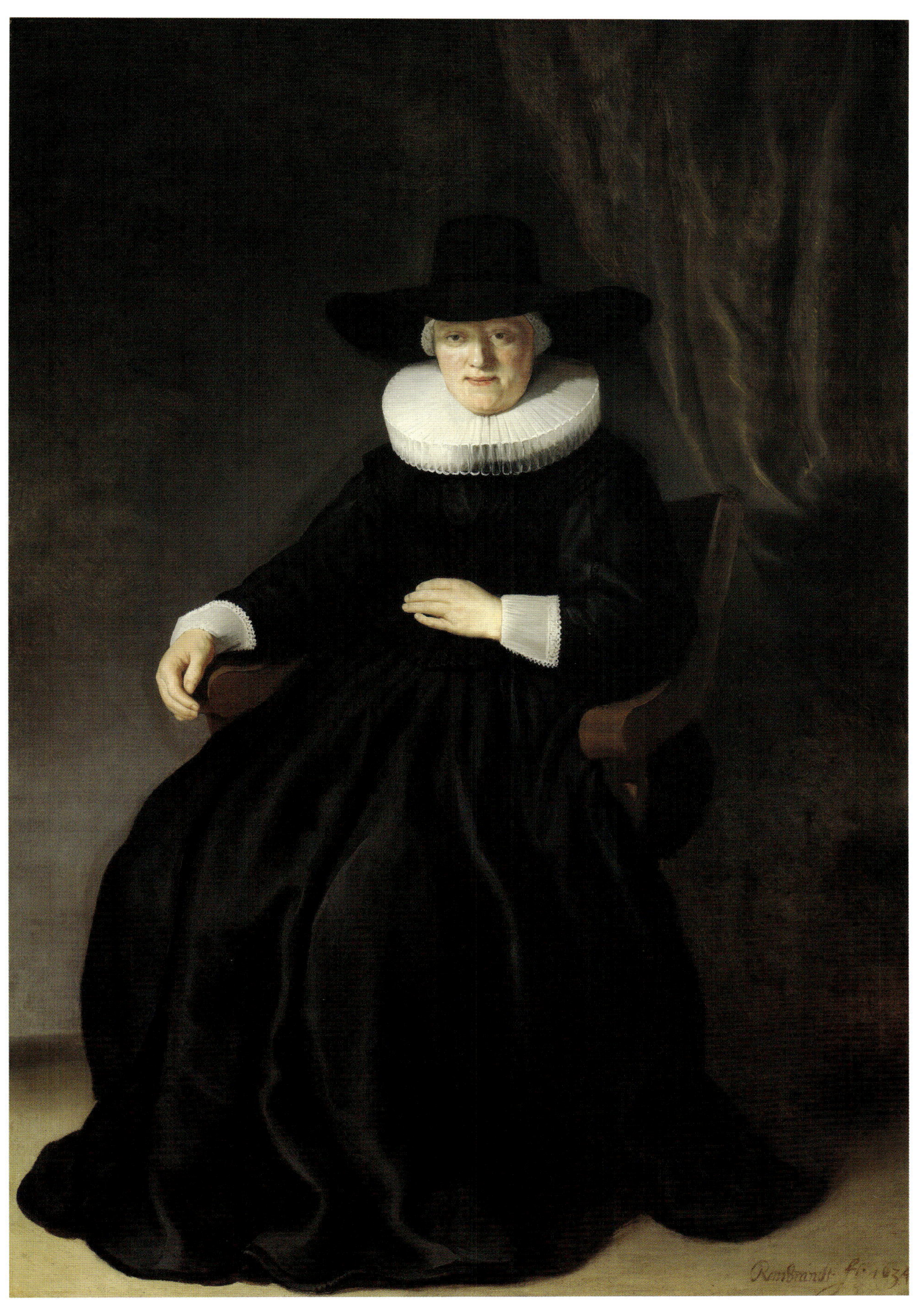

PLATE 29 [CAT. 19]
Rembrandt van Rijn
Portrait of Maria Bockenolle (wife of Johannes Elison), 1634
Oil on canvas, 175.1 x 124.3 cm (68 ⅞ x 48 ⅞ in.)
Museum of Fine Arts, Boston

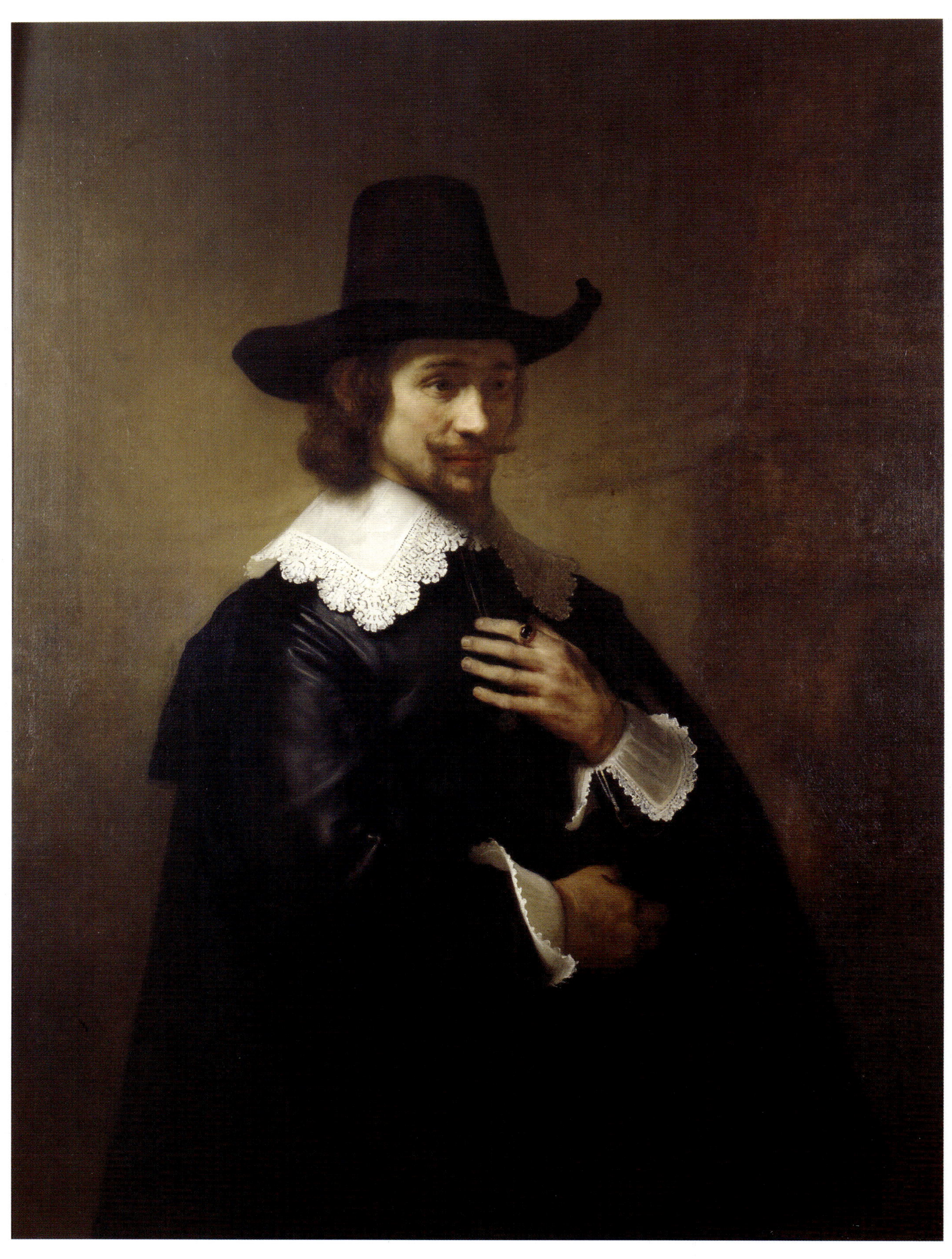

PLATE 30 [CAT. 27]
Rembrandt van Rijn (workshop of; Ferdinand Bol?)
Portrait of a Young Man in a Broad-brimmed Hat, 1643
Oil on canvas, 116.5 x 91.4 cm (45 7/8 x 36 in.)
Shelburne Museum, Vermont

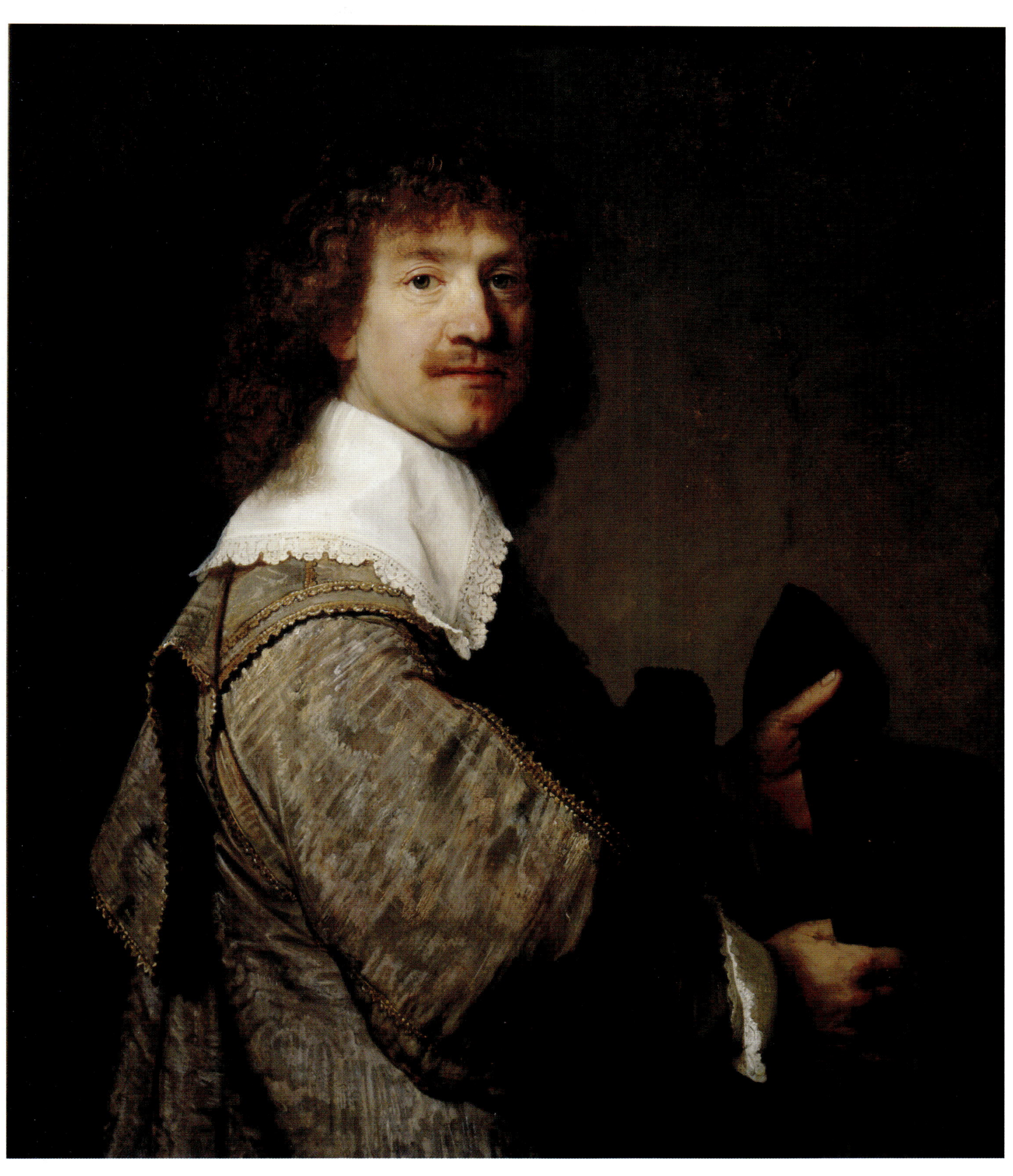

PLATE 31 [CAT. 25]
Rembrandt van Rijn
Portrait of a Man Holding a Black Hat, c. 1639
Oil on panel, 79.5 x 69.4 cm (31 3/8 x 27 3/8 in.)
The Armand Hammer Collection, Los Angeles

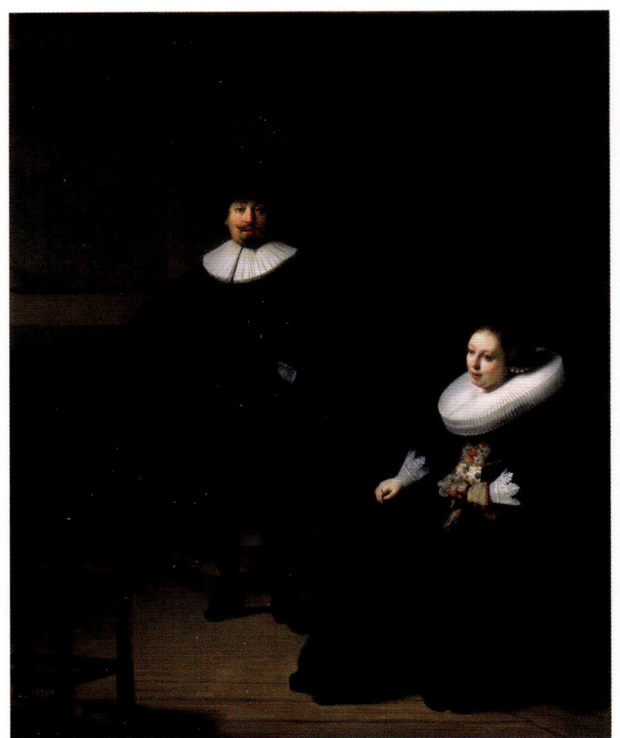

FIG. 60

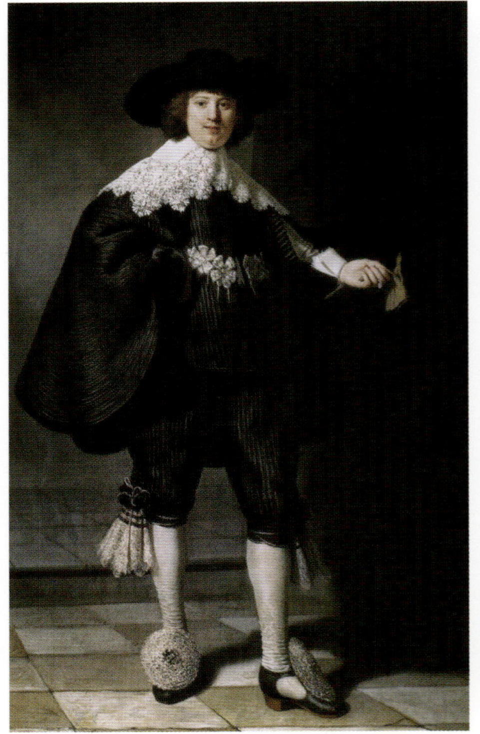

FIG. 61

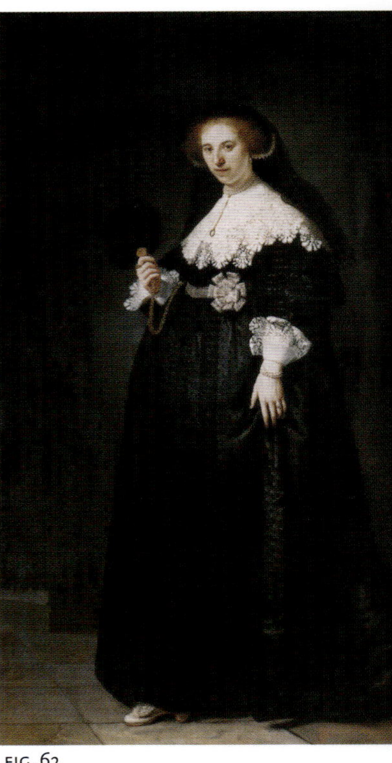

FIG. 62

visual transition between the face above and the red garment below, Rembrandt energized the subject in a discreet yet captivating way.

Rembrandt created a very different mood in his more modestly scaled *A Lady and a Gentleman in Black* of 1633 (FIG. 60), one of the paintings stolen from the Gardner Museum in Boston. The standing husband and his demurely seated wife, both dressed fashionably in black, hold gloves. While the man gazes out at the viewer, the woman gazes downward, seemingly caught up in her thoughts.[8] The substantially less than life-size scale of the figures set within a somewhat formal interior finds a parallel in the portraiture of Thomas de Keyser, who was an undoubted source of inspiration.[9] For whatever reason, Rembrandt chose not to develop this type of portraiture further despite the obvious appeal of the Gardner Museum double portrait.

Instead, in 1634, Rembrandt produced two pairs of full-length portraits very different in character from each other. The first represents a young couple celebrating their marriage, whereas the second depicts a middle-aged pastor and his wife. Yet each pair appears in a formal interior—that of the young couple being more patrician in character. The young couple, Maerten Soolmans and his wife, Oopjen Coppit (FIGS. 61, 62), both now in a private collection in Paris, stand full-length turned toward each other. The husband gestures more emphatically than his wife. By contrast, the portraits of the Johannes Elison and his wife, Maria Bockenolle (PLATES 28, 29), both now in the Museum of Fine Arts, Boston, represent a considerably older couple, both seated. Johannes gazes pointedly outward as if addressing an intended audience. He also raises his left hand to his chest as if about to speak. The well-stocked bookcases and open tomes attest to his learning and the degree to which it is the source of his capabilities as a preacher. His wife sits demurely before a large curtain. Her beautifully articulated hands rest passively on her armchair and at her waist, in contrast to the more energized hands of her husband.

On rare occasion sitters' actions may, to the modern eye, transgress discretion. Nowhere is this more evident than in the pair of double portraits in the Wallace Collection in London, one representing Jan Pellicorne with his son Casper, and the other Pellicorne's wife, Susanna van Collen, and their daughter Eva Susanna (FIGS. 63, 64). These magnificently preserved, large-scale paintings display a patently obvious venal concern with wealth—the transfer of a coin-filled gunnysack to the son and the presentation of a large coin to the daughter. Such an overt display of wealth, tempered by our contemporary disgust with the immense bonuses paid to bankers, hedge fund managers, and CEOs, may unconsciously affect our assessment of these two large

FIG. 60
Rembrandt van Rijn, *A Lady and Gentleman in Black*, 1633, oil on canvas, 131.6 x 109 cm (51 ¾ x 42 in.). The Isabella Stewart Gardner Museum, Boston; inv. P21s9

FIG. 61
Rembrandt van Rijn, *Maerten Soolmans*, 1634, oil on canvas, 207 x 132.5 cm (81 ½ x 52 ⅛ in.). Private collection, Paris

FIG. 62
Rembrandt van Rijn, *Oopjen Coppit*, 1634, oil on canvas, 207 x 132 cm (81 ½ x 52 ⅛ in.). Private collection, Paris

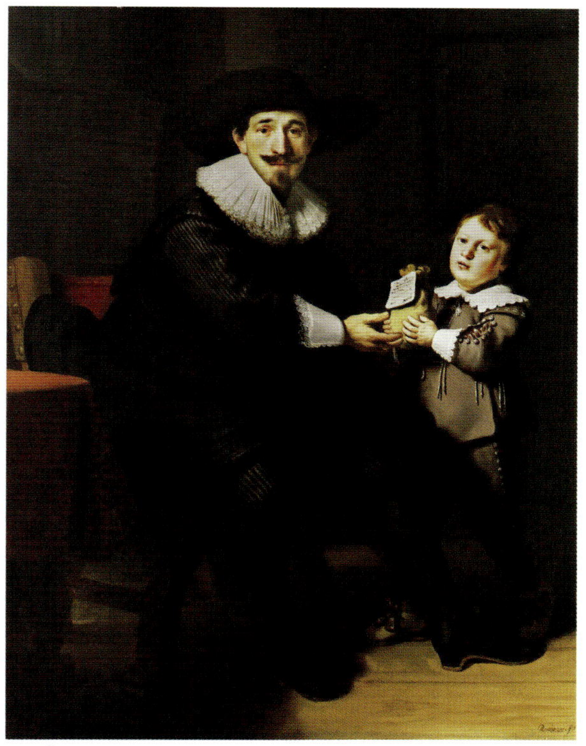
FIG. 63

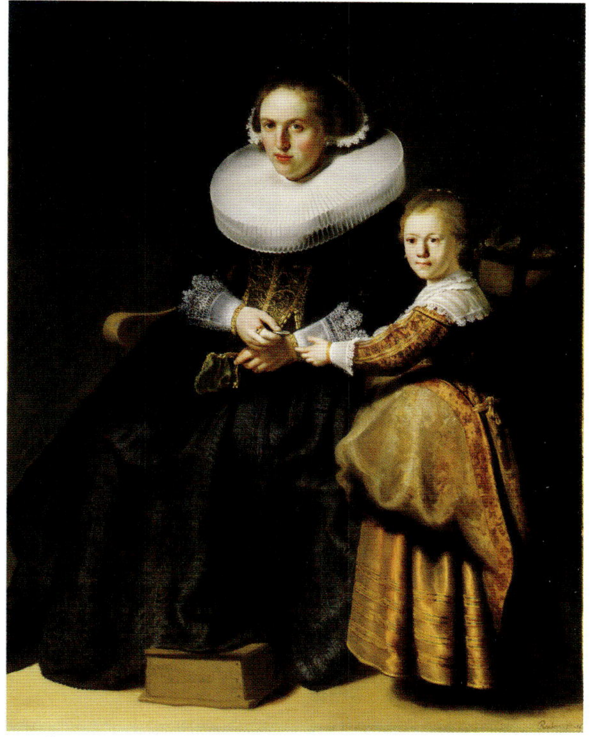
FIG. 64

canvases. In recent years their autograph status has been questioned;[10] yet, to my mind, they are unquestionably extremely well painted. Both pictures are remarkable in their distinctive coloration and both appear to bear authentic Rembrandt signatures. Perhaps here we are witnessing a commission that exploited Rembrandt's talents in a direction that is, even unconsciously, psychologically somewhat off-putting—or conversely, morbidly fascinating. Vulgarity causes unease and here one may understandably feel in the midst of it.

The large number of portraits produced in Rembrandt's studio during the 1630s raises the difficult question of collaboration. In volume two of the Rembrandt Research Project, a large number of portraits hitherto universally accepted as autograph paintings by Rembrandt were downgraded by the team of specialists involved in producing the *Corpus of Rembrandt Paintings*.[11] Critical to our understanding of this issue is the potential range of working methods in composing and completing portrait likenesses. One clear example of this process is *Portrait of a Woman* (see PLATE 13, p. 69), now in the Cleveland Museum of Art. Although this picture has suffered from severe abrasion, it is clear that the panel was prepared with a reserve left around the head. The face and hair were carefully finished, at which point the elaborate lace collar and hairpiece were added in the second phase of the production of this portrait. Then the background was carefully painted up to these highly ornamented lace fabrics and to the lady's coiffure. Whether these different phases of production were done by different hands or reflect the working procedures of the master still remains unclear, but the possibility for specialist collaboration in the production of such pictures certainly exists.

In his assessment of certain paintings in the National Gallery of Art, Arthur Wheelock Jr. posits that they likely involve studio collaboration.[12] Another picture, more demonstrably a studio product, is *Portrait of a Young Man in a Broad-brimmed Hat* (PLATE 30), now in the Shelburne Museum in Vermont. This canvas was acquired by Henry Havemeyer and once graced his famous Rembrandt Room. It later passed by inheritance to his daughter, Electra Havemeyer Webb, the founder of the Shelburne Museum.[13] The subject of this male portrait stands, turned to the right. His hand gestures call attention to his refined and costly attire—especially his elaborate starched collar and cuffs. He gazes not at the viewer but toward his wife, who stands by a table (FIG. 65). Her gaze and hand gestures seem to indicate that she is addressing her husband. She is also dressed in elegant finery. The painter of these companion portraits has captured the complex and intimate psychological interplay between these two sitters.

FIG. 63
Rembrandt van Rijn, *Jan Pellicorne with His Son Casper*, c. 1633, oil on canvas, 156 x 123 cm (61 ⅜ x 48 ⅜ in.). The Wallace Collection, London, inv. P82

FIG. 64
Rembrandt van Rijn, *Susanna van Collen with Her Daughter Eva Susanna*, c. 1633, oil on canvas, 155 x 123 cm (61 x 48 ⅜ in.). The Wallace Collection, London; inv. P90

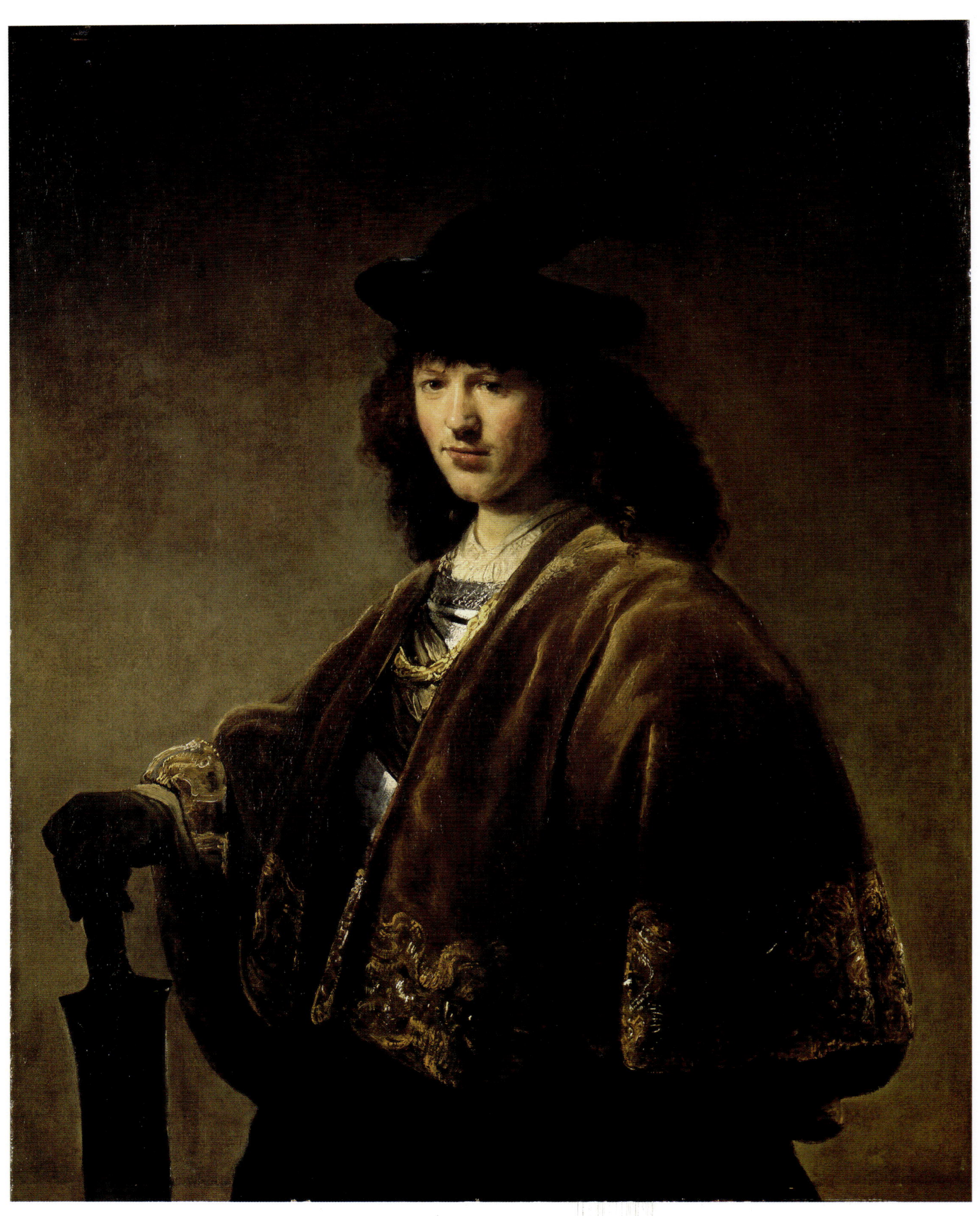

PLATE 32 [CAT. 24]
Rembrandt van Rijn (circle of)
Young Man with a Sword, c. 1633–45
Oil on canvas, 118 x 96.5 cm (46 ½ x 38 in.)
North Carolina Museum of Art, Raleigh

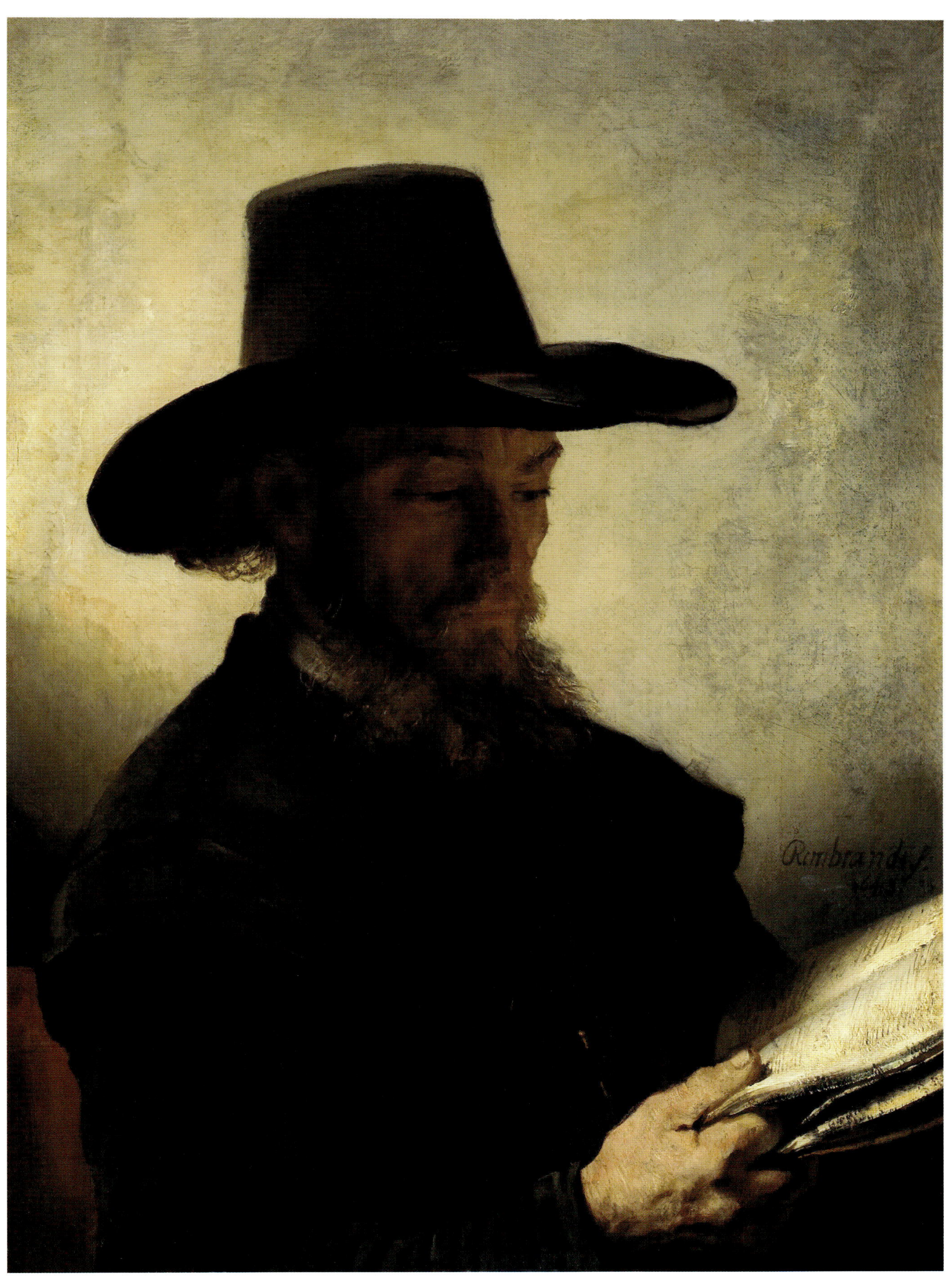

PLATE 33 [CAT. 28]
Rembrandt van Rijn (?) and workshop
Portrait of a Man Reading, c. 1648
Oil on canvas, 66.5 x 58 cm (26¼ x 22⅞ in.)
The Sterling and Francine Clark Art Institute, Williamstown

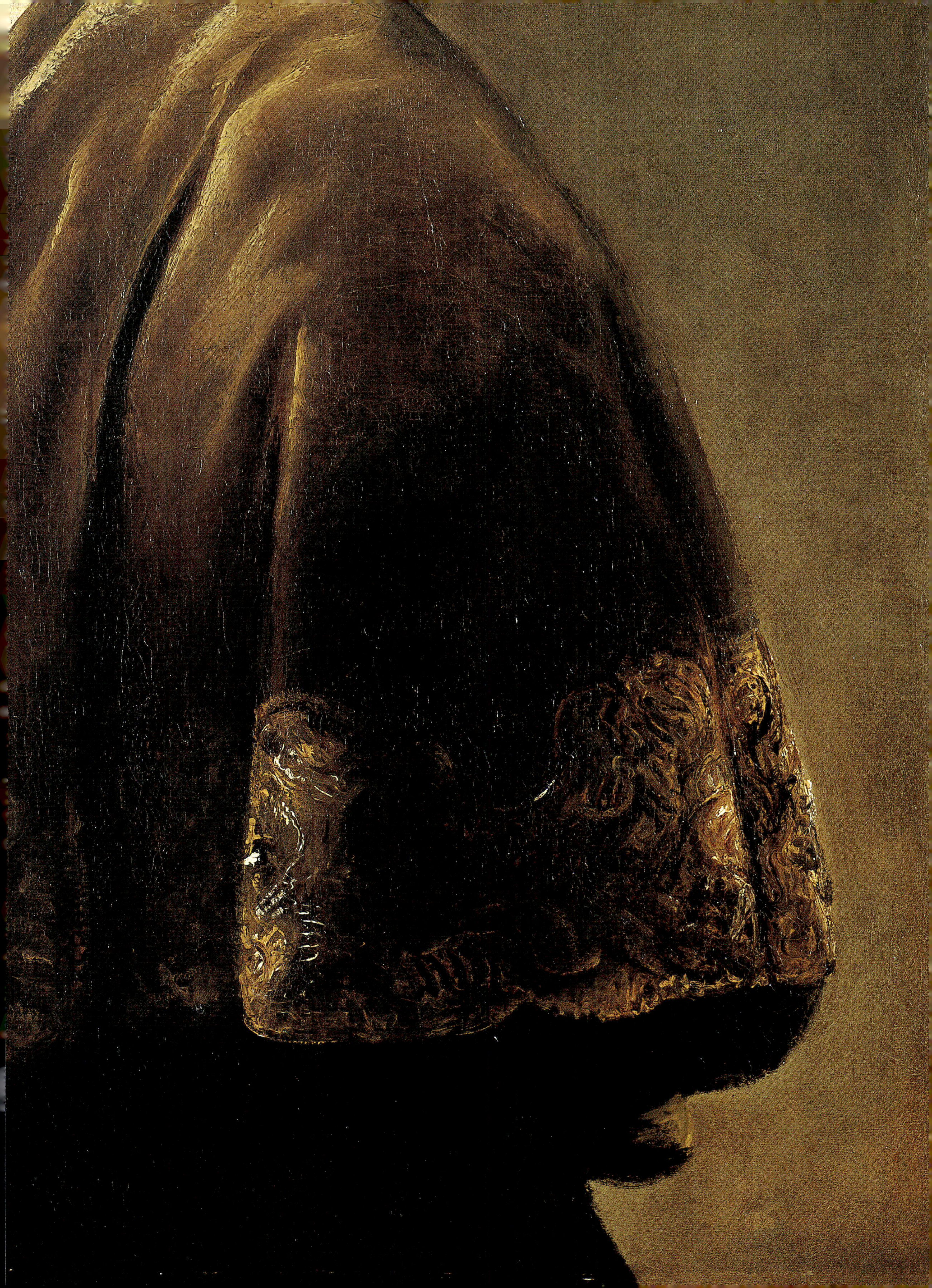

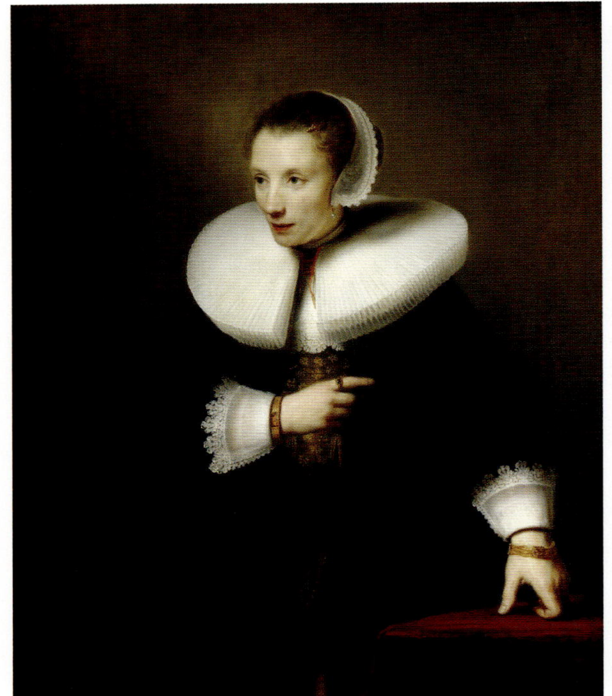

FIG. 65

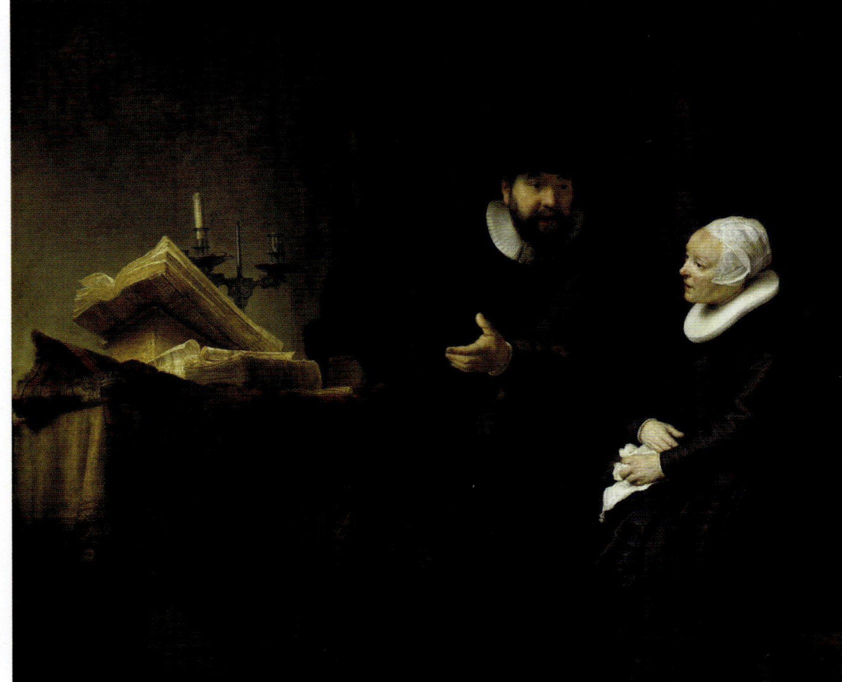

FIG. 66

In *Portrait of a Man Holding a Black Hat* (PLATE 31),[14] now in the Hammer Museum in Los Angeles, Rembrandt represents his subject in a particularly arresting fashion. Although the man is almost in right profile, he gazes steadily at the viewer. The sharp turn of his head causes his falling white ruff to crease and buckle. Like that in the *Portrait of a Man in a Red Doublet* (see PLATE 27, p. 115), this collar becomes a luminous foil setting off the sitter's head. At the same time it contrasts with the gentleman's magnificent jacket. Rembrandt paints the sleeve in an audacious display of energetic broken brushwork and enhances this bravura display by setting the standing figure before a warm background.

Rembrandt's activities as a portraitist fell off sharply during the late 1630s and 1640s.[15] Yet at this time he produced two masterpieces in this genre. The first is the monumental *Mennonite Preacher Anslo and His Wife* of 1641 (FIG. 66), now in Berlin. The second is the artist's most celebrated painting, *The Company of Captain Frans Banning Cocq ("The Night Watch")* completed in 1642, now in Amsterdam's Rijksmuseum. In both, the chief protagonist—Anslo the preacher and Banning Cocq the commander—are in the process of speaking, gesturing to an intended listener.[16] In both works Rembrandt's skill in employing gesture as a means of underscoring the power of speech creates, to an unparalleled degree, his ability to realize intentionality. All the experimentation he had shaped heretofore finds definitive expression in these two sublimely accomplished works—one seemingly private and the other spectacularly public.

Certain of Rembrandt's single-figure portraits from this period maintain the same high degree of quality infused with the characteristic degree of discrete alertness that makes these likenesses so sympathetic. Among them are *Portrait of Herman Doomer* of 1640 (see FIG. 4, p. 22), in the Metropolitan Museum of Art, and the novel pair, *Nicolaas van Bambeeck and His Wife, Agatha Bas* of 1641, now divided between the Royal Museum of Fine Arts in Brussels and the British Royal Collection in London. Each sitter appears at an arched opening that, in the case of Van Bambeeck's portrait, sets off a monumental architectural backdrop.

Rembrandt's remarkable career as a portraitist in Amsterdam in the 1630s spawned emulations that often remain nettlesome as certain of them bear Rembrandt "signatures" and dates. Among them count *Portrait of a Woman in Profile* (see PLATE 16, p. 80), traditionally identified as the artist's wife, Saskia. The painting, now in Hartford, is inscribed "Rembrandt f 1636." It has most recently been attributed to Govaert Flinck (1615–1660).[17] On a larger scale is the imposing *Young Man with a Sword* (PLATE 32), bearing the inscription "Rembrandt/1633." This picture, which entered the North Carolina Museum of Art in 1960 as part of the Samuel H. Kress

FIG. 65
Rembrandt van Rijn (workshop of; Ferdinand Bol?), *Portrait of a Woman Standing by a Table*, c. 1643, oil on canvas, 106 x 91.5 cm (41 ¾ x 36 in.). Kenwood House, London, the Iveagh Bequest

FIG. 66
Rembrandt van Rijn, *The Mennonite Preacher Anslo and His Wife*, 1641, oil on canvas, 176 x 210 cm (69 ¼ x 32 ⅝ in.). Gemäldegalerie, Berlin

Collection, had been attributed to Rembrandt by William Valentiner in 1933. The subsequent range of attributions—to Flinck, circle of Rembrandt, and anonymous but not from the circle of Rembrandt—demonstrates how divergent opinion concerning this picture has been.[18]

The decade of the 1640s involved emotionally wrenching personal losses for Rembrandt. One consequence was a shift in the artist's approach to subject matter. His art became more ruminative, replacing the exuberance of his earlier Amsterdam production best exemplified by *The Blinding of Samson* of 1636 (see FIG. 76, p. 146), now in Frankfurt. Instead, Rembrandt selected subjects demonstrably more meditative in mood, commencing with *The Visitation* of 1640 (see FIG. 88, p. 156), now in Detroit, and culminating at the end of the decade in the *Christ at Emmaus* of 1648 (see FIG. 77, p. 147) in Paris and the etching *The Hundred Guilder Print,* which he must have completed at roughly the same time. During this period, Rembrandt continued to attract students, including Ferdinand Bol (1616–1680), Samuel van Hoogstraten (1627–1678), Carel Fabritius (1622–1654), and others.

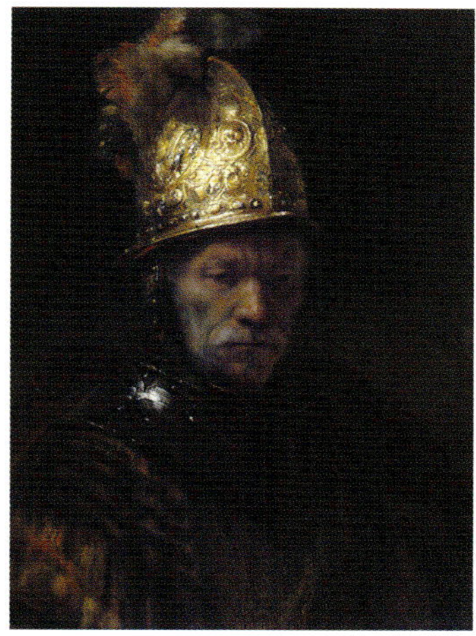

FIG. 67

The attribution of a number of pictures produced in Rembrandt's studio during this decade has been questioned in recent years. One such work, traditionally cited as *Portrait of a Man Reading* (PLATE 33), now in the Clark Art Institute in Williamstown, bears the "signature" and date 1645, and has in recent years been attributed to Fabritius. Yet close examination of the subject of this work raises interesting questions while challenging several assumed suppositions. The most important is why this painting is thought a priori to be a portrait. It could more appropriately be considered a visual representation of comprehension—the apprehension of an idea gleaned from the text on a printed page. Specialists have commented on the fact that the man's face seems thinly painted and lacking clear definition. Likewise, it should be noted that the face is cast entirely in shadow in contrast to the powerfully delineated right hand, which is in full light as he firmly grips the text he studies with such concentration. In its current state this picture is startling because of the luminosity created by the juicily applied yellow ocher coloration surrounding the reader's head and hat. Close examination indicates that this ocher appears to be a substantial overlay carefully painted up to the silhouetted hat and proper left forehead and cheek. This disconcertingly intense color appears to be applied over a more subdued background coloration. Why this change should have taken place is a mystery, but it certainly does not detract from the picture's appeal. Many copies exist, several of which appear to date from the nineteenth century. Most fail to capture the sense of intense concentration, largely because they attempt to define the reader's face in greater detail in order to make it more portrait-like. We may here be dealing with another novel variant of Rembrandt's experimentation with tronies. In this instance the subject is not about likeness—not about characterization—but instead a visualization of a state of mind.

By happenstance another now-suspect Rembrandt, *The Man with the Golden Helmet* (FIG. 67), now in Berlin, is very similar in size to the Clark's *Man Reading.* Although the face of the man in the Berlin painting is caught in a raking light, it is also relatively thinly painted, especially in contrast to the liberal, pastiglia-like layering of paint defining the helmet. Should this figure, in fact, be interpreted as a depiction of Mars, the god of war, then the *Man with the Golden Helmet* might be interpreted as personifying the active versus the contemplative life—the man of action versus the man of quiet learning. Yet he, too, is strangely introspective and ruminative. Although the pictures in Berlin and Williamstown are no longer accepted as Rembrandts, both embody a concept fully worthy of his imagination. How ideas that appear to have been fostered in his studio during the 1640s come to be produced in such a startling range of styles remains an enigma. Yet the ideas themselves are worthy of Rembrandt, and his degree of involvement in such creations seems tantalizingly evident yet paradoxically difficult if not impossible to pinpoint.

Rembrandt's later portraiture displays a broadening of style in which his display of brushwork becomes more evocative and suggestive. His figures are projected into a densely atmospheric realm that tends to blur detail. Yet his representation of each sitter's face, and often to a lesser degree, hands, is constructed using a complex layering of small dabs of paint that creates a palpable sense of a living presence. Although no longer aiming to achieve the smooth, licked paint surface of flesh tones so characteristic of his early Amsterdam portraits, the effect is evocative and visually arresting in its complexity and depth of color.

FIG. 67
Rembrandt van Rijn (circle of), *The Man with the Golden Helmet*, c. 1650–55, oil on canvas, 67.5 x 50.7 cm (26 ½ x 20 in.). Gemäldegalerie, Berlin

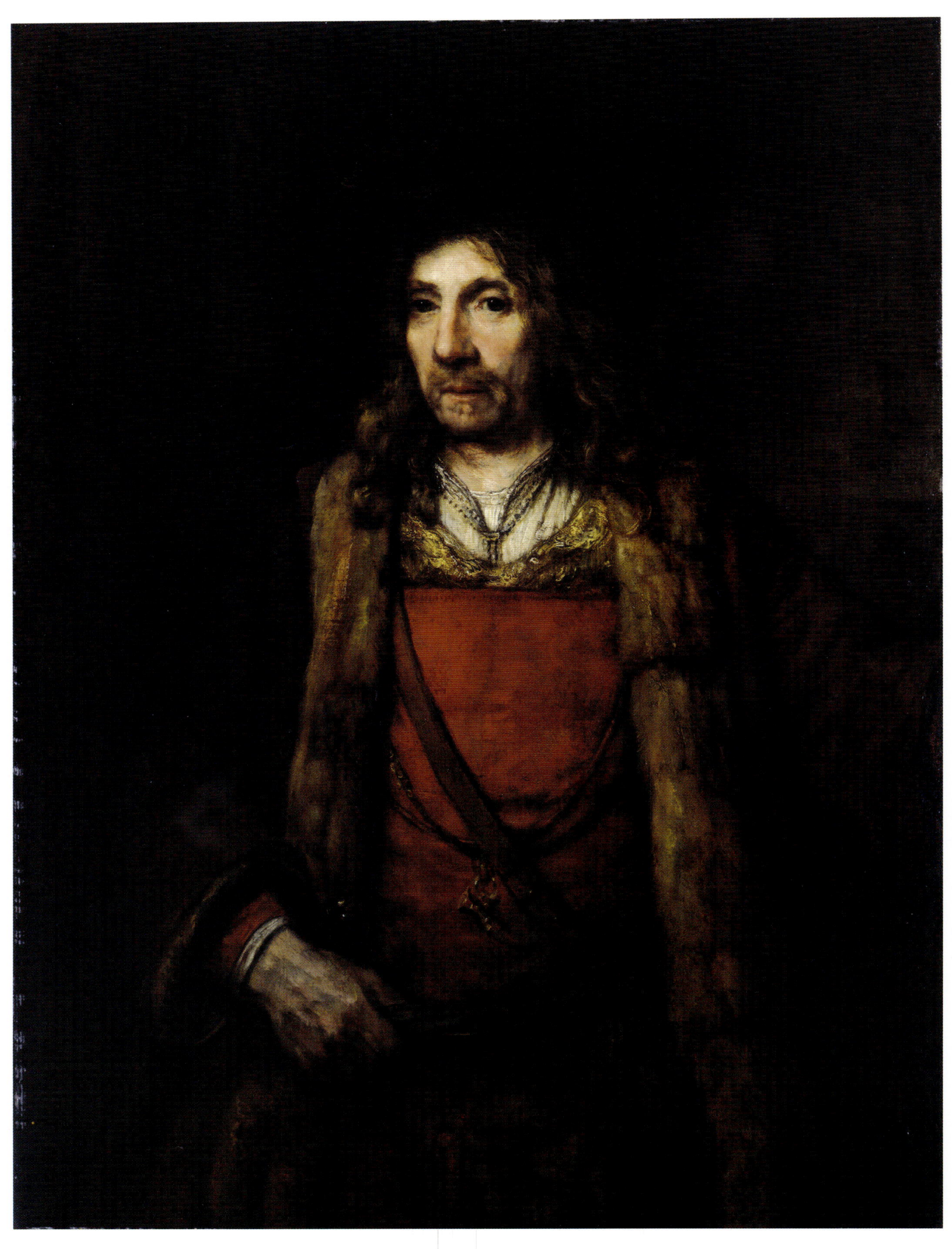

PLATE 34 [CAT. 32]
Rembrandt van Rijn
Man in a Fur-lined Coat, c. 1655–60
Oil on canvas, 114.9 x 88.3 cm (45 ¼ x 34 ¾ in.)
The Toledo Museum of Art

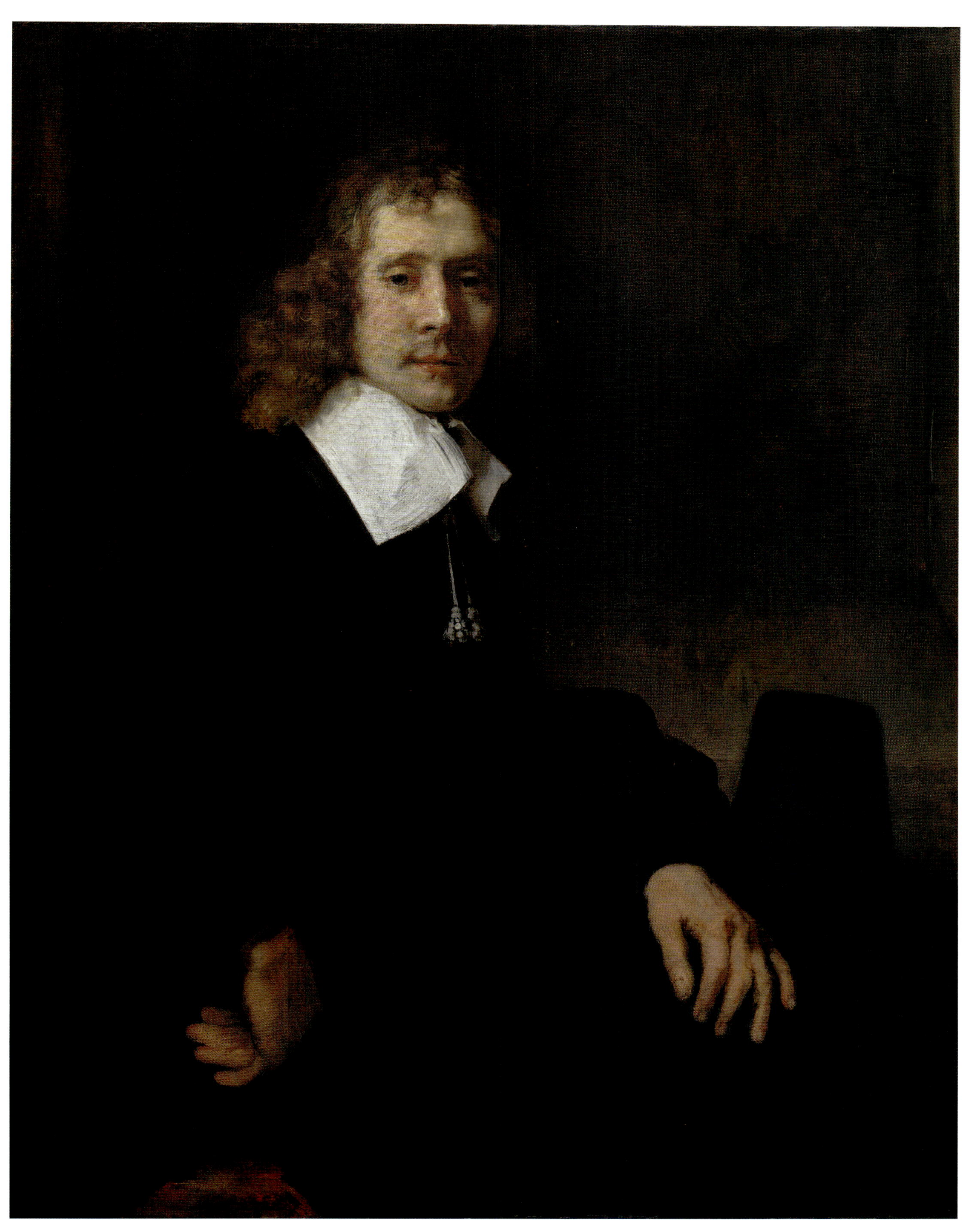

PLATE 35 [CAT. 36]
Rembrandt van Rijn
A Young Man Seated at a Table (possibly Govaert Flinck), c. 1660
Oil on canvas, 109.9 x 89.5 cm (43 ¼ x 35 ¼ in.)
National Gallery of Art, Washington

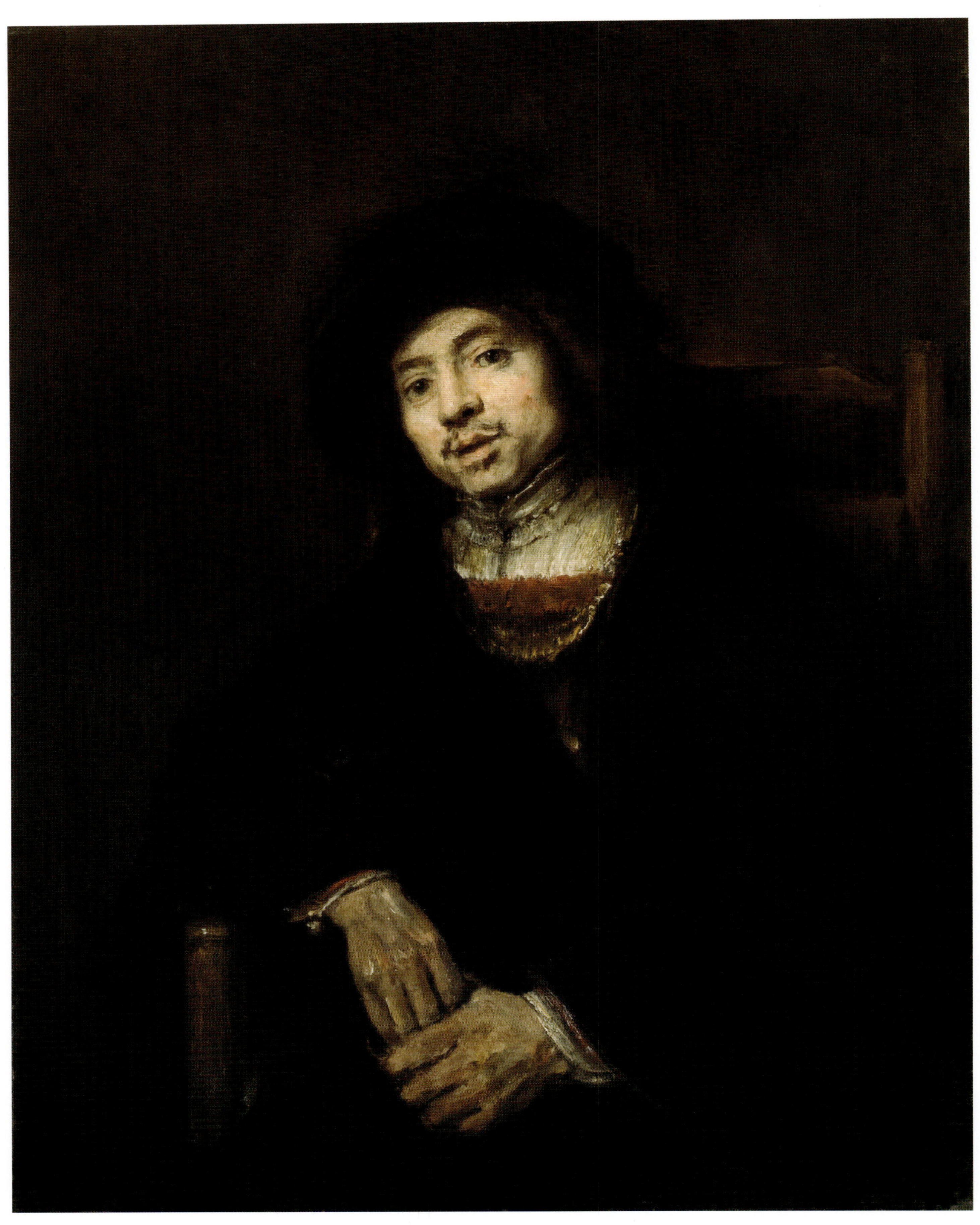

PLATE 36 [CAT. 37]
Rembrandt van Rijn
Portrait of a Young Man in an Armchair, c. 1660–65
Oil on canvas, 104.1 x 85.1 cm (41 x 33 ½ in.)
Memorial Art Gallery,
George Eastman Collection of the University of Rochester

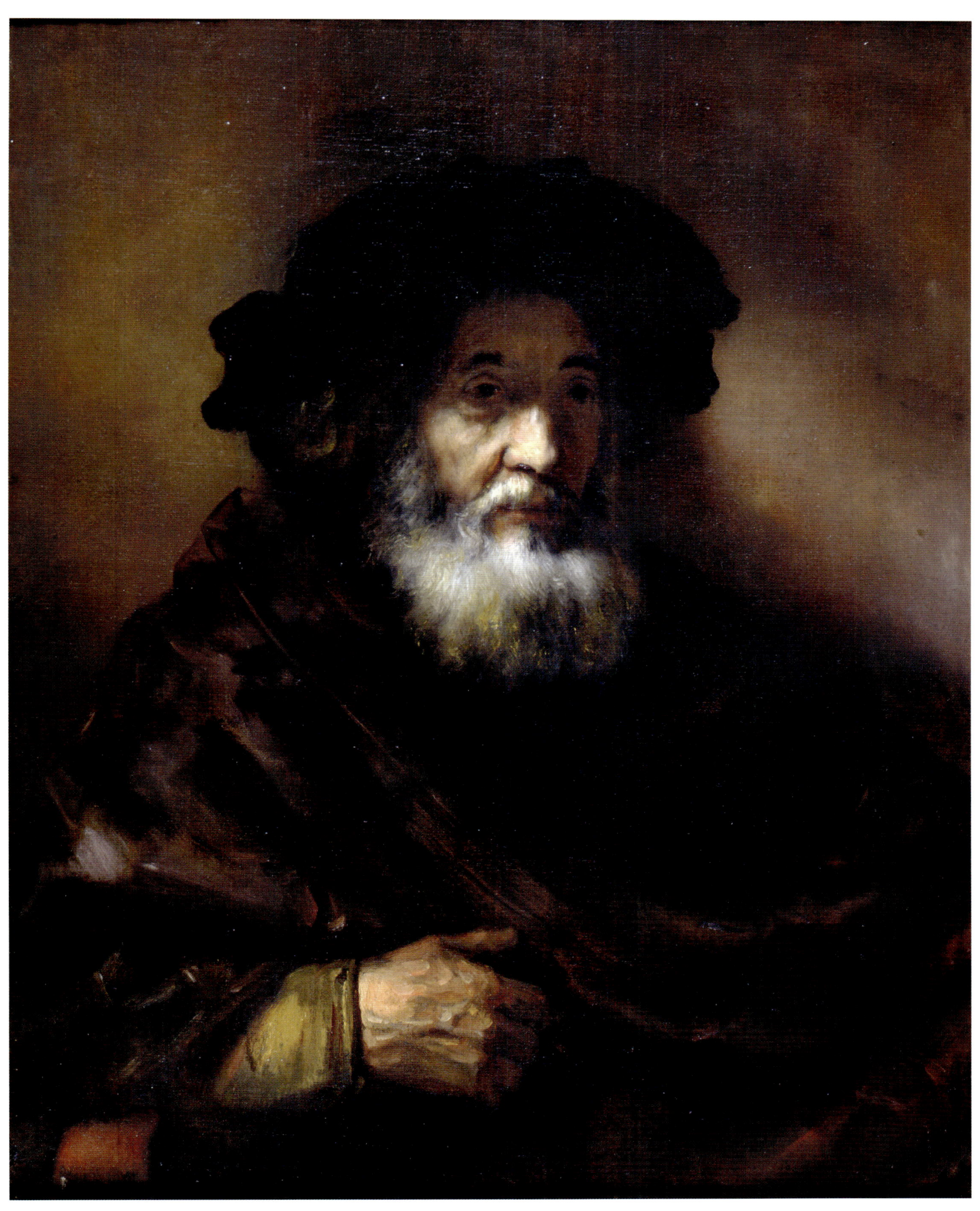

PLATE 37 [CAT. 30]
Rembrandt van Rijn (follower of)
Portrait of an Old Man in a Cape, c. 1650–55
Oil on canvas, 85.8 x 65.4 cm (33 ¾ x 25 ¾ in.)
Fogg Art Museum, Harvard Univerity, Cambridge

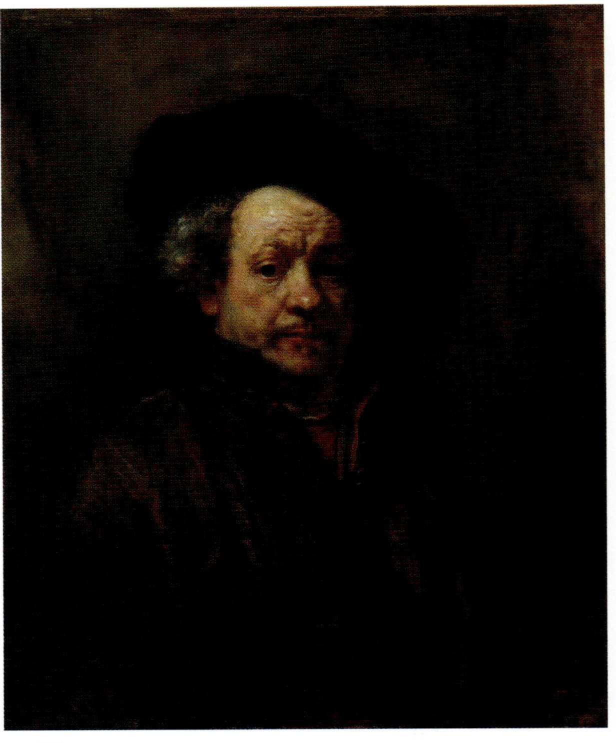

FIG. 68

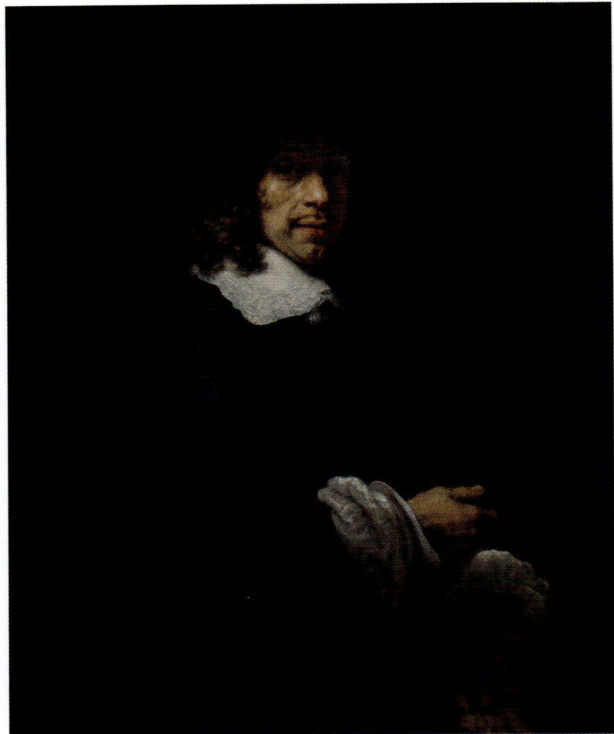

FIG. 69

The artist's most available model was himself, and Rembrandt's self-portraits from the 1650s until about 1661—especially commencing with his *Self-portrait* of 1657 in the Sutherland Collection, on loan to the National Gallery of Scotland in Edinburgh, the regal seated *Self-portrait* of 1658 (see FIG. 35, p. 73) in the Frick Collection in New York, the *Self-portrait* (see PLATE 9, p. 55) in the National Gallery of Art in Washington, and his two self-portraits of 1660 now in the Musée du Louvre and the Metropolitan Museum of Art (FIG. 68)—are all concentrated studies in intense self-analysis. Whether such pictures ever could have served as self-promotion will probably never be ascertained, yet Rembrandt found clients during his later career who clearly admired such an approach to the visual representation of their own likenesses. Fortunately certain pairs of portraits remain together and count among Rembrandt's most sublime achievements within the realm of portraiture. They include the portraits of Jacob Trip and his wife, Margaretha de Geer, in the National Gallery in London and the regrettably unidentified pairs in the Metropolitan Museum of Art—*Man with a Magnifying Glass*[19] and *Woman Holding a Pink* (see FIGS. 36, 37, pp. 74)—and the National Gallery of Art—*Portrait of a Gentleman with a Tall Hat and Gloves* (FIG. 69) and *Portrait of a Lady with an Ostrich-feather Fan* (FIG. 70).

Unfortunately the pairs in New York and Washington could not be lent to the exhibition, but we are fortunate to have fine representative examples of Rembrandt's late style of portraiture from Kansas City (see PLATE 15, p. 77), Toledo (PLATE 34), Washington (PLATE 35) and Rochester (PLATE 36). In most instances the actions of the sitters are relatively subdued, but their projection of intentionality is, nonetheless, clearly felt. This is particularly evident in the celebrated pairs in New York and Washington where hand gestures play such a significant role. In all instances they convey a sense of restraint and assurance that beautifully underscores the sitters' steady, unwavering gazes.

Certain sitters represented by Rembrandt in his later years assume a more active stance. The most celebrated is Rembrandt's *Portrait of Jan Six* dated 1654 (FIG. 71),[20] in which the sitter is in the process of putting on his gloves. Rembrandt's *Young Man Seated at a Table* of c. 1660 (PLATE 35) in the National Gallery of Art in Washington also assumes a somewhat active pose by turning to his right, casting his right hand akimbo, and gazing inquiringly toward the viewer. His tousled hair, flat open collar, and dangling tassels suggest a frisson of movement that wonderfully sets off his youthful face. By contrast Rembrandt's representation of a somewhat older man, now in Toledo, is impressive for the grandeur of his monumental standing bulk, which supports several

FIG. 68
Rembrandt van Rijn, *Self-portrait*, 1660, oil on canvas, 80.3 x 67.3 cm (31 5/8 x 26 1/2 in.). The Metropolitan Museum of Art, New York; 14.40.618

FIG. 69
Rembrandt van Rijn, *Portrait of a Gentleman with a Tall Hat and Gloves*, c. 1658–60, oil on canvas, 99.5 x 82.5 cm (39 1/8 x 32 1/2 in.). National Gallery of Art, Washington; 1942.9.67

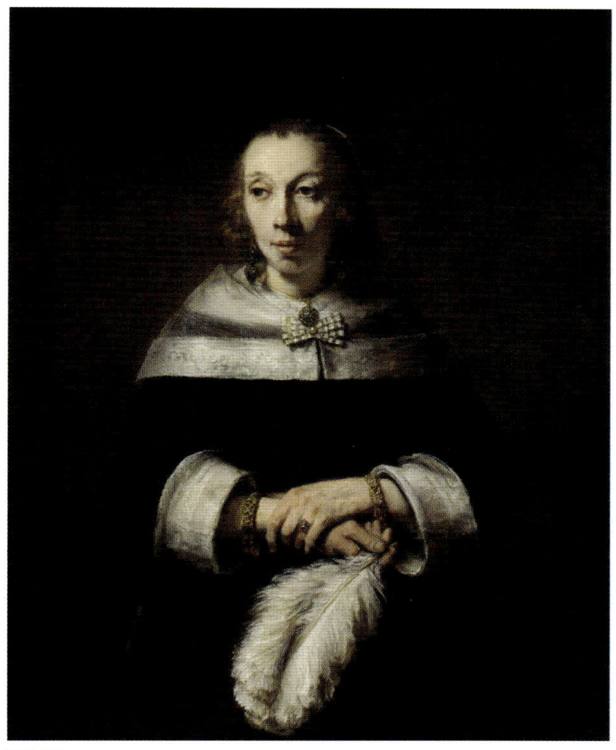

FIG. 70

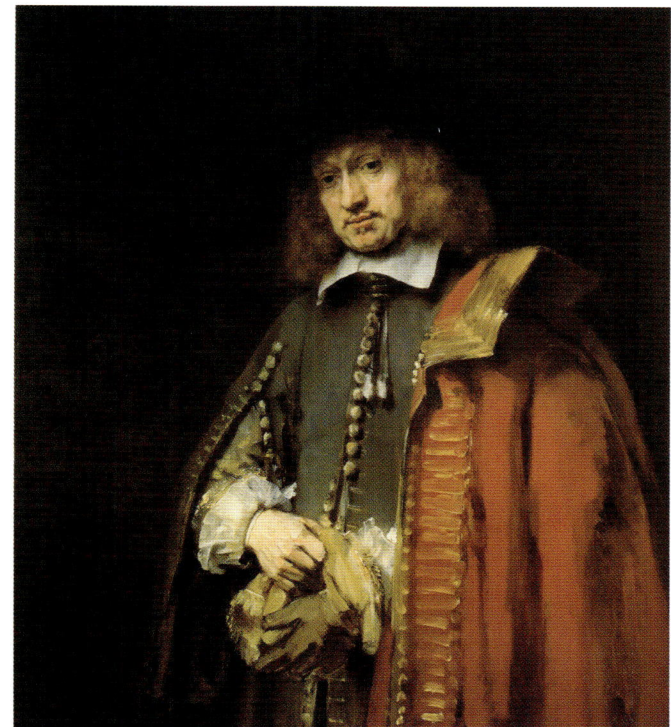

FIG. 71

layers of heavy garments. His powerful right hand, which firmly grips a belt-like sash, conveys power and energy. Whereas the young man's black attire in the picture in Washington has become thin and has lost its luminosity, the many layered garments worn by the man in Toledo are bathed in reasonably strong light that is most concentrated on the sitter's face and throat. His fur-trimmed coat, parted widely at the middle, reveals a deep, resonant red vest. Rembrandt does not flatter this sitter's somewhat homely face, yet the man's wide, searching eyes convey an assuredness that the painter reinforces by the large gripping right hand. The sitter's head, turned slightly to the left and set off by his long, wavy hair, adds a three-dimensionality enhanced by the broad play of light across the entire front of his body. This effect is somewhat diluted in that his hat has largely become illegible because its black paint layer has become extremely thin through abrasion. The end result is a masterful portrait of great visual complexity and emotional restraint captivating in its presence and in its array of luxurious attire.

As indicated earlier, the vast majority of Rembrandt's paintings available to American collectors were portraits. Many of the first collectors were more attracted to the artist's earlier oeuvre, but the vogue for later Rembrandt became more pronounced as the twentieth century progressed. While Henry Clay Frick bought the celebrated *Self-portrait* in 1906 (see FIG. 35, p. 73) and Benjamin Altman acquired his great late pair of portraits by 1909 (see FIGS. 36, 37, p. 74), the Widener pair (see FIGS. 69, 70), bought from Prince Youssoupoff, only entered that collection in 1921.

In their quest to represent Rembrandt in their collections, several leading American civic art museums acquired portraits. Most of these represented the painter's later style or, in many instances, an approximation thereof. This collecting activity coincided with a phase in Rembrandt connoisseurship that was at its most expansionist in defining the canon of autograph works. William Valentiner, who had already established his reputation as a Rembrandt scholar by his curatorial role in shaping the section of Dutch paintings in the Hudson-Fulton exhibition of 1909, continued adding to the artist's painted oeuvre in his publication of 1921, *Rembrandt wiedergefundene Gemälde (1910–1920)* (Klassiker der Kunst) [Further rediscovered Rembrandt paintings]. His Rembrandt exhibitions of 1930 in Detroit and *Rembrandt and His Pupils* of 1956 in Raleigh (see FIG. 7, p. 26) followed. The resulting overly optimistic expansionism only finally began to abate when Horst Gerson, in his 1969 revised edition of the catalogue raisonné compiled by Abraham Bredius, began the substantial process of pruning and rejection.[21]

FIG. 70
Rembrandt van Rijn, *Portrait of a Lady with an Ostrich-feather Fan*, c. 1658–60, oil on canvas, 99.5 x 83 cm (39 ⅛ x 32 ⅝ in.). National Gallery of Art, Washington; 1942.9.68

FIG. 71
Rembrandt van Rijn, *Portrait of Jan Six*, 1654, oil on canvas, 112 x 102 cm (44 ⅛ x 40 ⅛ in.). The Six Collection, Amsterdam

Within this expansionist period (prior to 1969) several museums as well as collectors made their acquisitions of Rembrandt paintings. Certain paintings such as *Portrait of a Young Man* (see PLATE 15, p. 77) purchased by the Nelson-Atkins Museum of Art in Kansas City, are splendid examples of the artist's late style of the 1660s. Unfortunately the Saint Louis Art Museum, which acquired its *Portrait of a Young Man* (see FIG. 42, p. 78) bearing a putative "signature" and date "166[.]," fared less well. This picture, purchased in 1950 and well preserved, is no longer accepted as an original. Its still-unidentified author concentrated attention on the sitter's head, setting it off under an elaborately configured floppy beret. The rest of the man's attire is summarily articulated and lacks internal structure. The sitter's gaze also lacks the inventiveness found, for example, in the *Man in a Fur-lined Coat* (PLATE 34, p. 130) in Toledo. This is particularly disconcerting as the eyes of the man in St. Louis fully catch the light. Rembrandt's employment of light, especially is it plays across a face, has subtle consequences. The degree to which this manipulation of light affects the character of a likeness is found in *Portrait of a Young Man (possibly Titus)* (FIG. 72), acquired by the Wadsworth Atheneum Museum of Art in 1954.[22] Like the portrait in St. Louis, this sitter sports an elaborately shaped floppy hat. The light playing across his face, which in a Rembrandt would spark an alertness and intensity, here has the opposite effect—to mask any sense of interiority and any kind of interaction with the viewer. Instead, the youth seems vacuous, an expression further underscored by his chain of improbably huge discs and by his impossible bulk. His garment seems to billow about him. By all logic his right hand drawn across his chest should have reduced the projecting bulk of his robe below his proper right shoulder. Instead it extends outward leaving the definition of the arm under the garment impossible to ascertain. Like the painting in St. Louis certain visual features come to the fore—a reduction of colors concentrated in a range of warm browns, strong light playing across the face, and to a much lesser degree elsewhere, a warm, modulated background, and a focus on idiosyncratically shaped floppy hats more appropriate to tronies than portraits.

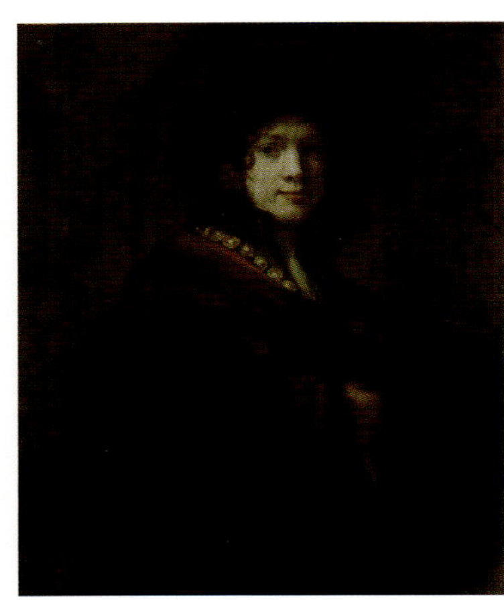
FIG. 72

We encounter a slightly but tellingly different approximation of Rembrandt in *Portrait of an Old Man in a Cape* (see PLATE 37, p. 133) in the Harvard University Art Museums. The elderly bearded sitter wears a heavily scalloped floppy hat that the painter accentuates by the illuminated, modulated background. The light source is stronger in this picture and plays across much of the figure while leaving his eyes in shadow. His large hand is strongly emphasized and, like its counterpart in the *Man Wearing a Fur-lined Coat* in Toledo, has a powerful visual attraction. Yet the sitter's garment is broadly and relatively thinly painted and does not effectively capture the sense of bulk of the body underneath. The rendering of the sitter's proper right arm is strangely inchoate. Yet in its general effect this painting is sympathetic and appealing. It captures a sense of probity that approximates Rembrandt closely. As a result it typifies the kind of painterly facture, mysterious lighting, and sentiment associated with Rembrandt's representations of elderly men, which were sufficiently widely emulated to have long masqueraded as autograph originals.

The Cleveland Museum of Art possesses two such pictures. The first, *Portrait of a Man* (see PLATE 17, p. 81), has been exhibited as a characteristic canvas by Rembrandt. In technique, the warm, modulated background silhouetting the sitter's idiosyncratically shaped cap, and the play of light on his face leaving his eyes in shadow, are all analogous in execution and visual effect to the *Portrait of an Old Man* at Harvard. Both evoke Rembrandt's style of the 1650s. The young man's attire is more fully resolved than that worn by the *Portrait of an Old Man* but is painted in a similar thin yet broad manner. Such pictures, essentially introspective in mood, are accomplished works in their own right.

Cleveland's second picture, *Old Man Praying* (see PLATE 49, p. 162), bearing a spurious signature and date 1661, has been linked to one or more of the putative, informally structured works from the "Apostle" series; it is now considered to be by a follower of Rembrandt.[23] The artist responsible for this picture has a very different painterly approach to representing detail from the two emulations from the 1650s discussed above. The sitter's hair, particularly his beard, is actually surprisingly superficially painted, suggesting strands applied over a darker layer of underlying paint. As a result the hair and even the face lack true volume or an underlying sense of cranial structure. The broadly painted garment is also curiously flat; its brushwork plays out on the surface. Even the hands are blocked out with a lack of transition between the strongly

FIG. 72
Rembrandt van Rijn (imitator of), *Portrait of a Young Man (possibly Titus)*, 1655, oil on canvas, 98.5 x 84 cm (38 ¾ x 33 in.). Wadsworth Atheneum Museum of Art, Hartford; 1954.83. Photo: Wadsworth Atheneum Museum of Art/Art Resource, NY

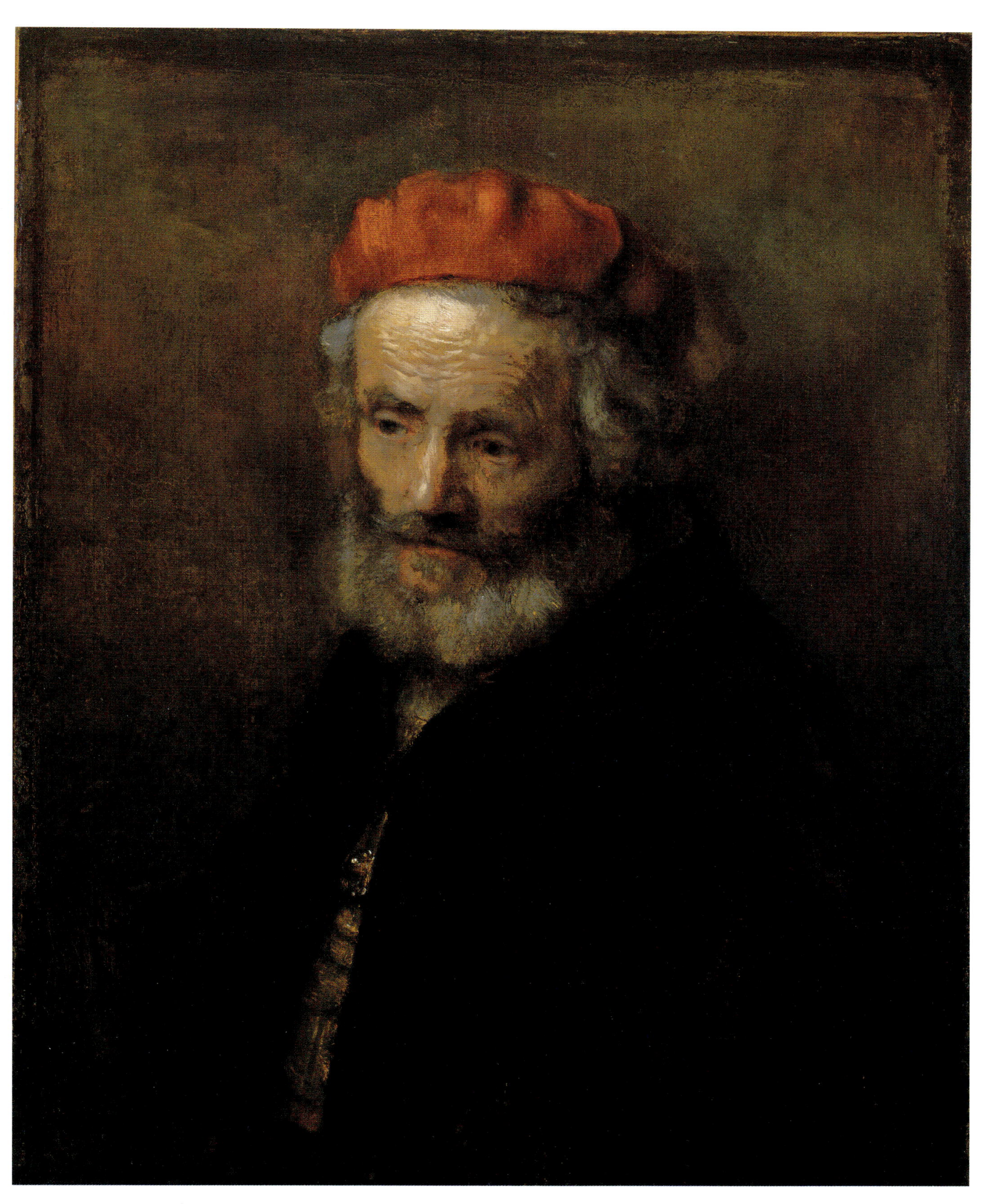

PLATE 38 [CAT. 29]
Rembrandt van Rijn (circle or follower of)
Old Man Wearing a Red Hat, 1650
Oil on canvas, 68 x 56 cm (25¾ x 22 in.)
Baltimore Museum of Art

illuminated highlights on the fingers that contrast so abruptly with the shaded passages adjacent to them. The thick application of paint defining the hands—especially the sitter's right hand—actually exaggerates the perception of weakness that results in such a degree of awkwardness and lack of visual refinement. A strong sentiment is captured here, but it lacks the intentionality of Rembrandt's undisputed apostles from the same period.

In a different vein the *Old Man Wearing a Red Hat* (PLATE 38), now in the Baltimore Museum of Art, was acquired by Jacob Epstein in 1924 as a work by Rembrandt. It bears the remains of an inscription "[.]embrandt f 1650." Its palette, introspection, and careful emulation of Rembrandt's complex dabbing and layering of paint in the man's face may suggest that this canvas is an old copy after a now-lost Rembrandt original. Its sympathetic appeal, although at a considerable remove from Rembrandt, may nonetheless document a characteristic work typifying the emergence of Rembrandt's later style. Another more problematic example, *An Old Man with a Gold Chain,* now in the Fine Arts Museums of San Francisco, appears to be closely related to Rembrandt's *Bearded Man in a Cap* in the National Gallery in London.[24] Yet its execution is slapdash and flaccid, especially evident in the representation of the gold chain and garments. This picture bears the "signature" "Rembrandt f 1657." Perhaps it, like the picture in Baltimore, copies a now-lost original.[25]

These types of pictures typify the challenges that faced and continue to face museums and collectors as they conduct research in order to understand and clarify the nature of the relationship of their paintings to Rembrandt but also to determine these pictures' roles in furthering our understanding of this celebrated artist and his impact on his students and emulators.

NOTES

1 Liedtke 2004, pp. 48–73, esp. p. 60.

2 As Jaap van der Veen indicates, it would appear that more often than not young men in the studio served as models for tronies, yet their accoutrements such as plumed hats endowed these figures with attributes that solely stemmed from the painter's imagination; Veen 1997, pp. 69–70.

3 In recent years the role of the tronie in Rembrandt's creative process has been the subject of considerable interest; see Vries 1989; Bruyn 1991; Veen 1997, pp. 69–80; Liedtke 2007, 2: discussed under no. 142, p. 562.

4 For further discussion of Rembrandt's self-portraits, see Chapman 1990. Wetering 1999, esp. pp. 31, 36, stresses the dual function of Rembrandt's self-portraits as representations of a famous man and as autograph specimens of his distinctive, virtuoso technique. Wetering also stresses the link between self-portraits and tronies.

5 For a brief and cogent assessment of the importance of these painters for Rembrandt, see Ekkart, pp. 39–42.

6 Veen 2006, esp. p. 128, stresses that three major portraits from 1631–32—namely *Nicolaes Ruts, Marten Looten* (see plate 26, p. 114) and *A Man Writing at a Desk*— in all likelihood stemmed from Uylenburgh's connections with key Mennonite merchants centered in Amsterdam.

7 It has been suggested that this picture may be the companion painting to the *Portrait of a Young Woman* (Corpus 1982–89, 2: no. A84, pp. 418–21) recently acquired by the Museum of Fine Arts, Houston. Other separated pairs include Rembrandt's *Portrait of a Forty-one-year-old Man* (Corpus 1982–89, 2: no. A86) now in the Norton Simon Museum in Pasadena, and its mate the *Portrait of a Forty-year-old Woman* (see fig. 44, p. 79) now in the Speed Art Museum in Louisville. Likewise, the *Portrait of Dick Jansz Pesser* (Corpus 1982–89, 2: no. A102) in the Los Angeles County Museum of Art has as its mate the *Portrait of Haesje Jacobsdr van Cleyburg* (Corpus 1982–89, 2: no. A103) now in the Rijksmuseum in Amsterdam. The Museum of Fine Arts, Boston retains the only pair in this bust format still together in the United States—Corpus 1982–89, 2: nos. C72 and C73. Other examples include the *Portrait of a Woman* in the Cleveland Museum of Art (see plate 13, discussed on p. 75), which is believed to have as its companion the *Portrait of a Man in a Slouched Hat* (Corpus 1982–89, 3: no. C104, pp. 657–60) whose current whereabouts are unknown.

8 A child, now painted out, was assuredly the object of the woman's attention; see Walsh 1976. Smith 1982, 259–88, esp. pp. 260–69. Veen 2006, esp. p. 165, provisionally identifies the two remaining sitters as Jan Pietersz. Bruyningh and his wife, Hillegond Pietersdr. Moutmaker.

9 Interestingly, when Thomas de Keyser painted his *Family Portrait,* monogrammed and dated 1640 and now in the Wallraf-Richartz-Museum in Cologne, he seems to have been inspired by Rembrandt's painting in the Gardner Museum—see Vey and Kesting, 1967.

10 Corpus 1982–89, 2: nos. C65, C66, pp. 710–27. Ingamells 1992, esp. p. 149 (as studio of Rembrandt).

11 Corpus 1982–89, 2: p. 198. Walter Liedtke has raised strenuous objections to many of the suppositions of the Rembrandt Research Project; see Liedtke 1989; Liedtke 1992; Liedtke 1995; New York 1995, 2: esp. pp. 16, 24, 46; Liedtke 1996; Liedtke 2004, nos. 1, 2, pp. 48–73. Other specialists sharing this concern include M. Kirby Talley Jr. (Talley 1989) and Ben Broos (Broos 1983). Jaap van der Veen posits a different view arguing for a certain degree of anticipated studio collaboration; see Veen 2006, esp. p. 136, where he argues for several collaborators working under Rembrandt as head of the workshop with Hendrick Uylenburgh running the business end of things. Yet Veen also points out that no actual documentation exists pertaining to the Uylenburgh enterprise during the period of Rembrandt's involvement.

12 Wheelock 1995, inv. 1940.1.13, pp. 215–21; inv. 1937.1.73, pp. 226–30; plus other works later in date.

13 This painting has as its likely pendant *A Portrait of a Woman Standing by a Table*, now part of the Iveagh Bequest, Kenwood House, London; see Corpus 1982–89, 3: pp. 12–50, esp. figs. 29, 30, pp. 37–38 (as still-unidentified hand within the Rembrandt workshop).

14 Corpus 1982–89, 3: no. A130, pp. 305–11.

15 Veen notes that Rembrandt's production of portraits fell off sharply after 1635 and his interest in portraiture was sporadic until the 1650s and early 1660s; Veen 1997, pp. 73, 76–77.

16 In one of his poems Joost van den Vondel makes specific reference to the power of speech in Rembrandt's double portrait of Cornelis Claesz. Anslo and his wife: "That's right. Rembrandt, paint Cornelis' voice! His visible self is second choice. The invisible can only be known through the word. For Anslo to be seen, he must be heard"; Schwartz 1985, p. 218.

17 Hartford 2009, no. 8 (repr.), pp. 20–21.

18 For the most recent discussion of this picture, see Weller 2009, no. 37 (repr.), pp. 170–73.

19 Liedtke 2007, 2: pp. 693–703, esp. no. 158, pp. 698–99, has proposed that the man may represent Jacob Haring the Younger.

20 Winkel 2006, pp. 93–134.

21 Gerson/Bredius 1969.

22 This painting has most recently been classified as an anonymous imitator of Rembrandt; Hartford 2009, no. 9 (repr.), pp. 22–23.

23 Washington and Los Angeles 2005, fig. 9 (as follower of Rembrandt), p. 22.

24 Gerson/Bredius 1969, no. 259A, p. 201.

25 Other versions exist that may help support this hypothesis.

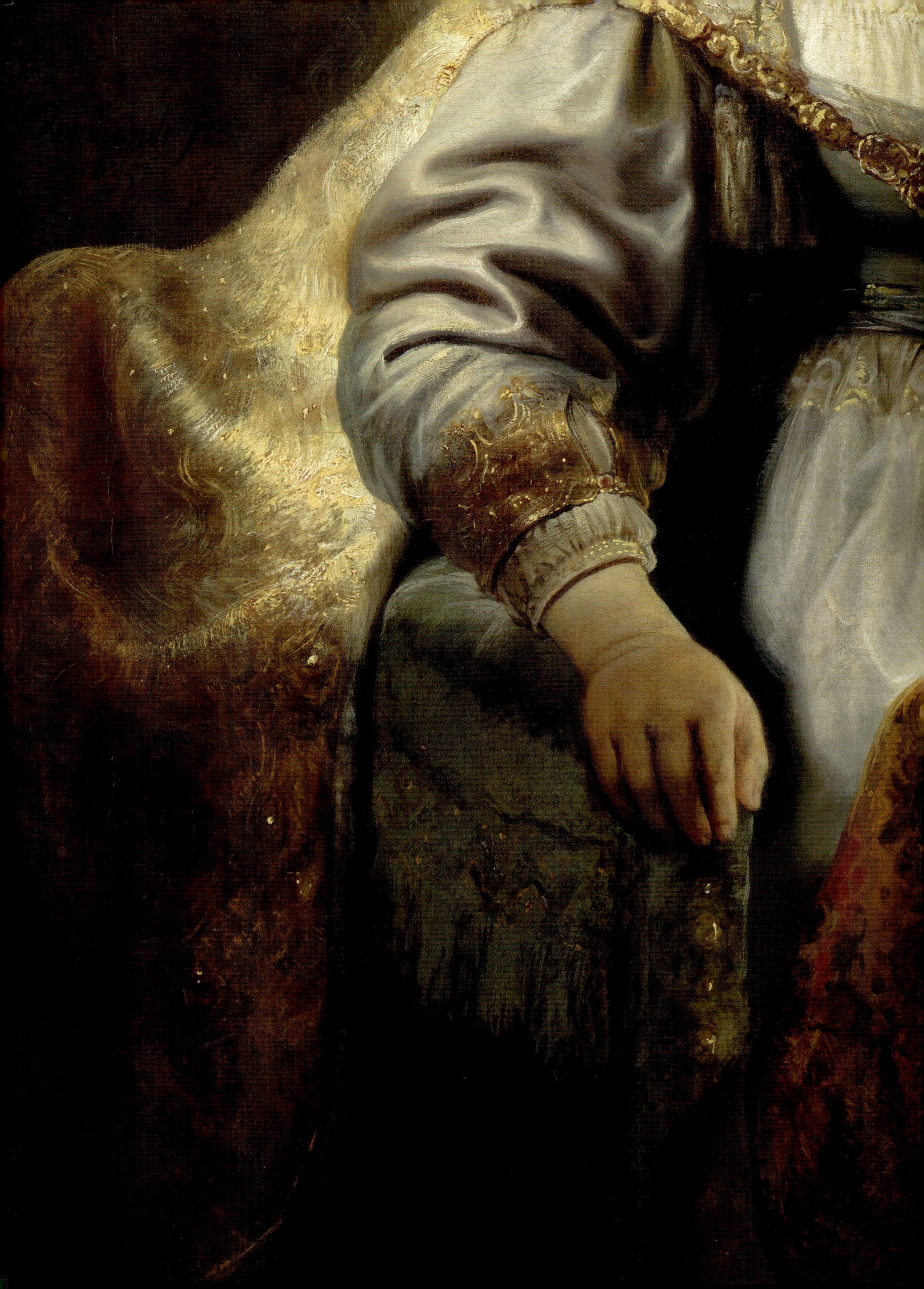

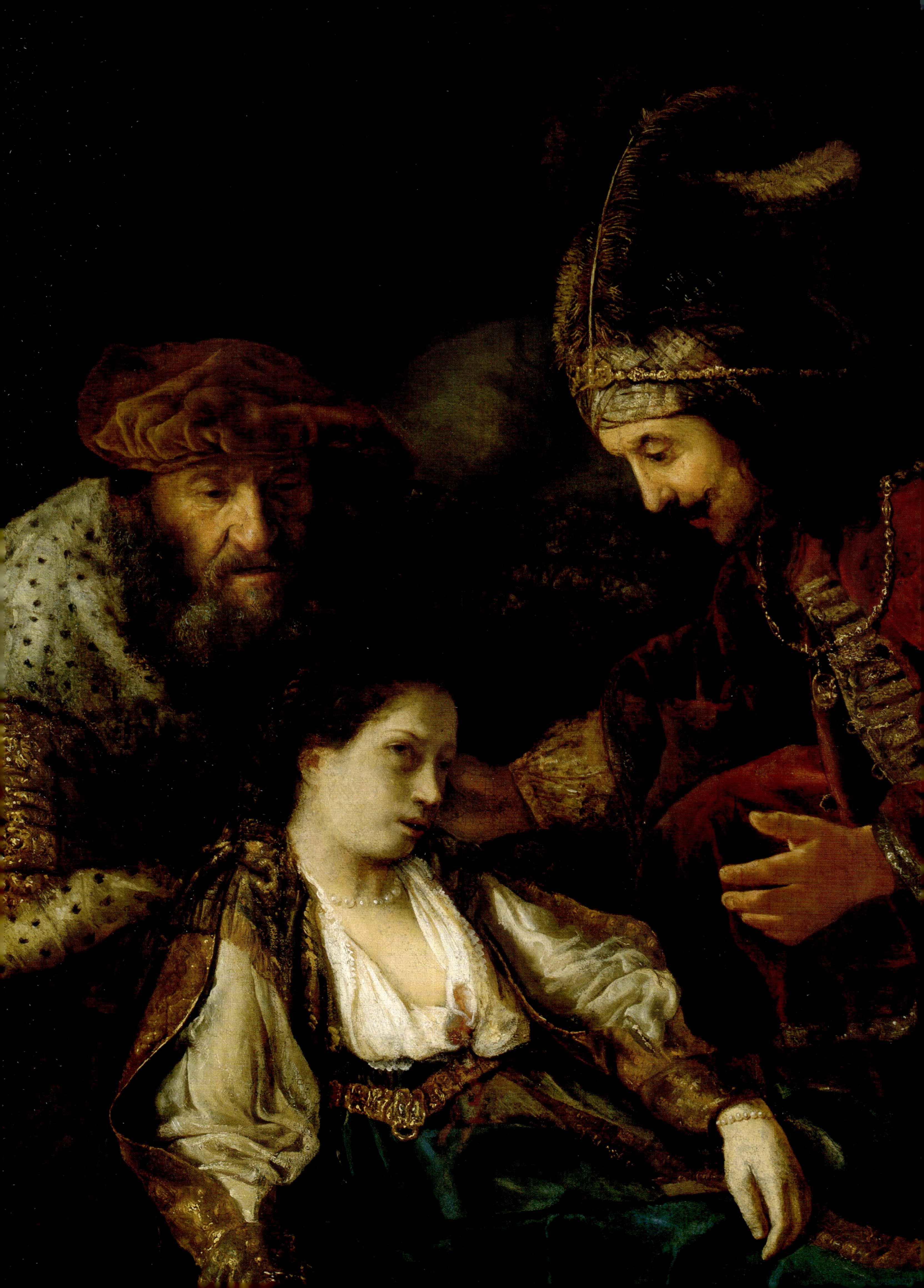

Rembrandt's History Paintings in America

DENNIS P. WELLER

Rembrandt, like many of the gifted and ambitious artists active during the Dutch Golden Age, considered himself a history painter. By the end of his career works in this category would account for roughly one-third of his painted oeuvre. Pictures based on subjects gleaned from classical mythology, ancient history, and above all the Bible—no other painter was more scriptural in his approach—were infused with a timelessness and humanity unequaled by his contemporaries. In capturing the precise moment protagonists struggled with powerful and conflicting emotions, his pictures support words he penned to Constantijn Huygens in a letter dated 12 January 1639. "Rembrandt himself spoke of a striving after 'de naetuereelste beweechgelickhijt' [most natural and moving emotion] in his Biblical history paintings."[1]

Portrait commissions, by contrast, largely paid the bills. In terms of numbers, works in this genre represent the vast majority of Rembrandt paintings now in America. Still, his history pictures held a special attraction for both Rembrandt and collectors during the seventeenth century. History subjects, it must be remembered, stood at the core of Dutch humanistic traditions.[2] Rembrandt, in accord with the aspirations of patrons and the opinions of art theorists, placed history subjects at the summit of the hierarchy of things to paint. Landscape, scenes of everyday life, still life, and portraiture were generally considered, at least from a theoretical viewpoint, of lesser importance within the republic's expanding art market. The artist and theorist Gerard de Lairesse (1641–1711), who sat for Rembrandt in a portrait from the mid-1660s (FIG. 73), was among those writers who took portrait painters to task. He suggested in his *Groot Schilderboeck* that artists "surrendered their freedom in representing portraits as no imagination is involved."[3]

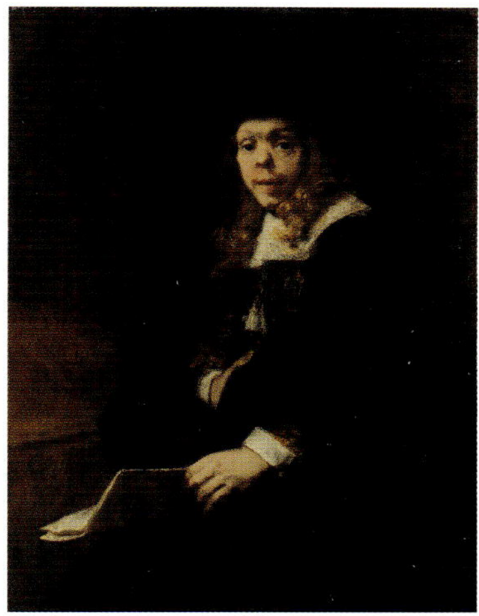

FIG. 73

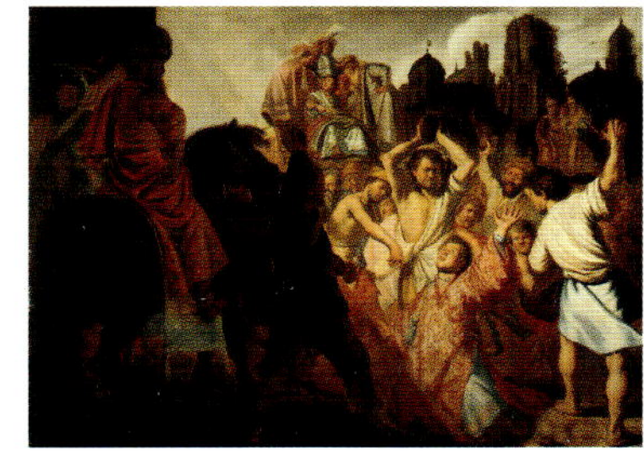

FIG. 74

Rembrandt's efforts as a history painter count among his greatest achievements. His engagement with these subjects also serves as a road map in tracing his stylistic development. The story began with a handful of unceremonious examples painted in his hometown of Leiden. Naïve in character and reflective of a young painter in search of his voice, these pictures appear to offer a critique on the work of one of his teachers, Pieter Lastman (1583–1633). Early paintings reflect such youthful inconsistencies; among them is *The Stoning of St. Stephen* (FIG. 74) with its high-pitched palette, crowded composition, and awkward light and dark contrasts.

Rembrandt, however, quickly developed his artistic skills. Refinements he made to his style culminated with his early masterpiece, *Judas with the Thirty Pieces of Silver* (FIG. 75), dated 1629. Huygens, in fact, cited the picture in his autobiography written shortly after the picture left the painter's easel. With high praise of Rembrandt's treatment of the despairing Judas, Huygens favorably compared the painting "with all Italy, indeed, with all the wondrous beauties that have survived from the most ancient of days."[4]

By the second half of the 1630s, and following his transition to Amsterdam earlier in the decade, Rembrandt produced a number of large and highly theatrical history compositions in emulation of the work of Antwerp painter Peter Paul Rubens (1577–1640). Counted among these masterpieces are the Passion series he painted for the Stadtholder Frederik Hendrik in The Hague, *The Blinding of Samson* (FIG. 76), *Belshazzar's Feast* (National Gallery, London), *The Sacrifice of Isaac* (see FIG. 15, p. 43), and *The Abduction of Ganymede* (Gemäldegalerie, Dresden).[5]

The following decade Rembrandt's approach to narrative compositions, one that began about the time of the death of his wife Saskia in 1642, changed. Works such as *The Holy Family with Angels* of 1642 in St. Petersburg or *Christ at Emmaus* (FIG. 77), painted six years later, are approached in hushed tones rather than as part of a boisterous spectacle. Tranquility reigns in these pictures, as both the human dimension and the spirituality of the narrative take center stage.

Rembrandt's remarkable understanding of human empathy and his growing spiritual engagement with his subjects intensified as his career progressed. In artworks from the last two decades of his life, he increasingly distilled the narrative element of his scriptural source to the point that the specific subject remains open to debate. What is lost in iconographic clarity,

FIG. 73
Rembrandt van Rijn, *Gerard de Lairesse*, c. 1665, oil on canvas, 112.7 x 87.6 cm (44 3/8 x 34 1/2 in.). The Metropolitan Museum of Art, New York; Robert Lehman Collection, 1975; 1975.1.140

FIG. 74
Rembrandt van Rijn, *The Stoning of St. Stephen*, 1625, oil on panel, 89.2 x 123.2 cm (35 1/8 x 48 1/2 in.). Musée des Beaux-Arts, Lyon; A 2735

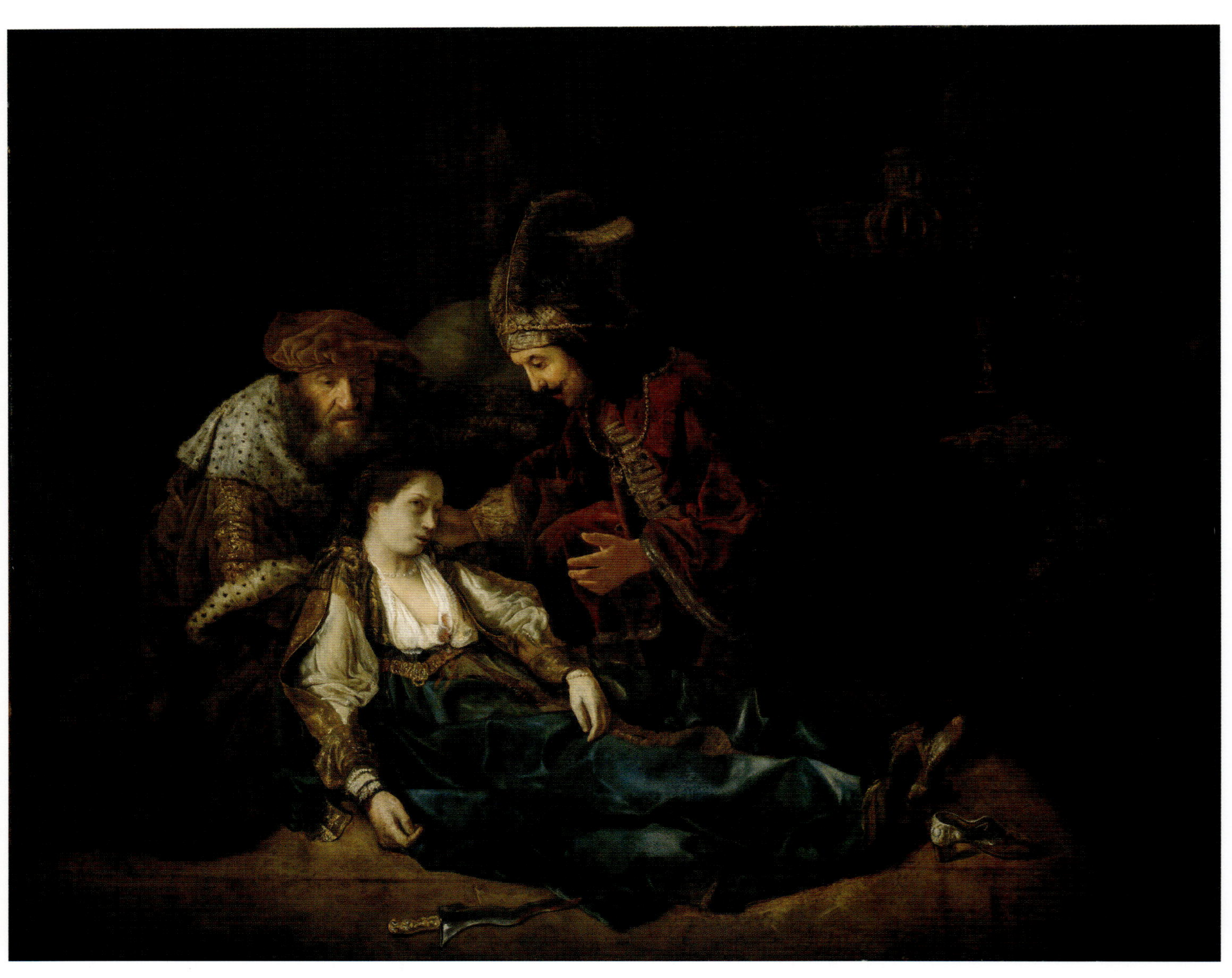

PLATE 39 [CAT. 41]
Rembrandt van Rijn (follower of)
The Death of Lucretia(?), c. mid-1640s
Oil on canvas, 174 x 219.7 cm (68 1/2 x 86 1/2 in.)
The Detroit Institute of Arts

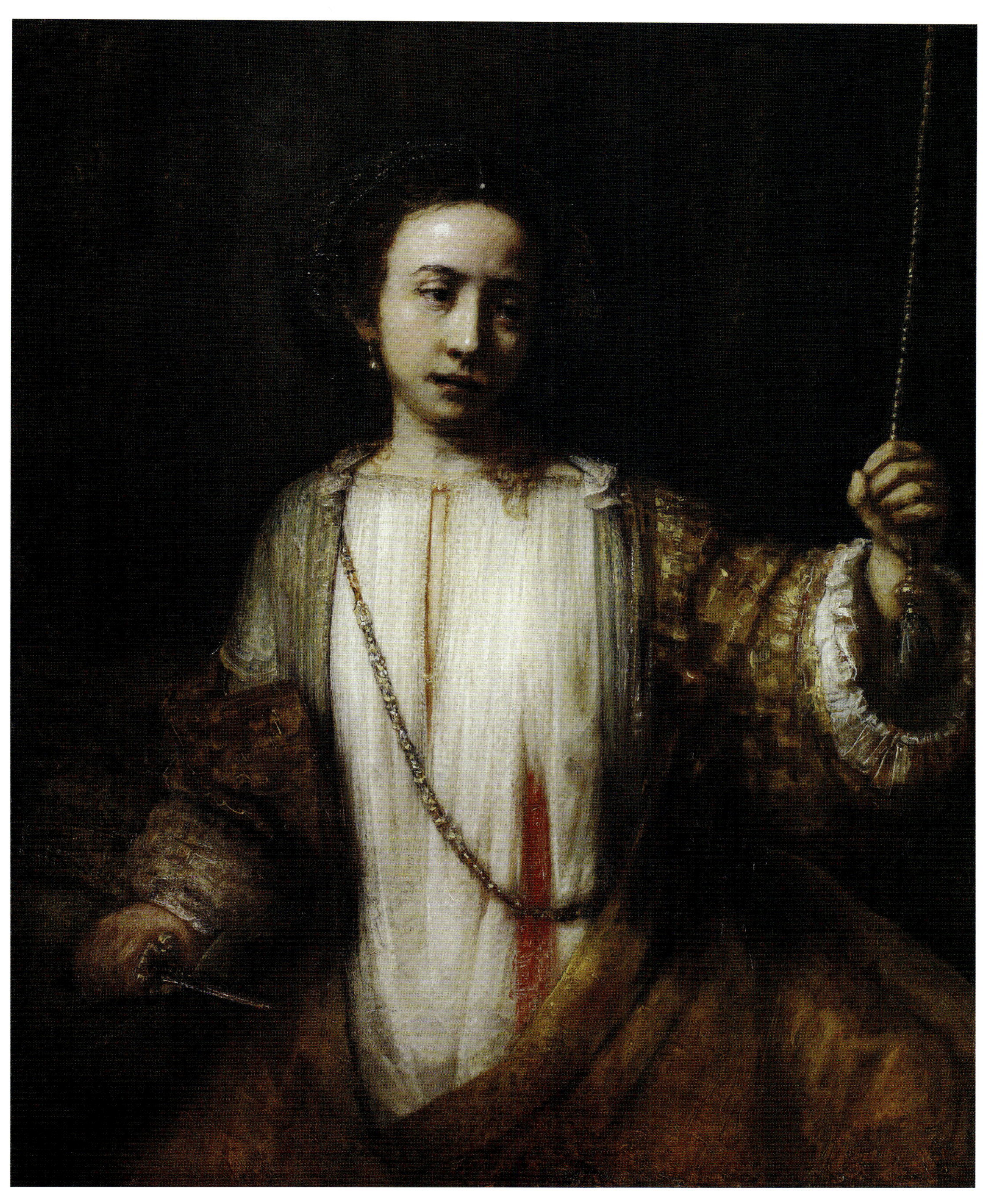

PLATE 40 [CAT. 50]
Rembrandt van Rijn
Lucretia, 1666
Oil on canvas, 110.2 x 92.3 cm (43 3/8 x 36 3/8 in.)
Minneapolis Institute of Arts

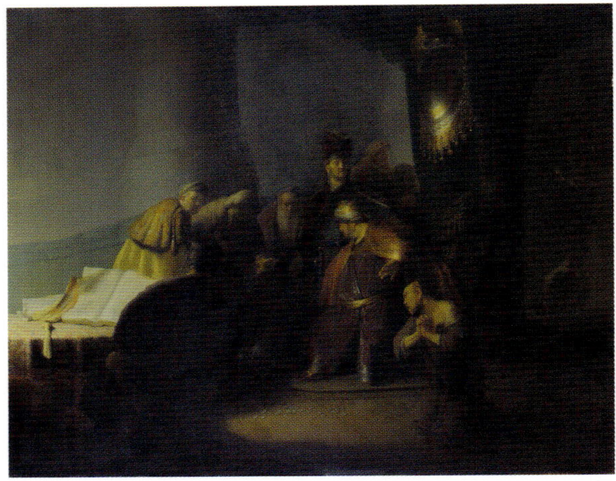

FIG. 75

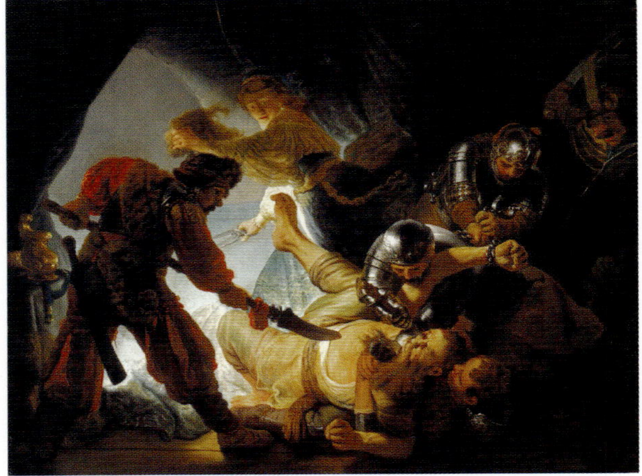

FIG. 76

however, is gained in exposing the inner conflict and spiritual turmoil of the protagonists and their relationship with others. Rembrandt enlisted these qualities in *Bathsheba* (Musée du Louvre, Paris), *Jacob Blessing the Children of Joseph* (Staatliche Kunstsammlungen, Dresden), *The Jewish Bride* (Rijksmuseum, Amsterdam), *The Denial of St. Peter* (Rijksmuseum, Amsterdam), and *The Return of the Prodigal Son* (FIG. 78).[6]

Rembrandt remained committed to history painting until his last days. Many believe his last picture, one left unfinished at the time of his death, was *Simeon with the Christ Child in the Temple* (FIG. 79), now in Stockholm. Interestingly, this picture had made its way into a New York collection by the early twentieth century, only to return to Europe in the 1940s.[7] Its provenance reminds us that not all the Rembrandt paintings that came to the United States have remained within its borders.

Sadly, American collections can claim few of Rembrandt's major history paintings. Since many of these masterpieces were firmly ensconced in European royal or national institutions long before Americans entered the competition in the late nineteenth century, one is largely correct in linking this paucity to the capriciousness of the art market. Still, such an assumption only partly explains the disproportionally small number of these works making their way from Europe during these years and in the decades to follow. Evidence also suggests some early collectors were reluctant to acquire religious pictures.[8] A revealing example in this regard centers on the marketing of *Saul and David* (FIG. 80) more than a century ago.

The French dealer Paul Durand-Ruel brought *Saul and David* to America in the 1890s, hoping to find a suitable buyer among the country's growing number of collectors eager to acquire Rembrandts. He failed in his efforts, however, and the work returned to Paris and was quickly purchased by Abraham Bredius in 1898.[9] Questions arise about whether it was the subject matter that failed to elicit a buyer in America, or the high asking price of more than 200,000 French francs (approximately $1.7 million today).

While these questions can be debated, one can assume the reputation of the artist was not a factor. By the end of the nineteenth century the market for Rembrandts was robust and growing. The number of paintings assigned to the artist was also expanding at an alarming rate, with the imposing *Saul and David* then seen as an important example of his oeuvre from the late 1650s.[10] In light of its somewhat recent change of attribution removing the work from the Rembrandt column, perhaps some of the potential buyers who had passed on the picture in the 1890s should be credited with insights not normally associated with them.

The story of Rembrandt's history paintings in America is marked by a slow start. This lukewarm interest stood in contrast to the enthusiasm shown by collectors for his portraits. To a large extent, this reality reflected both a good news and bad news scenario. Although far fewer history paintings steamed toward America, there were also fewer questionable, if not outright spurious, attributions. History painting acquisitions, for example, carried an approximately fifty percent chance of being by the master, while the success rate was considerably lower for portraits and other subjects.

FIG. 75
Rembrandt van Rijn, *Judas with the Thirty Pieces of Silver*, 1629, oil on panel, 79 x 102.3 cm (31 1/8 x 30 3/8 in.). Private collection, England

FIG. 76
Rembrandt van Rijn, *The Blinding of Samson*, 1636, oil on canvas, 206 x 276 cm (81 1/8 x 108 3/4 in.). Städelsches Kunstinstitut and Städtische Galerie, Frankfurt; inv. 1383

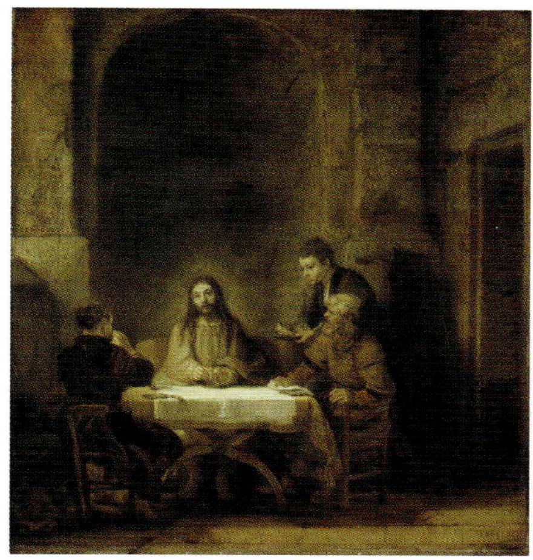

FIG. 77

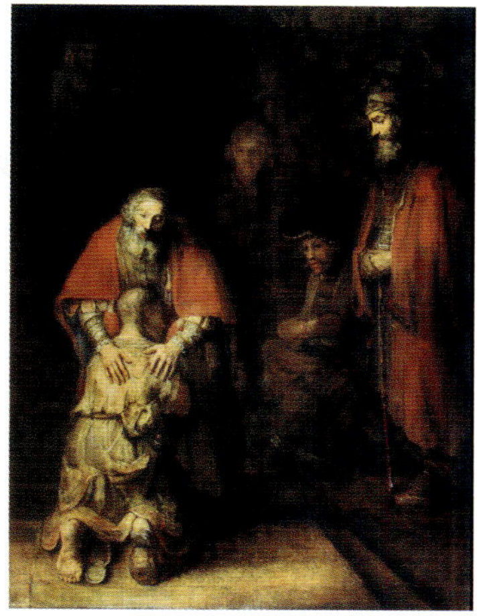

FIG. 78

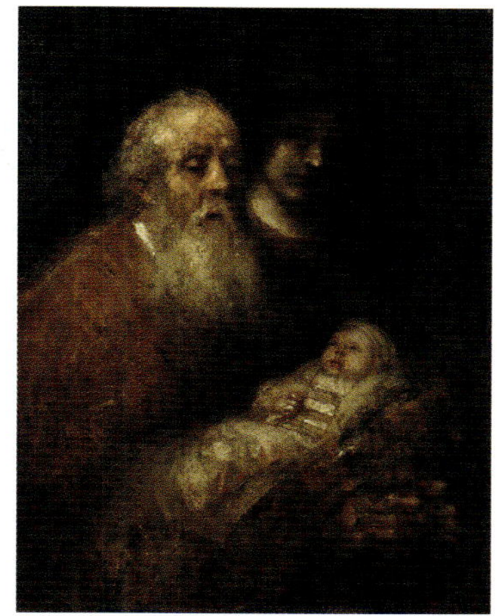

FIG. 79

Arguably, the two most reliable early benchmarks in assessing the status of Rembrandts in America occurred in 1909 and 1931. The exhibition of paintings by Dutch old masters in the Hudson-Fulton Celebration of 1909 contained thirty-six paintings then thought to be by Rembrandt. Of the nine pictures that might reasonably be included in the history painting category, five are accepted as autograph today. In 1931, with William Valentiner's ambitious yet problematic book *Rembrandt Paintings in America*, the number of "histories" rose to thirty-two, with more than half still considered as by the master.[11]

Unlike the previous catalogue essays by Tom Rassieur and George Keyes, which emphasize aspects of Rembrandt's ongoing stylistic development, the following survey of the master's history paintings has been organized by the date in which they entered American collections. In doing so, overall tendencies in collecting emerge. The one area in which American collectors proved to be enormously successful—in both their numbers and the fact that most were autograph Rembrandts—was in the depiction of single-figure history subjects. These pictures featured apostles, goddesses, and heroines from ancient history. Often straddling the boundary between history and portraiture, such works were not immune to causing confusion regarding their iconography, a situation not unlike the dilemma still facing experts in identifying the figures in *The Jewish Bride* (Rijksmuseum, Amsterdam; on loan from the city of Amsterdam since 1885).[12]

The story of Rembrandt's history paintings in America, to include works attributed to the master at the time of their arrival, seems to have begun in the middle of the nineteenth century with *Mercury and Aglauros* (FIG. 81). The picture, depicting an episode from Ovid's *Metamorphoses*, came to America from Paris shortly after its purchase by Francis Brooks in 1854. Bought as a Rembrandt, the painting was sold by the heirs of Brooks in 1903 to the Museum of Fine Arts, Boston. By 1908 the Rembrandt attribution had been questioned, with scholars first assigning it to Govaert Flinck (1615–1660) and then to Gerbrand van den Eeckhout (1621–1674) in the decades to follow. More recently, Carel Fabritius (1622–1654) has convincingly been identified as the painter.[13]

In hindsight, paintings such as *Mercury and Aglauros* clearly serve as cautionary tales with regard to overly ambitious attributions to Rembrandt. Another example, perhaps one more Rembrandt-worthy at first glance, is *The Death of Lucretia(?)* (PLATE 39). James E. Scripps, a Detroit newspaperman and collector of old master paintings, bought the picture shortly after it had sold in a London sale on 12 May 1888. Scripps, who became one of the founding trustees of the Detroit Museum of Art (the precursor of the Detroit Institute of Arts), acquired the work just before donating it, along with more than seventy other pictures, to the museum in October 1889. Then thought to be entirely by the master's hand, it wasn't until 1934 that Detroit director William Valentiner associated the painting with Rembrandt's pupil Jan Victors (1619–1676).[14] Valentiner, who it must be remembered was among those scholars most responsible for expanding Rembrandt's painted oeuvre, must be given credit here for removing the picture from the master.

FIG. 77
Rembrandt van Rijn, *Christ at Emmaus*, 1648, oil on panel, 68 x 65 cm (26 3/4 x 25 5/8 in.). Musée du Louvre, Paris; inv. 1739

FIG. 78
Rembrandt van Rijn, *The Return of the Prodigal Son*, c. 1668, oil on canvas, 262 x 205 cm (103 1/8 x 80 3/4 in.). The State Hermitage Museum, St. Petersburg

FIG. 79
Rembrandt van Rijn, *Simeon with the Christ Child in the Temple*, c. 1669, oil on canvas, 98.5 x 79.5 cm (38 3/4 x 31 1/4 in.). Nationalmuseum, Stockholm; 4567

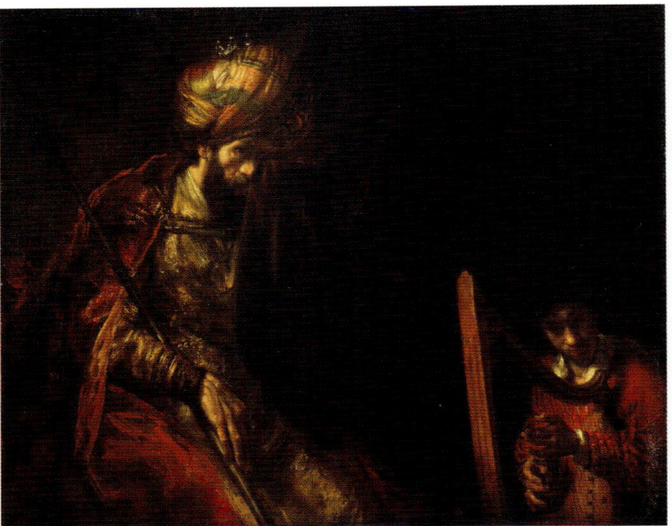

FIG. 80

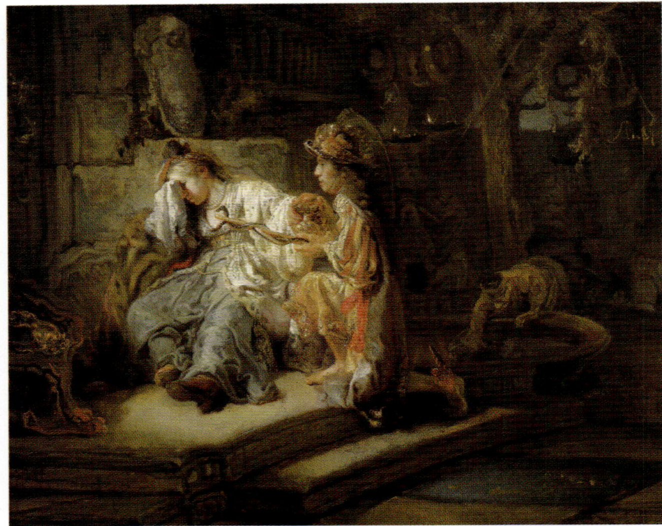

FIG. 81

George Keyes recently catalogued *Death of Lucretia(?)*, assigning it to an unnamed follower of Rembrandt. He summarized the issues involved with this perplexing picture. "Despite its large scale and the ambitions of the painter, this picture defied easy identification as to its subject, author, or relationship to Rembrandt."[15] The composition shows a recumbent woman, near death, with a dagger lying next to her. Two male figures in antique costumes—one younger, one older—attend to her. If the traditional identification of Lucretia is correct, then the pair represent the heroine's father and husband. They were called to the scene moments after the virtuous Roman matron stabbed herself following her rape by Tarquin.

Rather than arguing for the identification of the protagonists, a more relevant question here centers on the stylistic markers that led to its Rembrandt attribution in the late nineteenth century. The palette, character of the light and shadow, and some elements of the brushwork suggest Rembrandt's style, especially the "extensive use of incisions through still-wet paint to define detail."[16] Nevertheless, the work stands largely alone, clearly isolated from both Rembrandt and his known pupils.

The Death of Lucretia(?) likely dates to the early 1640s, as its composition drew inspiration from the more dynamic and exotic baroque compositions painted by Rembrandt during the late 1630s. In assessing the human dimension of the figures represented, it seems evident that the heartfelt emotion one associates with Rembrandt's genius is missing. The heroine, whether Lucretia or not, wears an expression that might be better associated with extreme indigestion rather than death. To better gauge the emotion Rembrandt brought to Lucretia's dying moments, one need only consider *Lucretia*, now in Minneapolis (PLATE 40).

The first autograph history painting by Rembrandt to come to America arrived in 1893. *Philemon and Baucis* (PLATE 41), signed and dated 1658, comes from the Widener Collection at the National Gallery of Art. Its journey to Washington began in Chicago when Charles T. Yerkes bought it for his collection through the Paris dealer Charles Sedelmeyer. The picture eventually made its way into the Joseph E. Widener collection in Elkins Park, Pennsylvania, after which it was presented to the fledgling National Gallery of Art in 1942.

The subject was one seldom portrayed by Dutch painters. The story, described by Ovid in the eighth book of his *Metamorphoses*, details a visit by the Roman gods Jupiter and Mercury to the home of Philemon and Baucis. The elderly couple received their guests with hospitality, unlike their neighbors who had shunned the disguised gods. A series of events soon led Philemon and Baucis to recognize the divinity of their visitors, after which they offered their only goose as the main course of their humble meal. Rembrandt depicted the moment "in which Jupiter both commands them not to kill the goose and blesses their offering with a firm yet comforting gesture."[17] Philemon and Baucis were rewarded for their generosity by having their home turned into a temple, with the pair serving as attendants. The two were also granted their wish to die at the same moment, after which they were transformed into oak and linden

FIG. 80
Rembrandt van Rijn (studio of?), *Saul and David*, c. 1650–55, oil on canvas, 130 x 164.3 cm (51 ⅛ x 64 ⅝ in.). Royal Cabinet of Paintings Mauritshuis, The Hague; inv. 621

FIG. 81
Carel Fabritius, *Mercury and Aglauros*, c. 1645–47, oil on canvas, 72.4 x 91 cm (23 ½ x 35 ⅞ in.). Museum of Fine Arts, Boston; Martha Ann Edwards Fund; 03.1143

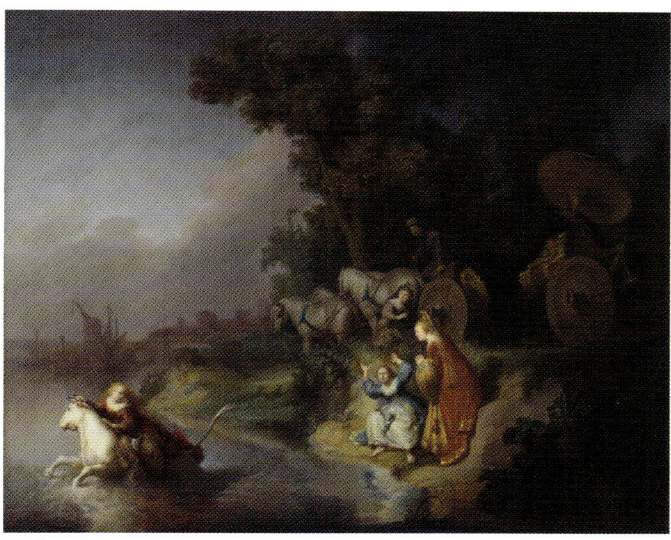

FIG. 82

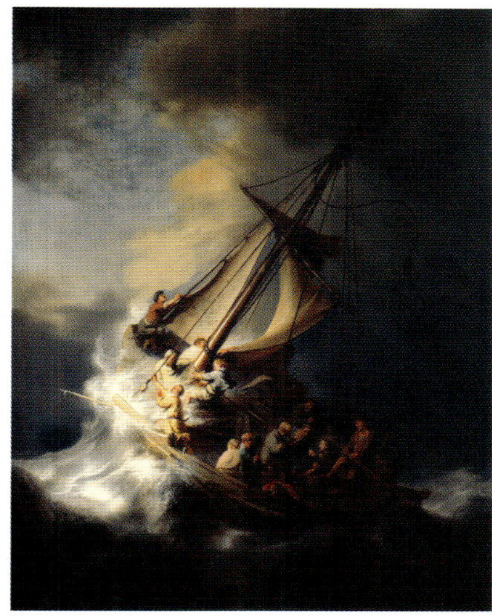

FIG. 83

trees flanking the entrance to the temple. The artist, art theorist, and biographer Karel van Mander (1548–1606) interpreted the moral of the story as one in which hospitality and virtue are rewarded and evil punished.[18]

Stylistically, *Philemon and Baucis* is consistent with examples of Rembrandt's paintings in the late 1650s. A dramatic light behind Mercury draws the viewer's attention to the events taking place around the table, while the rest of the composition is cast largely in shadow. Broadly applied brushwork is evident throughout. Unfortunately, the picture has suffered from abrasion and the effects of a transfer of the paint layers to a cradled wood panel.

The Washington picture represents Rembrandt's only extant painted image of Philemon and Baucis. Like many of his contemporaries, however, the artist drew upon other stories from the *Metamorphoses* for inspiration. His masterful *The Abduction of Europa* (FIG. 82) at the J. Paul Getty Museum is one such example. The painting carries a date of 1632 and came to America only in 1995. In many respects, *The Abduction of Europa* represents the polar opposite of *Philemon and Baucis*. Although not much larger in size, one finds in its brash imagery, brighter palette, polished brushwork, and erotic subject a far different stylistic approach.

In his decision to acquire *Philemon and Baucis*, one wonders if in 1893 Charles Yerkes was attracted more to the subject matter or to the Rembrandt name attached to it. One might suspect the latter, as it joined three other "Rembrandts" from the Yerkes collection to appear in his collection catalogue of 1893. In addition to the Washington painting, he had acquired *Joris de Caulerij* (see PLATE 12, p. 68) and two other pictures then misattributed to Rembrandt, *Portrait of a Rabbi* (private collection; previously on loan to the Brooklyn Art Museum) and *The Raising of Lazarus* (The Art Institute of Chicago).[19]

Another collector entered the competition for Rembrandts just a few years after Yerkes had acquired his pictures: the Bostonian Isabella Stewart Gardner. She no doubt shared some of the same motivations as Yerkes, but with even more impressive results. Among her Rembrandt acquisitions was *Christ in the Storm on the Sea of Galilee* (FIG. 83). Given the seal of approval by Gardner's advisor Bernard Berenson, the picture arrived in America in 1898 from the London dealer Colnaghi. Sadly, the whereabouts of the large and unique painting remain a mystery following its theft from the Gardner Museum in March 1990.

Between the time Gardner came into possession of *Christ in the Storm on the Sea of Galilee* in 1898, and the opening of the Hudson-Fulton Celebration in New York in the fall of 1909, the battle for Rembrandts intensified significantly. Unfortunately, the ambition of collectors far surpassed the pictures available to them on the art market. Still, individuals such as Benjamin Altman, Peter A. B. Widener, J. Pierpont Morgan, and Henry Clay Frick, among others, were willing to pay exorbitant amounts for their "Rembrandt" masterpieces. Like their portrait counterparts, history painting acquisitions were mixed with regard to current opinions regarding the attributions.

FIG. 82
Rembrandt van Rijn, *The Abduction of Europa*, 1632, oil on oak, 62.2 x 77 cm (24½ x 30¼ in.). The J. Paul Getty Museum, Los Angeles; 95.PB.7

FIG. 83
Rembrandt van Rijn, *Christ in the Storm on the Sea of Galilee*, 1633, oil on canvas, 160 x 128 cm (63 x 50⅜ in.). The Isabella Stewart Gardner Museum, Boston; inv. P21S24

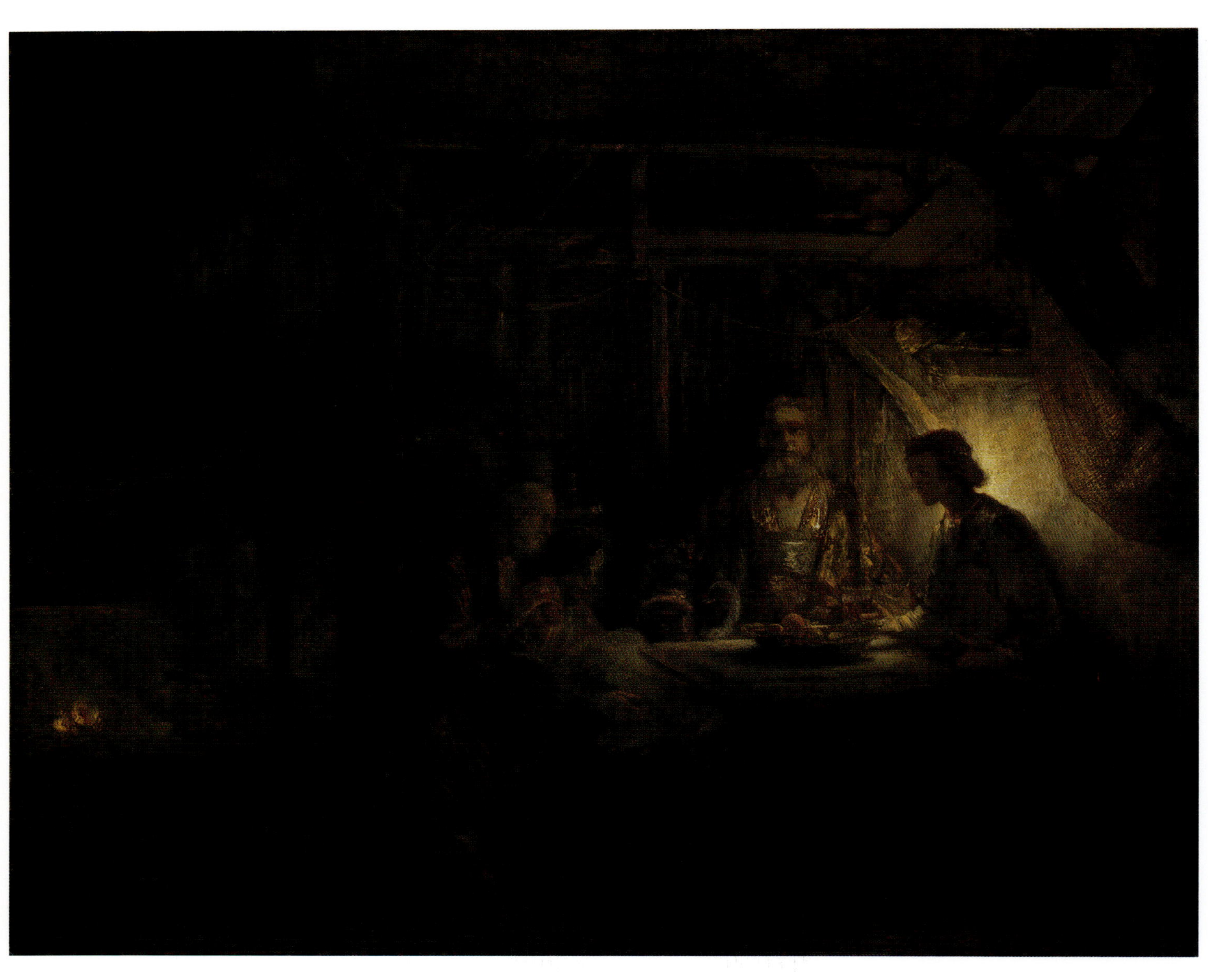

PLATE 41 [CAT. 46]
Rembrandt van Rijn
Philemon and Baucis, 1658
Oil on panel transferred from panel, 54.5 x 68 cm (21 ½ x 27 in.)
National Gallery of Art, Washington

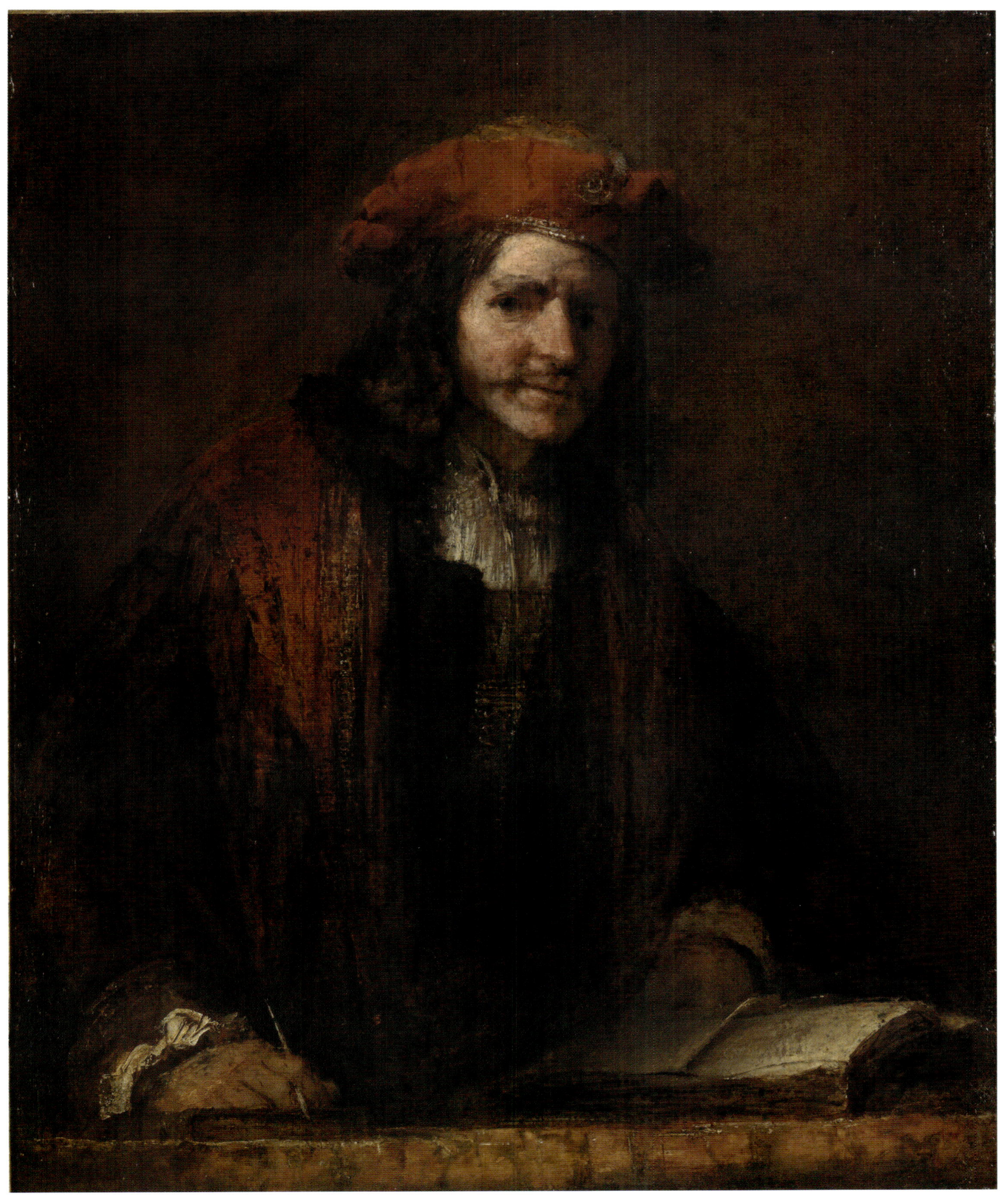

PLATE 42 [CAT. 47]
Rembrandt van Rijn (attributed to)
Man in a Red Cap (an evangelist?), c. 1660–62
Oil on canvas, 102 x 80 cm (40 ¼ x 31 ½ in.)
Museum Boijmans Van Beuningen, Rotterdam

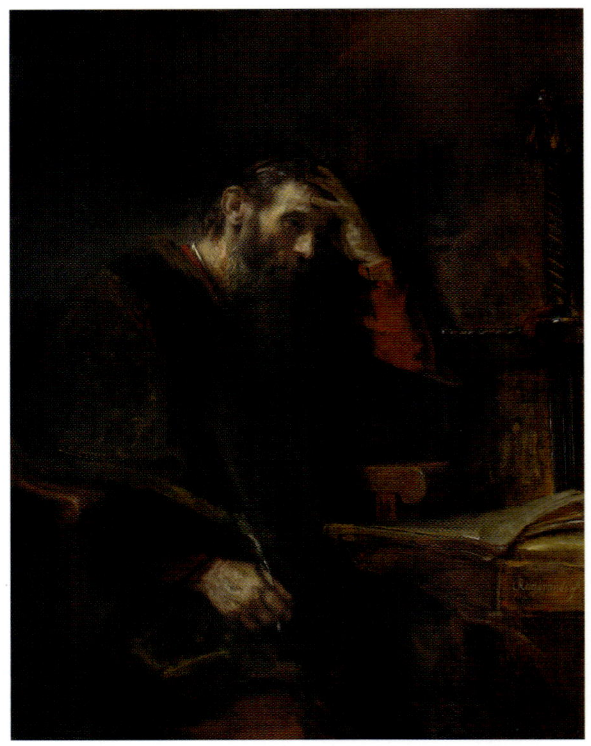

FIG. 84

From this group, and counted among the pictures appearing in the exhibition of paintings by Dutch old masters at the Hudson-Fulton Celebration, was *Man in a Red Cap (an evangelist?)* (PLATE 42). The picture serves as another example that made its American debut in Chicago, this time courtesy of the collector P. C. Hanford. By 1909, however, ownership had passed to the New Yorker Charles Schwab. Now residing at the Museum Boijmans van Beuningen in Rotterdam, *Man in a Red Cap* represents another Rembrandt returning to Europe via the art market after spending years in the United States. In many respects, the painting serves as a benchmark in the discussion of Rembrandt paintings in America. Both the work's subject and its attribution have remained open to interpretation in the century since it appeared in the New York exhibition.

Known as *The Accountant* in 1909, the figure shown holds a quill pen in his right hand and props open the pages of a book with his left. In the years to follow scholars theorized the sitter might represent an evangelist and linked the painting to a number of pictures identified as Rembrandt's "Late Religious Portraits."[20] Positioned on the cusp between history subject and portrait, such pictures became favorites among American collectors. Perhaps, as in this example, early owners ignored its purported identification as a biblical figure, opting instead to recognize it as a portrait. Does the sitter, in fact, represent an unidentified evangelist, or even St. Luke penning his gospel as Valentiner had written on various occasions?[21] Can he be identified as a *portrait historié,* or simply a portrait? Jeroen Giltaij, for example, argued that there "was nothing in the costume, gestures, or attributes of the figure to regard the image as anything other than the portrait of a professional, either a businessman or scholar."[22]

An equally intriguing issue concerns the attribution of the painting to Rembrandt. Giltaij and his colleague Guido Jansen cite various anomalies and weaknesses in paint application, while Ernst van de Wetering and the curators of the exhibition *Rembrandt's Late Religious Portraits* (see below) had cautioned against removing it from Rembrandt's oeuvre.[23] Condition issues have contributed to this split decision of attribution. A recent cleaning of the painting removed old varnish and overpaint, but losses to the paint surface over the centuries continue to cloud the issue.[24] Interestingly, when *Man in a Red Cap* last visited America in 2005 (Washington and Los Angeles), it was catalogued as autograph. Back at home in Rotterdam, however, it now carries the label "studio of Rembrandt van Rijn."

Examples from the "series" of religious portraits assigned to Rembrandt became a well-established commodity in American old master art collecting circles by the second decade of the

FIG. 84
Rembrandt van Rijn (and workshop of ?), *The Apostle Paul*, c. 1657, oil on canvas, 131.5 x 104.4 cm (51 ¾ x 41 ⅛ in.). National Gallery of Art, Washington; Widener Collection; 1942.9.59

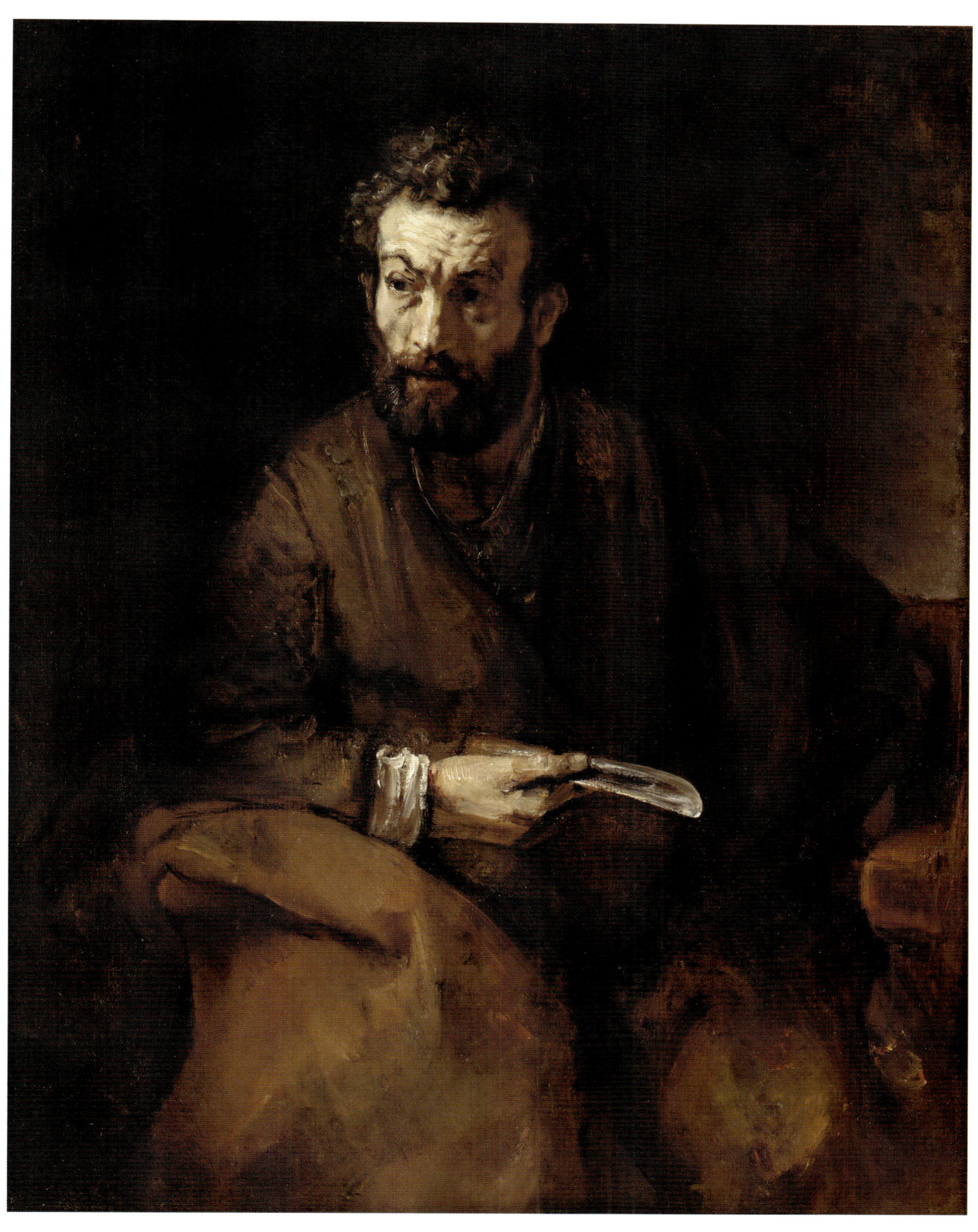

PLATE 43 [CAT. 45]
Rembrandt van Rijn
St. Bartholomew, 1657
Oil on canvas, 122.7 x 99.7 cm (48 3/8 x 39 1/4 in.)
The Putnam Foundation, Timken Museum of Art, San Diego

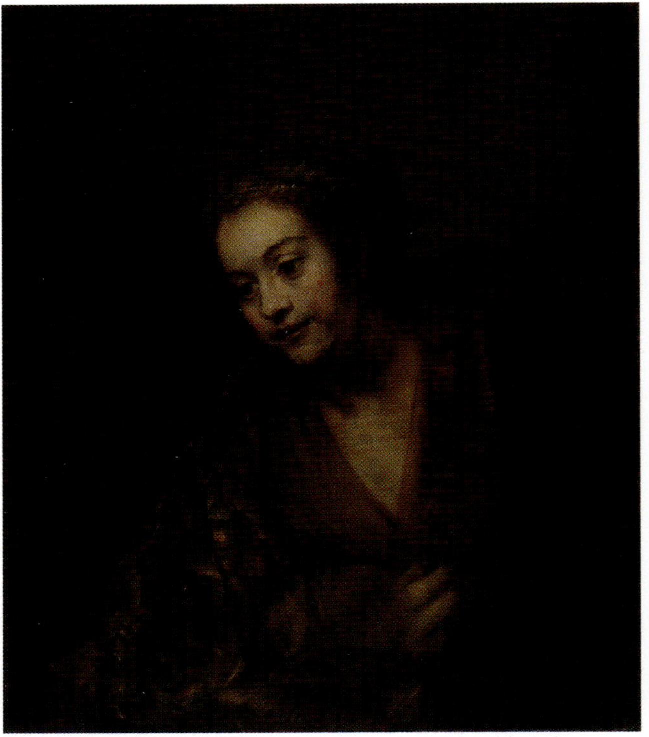

FIG. 85

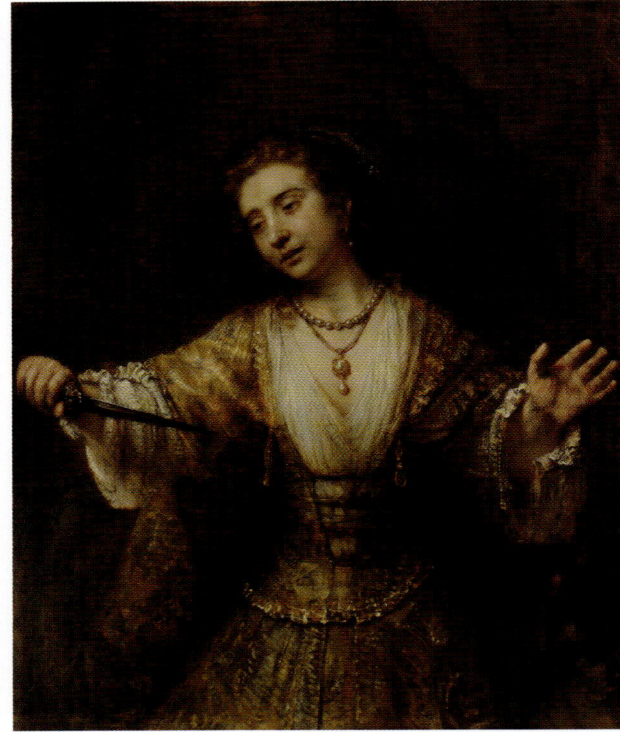

FIG. 86

twentieth century.[25] Soon to join the *Man in a Red Cap* was *The Apostle Paul* (FIG. 84), a purchase by Peter A. B. Widener around 1912, and *St. James the Major* (private collection) when it appeared on the New York art market in 1913.[26]

It was also around 1913 that *St. Bartholomew* (PLATE 43) crossed the Atlantic and entered the Henry Goldman collection in New York. The work was subsequently acquired by the Putnam Foundation and now is one of the treasures of the Timken Museum of Art in San Diego. Fully signed and dated "Rembrandt / f. 1657," its attribution has never been questioned. The seated Bartholomew appears in three-quarter length and holds a knife in his right hand, the symbol of his martyrdom as he was flayed alive. A simple turn of the saint's head animates the figure. According to Arthur Wheelock, "Rembrandt's portrayal of a relatively youthful man with rugged features reflects his own vision of biblical figures as unidealized, real people."[27]

Outwardly, Bartholomew appears to focus on an unseen external presence, perhaps his approaching executioners. At the same time, and displaying the genius Rembrandt brought to the subject, the figure also appears lost in thought. The message of faith conveyed in this remarkable canvas is further underscored by its execution and limited palette. "The combination of vigorous, sculpting brushwork in the face contrasts with the broader, planar application in the cuff and hand, while the roughly indicated bulk of the figure serves as a rich foil for these two descriptive elements."[28]

Early collectors seem to have been equally committed to the acquisition of female single-figure history paintings. They include Mrs. Collis P. (Arabella D.) Huntington's purchase of *Hendrickje Stoffels (as the Sorrowing Virgin)* (FIG. 85) in 1907 for $135,000 (more than $2.5 million today). This canvas represents another autograph picture in which possible religious content has been questioned. Is the picture simply a portrait of Rembrandt's common-law wife, Hendrickje Stoffels, or Hendrickje in the guise of the sorrowing virgin?[29]

Arguably, the most important of the early acquisitions in the category of female history subjects were neither biblical nor mythological, but instead representations of an episode from Roman history. Two paintings of Lucretia, one in Washington (FIG. 86), the other in Minneapolis (see PLATE 40), rank among the most moving and powerful female images ever produced by Rembrandt. Carrying dates of 1664 and 1666, respectively, both showcase the genius of Rembrandt's late painting style. The exhibited painting was purchased in the mid-1920s by Herschel V. Jones from a New York dealer. It remained in the family until 1934, after which the picture was acquired by the Minneapolis Institute of Arts.

FIG. 85
Rembrandt van Rijn, *Hendrickje Stoffels (as the Sorrowing Virgin)*, mid-1650s, oil on canvas, 78.4 x 68.9 cm (30⅞ x 27⅛ in.). The Metropolitan Museum of Art, New York; Gift of Archer M. Huntington, in memory of his father, Collis Porter Hunnington; 1926 26.101.9

FIG. 86
Rembrandt van Rijn, *Lucretia*, 1664, oil on canvas, 120 x 101 cm (47¼ x 39¼ in.). National Gallery of Art, Washington; Andrew W. Mellon Collection; 1937.1.76

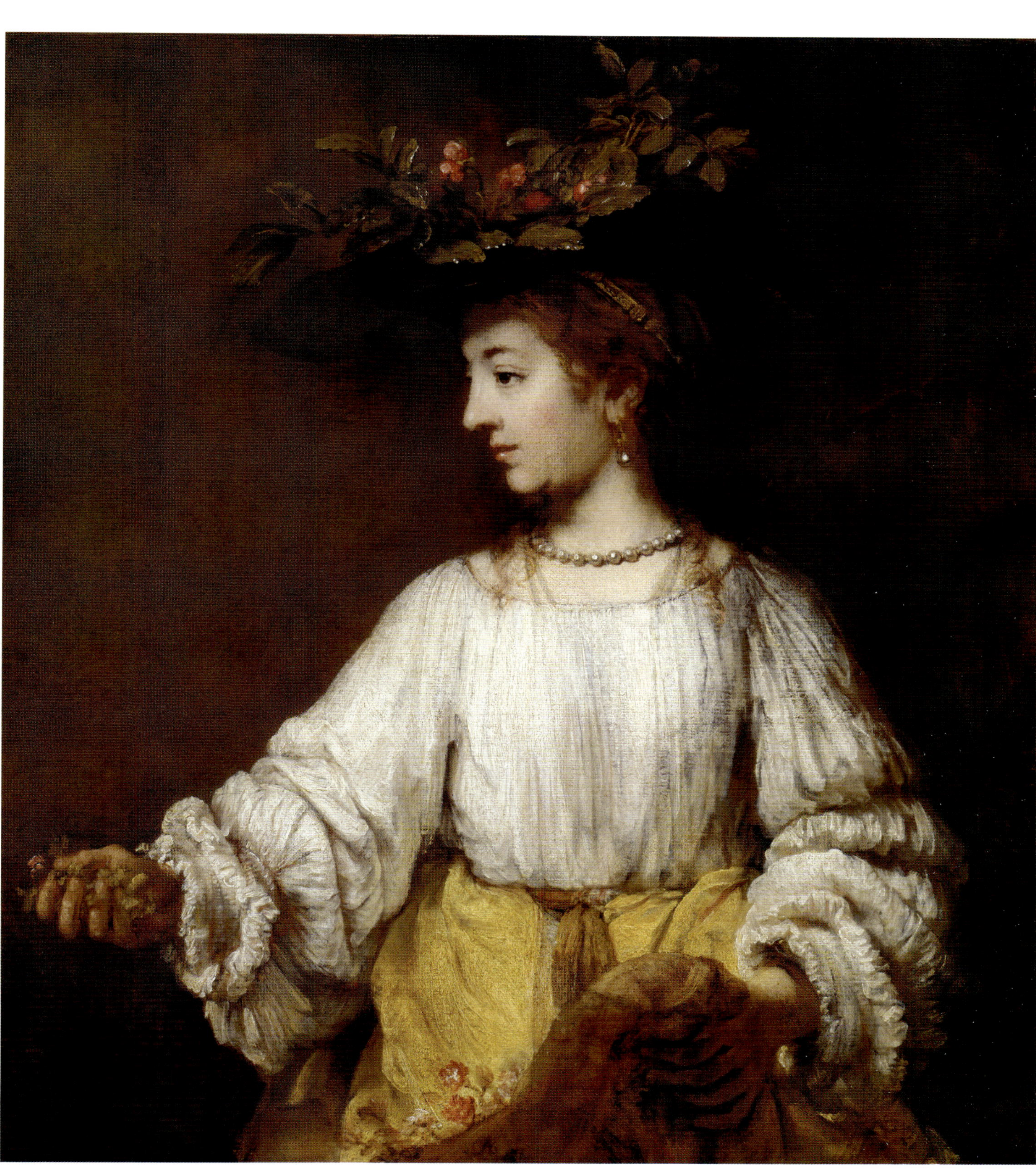

PLATE 44 [CAT. 44]
Rembrandt van Rijn
Flora, c. 1654
Oil on canvas, 100 x 91.8 cm (39 3/8 x 36 1/8 in.)
The Metropolitan Museum of Art, New York

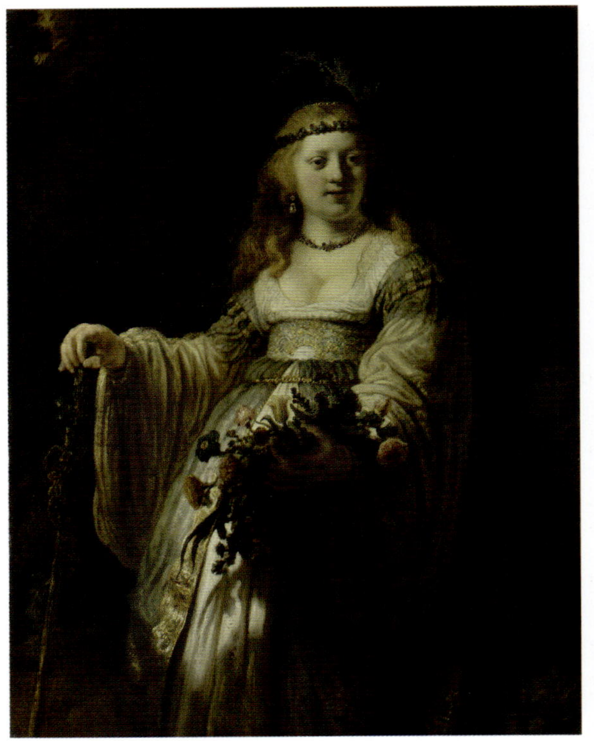

FIG. 87

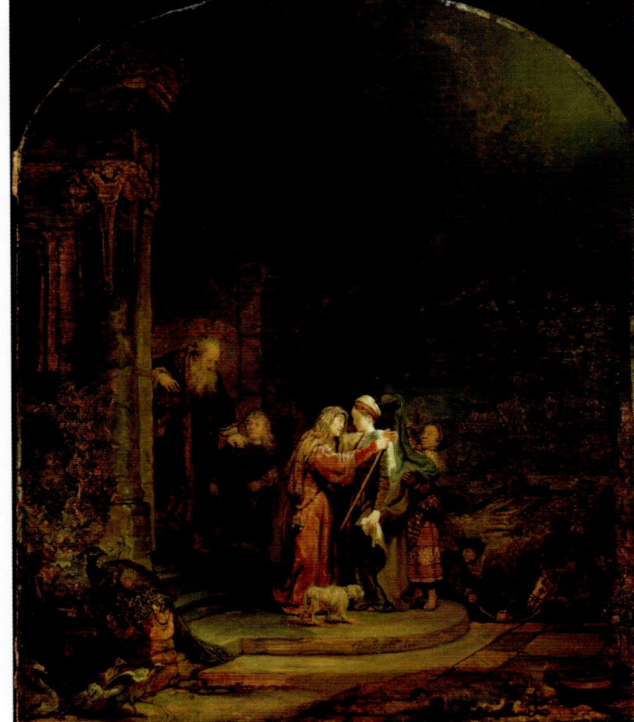

FIG. 88

The Washington *Lucretia*, by contrast, took a more circuitous route before reaching its current home at the National Gallery of Art. M. C. D. Borden was its first American owner in 1906. Following his death the canvas was sold in 1913 at auction in New York. Passing through the hands of the dealers Knoedler & Company (New York and Paris), and Frederik Müller (Amsterdam), the painting soon found new homes in Europe. First a Dutch, and then a Danish collector took possession of *Lucretia*, after which it appeared again on the New York art market in 1921. Three years later Knoedler sold the picture to Andrew W. Mellon. Unlike the previously discussed examples that left American collections, *Lucretia*, after returning to Europe for less a decade, retraced its steps back across the Atlantic.

Returning to the Minneapolis *Lucretia*, one is witness to the moment just after the heroine plunged a dagger into her heart. Blood has stained her white chemise as she makes the transition from life to death. Her expression conveys an understanding and acceptance of her actions. Like its counterpart in Washington, where the painter captured the moment just before Lucretia's self-sacrifice, Rembrandt mustered the full genius of his mature style in describing the figure. He varied his paint application from smooth to rough—the latter with a frequent use of the palette knife—and carefully controlled the play of light across the form. Highlights fall on her forehead and nose, the white of her sleeve, and the blood-soaked chemise.

Far different in temperament from the emotionally arresting and deeply moving *Lucretia* painted just a few short years before the artist's death in 1669, is *Flora* (PLATE 44). Rembrandt likely executed this depiction of the ancient Roman goddess of flowers about 1654. Although some scholars have attempted to link her features to those of Saskia, perhaps with hints of Hendrickje thrown in for good measure, there seems to be no foundation for such a conclusion. As Walter Liedtke wrote, "There was certainly no intention of depicting either woman. The figure is an ideal type that goes back to earlier pictures by Rembrandt."[30]

Flora shows a woman appropriately adorned with a flowering cherry branch on her hat and holding flowers in her hand and apron. The picture came out of the Spencer collection at Althorp just after World War I. Sold to Mrs. Henry E. Huntington (formerly Mrs. Collis P. Huntington) of New York, by 1920 it had passed to her son, Archer M. Huntington. He gave the work to the Metropolitan Museum of Art in 1926.

Although the subject was one familiar to Rembrandt, the sentiments conveyed by the figure differ significantly from his earlier treatments of the theme. For example, a 1635 dated painting

FIG. 87
Rembrandt van Rijn, *Flora (Saskia van Uylenburgh in Arcadian Costume)*, 1635, oil on canvas, 123.5 x 97.5 cm (48 5/8 x 38 3/8 in.). The National Gallery, London; inv. 4930

FIG. 88
Rembrandt van Rijn, *The Visitation*, 1640, oil on panel, 56.5 x 47.9 cm (22 1/4 x 18 7/8 in.). The Detroit Institute of Arts; City of Detroit Purchase; 27.200

in London (FIG. 87) finds Saskia serving as the model, a smile passing her lips. The New York picture, by comparison, shows a more reserved figure, tender and feminine, yet lost in thought. Undoubtedly, circumstances in Rembrandt's life, including the death of Saskia more than a decade earlier, prompted his change in approach to the subject. No longer reflective of a celebration of spring, Flora seems better suited here to symbolize the passing of time.

American collectors would add to the tally of outstanding single-figure mythological and biblical pictures by Rembrandt as the years passed. By contrast, others were having far less success in their quest for large narrative paintings. Although few examples appeared on the art market during these decades, masterpieces did surface from time to time. Among them was *The Visitation* of 1640 (FIG. 88), one of the finest history paintings by Rembrandt in America.[31] Acquired by Valentiner in 1927 during his tenure as director of the Detroit Institute of Arts, it joined a handful of other autograph narrative pictures already in residence in the United States. The count included the previously discussed *Philemon and Baucis; The Circumcision* of 1661, a work acquired by P. A. B. Widener by 1912 and also now at the National Gallery of Art; and Benjamin Altman's gift to the Metropolitan Museum of Art in 1913, *The Toilet of Bathsheba*, signed and dated 1643.

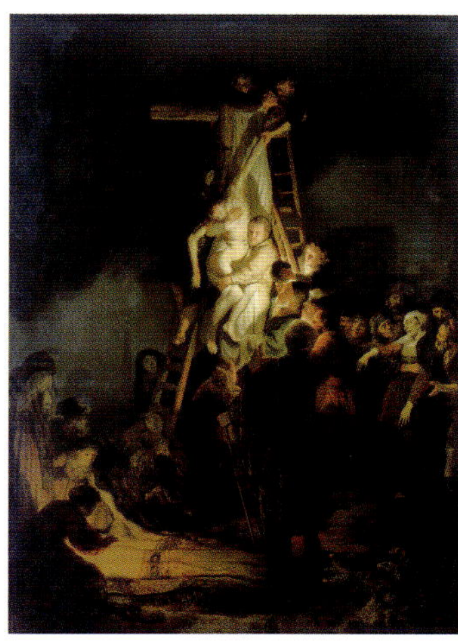
FIG. 89

These autograph narrative pictures were joined by paintings then misattributed to Rembrandt. A textbook example of the perfect storm swirling around high demand, scholarly missteps, and market accommodation was another acquisition by the estate of P. A. B. Widener by his son Joseph in the early 1920s, *The Descent from the Cross* (PLATE 45). At the time, the canvas was touted as a major rediscovered masterpiece by Rembrandt, having previously fetched a record auction price in 1909 for one of his paintings in London. The July 2nd sale came just a week after noted Rembrandt scholar Wilhelm von Bode had given his seal of approval to the picture. In his expertise he favorably compared it to other well-known versions of the same image—one from the "Passion" series commissioned from Rembrandt by Frederik Hendrik in the early 1630s (see FIG. 13, p. 42), the other a large canvas at the Hermitage in St. Petersburg (FIG. 89).

The attribution of the Washington painting to Rembrandt would not be seriously questioned until the late 1960s when Horst Gerson removed it from the corpus. In assessing the picture, he concluded "the gestures are lame, the expression sentimental and the composition as a whole lacks concentration."[32] His opinion could not be further from earlier assessments by scholars from Cornelius Hofstede de Groot to Jakob Rosenberg. The latter described the work in glowing terms as late as 1964, calling it a "highly important" autograph replica of the Hermitage *Descent from the Cross*.[33] He wrote, "Whatever his reasons, Rembrandt shows how, with a few significant changes, he can transform an old composition into something completely new in its emotional content and pictorial expression."[34]

Recent questions regarding the authenticity of the St. Petersburg canvas have cast further doubts on Rosenberg's conclusion that the painting at the National Gallery of Art is by Rembrandt. Arthur Wheelock has provided a plausible interpretation of the genesis of the picture, albeit one still open to debate.

> This painting is thus a fascinating document about the complexities that sometimes exist with works produced in Rembrandt's workshop. The evidence suggests that it was initially painted in a much larger size, with a composition that resembled that of the Hermitage *Descent from the Cross*. The exact date of the first period of execution cannot be precisely determined, but it probably was during the mid-1630s. Around 1650, or shortly thereafter, it was severely cropped at the left and bottom, and virtually the entire composition was reworked.[35]

Wheelock conjectured that Rembrandt may have had a hand in the composition's rethinking but did not participate in its execution. Identifying Constantijn van Renesse (1626–1680) as the painter likely responsible, he proposed a date of 1650–52 for the "Renesse" repainting, a timeframe consistent with the overpainted date of 1651 the picture once carried.

About the same time both versions of *Descent from the Cross* fell from the Rembrandt column, another large and ambitious narrative painting was removed from his oeuvre, the falsely signed

FIG. 89
Rembrandt van Rijn (?), *The Descent from the Cross*, 1634, oil on canvas, 158 x 117 cm (62 ¼ x 46 ⅛ in.). The State Hermitage Museum, St. Petersburg; inv. GE-753

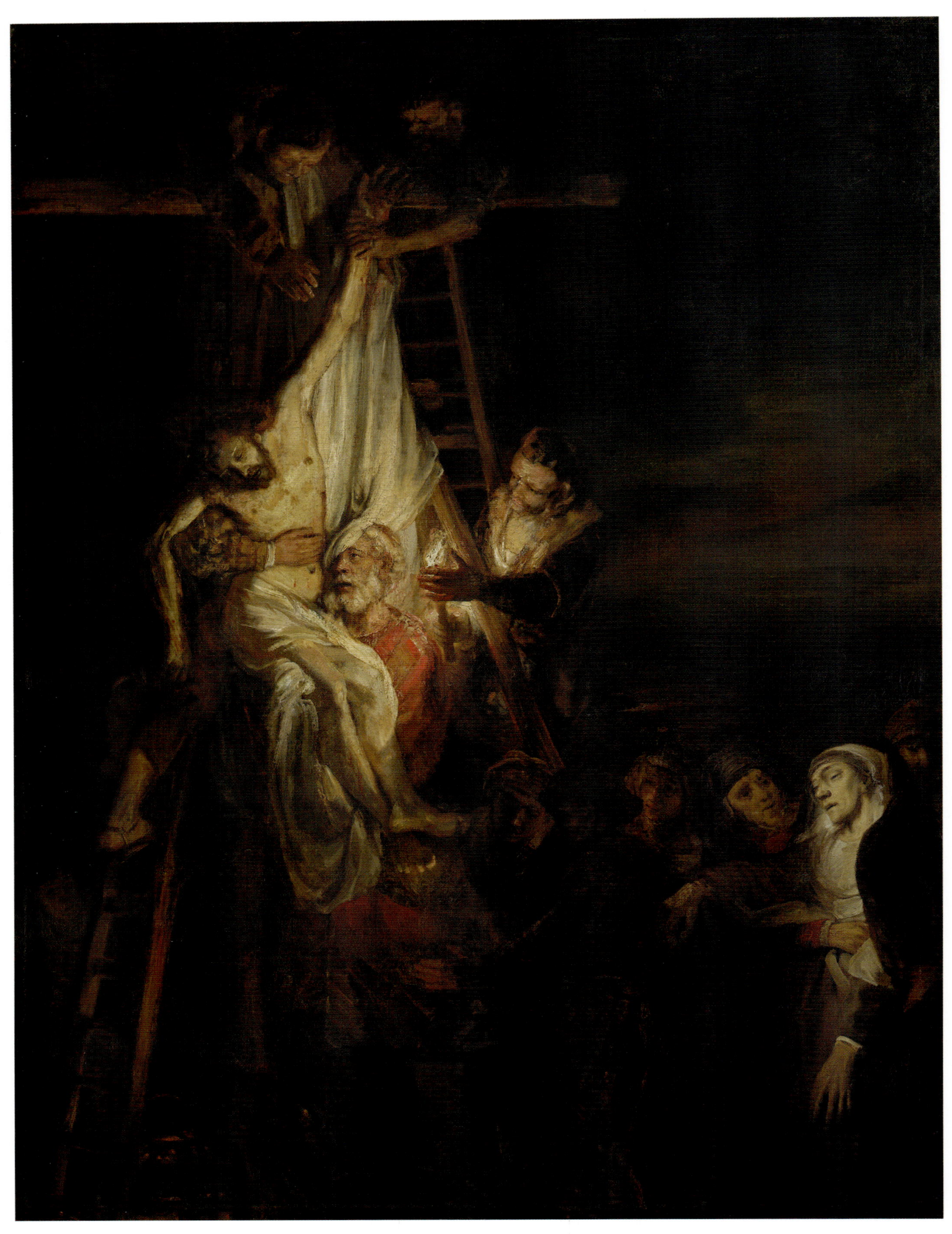

PLATE 45 [CAT. 43]
Rembrandt van Rijn (workshop of; probably Constantijn van Renesse)
The Descent from the Cross, c. 1650/52
Oil on canvas, 142 x 110.9 cm (55 7/8 x 43 5/8 in.)
National Gallery of Art, Washington

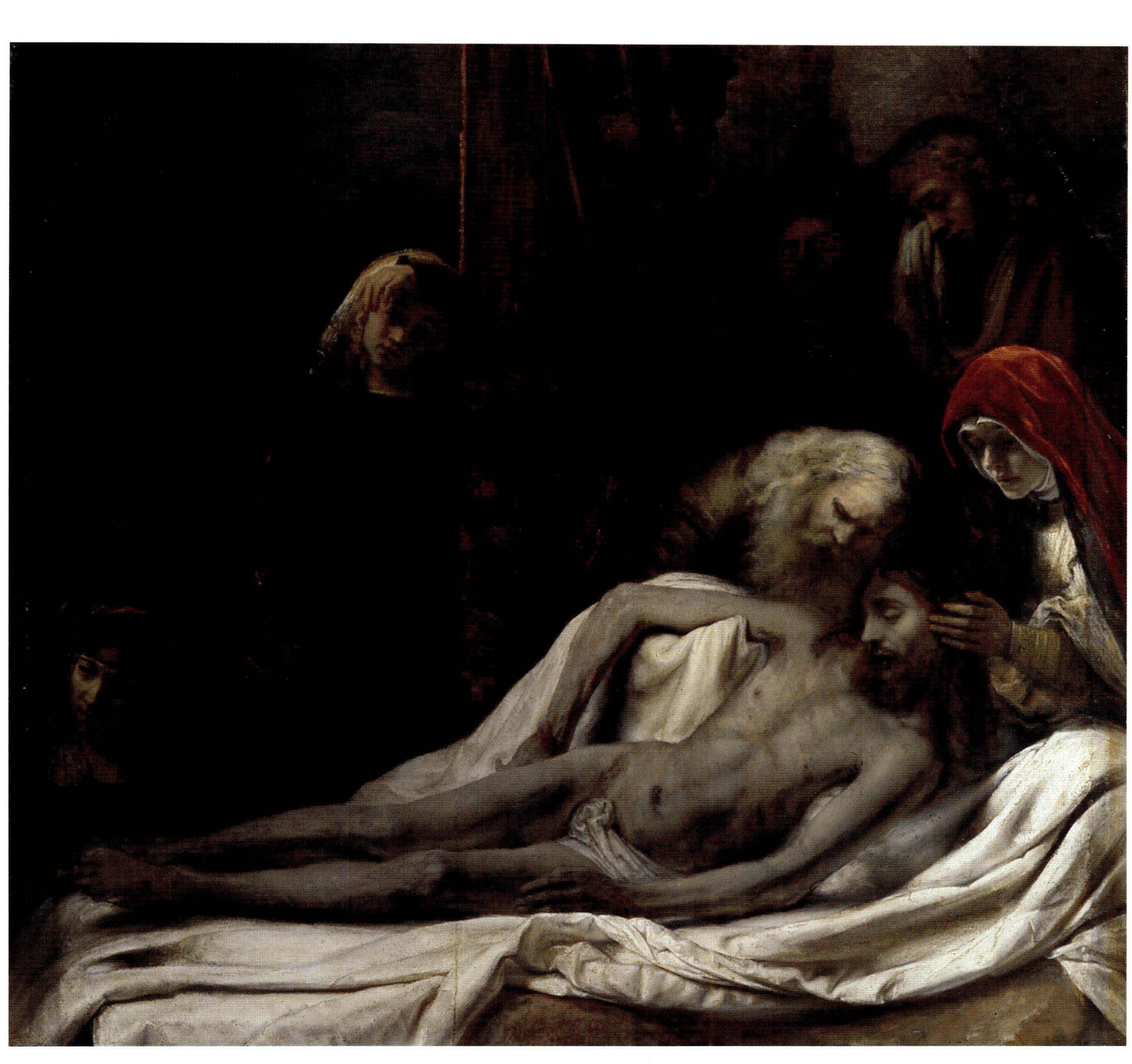

PLATE 46 [CAT. 42]
Rembrandt van Rijn (workshop of)
Lamentation, c. 1645–50
Oil on canvas, 180.3 x 198.8 cm (71 x 78 ¼ in.)
The John and Mable Ringling Museum of Art,
the State Art Museum of Florida, Sarasota

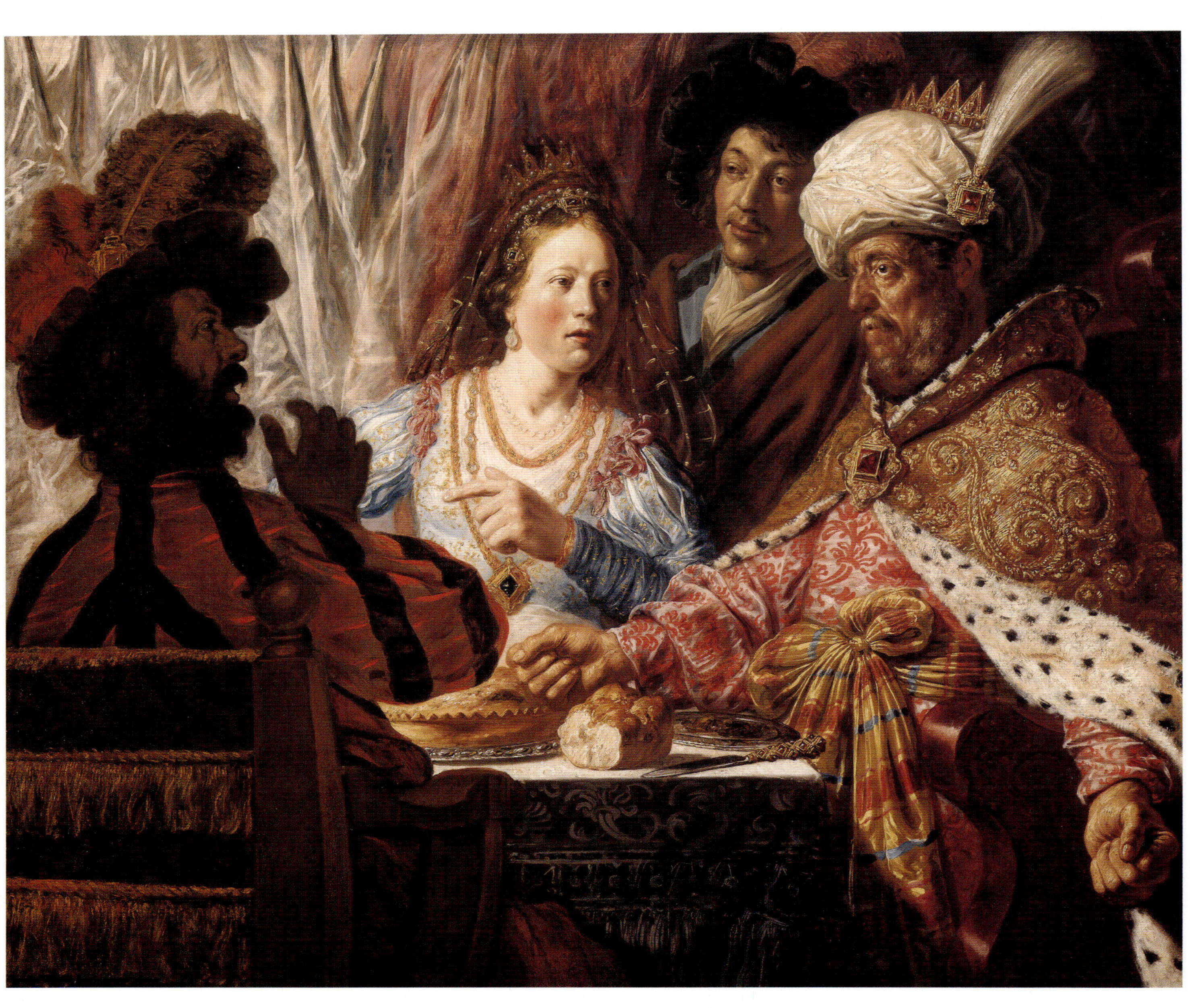

PLATE 47 [CAT. 39]
Jan Lievens
The Feast of Esther (Wrath of Ahasuerus), c. 1625
Oil on canvas, 130.9 x 163.2 cm (51 ½ x 64 ¼ in.)
North Carolina Museum of Art, Raleigh

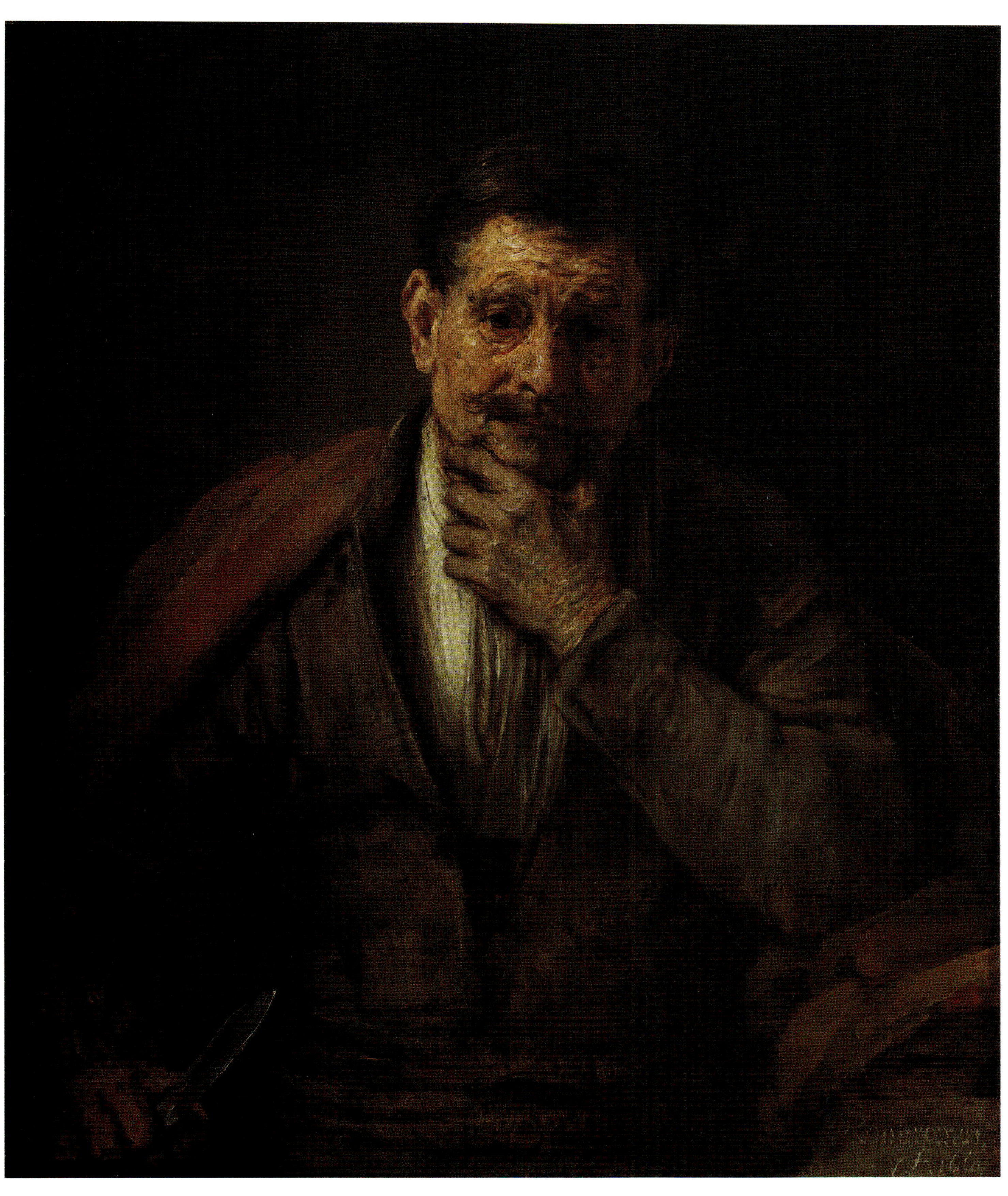

PLATE 48 [CAT. 48]
Rembrandt van Rijn
St. Bartholomew, 1661
Oil on canvas, 86.7 x 75.6 cm (34 1/8 x 29 3/4 in.)
The J. Paul Getty Museum, Los Angeles

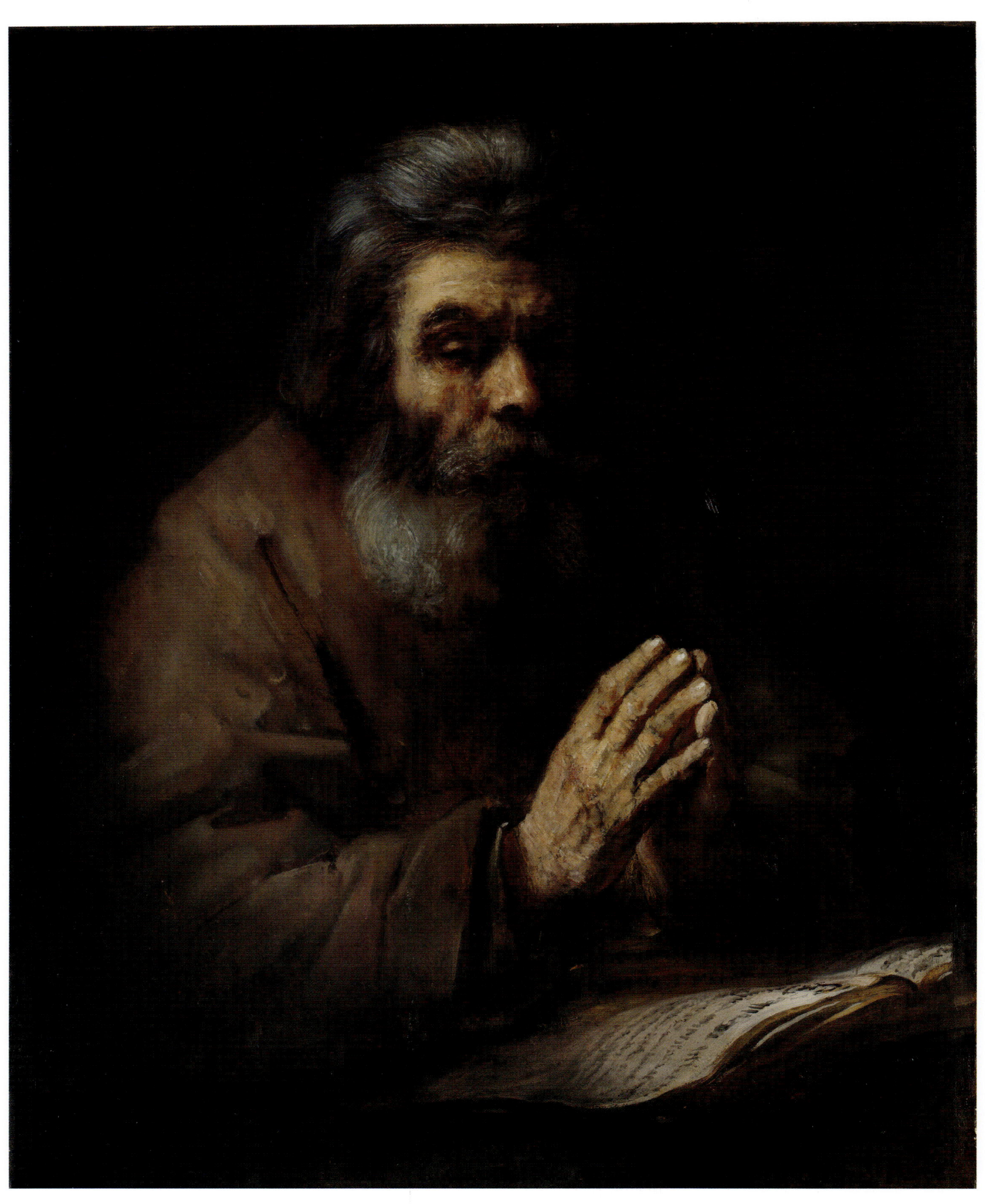

PLATE 49 [CAT. 49]
Rembrandt van Rijn (follower of)
Old Man Praying, c. 1661 or later
Oil on canvas, 87.3 x 72.1 cm (34 3/8 x 28 3/8 in.)
The Cleveland Museum of Art

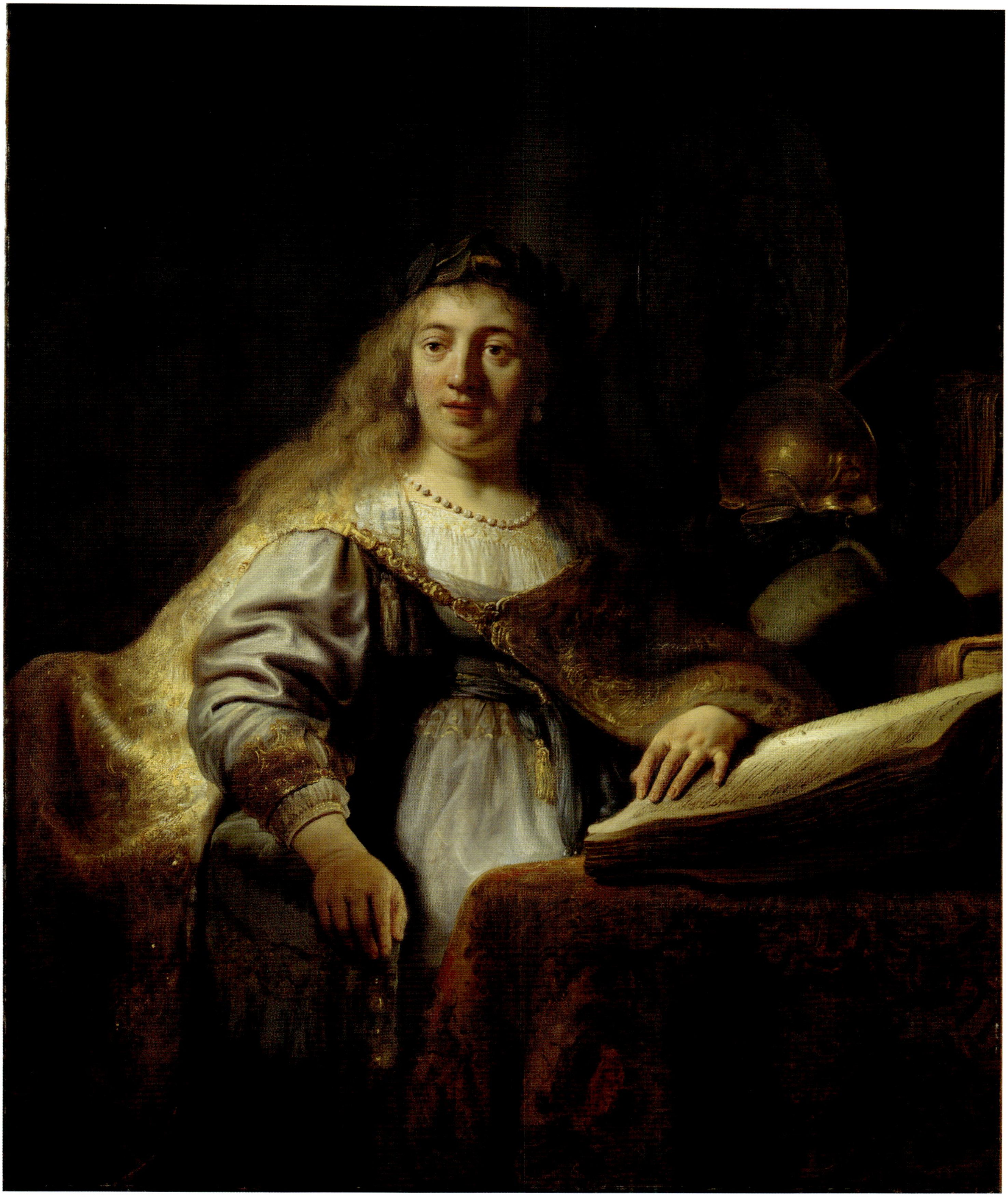

PLATE 50 [CAT. 40]
Rembrandt van Rijn
Minerva in Her Study, 1635
Oil on canvas, 137 x 116 cm (54 x 45 ⅝ in.)
Private collection, New York

and dated *Lamentation* (PLATE 46).[36] This large canvas was purchased by circus magnate John Ringling at a London sale the summer of 1929 and, following his death in 1936, subsequently bequeathed by Ringling to the museum in Sarasota that bears his name.[37] The provenance of this painting can be traced to at least 1835, and it often appeared as by Rembrandt in the literature and in a number of important exhibitions until downgraded to a school piece in the 1960s (see catalogue of the exhibition).

Cut down at the top and along the right side, the painting has suffered severe damage over the centuries. The composition shows the dead, emaciated body of Christ being prepared for entombment by his followers. Included in the group of mourners are Joseph of Arimathea, the Virgin Mary who gently pulls back Christ's hair from his face, the weeping John the Evangelist, Nicodemus, and Mary Magdalen at Christ's feet. All are grief stricken as they endure the tragedy of the event. Unfortunately, the unknown painter responsible for its execution did not share in Rembrandt's genius. Instead of capturing the emotional duress of the faithful, one is witness to a strange amalgam of melodrama and vacant stares.

Lamentation also stands at some distance from autograph pictures by Rembrandt from the late 1640s and early 1650s in terms of its brushwork, a reality already noted in 1969 when the work was seen in the exhibition *Rembrandt after Three Hundred Years*. There, for the first time, it was downgraded to "attributed to Rembrandt." In discussing the painting in the catalogue, J. Richard Judson took a cautionary approach. "Rembrandt builds up in powerful layers and his light effects are not made up of spotted highlights across the picture surface," as are seen in the Sarasota picture.[38] A few painters from the Rembrandt circle have been associated with its execution in the decades since, most notably Willem Drost (1633–1659). Nevertheless, Jonathan Bicker, in his recent monograph on Drost, convincingly rejected such an attribution.[39]

Authorship is no longer questioned for another large-scale biblical picture thought to be by Rembrandt when it entered the country shortly after World War II. *The Feast of Esther* (PLATE 47) in Raleigh is now considered the youthful masterpiece of the precocious Leiden painter Jan Lievens (1607–1674). In 1956, however, Valentiner touted its acquisition by the newly opened North Carolina Museum of Art, claiming it to be a major painting from the early career of Rembrandt (see FIG. 1, p. 19).

The Rembrandt attribution must be seen within the context of the accepted connoisseurship practices when the painting was rediscovered in the 1930s. In general, an expansionist view of the artist's oeuvre was in vogue during the first half of the twentieth century. This phenomenon, particularly as it related to this painting, can be partly explained by a strong desire by scholars to uncover works from early in Rembrandt's career. Considering that youthful works by Lievens were little understood and of far less interest to researchers, it is not surprising that Rembrandt was assigned this ambitious, albeit flawed, work.[40]

Questions, in fact, were being raised regarding the authorship of the painting even before it made its journey to Raleigh. The composition clearly aligns itself with the artistic approach found in pictures by Lievens rather than Rembrandt from the mid-1620s. The aforementioned Constantijn Huygens, who described the strengths and weaknesses of this "pair of young and noble painters" in his autobiography, could have been speaking of *The Feast of Esther* as he described works by Lievens. "Conversely, Lievens is the greater in inventiveness and audacious themes and forms. Everything his young spirit endeavors to capture must be magnificent and lofty. Rather than depicting his subject in true size, he chooses a larger scale."[41] (see also p. 35).

Certainly the compressed space, a garish palette, and aggressive brushwork are among the features found in Lievens's early narrative works. These stylistic markers stand at some distance from the more modest examples by Rembrandt, with their "sure touch and liveliness of emotions," again using the words of Huygens.[42]

Esther, risking her life to save her people, revealed to King Ahasuerus the treachery of Haman, the king's chief minister who plotted to slaughter all the Jews in Persia (Esther, 7:1–7). Her story remained a popular one for the Dutch throughout the seventeenth century, as in their struggle with the Spaniards the citizens of the young republic came to identify with the children of Israel. The composition shows the moment that Esther reveals the plot, as she points to the figure of Haman cast in shadow to the left. Ahasuerus responds in anger, and eventually the traitor to the Jews would die on the gallows.

In many respects, *The Feast of Esther* represents another cautionary tale regarding "Rembrandts" entering American collections since the 1950s. Not only have opportunities on the market become much more rare, but intense scrutiny of lofty attributions is now commonplace. The bloated oeuvre catalogues popular earlier in the century have increasingly become a thing of the past, often with dramatic effect.[43]

Still, opportunities, while far less frequent, have arisen. Close to the time the North Carolina museum acquired the *Feast of Esther,* another picture, one possibly featuring Esther as well, appeared on the art market. Titled simply *A Young Woman at Her Toilet* (FIG. 90), the identity of the sitter remains open to interpretation. Is she Esther, Judith, or another Old Testament heroine? While the specifics of the subject are unresolved, its authorship by Rembrandt is certain. Arriving at the National Gallery of Canada in 1953, the picture had previously been in the collection of the Prince of Liechtenstein.[44]

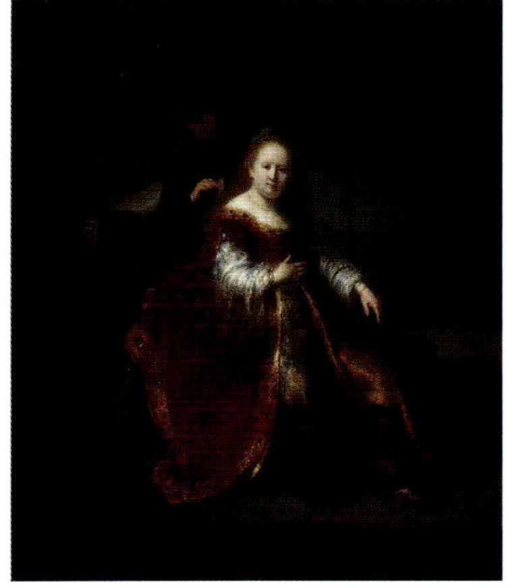

FIG. 90

In turning to the more recent Rembrandt history acquisitions in America, the deep pockets of J. Paul Getty enabled the institution bearing his name to make the greatest inroads among museums. In 1995, the Getty acquired the previously discussed *Abduction of Europa* (see FIG. 82), as well as *Daniel and Cyrus before the Idol Bel* (FIG. 91), a subject taken from the book of Daniel. The pair joined another history painting already in the collection, *St. Bartholomew* (PLATE 48). Signed and dated 1661, *St. Bartholomew* had arrived at the Getty years earlier, in 1971. With it, America added another important example of a single-figure religious "portrait."[45]

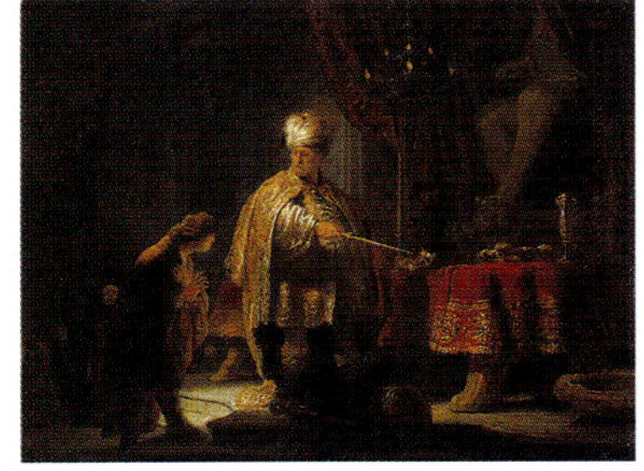

FIG. 91

Bartholomew sits pensively before the viewer and, like his counterpart in San Diego (see PLATE 43, p. 153), holds in his right hand a knife to symbolize his impending martyrdom. Rembrandt again plumbed the depth of the apostle's faith as he ponders his fate. Dating four years later than the comparable work in San Diego, the canvas represents further developments in Rembrandt's painting style. Here, thinly applied paint layers serve to define the saint's torso. The brushwork in these passages contrasts with the "short, thick, impastoed strokes that sculpt the face of Bartholomew."[46]

The bravado execution Rembrandt brought to *St. Bartholomew* differs in significant ways with another work linked to the group of religious portraits now in America. *Old Man Praying* (an apostle?) (PLATE 49) was purchased by the Cleveland Museum of Art in 1967. It came via a New York dealer following its appearance in a London sale of 1964 and was envisioned as filling a major gap in Cleveland's collection. Few consider the painting as autograph today. Horst Gerson had expressed doubts about the attribution by 1969. He wrote "there is a kind of looseness of surface texture that I have not observed in other works by Rembrandt."[47]

His remarks came the same year the picture, still assigned to Rembrandt, was included in *Rembrandt after Three Hundred Years* in 1969. Labeled simply as *Old Man Praying,* arguments for recognizing the figure as an apostle have been expressed by various scholars.[48] Unfortunately, the lack of a symbol such as the knife in the *St. Bartholomew* clouds concrete identification. Like a number of its counterparts, it, too, straddles the boundary between a portrait and a history painting.

Examples from the so-called series of Christian apostles from the 1650s and 1660s find their opposites in the group of large-scale, vivacious female goddesses Rembrandt painted throughout his career. Such works had their early admirers in America, for example, Michael

FIG. 90
Rembrandt van Rijn, *A Young Woman at Her Toilet*, c. 1632–33, oil on canvas, 109.2 x 94.4 cm (43 x 37 ¼ in.). The National Gallery of Canada, Ottawa; Museum Purchase; inv. 6089

FIG. 91
Rembrandt van Rijn, *Daniel and Cyrus before the Idol Bel*, 1633, oil on panel, 23.5 x 30.2 cm (9 ¼ x 11 ⅞ in.). The J. Paul Getty Museum, Los Angeles; inv. 95.PB.15

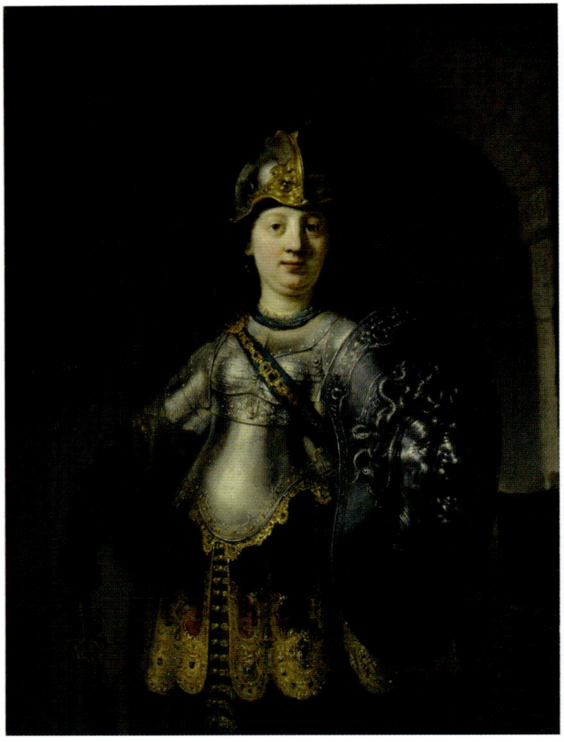

FIG. 92

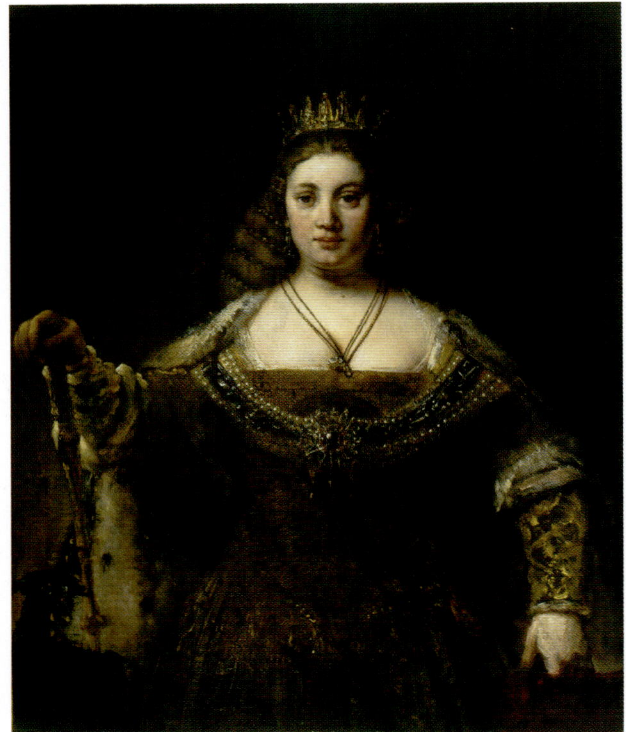

FIG. 93

Friesdam with his purchase of *Bellona* (FIG. 92) in the early 1920s. The interest was revived more than a half-century later when Armand Hammer made headlines with the acquisition of *Juno* (FIG. 93) for a record Rembrandt price, and has continued into the present century with the arrival in America of *Minerva in Her Study* (PLATE 50).

Minerva in Her Study emerged from shadows of a Scottish collection less than a century ago. Traveling through various private collections in the years since, evidence suggests the work may have been in the New York collection of Jules S. Bache in 1929.[49] More recently, the painting was on loan from a Japanese corporation to the Bridgestone Museum of Art in Tokyo between 1988 and 2001. Its current American owner purchased it from the Japanese in 2001.

Minerva (Pallas Athena in Greek) appears as a golden-haired beauty in her role as goddess of wisdom. She is also known as the goddess of victory in war and peace, and quite appropriately as a protector of painters. Here, Rembrandt strove to represent the multifaceted nature of the goddess. She stands before the viewer with a striking physical presence and monumentality; among the objects discarded in the right background are her shield, helmet, and spear. Like so many of Rembrandt's pictures, scholars have raised authorship and whether or not the figure represented is Saskia.[50]

Signed and dated 1635, the work fits comfortably with the handful of other images of life-sized female historical figures from the painter's early years in Amsterdam, including *Bellona* from two years earlier. Each is marked by a bold and textured application of paint, and dramatic contrasts of light and shadow with strong three-dimensional effects. *Minerva* displays both warm and cool harmonies, and a limited palette centering on creams, grays, and rusty browns.

Valentiner introduced the painting to the art world in the mid-1920s, and as one might expect, he saw it as autograph. Its theatrical undercurrent prompted him to see her as having "descended from the stage."[51] Over the decades others either ignored the painting or questioned the attribution to Rembrandt. Any confusion about the picture's authorship seems to have been laid to rest after extensive examination by the Rembrandt Research Project. In its summary, the RRP found that *Minerva in Her Study* represents a "wholly autograph work from the 1635."[52] A recent cleaning of the picture only served to reinforce that conclusion and to highlight the excellent condition of the paint surface.

Minerva in Her Study comes from the same private collector who so generously lent a number of other Rembrandt paintings to the exhibition. Among these loans are the *Three Singers (Hearing)*

FIG. 92
Rembrandt van Rijn, *Bellona*, 1633, oil on canvas, 127 x 97.5 cm (50 x 38 3/8 in.). The Metropolitan Museum of Art, New York; the Friedsam Collection, Bequest of Michael Friedsam; 1931 31.100.23

FIG. 93
Rembrandt van Rijn, *Juno*, c. 1662–65, oil on canvas, 127.1 x 107 cm (50 x 42 1/8 in.). The Armand Hammer Collection, Los Angeles; Gift of the Armand Hammer Foundation

and *The Operation (Touch)* (see PLATES 18, 19, pp. 90, 91), two pictures from an incomplete set of the five senses painted by the young artist at the outset of his career. Both are discussed in Tom Rassieur's essay surveying Rembrandt's Leiden activity. As allegories, one can argue that *Hearing* and *Touch* fall within the realm of history painting. Regardless of their category, this pair of intriguing pictures again places a focus on collecting and connoisseurship, the core issues of this exhibition. As recent arrivals to our shores, and following decades of debate regarding their attribution to Rembrandt, they seem to have found a home within the painter's early oeuvre.[53]

Within the larger context of Rembrandt collecting, these two small panels, as well as *Minerva in Her Study* and a handful of other recent acquisitions, speak volumes about opportunities available in today's marketplace. The fact that a single collector has been able to amass a significant collection of Rembrandt paintings in just a few years will certainly come as a shock to most readers. But unlike the distant past when Benjamin Altman, Henry Clay Frick, Isabella Stewart Gardner, Joseph E. Widener, Andrew Mellon, and others competed in a robust market for comparatively large numbers of Rembrandt paintings, collectors today operate in a much smaller and more carefully policed arena. Still, opportunities such as *Minerva in Her Study* have not entirely disappeared from the art market. For the lucky few with the means to acquire pictures by the master, the story of Rembrandt paintings in America continues to be written.

NOTES

1 Broos 1993, p. 260.
2 One can define a history as any composition in which the human figure plays the main role and the subject matter is derived from the Bible, history, mythology, or literature, including allegory.
3 Lairesse 1707/1740, part 2, p. 5. For an overview of the theories pertaining to subject matter, see Blankert, in Washington, Detroit, Amsterdam 1980, pp. 15–33. This exhibition focused attention on the long-neglected subject of Dutch history painting from the seventeenth century.
4 Leiden 1991, p. 132. Huygens's autobiographical notes appear to have been written shortly after he visited Rembrandt and Lievens in the winter of 1628. They were first published in 1891. For a translation of the full text Rembrandt and Lievens, see ibid., pp. 132–34.
5 All these pictures and others discussed below are usually illustrated and discussed in the catalogues devoted to Rembrandt's paintings. For an excellent overview of this material, see Schwartz 2006.
6 In addition to these biblical examples, his much-truncated *Oath of Claudius Civilus*, now in Stockholm but originally commissioned for Amsterdam's new city hall, also falls into this category. See color illustration in ibid., fig. 308, p. 180.
7 The painting was in the collection of Carel F. de Wild, New York, during the second half of the 1910s. It then came to the New York art market before landing in the collection of Nils B. Hersloff, West Orange, N.J., and Stockbridge, Mass., by the 1930s. The painting was acquired by the Nationalmuseum, Stockholm, in 1949.
8 A lack of interest in religious pictures was not uncommon. Another case in point was an early disdain by American collectors for examples by Peter Paul Rubens whose Catholicism flavored his works. There were exceptions, however, most notably the purchases by John Ringling, of traveling circus fame.
9 The painting, after being on loan for decades, was given to the Mauritshuis, The Hague, following the death of Bredius in 1946. For a discussion of *Saul and David* within the context of American collecting, see Quodbach 2004–5, p. 106.
10 Elsewhere in this volume are discussions of the expansive nature of the oeuvre catalogues devoted to paintings by Rembrandt. The number of "autograph" pictures exceeded 700 in William Valentiner's catalogue of 1921. See Schwartz 2006 (pp. 14–15) for a graph charting the number of assigned pictures in the various catalogues.
11 See New York 1909 and Valentiner 1931 for discussions and illustrations of the paintings in question.
12 *The Jewish Bride*, c. 1665, may represent the biblical couple Isaac and Rebecca.
13 See discussion and color plate in The Hague and Schwerin 2004, no. 6, pp. 106–10. See also, in this volume, the discussion by George Keyes in his essay "Rembrandt Paintings and America," p. 61.
14 Valentiner 1934, 2: xxix and pl. 27, xxxi.
15 Keyes et al., 2004, p. 184.
16 Ibid.
17 Wheelock 1995, p. 248 (as part of the entry for the systematic catalogue *The Dutch Paintings of the Seventeenth Century* at the National Gallery of Art, pp. 247–52). In addition to *Philemon and Baucis*, the Wideners (in this case Joseph's father, Peter A. B. Widener), had acquired in 1912 another small history painting, *The Circumcision*, 1661, oil on canvas, inv. 1942.9.60.
18 Van Mander 1604/1618, "Uytleggingh op den *Metamorphosis*," chap. 8, folio 64.
19 Yerkes 1893, nos. 45–48. *Lazarus* is particularly noteworthy, as it represents a copy of a Rembrandt composition dating to about 1630/31. The autograph Rembrandt is in the collection of the Los Angeles County Museum of Art. It was a gift to LACMA from Howard F. Ahmanson & Company in 1972, having previously been in a Swiss collection until purchased by Ahmanson. The copy, previously owned by Yerkes, has found a home at the Art Institute of Chicago.
20 *Rembrandt's Late Religious Portraits* served as the title to a recent exhibition devoted to these paintings (Washington and Los Angeles 2005).
21 Valentiner 1920–21, pp. 219, 221.
22 Giltaij, in Frankfurt and Kyoto 2003, no. 44, pp. 222–24.
23 Sutton, in Washington and Los Angeles 2005, no. 13, cites the various arguments outlined here, and provides bibliographic sources.
24 For a discussion of the painting's history and recent conservation treatment, see Giltaij 2009.
25 Such works were thought to form either one or two series of apostles, an idea first suggested by William Valentiner in 1920–21 (see note 21 above). As Liedtke (San Diego 1996, p. 90) has noted, however, the works brought into such discussions "present so many problems of attribution, conflicting sizes, and contrasting compositions that the idea of an intended series remains completely hypothetical."
26 The *St. James the Major*, after a lengthy stay in America, was recently purchased by a private collector abroad when offered at a Sotheby's sale in New York on 25–26 January 2007. For a discussion of this picture, see the auction catalogue and Washington and Los Angeles 2005, no. 9.
27 Wheelock, in Washington and Los Angeles 2005, p. 80.
28 Ibid.
29 Illustrated and discussed in Liedtke 2007, 2: no. 154, pp. 669–76. Joining this exclusive club of single-figure female history pictures by Rembrandt in America was *Bellona*, representing the Roman goddess of war, a

purchase by Michael Friedsam in early 1920. Both *Bellona* and *Hendrickje Stoffels (as the Sorrowing Virgin)* have found permanent homes at the Metropolitan Museum of Art, New York.

30 Ibid, p. 661. It not surprising that features of both Saskia and Hendrickje Stoffels have been linked with the picture. Rembrandt collectors have long been drawn to compositions thought to feature portraits of Rembrandt or various family members.

31 For a discussion of *The Visitation*, see Keyes et al. 2004, no. 71, pp. 172–75. This picture represents a rare example from the first half of the twentieth century in which an acquisition by a museum came as a purchase rather than a gift. By comparison, all the Rembrandts acquired by the Metropolitan Museum of Art and the National Gallery of Art came via gifts. The only exception is *Aristotle with a Bust of Homer*, a purchase by the Met in 1961 for a record price of $2,300,000 (see fig. 2, p. 20).

32 Gerson/Bredius 1969, no. 584, p. 610.

33 Rosenberg 1948 (rev. ed. 1964, p. 220).

34 Ibid.

35 Wheelock 1995, p. 307.

36 In addition to the spurious signature, the picture shows a date of 1650.

37 Interestingly, Ringling had also purchased another "Rembrandt" during his lifetime. *An Evangelist Writing (St. John?)* did not remain in his collection following his death. Today, it is housed at the Museum of Fine Arts, Boston, inv. 39.581, where it is catalogued as an "Imitator of Rembrandt."

38 Judson, in Chicago 1969, pp. 43–44.

39 Bikker 2005, R4, pp. 133–34.

40 Weller 2009, pp. 109–10.

41 Translation from Leiden 1991, p. 132 (see note 4 above).

42 Ibid.

43 Horst Gerson's revision of Bredius (Gerson/Bredius 1969), and especially the results of the ongoing Rembrandt Research Project (RRP), have removed scores of misattributed pictures from Rembrandt's oeuvre.

44 Another painting now at the National Gallery of Canada also needs to be mentioned within the context of Rembrandt's history paintings. In 1967 the same institution acquired *The Tribute Money* as a Rembrandt. The picture can no longer be assigned to him. The work is discussed by the RRP (Corpus 1982–89, 1: C7, pp. 488–96).

45 It should be noted that the St. Bartholomew painting was previously thought to represent either a genre figure or a portrait. For reasons outlined below, the identification of the saint now seems secure. Interestingly, and until it was recently downgraded to "attributed to Rembrandt," a third image of St. Bartholomew thought to be by Rembrandt had found a home in an American museum (*St. Bartholomew*, c. 1633, oil on panel, Worcester Art Museum).

46 Anne T. Woollett, in Washington and Los Angeles 2005, p. 101.

47 Gerson/Bredius 1969, no. 616, p. 613.

48 Chicago 1969, no. 19, p. 40.

49 The evidence of the Bache ownership comes from a photo mount housed at the Frick Art Reference Library, New York.

50 Manuth and De Winkel 2002, p. 12.

51 Valentiner 1925–26, p. 270.

52 Corpus 1982–89, 3: p. 174.

53 In volume one of the Corpus (1982, B1 and B2), the pair fell into the "B" category in which authorship by Rembrandt could not "be positively either accepted or rejected." In the years since, opinions have moved toward accepting them as autograph examples by Rembrandt.

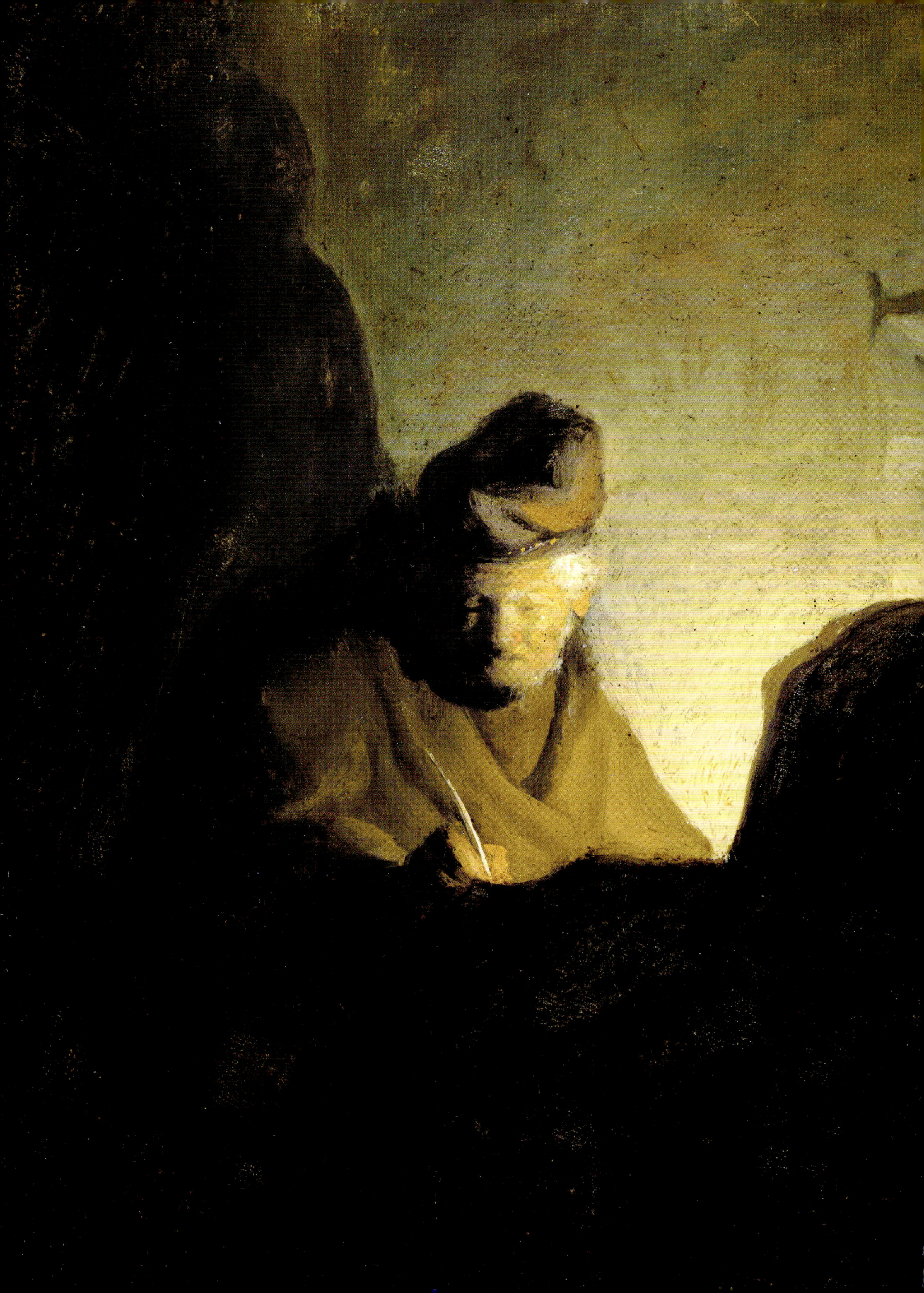

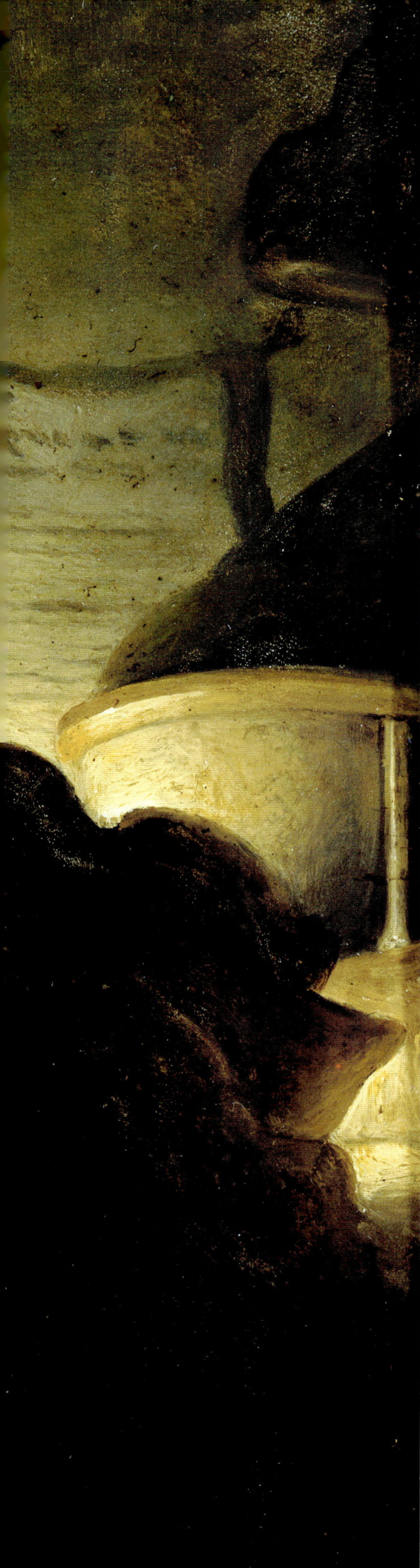

Catalogue of the Exhibition

Compiled by DENNIS P. WELLER

The following entries provide basic catalogue information for the exhibited paintings. Within each grouping the material is organized chronologically by artist, title of work, inscriptions, date, support, dimensions (fractions are rounded up to the nearest eighth), current location, provenance (beginning with ownership just prior to entering an American collection), selected exhibitions, and selected literature. The exhibitions and literature listings also focus on the period after the paintings came to America. Pictures previously but no longer considered as autograph paintings by Rembrandt have been integrated with accepted examples by the master. They are presented in three groupings—the Leiden Years, Amsterdam Portraiture, and History Paintings.

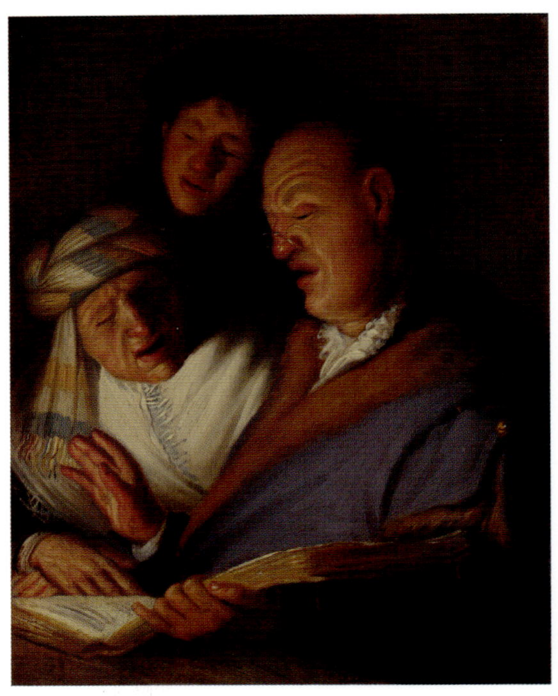

CAT. 1

Rembrandt van Rijn
The Three Singers (Hearing), c. 1624/25
Oil on oak, 21.6 x 17.8 cm (8 ½ x 7 in.)
Private collection, New York
PLATE 18

Inscriptions
None

Provenance
Collection Dr. C. J. K. van Aalst, Hoevelaken, by 1935; (Hans Cramer, The Hague, 1965–79). Dutch private collector, by 1995; (Johnny van Haeften, London, by 2007); acquired by the current owner, December 2007.

Selected Exhibitions
Leiden 1956, no. 2; Leiden 1976, no. S28a; Montreal and Toronto 1969, no. 2; Stockholm 1992, no. 46; Kassel and Amsterdam 2001, no. 9.

Selected Literature
Bredius 1936, no. 421; Gerson/Bredius 1969, no. 421A; Schwartz 1985, p. 34; Tümpel 1986, no. A28; Corpus 1982–89, 1: no. B1, pp. 399–404; Corpus 2005, p. 627.

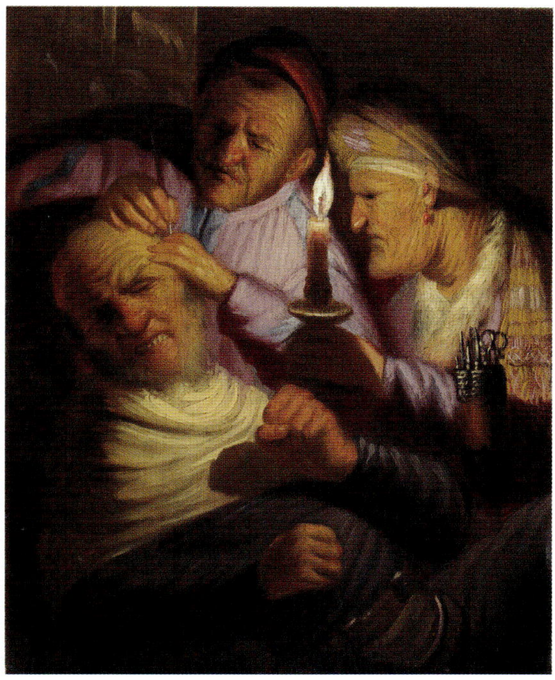

CAT. 2

Rembrandt van Rijn
The Operation (Touch), c. 1624/25
Oil on oak, 21.5 x 17.7 cm (8½ x 7 in.)
Private collection, New York
PLATE 19

Inscriptions
None

Provenance
Collection Dr. C. J. K. van Aalst, Hoevelaken, by 1939; (art dealer, Hans Cramer, The Hague, 1968–79). English private collection, by 1995; (sale, Christie's, New York, 7 July 1995, lot 57); acquired by the current owner, January 2007.

Selected Exhibitions
Leiden 1956, no. 3; Leiden 1976, no. S28b; Stockholm 1992, no. 47.

Selected Literature
Gerson/Bredius 1969, no. 421A; Schwartz 1985, p. 34; Tümpel 1986, no. A27; Corpus 1982–89, 1: no. B2, pp. 405–7; Kassel and Amsterdam 2001, no. 10 (not in exhibition); Corpus 2005, p. 627.

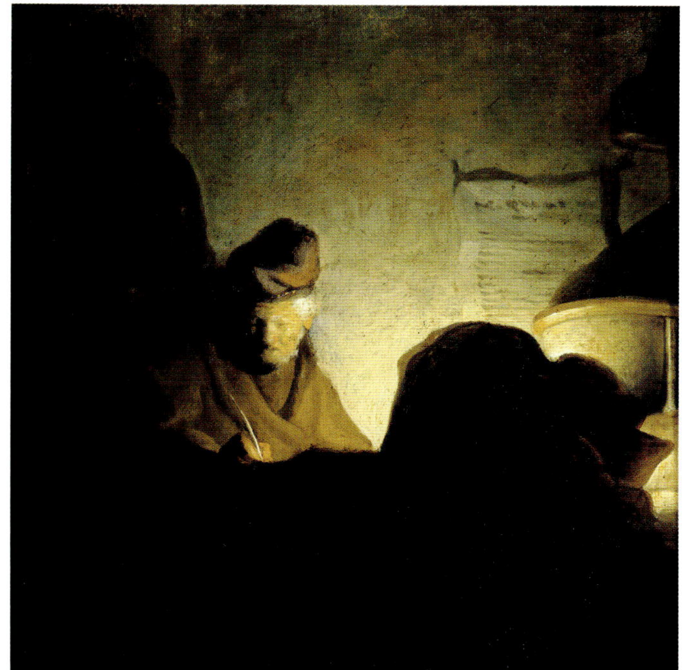

CAT. 3

Rembrandt van Rijn (attributed to)
A Scholar by Candlelight, c. 1628/29
Oil on copper, 13.9 x 13.9 cm (5½ x 5½ in.)
Collection of Isabel and Alfred Bader, Milwaukee
PLATE 20

Inscriptions
None

Provenance
Collection Norbert Mayer; acquired by current owner in 1959.

Selected Exhibitions
Amsterdam 1898, no. 1; Kingston 1984, no. 7; Yokohama, Fukuoka, Kyoto 1986, no. 3; Milwaukee 1989, no. 12; Kingston 1996, no. 14; Boston 2000, no. 20 (as Circle of Rembrandt); Kassel and Amsterdam 2001, no. 59 (as Circle of Rembrandt).

Selected Literature
Smith 1829–42, 7: no. 185, pp. 76–77; Hofstede de Groot 1908–27, 6: no. 240, p. 153; Valentiner 1909, p. 14; Bredius 1936, no. 425; Gerson/Bredius 1969, no. 425, pp. 541, 588; Corpus 1982–89: 1: no. C18, pp. 554–58; De Witt 2008, no. 164, pp. 269–72.

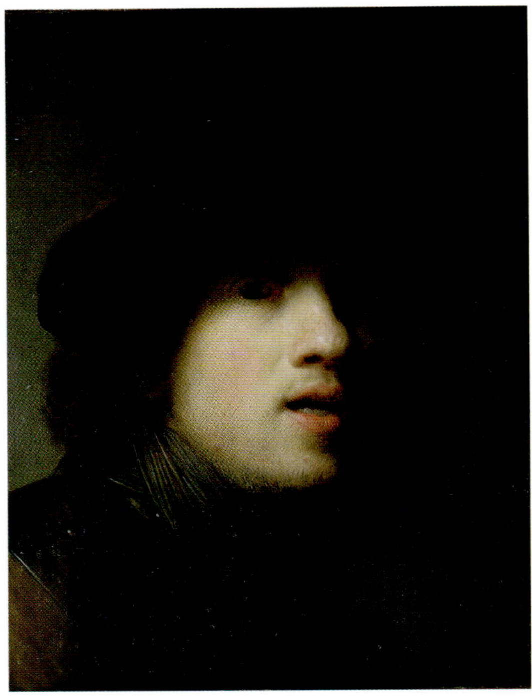

CAT. 4

Rembrandt van Rijn
Self-portrait (Study in a Mirror), c. 1629
Oil on panel, 44.5 x 34.3 cm (17 ½ x 13 ½ in.)
Indianapolis Museum of Art, The Clowes Fund Collection
Raleigh only
PLATE 21

Inscriptions
At lower right: *RHL* [in ligature]

Provenance
(Frederick Mont and Newhouse Galleries, Inc., New York, 1951); Dr. G. H. A. Clowes (1877–1958), Indianapolis; The Clowes Fund Collection, Indianapolis, 1959–present, the Indianapolis Museum of Art.

Selected Exhibitions
New York, Toledo, Toronto 1954, no. 60; Raleigh 1956, no. 3; Indianapolis and San Diego 1958, no. 2; London and The Hague 1999, no. 8; Indianapolis 2006, no. 1; Cincinnati 2008, no. 1.

Selected Literature
Bode 1897–1906, 8: no. 546; Hofstede de Groot 1908–27, 6: no. 549; Bredius 1936, no. 3; Bauch 1966, no. 289; Gerson/Bredius 1969, no. 3; Corpus 1982–89, 1: pp. 235–40 (under A22); Chapman 1990, pp. 146–47; Corpus 2005, Corrigenda, pp. 598–601.

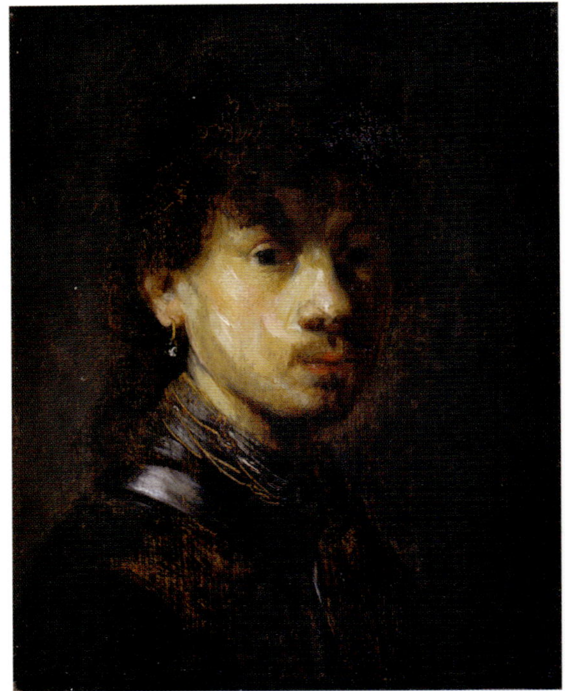

CAT. 5

Rembrandt van Rijn (imitator of)
Bust of a Young Man, after 1629
Oil on oak, 22.9 x 18.3 cm (9 x 7 ¼ in.)
Fogg Art Museum, Harvard University, Cambridge, Bequest of James P. Warburg, 1969.56
PLATE 22

Inscriptions
On right above neck in black: *RHL 1629*

Provenance
(Thomas Agnew & Sons, London, before 1926); Paul M. Warburg, New York, 1929; gift to the Fogg Art Museum, Harvard University, 1969.

Selected Exhibitions
Detroit 1930, no. 1 (as Self-portrait); Cambridge 1969; New York 1973; Cambridge 1977.

Selected Literature
Valentiner 1926, pp. 117–19; Valentiner 1931, no. 3, pl. 3; Bredius 1936, no. 4; Bauch 1966, no. 291; Gerson/Bredius 1969, no. 4, pp. 4, 547; Corpus 1982–89, 1: no. C35, pp. 633–37; Bowron 1990, no. 122, p. 177.

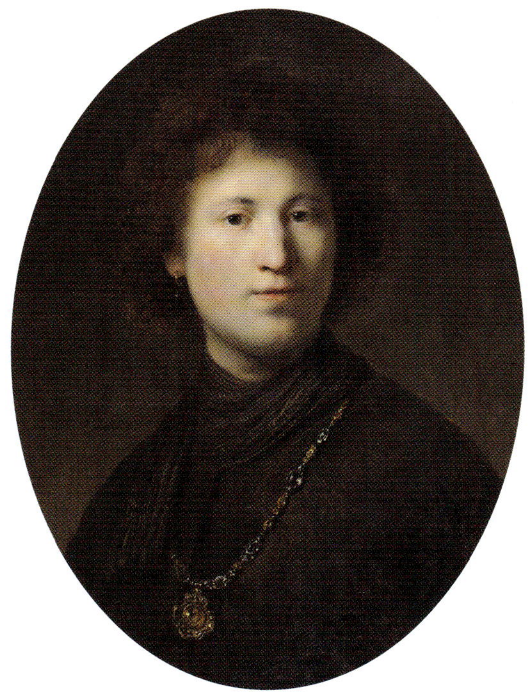

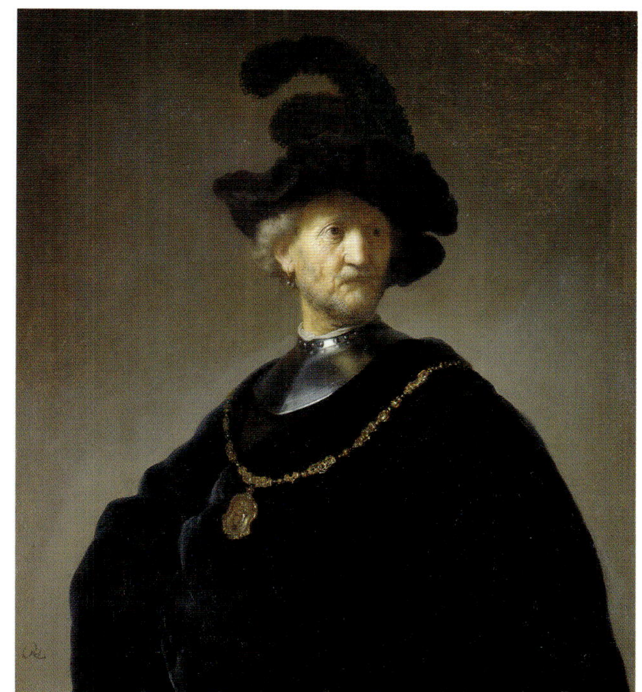

CAT. 6

Rembrandt van Rijn and workshop
Bust of a Young Man with a Gold Chain, c. 1629 or 1632
Oil on oval panel, 57.7 x 43.9 cm (22 ¾ x 17 ¼ in.)
The Cleveland Museum of Art, Bequest of John L. Severance, 1942.644
PLATE 23

Inscriptions
At center right edge: *RHL* [in ligature] *van Rijn 1632*

Provenance
(Knoedler & Co., London); John L. Severance, Cleveland, 1921; his estate; 1936, his bequest to the Cleveland Museum of Art, 1936.

Selected Exhibitions
Detroit 1930, no. 11.

Selected Literature
Hofstede de Groot 1908–27, 6: nos. 557, 558; Valentiner 1921, p. 23 (as Self-portrait); Valentiner 1931, no. 16; Bredius 1936, no. 156, p. 7; Bauch 1966, no. 142, p. 9; Gerson/Bredius 1969, no. 156, p. 135; Cleveland 1982, no. 111, pp. 254–56; Corpus 1982–89, 1: no. A23, pp. 246; 2: Corrigenda, p. 838; Cleveland 1993, p. 193.

CAT. 7

Rembrandt van Rijn
Old Man with a Gold Chain, c. 1631
Oil on panel, 83.1 x 75.7 cm (32 ¾ x 29 ¾ in.)
Mr. and Mrs. W. W. Kimball Collection
The Art Institute of Chicago, 1922.4467
Minneapolis only
PLATE 24

Inscriptions
At lower left: *RHL*

Provenance
(Julius Böhler, Munich, by 1913); (H. Reinhardt, New York, 1913 or 1914); Evalyne M. Cone Kimball (d. 1921), Chicago, by 1914; her bequest to the Art Institute of Chicago, 1922.

Selected Exhibitions
Detroit 1930, no. 8; Chicago and Worcester 1935; New York 1950, no. 2; Boston and Chicago 2003, no. 30.

Selected Literature
Hofstede de Groot 1908–27, 6: no. 675, pp. 321–22; Valentiner 1921, no. 19, pp. xvi, 17; Valentiner 1931, no. 5; Bredius 1936, no. 81; Rosenberg 1964, pp. 43, 71, 256, fig. 60; Bauch 1966, no. 129, p. 9; Gerson/Bredius 1969, no. 81, pp. 73, 554; Corpus 1982–89, 1: no. A42; Schwartz 1985, p. 65, fig. 54; Boston 2000, p. 123 (illus. p. 121).

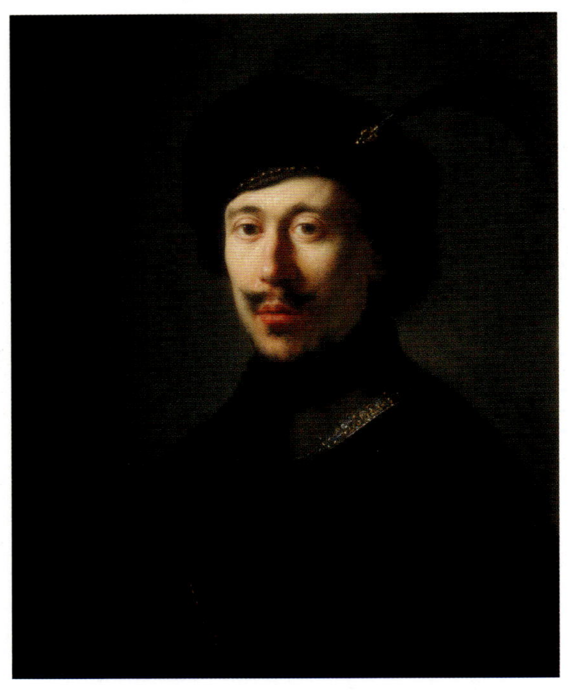

CAT. 8

Rembrandt van Rijn (workshop of; Isaac de Joudreville?)
Bust of a Young Man in a Gorget and Plumed Cap, c. 1631/32
Oil on oak, 57.7 x 46 cm (22¾ x 18⅛ in.)
The San Diego Museum of Art, anonymous gift to Fine Arts Gallery, San Diego, 1939
PLATE 3

Inscriptions
At bottom left: *RHL 1631*

Provenance
(Eugene Glaenzer & Co., New York, 1906); Henry Reinhardt, 1906; Frank G. Logan, Chicago, 1906–39; (Robert C. Vose Galleries, Boston, 1939); Anne R. and Amy Putnam, San Diego, for the Fine Arts Gallery, San Diego, 1939 (1939:019).

Selected Exhibitions
New York 1909, no. 76; Detroit 1930, no. 8; Los Angeles 1947, no. 5.

Selected Literature
Hofstede de Groot 1908–27, 6: no. 375a; Valentiner 1931, no. 11 (as Self-portrait); Bredius 1936, no. 144; Bauch 1966, no. 137; Gerson/Bredius 1969, no. 144; Corpus 1982–89, 2: no. C55, pp. 659–65.

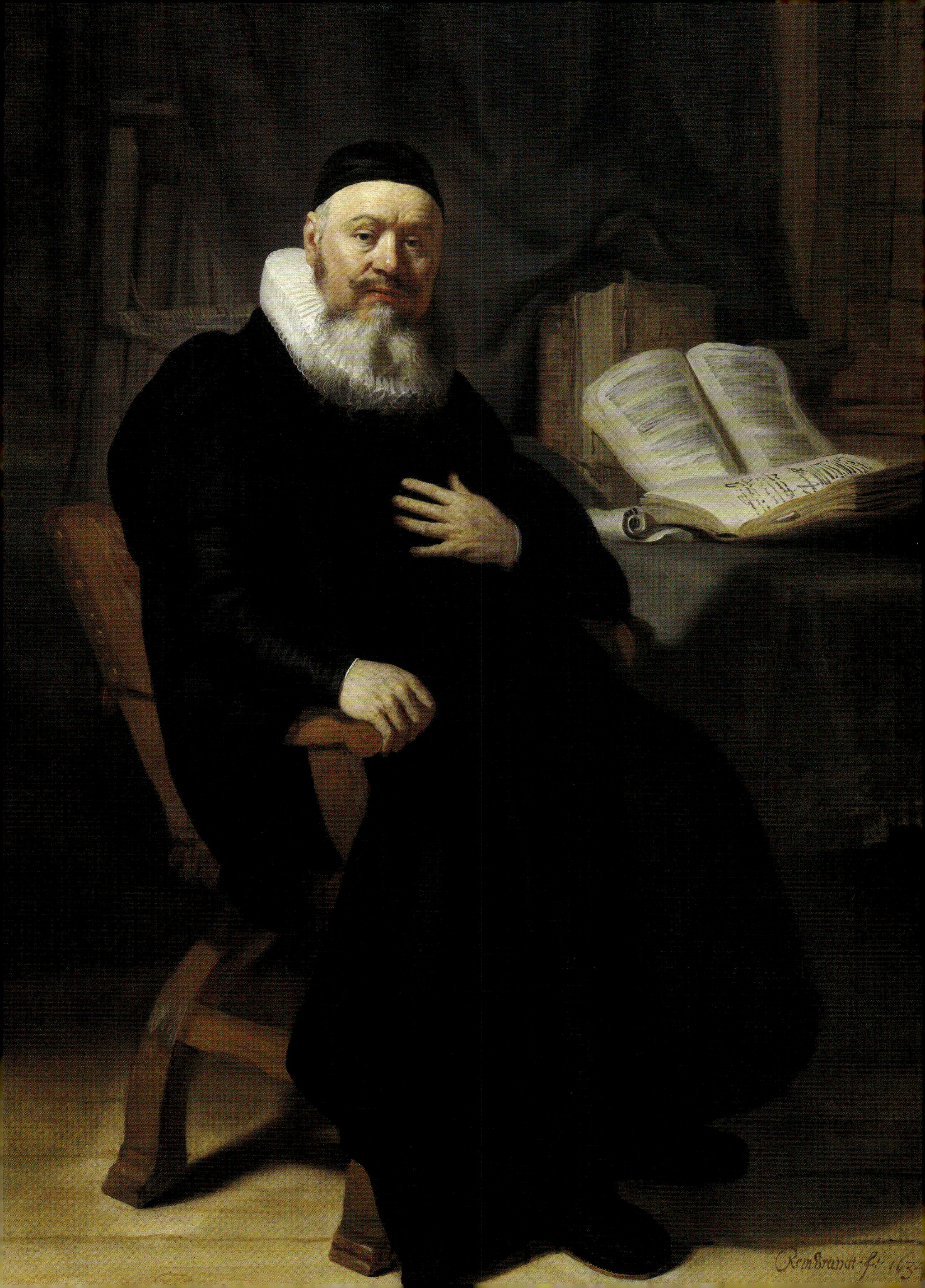
Rembrandt f. 1634

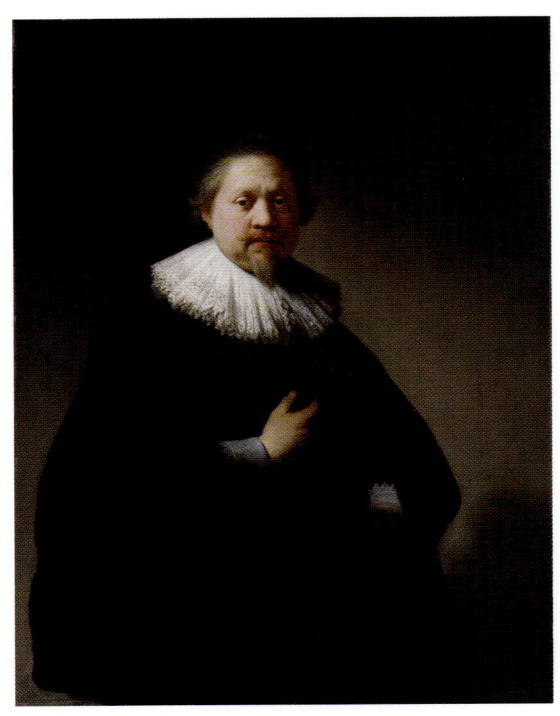

CAT. 9

Rembrandt van Rijn
Portrait of a Man, Probably a Member of the Van Beresteyn Family, 1632
Oil on canvas, 111.8 x 88.9 cm (44 x 35 in.)
The Metropolitan Museum of Art, New York; H. O. Havemeyer Collection, Bequest of Mrs. H. O. Havemeyer (29.100.3)
PLATE 10

Inscriptions
Lower right: *RHL van Rijn / 1632*

Provenance
(Cottier & Co., London and New York, 1888); sold 8 December 1888 to H. O. Havemeyer (1847–1907), New York; by inheritance to his wife, Mrs. H. O. Havemeyer (d. 1929), New York; bequest to the Metropolitan Museum of Art, 1929.

Selected Exhibitions
New York 1890, no. 5; Birmingham 1951, unnumbered; Chattanooga 1952, unnumbered; New York 1973, no. 5; New York 1993, no. A445; New York 1996, no. 3.

Selected Literature
Bode 1897–1906, 2: no. 82, pl. 82, pp. 6, 44, 46; Valentiner 1909, pp. 74 (ill.), 551, 568; Hofstede de Groot 1908–27, 6: no. 624, p. 301; Valentiner 1931, no. 23, pl. 23; Bredius 1936, no. 167, p. 8; Bauch 1966, no. 360, pl. 360, p. 19; Gerson/Bredius 1969, no. 167, pp. 142 (ill.), 561, 576 (under no. 331); Schwartz 1985, p. 163, fig. 159; Corpus 1982–89, 2: no. C68 (as not by Rembrandt), pp. 26, 38, 74, 740–51; Tümpel 1986, no. A81 (as Rembrandt workshop), pp. 82 (ill.), 428–29, 431; Liedtke 2007, pp. 568–83 (and pages for pendant below).

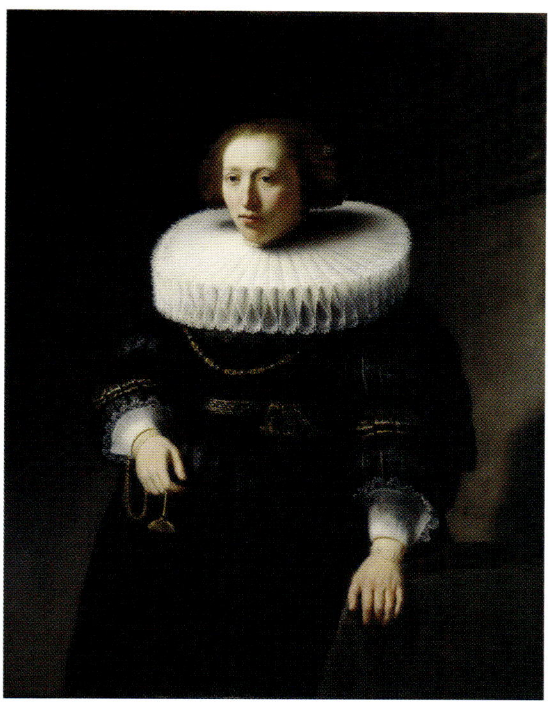

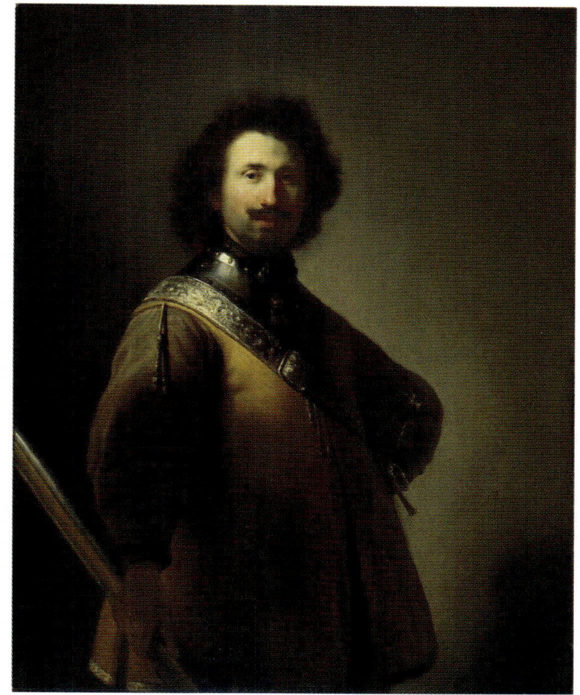

CAT. 10

Rembrandt van Rijn
Portrait of a Woman, Probably a Member of the Van Beresteyn Family, 1632
Oil on canvas, 111.8 x 88.9 cm (44 x 35 in.)
The Metropolitan Museum of Art, New York; H. O. Havemeyer Collection, Bequest of Mrs. H. O. Havemeyer (29.100.4)
PLATE 11

Inscriptions
Lower right: *RHL· van Rijn / 1632*

Provenance
(Cottier & Co., London and New York, 1888); sold on 8 December 1888 to H. O. Havemeyer (1847–1907), New York; by inheritance to his wife, Mrs. H. O. Havemeyer (d. 1929), New York; bequest to the Metropolitan Museum of Art, 1929.

Selected Exhibitions
New York 1890, no. 8; Toronto 1950, no. 36; Birmingham 1951, unnumbered; Chattanooga 1952, unnumbered; New York 1973, no. 5; Bordeaux 1981, no. 106; New York 1993, no. A446; New York 1995, no. 4.

Selected Literature
Bode 1897–1906, 2: no. 83, pl. 83, pp. 6, 44, 46; Valentiner 1909, pp. 75 (ill.), 551, 568; Hofstede de Groot 1908–27, 6: no. 625, pp. 301–2; Valentiner 1931, no. 24, pl. 24; Bredius 1936, no. 331, p. 14, pl. 331; Bauch 1966, no. 459, pl. 459, p. 24; Gerson/Bredius 1969, pp. 262 (ill.), 561 (under no. 167); Schwartz 1985, p. 163, figs. 160, 161; Corpus 1982–89, 2: no. C69 (as not by Rembrandt), pp. 26, 38, 73–74, 740, 742–43, 747–59; Tümpel 1986, no. A103 (as Rembrandt workshop), pp. 83 (ill.), 429, 431; Liedtke 2007, pp. 583–84 (and pages for pendant above).

CAT. 11

Rembrandt van Rijn
Joris de Caulerij, 1632
Oil on canvas, transferred to panel, 102.9 x 84.3 cm (40½ x 33¼ in.)
Fine Arts Museums of San Francisco, Legion of Honor; Roscoe and Margaret Oakes Collection (66.31)
PLATE 12

Inscriptions
At lower right: *RHL. van Ryn / 1632* [RHL in ligature]

Provenance
(A. Preyer, Amsterdam, 1890); Charles T. Yerkes (1839–1905), Chicago, 1890–1905; (sale, New York, American Art Association, 5–8 April 1910, lot 84); (Jacques Seligmann, Paris and New York, 1910–11); G. Rassmussen, Chicago, by 1925; (John Levy Galleries, New York, 1937); Edwin D. Levinson, New York, 1937–54; by inheritance to his daughters Mrs. Edna (Levinson) Ripin and Mrs. Evelyn A. (Levinson) Stein, New York, 1954–55; (Knoedler & Co., New York, 1955, consignment from the Levinson estate through Julius H. Weitzer, New York); Roscoe and Margaret Oakes, San Francisco, 1955; Fine Arts Museums of San Francisco (previously the M. H. de Young Memorial Museum), gift of the Roscoe and Margaret Oakes Foundation, 1966.

Selected Exhibitions
New York 1940, no. 86; The Hague and San Francisco 1990, no. 50; Amsterdam 2006B, no. 20; The Hague and London 2007, no. 51.

Selected Literature
Yerkes 1893, no. 48; Bode 1897–1906, 2: no. 84, pp. 49–50; Hofstede de Groot 1908–27, 6: no. 633, p. 270; Valentiner 1931, no. 21; Bredius 1936, no. 170; Gerson/Bredius 1969, no. 170, pp. 145, 562; Corpus 1982–89, 2: no. A53, pp. 7, 8, 26, 92, 97, 106, 199–205; Tümpel 1986, no. 196, pp. 99, 412; Van der Veen, in London and Amsterdam 2006, pp. 135–36.

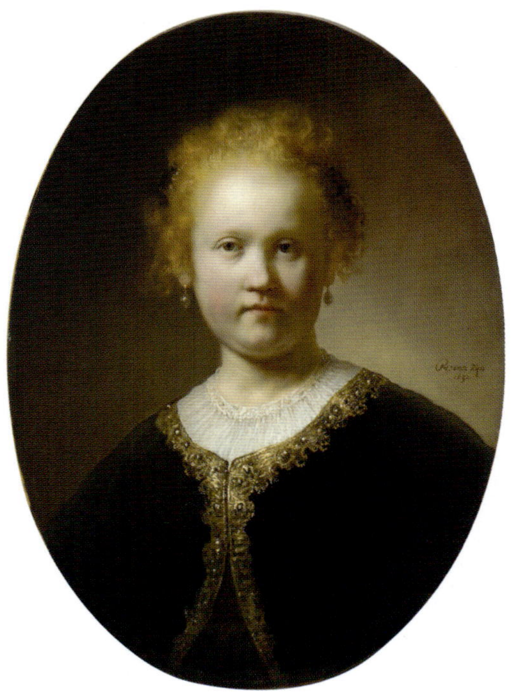

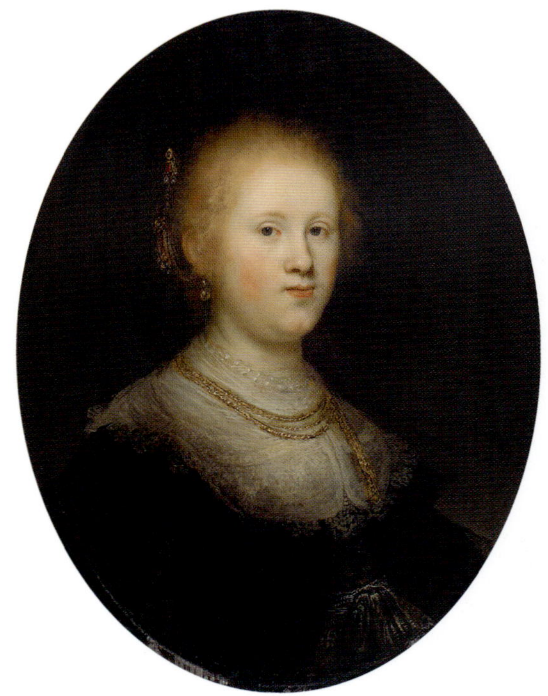

CAT. 12

Rembrandt van Rijn
Portrait of a Girl Wearing a Gold-trimmed Cloak, 1632
Oil on oval panel, 59 x 44 cm (23 ¾ x 16 ⅞ in.)
Private collection, New York
PLATE 5

Inscriptions
At center right: *RHL van Rijn / 1632*

Provenance
Rt. Rev. Dr. Georgius Schmid von Grüneck, Chur, Switzerland, 1908–32; (consigned to Robert C. Vose, Boston, 1929); Robert Treat Paine II (d. 1943), Boston; by descent; (sale, Sotheby's, London, 10 December 1986, lot 44); private collection, 1986–2008; acquired by current owner, 2008.

Selected Exhibitions
Chicago and Worcester 1935, no. 3; Long-term loan to the Museum of Fine Arts, Boston, 1966–86.

Selected Literature
Hofstede de Groot 1908–27, 6: no. 699; Valentiner 1909, no. 56; Valentiner 1931, no. 17; Bredius 1936, no. 89; Bauch 1966, no. 452; Gerson/Bredius 1969, no. 89; Corpus 1982–89, 2: no. A50, pp. 166–71; Tümpel 1986, no. 227; Corpus 2005, pp. 629, 632 fig. 4.

CAT. 13

Rembrandt van Rijn (workshop of)
Portrait of a Young Woman, 1632
Oil on oval panel, 63.8 x 49.2 cm (25 ⅛ x 19 ⅜ in.)
Allentown Art Museum, Samuel H. Kress Collection, 1961 (inv. 61.35)
PLATE 6

Inscriptions
At lower right: *RHL van Rijn / 1632*

Provenance
A. Contini-Bonacossi (d. 1955), Rome, by 1928; Samuel H. Kress, New York, 1928; Kress Foundation gift to the Allentown Art Museum, 1961.

Selected Exhibitions
Detroit 1930, no. 13; New York 1933, no. 2; Indianapolis 1937, no. 58; New York 1940, no. 85; New York 1942B, no. 40; New York 1950, no. 6; Tucson 1951, no. 16.

Selected Literature
Hofstede de Groot 1908–27, 6: no. 696; Valentiner 1931, no. 19; Bredius 1936, no. 86; Allentown 1960, pp. 116–19; Bauch 1966, no. 453; Gerson/Bredius 1969, no. 86; Eisler 1977, no. K39 (as attributed to Rembrandt), pp. 136–38, fig. 125; Corpus 1982–89, 2: no. C59.

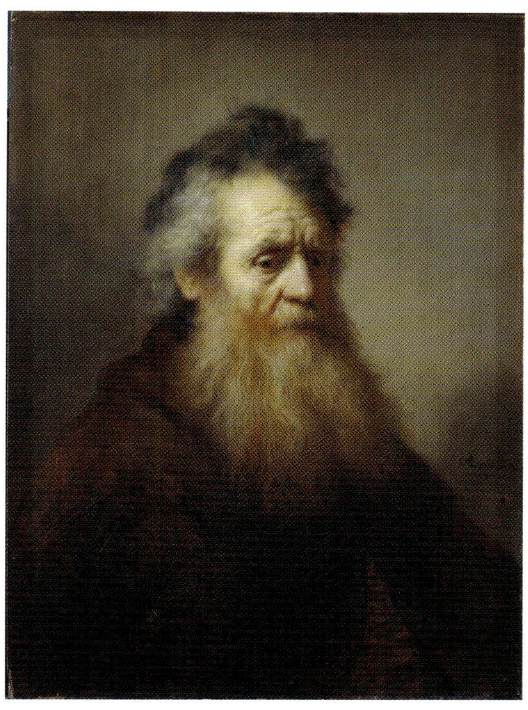

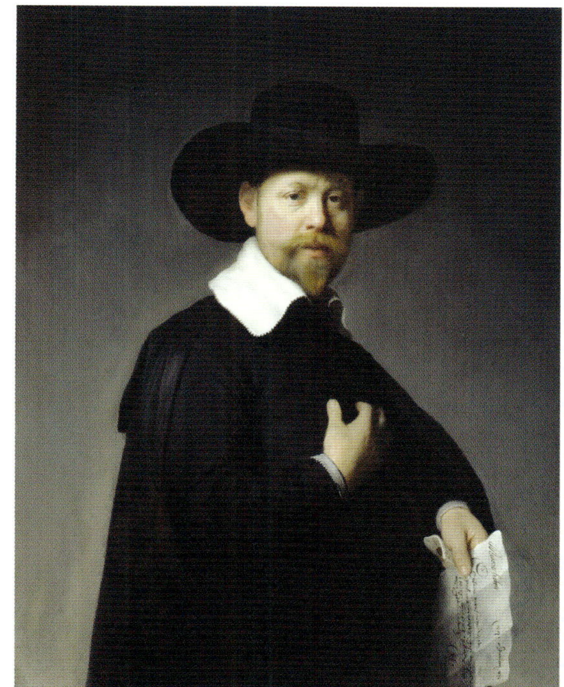

CAT. 14

Rembrandt van Rijn
Portrait of an Old Man, 1632
Oil on cradled oak, 66.9 x 50.7 cm (26 3/8 x 20 in.)
Fogg Art Museum, Harvard University, Cambridge, Bequest of Nettie G. Naumburg (1930.191)
PLATE 25

Inscriptions
At lower right: *RHL* [in monogram] *van Ryn / 1632*

Provenance
Collection Grand Dukes of Oldenburg, by 1823 and until after World War I; (Ehrich Galleries, New York, by 1928); Mrs. Aaron (Nettie G.) Naumburg, New York; gift to the Fogg Art Museum, 1930.

Selected Exhibitions
None

Selected Literature
Hofstede de Groot 1908–27, 6: no. 417; Bredius 1936, no. 147; Slive 1963, p. 137; Rosenberg 1964, p. 371; Bauch 1966, no. A8; Gerson/Bredius 1969, no. 147; Bauch 1977, no. A8 (as by Jacob Bacher and Rembrandt); Sumowski 1983, 4: no. 1919 (as anonymous Rembrandt school); Corpus 1982–89, 3: p. 24; Bowron 1990, no. 121, p. 126; Amsterdam and Berlin 2006, pp. 183–84, fig. 136.

CAT. 15

Rembrandt van Rijn
Portrait of Marten Looten, 1632
Oil on panel, 92.7 x 76.2 cm (36 1/2 x 30 in.)
Los Angeles County Museum of Art; Gift of J. Paul Getty, 53.50.3
PLATE 26

Inscriptions
On top of letter held by sitter: *Marten looten* [ ] *Jannuary 1632*
At bottom of letter: *RHL*

Provenance
A. W. M. Mensing, Amsterdam, before 1938; (sale, Amsterdam, Frederik Muller & Cie, 15 November 1938, lot 86); J. Paul Getty, Los Angeles; gift to the museum, 1953.

Selected Exhibitions
Amsterdam 1898, no. 20; Los Angeles 1947, no. 6; Raleigh 1956, no. 4; Los Angeles 2009, no. 8.

Selected Literature
Hofstede de Groot 1908–27, 6: no. 659; Bredius 1936, no. 166; Bauch 1966, no. 358; Gerson/Bredius 1969, no. 166; Corpus 1982–89, 2: no. A52, pp. 190–98; Tümpel 1986, no. 195; Los Angeles 1987, p. 82.

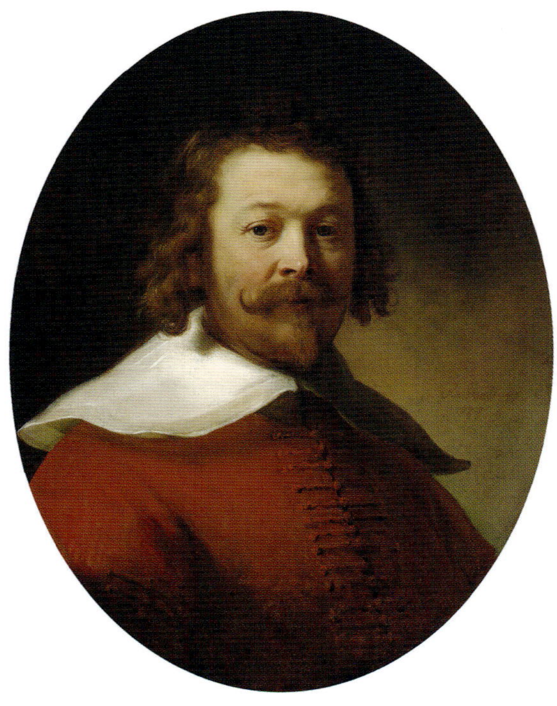

CAT. 16

Rembrandt van Rijn
Portrait of a Man in a Red Doublet, 1633
Oil on panel, 63.5 x 50.8 cm (25 x 20 in.)
Private collection, New York
PLATE 27

Inscriptions
At lower right: *Rembrandt · fec / 1633*

Provenance
(Vicars Brothers, London, 1929); (Howard Young Galleries, New York, by 1930); David Loew, Beverly Hills; (Findlay Gallery, New York, 1954); Amon Carter (1879–1955), Fort Worth; by descent; (sale, Sotheby's, New York, 30 January 1998, lot 18; acquired by Alfred Bader for Otto Naumann Ltd., New York); Bellagio Gallery of Fine Arts, Las Vegas, Nevada; (sale, Christie's, New York, 26 January 2001, lot 81); (Noortman Gallery, Maastricht); acquired by the current owner, January 2008.

Selected Exhibitions
(Listed in the literature as Detroit 1930, no. 23, but not in exhibition); The Bellagio Gallery of Fine Art, Las Vegas, 1999–2000; Denver and Newark 2001, no. 17a; London and Amsterdam 2006, fig. 89.

Selected Literature
Valentiner 1931, no. 37; Bredius 1936, no. 176; Bauch 1966, no. 364; Gerson/Bredius 1969, no. 176; Tümpel 1986, no. A83; Corpus 2005, Addendum 4, pp. 638–46.

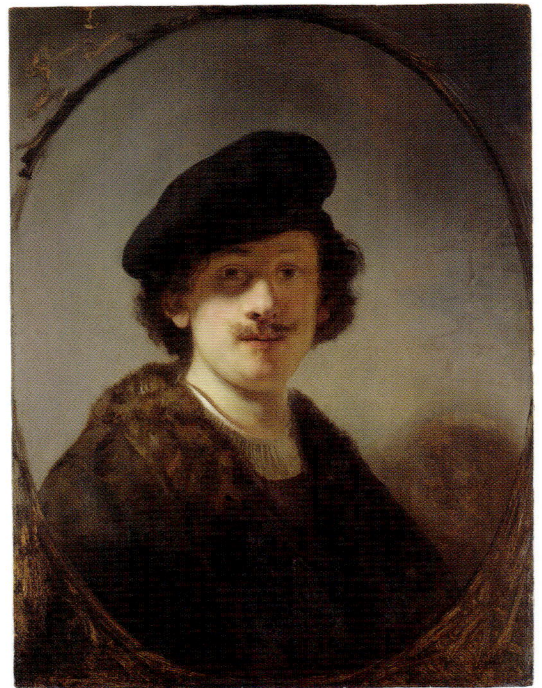

CAT. 17

Rembrandt van Rijn
Self-portrait with Shaded Eyes, 1634
Oil on panel, 70.8 x 55.2 cm (27 ⅞ x 21 ¾ in.)
Private collection, New York
PLATE 7

Inscriptions
At lower right: *Rembrandt · f* [three dots in triangle] / *1634*

Provenance
Paul Page, Moulins, France, 1966 and by descent; (sale, Sotheby's, London, 10 July 2003, lot 19); Steve Wynn, Las Vegas; acquired by current owner in February 2008.

Selected Exhibitions
Amsterdam 2003; extended loans to the Rembrandthuis, Amsterdam, 2003; Chrysler Museum, Norfolk, Virginia, 2009; the Ashmolean Museum, Oxford, 2010.

Selected Literature
Moltke 1965, no. 101 (as copy in style of Rembrandt), p. 247; Wetering 2002, pp. 16, 18–23; Corpus 2005, Addendum 2, pp. 615–26; Wetering 2008, pp. 212–13.

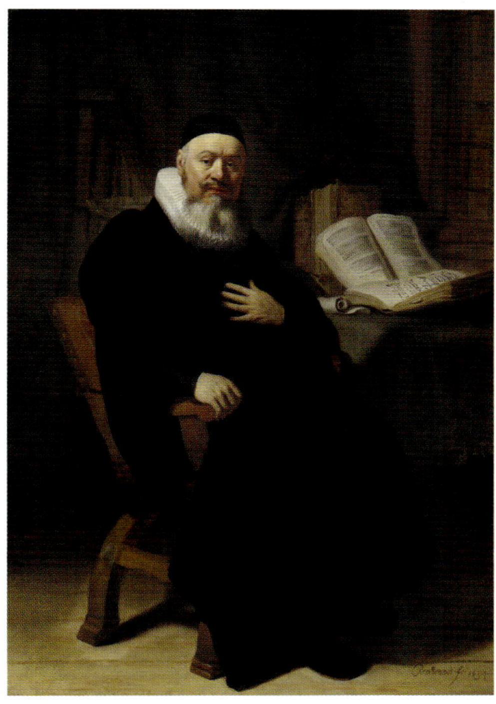

CAT. 18

Rembrandt van Rijn
Portrait of the Reverend Johannes Elison, 1634
Oil on canvas, 174.1 x 124.5 cm (68 ½ x 49 in.)
Museum of Fine Arts, Boston, William K. Richardson Fund, 56.510
PLATE 28

Inscriptions
Lower right: *Rembrandt · f[ ] · 1634*

Provenance
(Galerie Charpentier, Paris, by 1952); (Rosenberg and Stiebel, New York, by 1956); acquired by the Museum of Fine Arts, Boston, 1956.

Selected Exhibitions
New York 1950, no. 8; San Francisco 1966, no. 34.

Selected Literature
Hofstede de Groot 1908–27, 6: no. 645; Bredius 1936, no. 200; Rosenberg 1957; Bauch 1966, no. 372; Gerson/Bredius 1969, no. 200; Corpus 1982–89, 2: no. A98.

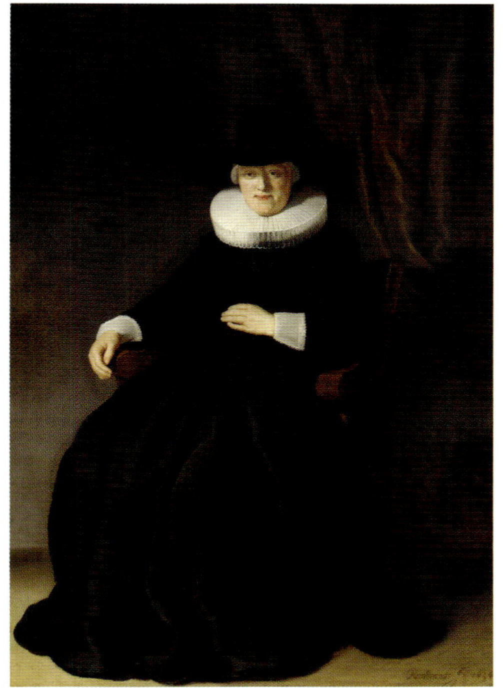

CAT. 19

Rembrandt van Rijn
Portrait of Maria Bockenolle (wife of Johannes Elison), 1634
Oil on canvas, 175.1 x 124.3 cm (68 ⅞ x 48 ⅞ in.)
Museum of Fine Arts, Boston, William K. Richardson Fund, 56.511
PLATE 29

Inscriptions
Lower right: *Rembrandt · f[ ] · 1634*

Provenance
(Galerie Charpentier, Paris, by 1952); (Rosenberg and Stiebel, New York, by 1956); acquired by the Museum of Fine Arts, Boston, 1956.

Selected Exhibitions
San Francisco 1966, no. 35.

Selected Literature
Hofstede de Groot 1908–27, 6: no. 646; Bredius 1936, no. 347; Rosenberg 1957; Bauch 1966, no. 477; Gerson/Bredius 1969, no. 347; Corpus 1982–89, 2: no. A99.

CAT. 20

Rembrandt van Rijn
Portrait of Anthonie Coopal, 1635
Oil on mahogany panel, 83.7 x 67 cm (32 7/8 x 26 3/8 in.)
Private collection, New York
PLATE 2

Inscriptions
At right: *Rembrandt·ft* [followed by three dots set as a triangle]/*1635*

Provenance
Baron Alphonse von Rothschild (d. 1942), Vienna; seized by Nazi forces in 1938 and later returned to the Rothschild family by Allied forces, 25 April 1946; (Frederick Mont, New York); Baron Neumann Collection, New York, by 1966; Mr. and Mrs. Charles H. N. De Vègvàr, Greenwich, Conn., 1969–2007; acquired by the current owner, 2007.

Selected Exhibitions
Long-term loan Museum of Fine Arts, Boston, 1984–2007; London and Amsterdam 2006, fig. 86; Hartford 2009, no. 2.

Selected Literature
Hofstede de Groot 1908–27, 6: no. 634; Bredius 1936, no. 203; Bauch 1966, no. 377; Gerson/Bredius 1969, no. 203; Schwartz 1985, no. 130; Tümpel 1986, no. A89; Corpus 1982–89, 3: no. C108, pp. 679–84 (as circle or workshop of Rembrandt).

CAT. 21

Rembrandt van Rijn and workshop
Portrait of a Woman, 1635 or earlier
Oil on oak panel, 77.5 x 64.8 cm (30 1/2 x 25 1/2 in.)
The Cleveland Museum of Art, The Elisabeth Severance Prentiss Collection, 1944.90
Cleveland and Minneapolis only
PLATE 13

Inscriptions
At right above shoulder: *Rembrandt. f. / 1635*

Provenance
Karl von der Heydt, Berlin, before 1898 and until at least 1908; (A. B. Antik, Stockholm, and Knoedler & Co., New York, by 1919); Elisabeth Severance Prentiss (1863–1944), Cleveland, 1919; bequest to the Cleveland Museum of Art, 1944.

Selected Exhibitions
Amsterdam 1898, no. 33; Los Angeles 1947, no. 12; New York 1950, unnumbered; Baltimore 1954, no. 81.

Selected Literature
Hofstede de Groot 1908–27, 6: no. 846; Valentiner 1931, no. 56; Bredius 1936, no. 350; Bauch 1966, no. 485; Gerson/Bredius 1969, no. 350; Cleveland 1982, no. 112; Corpus 1982–89, 2: no. C105; Cleveland 1993, p. 193.

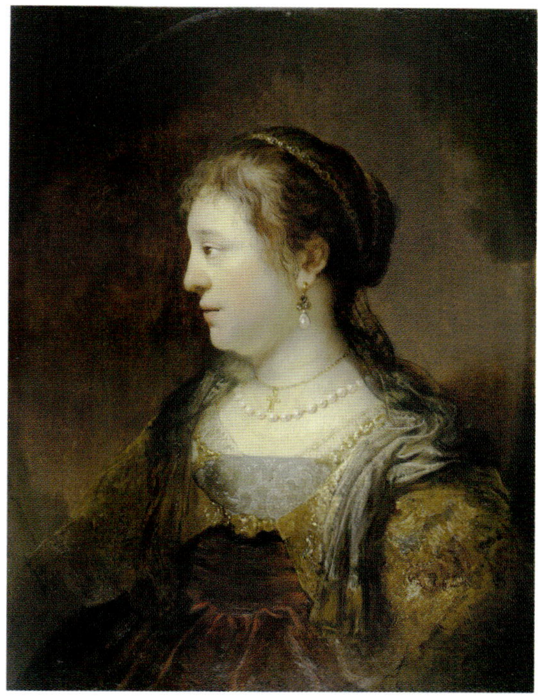

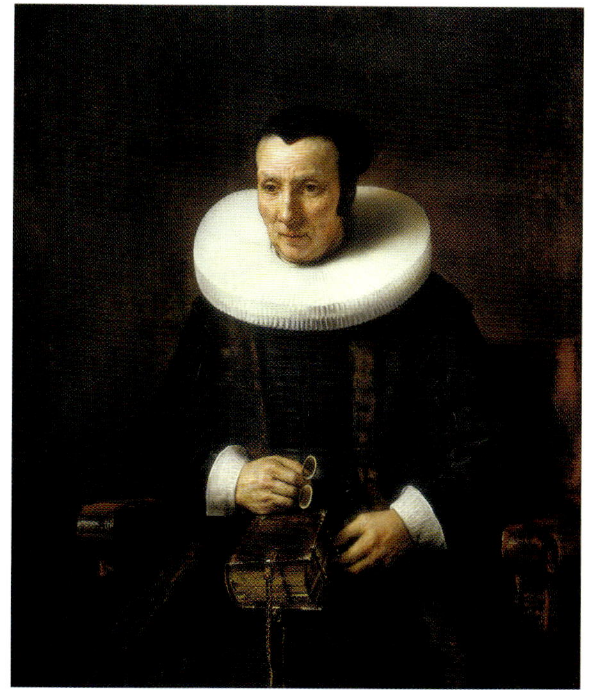

CAT. 22

Govaert Flinck (attributed to)
Portrait of a Woman in Profile (Saskia?), 1636
Oil on panel, 68.6 x 52.7 cm (27 x 20¾ in.)
Wadsworth Atheneum Museum of Art, Hartford, Gift in memory of Mae Cadwell Rovensky, 1961 (1961.191)
PLATE 16

Inscriptions
Faint signature at middle left: *Rembrandt. / f. 1636*

Provenance
Mrs. Samuel S. Joseph, London, by 1898; S. R. Berton, New York, by 1914; (Knoedler & Co., London, 1916); Mrs. William Hayward (formerly Mrs. Morton F. Plant), New York, by 1931; John E. Rovensky, Newport, R.I., and New York; gift to the Wadsworth Atheneum, 1961.

Selected Exhibitions
Hartford 2009, no. 8.

Selected Literature
Hofstede de Groot 1908–27, 6: no. 611; Valentiner 1909, pp. 130, 553; Valentiner 1931, no. 51; Bredius 1936, no. 105; Bauch 1966, no. 493; Gerson/Bredius 1969, no. 105; Hartford 1978, no. 120, pp. 175–77; Sumowski 1983, 5: no. 2082, p. 3099.

CAT. 23

Rembrandt van Rijn and workshop
An Old Lady with a Book, 1637
Oil on canvas, 109.7 x 91.5 cm (43¼ x 36 in.)
National Gallery of Art, Washington; Andrew W. Mellon Collection, 1937.173
PLATE 4

Inscriptions
On bottom left: *Rembr*[an]*dt. / f.1*[63]*7*·

Provenance
(Duveen Brothers, London and New York, in 1920); sold November 1924 to Andrew W. Mellon, Pittsburgh and Washington; deeded 28 December 1934 to the A. W. Mellon Educational and Charitable Trust, Pittsburgh; Andrew W. Mellon Collection, National Gallery of Art, 1942.

Selected Exhibitions
Pittsburgh 1925, no. 60; Detroit 1930, no. 36; Washington 1969, no. 4.

Selected Literature
Hofstede de Groot 1908–27, 6: no. 876; Valentiner 1931, no. 79; Bredius 1936, no. 362; Bauch 1966, no. 508; Gerson/Bredius 1969, no. 362; Tümpel 1986, no. 242; Wheelock 1995, pp. 226–30.

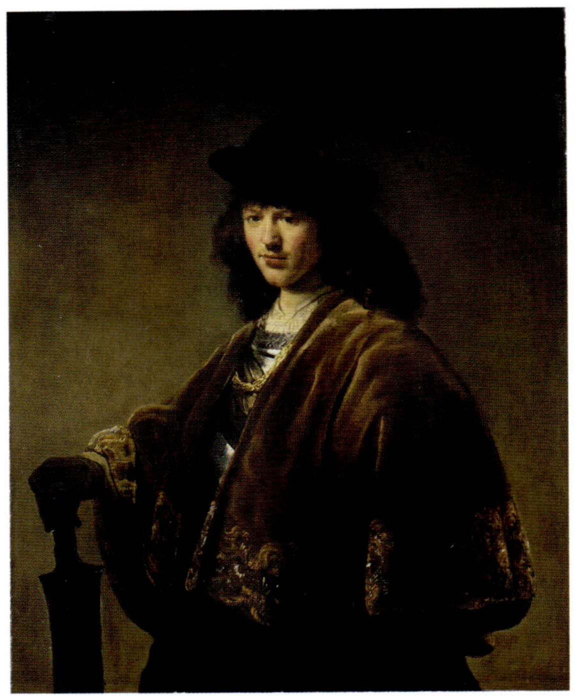

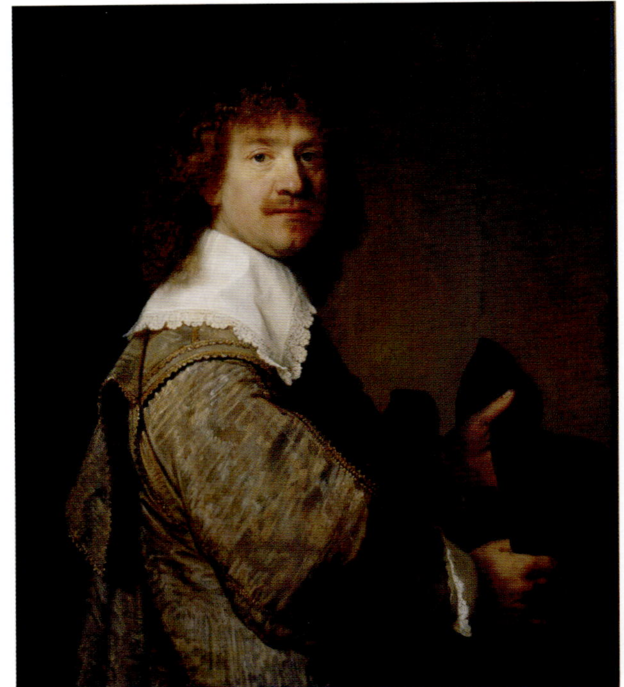

CAT. 24

Rembrandt van Rijn (circle of)
Young Man with a Sword, c. 1633–45
Oil on canvas, 118 x 96.5 cm (46 ½ x 38 in.)
North Carolina Museum of Art, Raleigh; Gift of the Samuel H. Kress Foundation (60.17.68)
PLATE 32

Inscriptions
Upper left corner: *Rembrandt / 163*[3]

Provenance
(Schaeffer Galleries, New York, by 1956); sold to the Samuel H. Kress Foundation, New York, February 1957; gift to the North Carolina Museum of Art, 1960 (as Rembrandt van Rijn).

Selected Exhibitions
Indianapolis and San Diego 1958, no. 8; New York 1961, no. 20; Washington 1961, no. 77; Montreal and Toronto 1969, no. 7; Kress 1994, no. 25 (as attributed to Govaert Flinck).

Selected Literature
Gerson/Bredius 1969, p. 548 (under no. 25); Eisler 1977, no. K2184, pp. 138–40; Sumowski 1983, 5: no. 2079, p. 3098; Corpus 1982–89, 3: p. 595 (as probably not from Rembrandt's circle); Weller 2009, no. 37, pp. 170–73.

CAT. 25

Rembrandt van Rijn
Portrait of a Man Holding a Black Hat, c. 1639
Oil on panel, 79.5 x 69.4 cm (31 ⅜ x 27 ⅜ in.)
The Armand Hammer Collection, Los Angeles, Gift of the Armand Hammer Foundation (AH.90.59)
Cleveland and Minneapolis only
PLATE 31

Inscriptions
At lower right: *Rembrandt*

Provenance
Prince Nicolas Gagarin, Moscow, by 1906; (sold through Prince Pierre Troubteskoy, 1925); Alfred W. Erickson, New York; (sale, Sotheby's, New York, 15 November 1961, lot 14); J. William Middendorf II (b. 1924), 1961–79; Armand Hammer (1898–1990), Los Angeles, 1979; the Armand Hammer Foundation, 1990.

Selected Exhibitions
Long-term loan Metropolitan Museum of Art, New York, until 1979; Melbourne and Canberra 1997, no. 12; Los Angeles 2009, no. 1.

Selected Literature
Hofstede de Groot 1908–27, 6: no. 751; Valentiner 1909, p. 217; Valentiner 1931, no. 62; Rosenberg 1948, p. 248; Bauch 1977, no. 379; Corpus 1982–89, 3: no. A130, pp. 305–11; Hammer 1985, no. 12, pp. 36–37, 223–24.

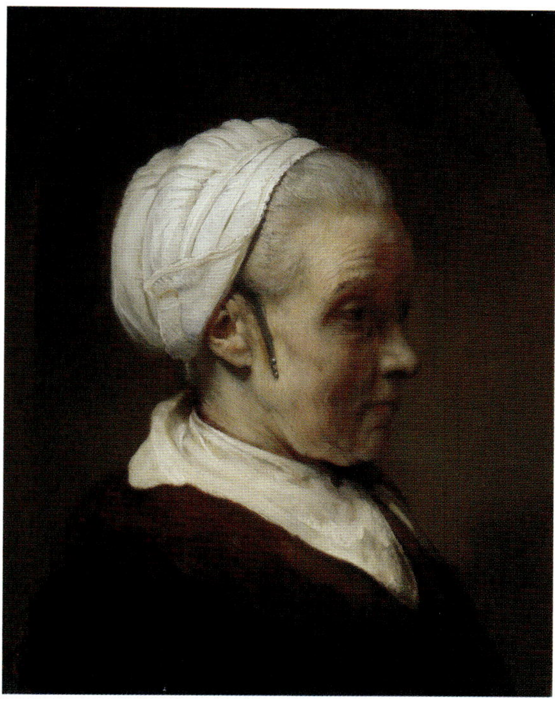

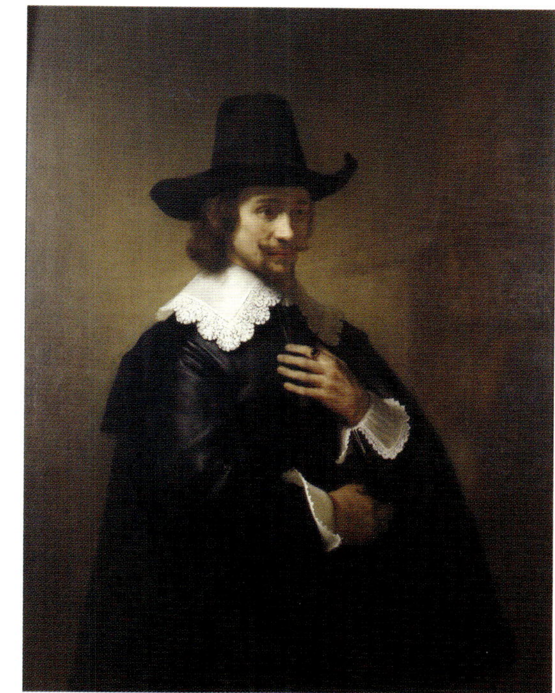

CAT. 26

Rembrandt van Rijn
Study of an Elderly Woman in a White Cap, c. 1640
Oil on panel, 53.3 x 36.5 cm (21 x 14 3/8 in.)
Private collection, New York
PLATE 1

Inscriptions
None

Provenance
Watson, Sanford Manor, Woodley, Berkshire, England; Eldridge R. Johnson, Moorestown, N. J., by 1930; by descent; (Newhouse Galleries, New York, by 1971); F. Howard and Mary D. Fleming Walsh, Forth Worth, 1971; by descent to family members; Walsh Art Trust, Fort Worth; (sale, Sotheby's, New York, 26 January 2006, lot 10); acquired by the current owner, 2006.

Selected Exhibitions
Detroit 1930, no. 40; Fort Worth 2009, no. 25.

Selected Literature
Hofstede de Groot 1908–27, 6: no. 328; Valentiner 1921, no. 13; Valentiner 1931, no. 92; Sumowski 1983, 4: no. 2881 n. 1; Wetering 2008, p. 211.

CAT. 27

Rembrandt van Rijn (workshop of; Ferdinand Bol?)
Portrait of a Young Man in a Broad-brimmed Hat, 1643
Oil on canvas, 116.5 x 91.4 cm (45 7/8 x 36 in.)
Shelburne Museum, Vermont; Electra Havemeyer Webb Collection, 27.1.1-150
PLATE 30

Inscriptions
At lower right: *Rembrandt f. 1643*

Provenance
Princesse de Sagan, Paris, by 1874; (sale through Durand-Ruel, Paris, about 1892); Mr. and Mrs. H. O. Havemeyer, New York, until 1907; Mrs. H. O. Havemeyer (d. 1929), New York, 1907–29; her daughter Electra Havemeyer (Mrs. Watson Webb), New York, 1929–60; gift to the Shelburne Museum, 1960.

Selected Exhibitions
Amsterdam 1932, no. 16.

Selected Literature
Hofstede de Groot 1908–27, 6: no. 766; Weitzenhoffer 1982, pp. 129, 149, 155, 166 n. 7; Corpus 1982–89, 3, p. 37, fig. 29; Sumowski 1983, 6: no. 2209, pp. 3695, 3793 (as F. Bol); New York 1993, no. 459, p. 375.

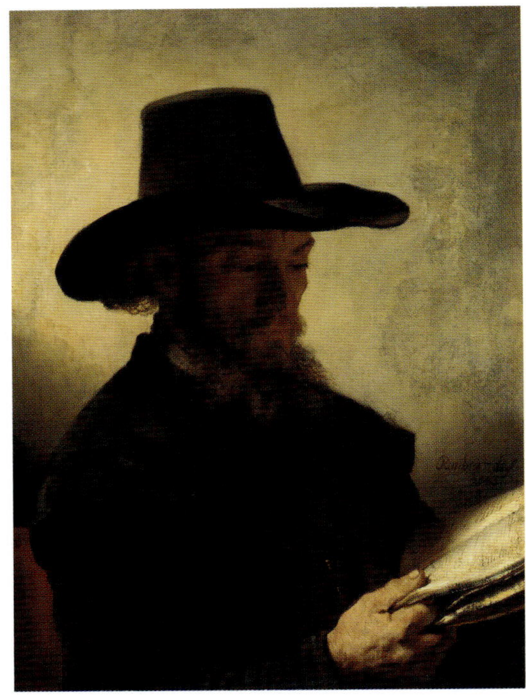

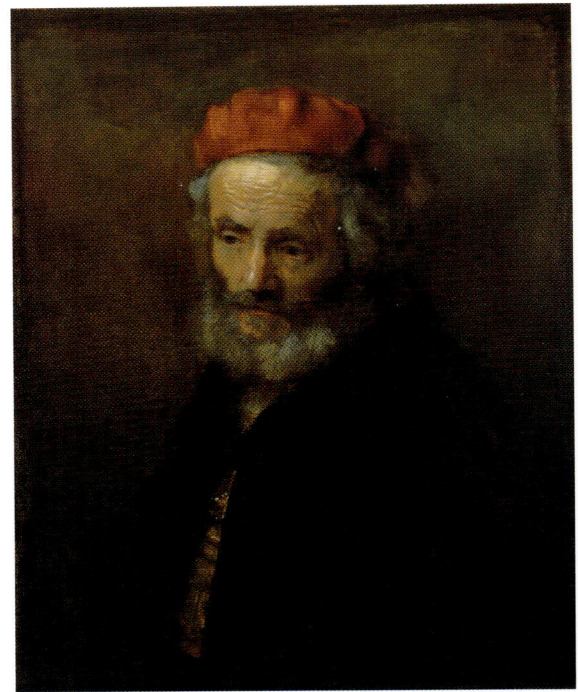

CAT. 28

Rembrandt van Rijn (?) and workshop
Portrait of a Man Reading, c. 1648
Oil on canvas, 66.5 x 58 cm (26 1/4 x 22 7/8 in.)
The Sterling and Francine Clark Art Institute, Williamstown, Mass., no. 841
PLATE 33

Inscriptions
Above book at bottom right: *Rembrandt. f: / 164*[8]. *5.*

Provenance
Count Demandolx-Dedons, Marseilles; (M. Knoedler & Co., New York); acquired by Robert Sterling Clark (1877–1956), 1923.

Selected Exhibitions
New York 1925, no. 14; Williamstown 1960, unnumbered cat; Chicago 1969, no. 22 (attributed to Rembrandt).

Selected Literature
Hofstede de Groot 1908–27, 6: p. 11; Valentiner 1921, no. 56; Valentiner 1931, no. 93; Bredius 1936, no. 238; Gerson/Bredius 1969, no. 238; Williamstown 1992, p. 86.

CAT. 29

Rembrandt van Rijn (circle or follower of)
Old Man Wearing a Red Hat, 1650
Oil on canvas, 68 x 56 cm (25 3/4 x 22 in.)
Baltimore Museum of Art, The Jacob Epstein Collection, 1951 (1951.108)
PLATE 38

Inscriptions
At upper right: [·]*embrandt f. 1650*

Provenance
(Thomas Agnew & Sons, London); George J. Gould, New York, by 1909; (Duveen Brothers, New York); Jacob Epstein, Baltimore, 1924; gift to the Baltimore Museum of Art, 1951.

Selected Exhibitions
New York 1909, no. 95; Detroit 1930, no. 47; Amsterdam 2006A, p. 69.

Selected Literature
Hofstede de Groot 1908–27, 6: no. 412; Bredius 1936, no. 258; Bauch 1966, no. 201; Gerson/Bredius 1969, no. 258.

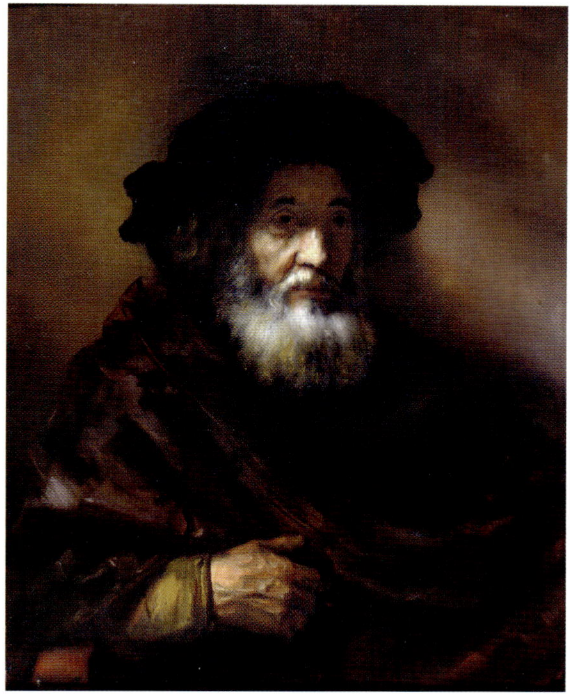

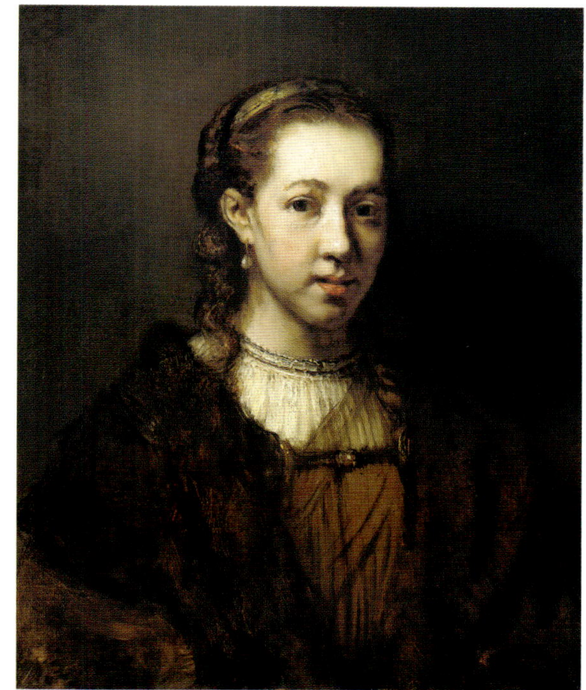

CAT. 30

Rembrandt van Rijn (follower of)
Portrait of an Old Man in a Cape, c. 1650–55
Oil on canvas, 85.8 x 65.4 cm (33¾ x 25¾ in.)
Fogg Art Museum, Harvard University, Cambridge, Gift of William A. Coolidge (1985.101)
PLATE 37

Inscriptions
None

Provenance
C. A. Waltner, Paris; W. A. Slater, Norwich, Conn., before 1889; (Knoedler & Co., New York, by 1936); Nathan R. Allen Sr., Kenosha, Wisc.; by descent to Mrs. Nathan R. Allen Sr., Kenosha; R. Whitacker, Kenosha (according to Bauch 1966, no. 220); Mr. and Mrs. Nathan R. Allen Jr., Greenwich, Conn., by 1969; William A. Coolidge, Ipswich, Mass., by 1973; gift to the Fogg Art Museum, Harvard University, 1985.

Selected Exhibitions
On loan Museum of Fine Arts, Boston, 1889; New York 1909, no. 100; on loan Corcoran Gallery, Washington, 1916; on loan Brooklyn Museum of Art, 1924; Detroit 1930, no. 56; Chicago 1969, no. 14; on loan Museum of Fine Arts, Boston, December 1986–March 1987.

Selected Literature
Hofstede de Groot 1908–27, 6: no. 454; Valentiner 1931, no. 122; Bredius 1936, no. 282; Bauch 1966, no. 220; Gerson/Bredius 1969, no. 282; Bowron 1990, no. 125, p. 178.

CAT. 31

Rembrandt van Rijn (follower of)
Portrait of a Woman (Hendrickje Stoffels?), c. 1653
Oil on canvas, 65.5 x 54 cm (25¾ x 21¼ in.).
Collection of Isabel and Alfred Bader, Milwaukee
PLATE 8

Inscriptions
None

Provenance
Lord Melchett of Landford, Romney, Hampshire, England, by 1929; (Joseph Duveen, New York, by 1935); Norton and Lucille Ellis Simon, Los Angeles, 1957; Lucille Ellis Simon, Los Angeles, after 1970–2002; (sale, Christie's, New York, 7 June 2002, lot 24); (Salomon Lilian and other dealers, New York); acquired by current owner, 2003.

Selected Exhibitions
Amsterdam 1935, no. 18; New York 1942B, no. 45; Milwaukee 1943, no. 26; Los Angeles 1947, no. 22; Chicago 1969, no. 10; on loan Los Angeles County Museum of Art, 1983–2001.

Selected Literature
Hofstede de Groot 1908–27, 6: no. 717; Bredius 1936, no. 112; Bauch 1966, no. 513; Gerson/Bredius 1969, no. 112; Schwartz 1985, p. 308; De Witt 2008, no. 15.

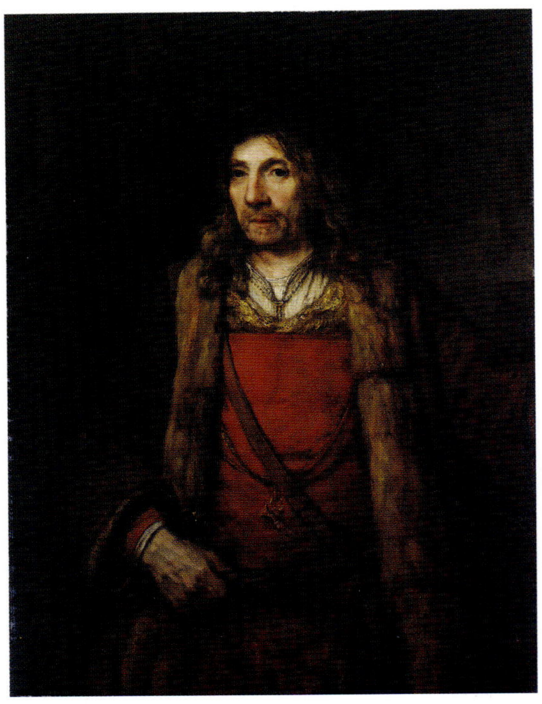

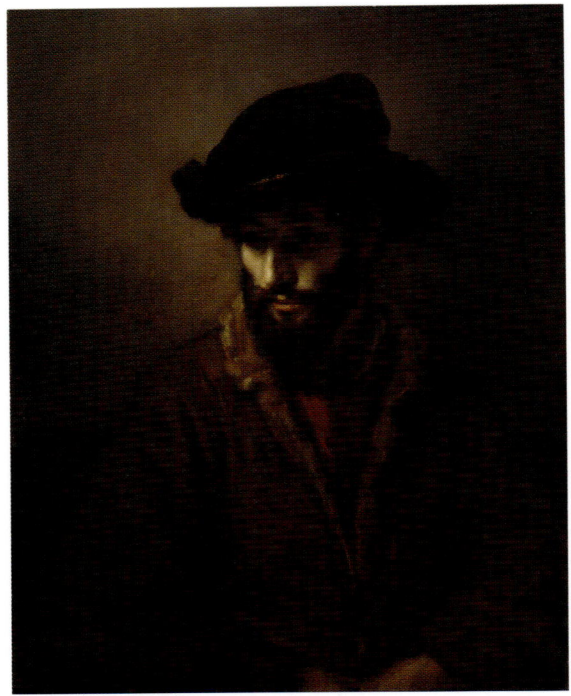

CAT. 32

Rembrandt van Rijn
Man in a Fur-lined Coat, c. 1655–60
Oil on canvas, 114.9 x 88.3 cm (45 ¼ x 34 ¾ in.)
The Toledo Museum of Art, Clarence Brown Fund (1977.50)
PLATE 34

Inscriptions
None

Provenance
(Sale, Galerie Sedelmeyer, Paris, 12 June 1890, lot 43); (W. Schaus, New York, by 1893); James Ross, Montreal; (sale, Christie's, London, 8 July 1927, lot 16); (Thomas Agnew & Sons, London); Alvan T. Fuller (1878–1958), Boston; Fuller Foundation, Boston; acquired by the Toledo Museum of Art, 1977.

Selected Exhibitions
New York 1909, no. 99; London 1929, no. 68; Chicago and Worcester 1935, no. 9; Boston 1959, no. 3; San Francisco 1966, no. 39; Amsterdam and Berlin 2006, pp. 52, 53, 56, fig. 55.

Selected Literature
Hofstede de Groot 1908–27, 6: no. 750; Valentiner 1931, no. 168; Bredius 1936, no. 278; Bauch 1966, no. 409; Gerson/Bredius 1969, no. 278; Schwartz 1985, p. 254, fig. 305; Toledo 2009, p. 175

CAT. 33

Rembrandt van Rijn (workshop of)
Portrait of a Man, c. 1655–60
Oil on canvas, 84.5 x 69.2 cm (33 ¼ x 27 ¼ in.)
The Cleveland Museum of Art, Gift of the Hanna Fund, 1950.252
PLATE 17

Inscriptions
Signed at right: *Rembrandt / 16*[..]

Provenance
Paul Delaroff, St. Petersburg (Leningrad), by 1906; (Thomas Agnew & Sons, London); (Scott & Fowles, New York); Otto H. Kahn (1867–1934), New York, 1910; presented by his children to the Metropolitan Opera Association, New York, 1950; (M. Knoedler & Co., New York); acquired by the Cleveland Museum of Art, 1950.

Selected Exhibitions
New York 1914, no. 13; Raleigh 1956, no. 28; Buffalo 1957, no. 24; Raleigh 1959, no. 74.

Selected Literature
Hofstede de Groot 1908–27, 6: no. 414; Valentiner 1931, no. 130; Bredius 1936, no. 246; Gerson/Bredius 1969, no. 246; Cleveland 1982, no. 113, pp. 258–61; Cleveland 1993, p. 193.

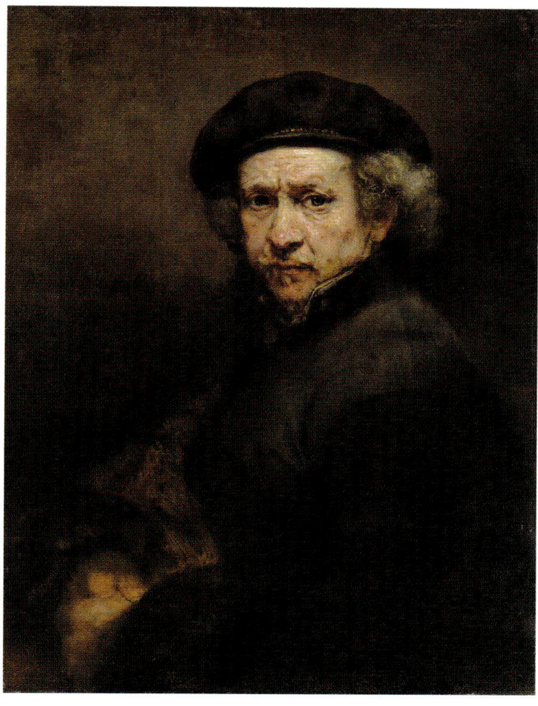

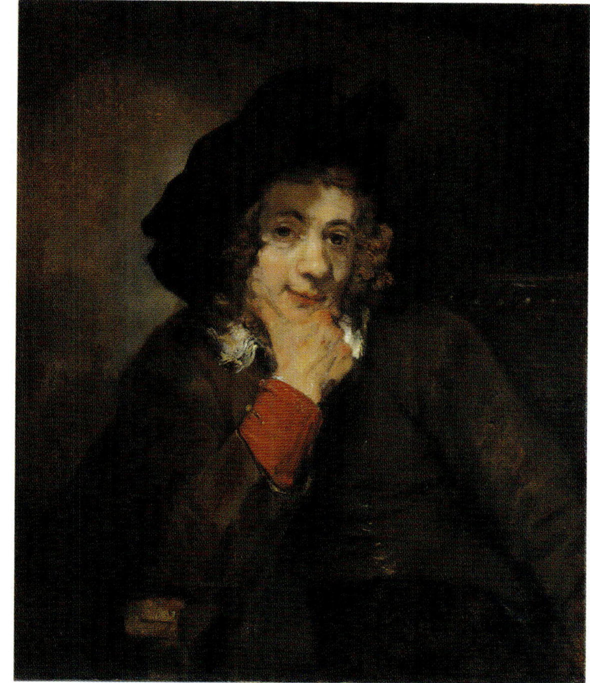

CAT. 34

Rembrandt van Rijn
Self-portrait, 1659
Oil on canvas, 84.5 x 66 cm (33 ¼ x 26 in.)
National Gallery of Art, Washington; Andrew W. Mellon Collection; 1937.1.72
PLATE 9

Inscriptions
At center left: *Rembrandt f. 1659*

Provenance
John Charles, 7th Duke of Buccleuch; (P. and D. Colnaghi and Co., New York, 1928); (Knoedler & Co., New York); sold January 1929 to Andrew W. Mellon, Pittsburgh and Washington; deeded 28 December 1934 to the A. W. Mellon Educational and Charitable Trust, Pittsburgh; Andrew W. Mellon Collection, National Gallery of Art, 1941.

Selected Exhibitions
Detroit 1930, no. 62; New York 1930, no. 8; Amsterdam 1935, no. 26; Chicago 1935, no. 6; New York 1939, no. 307; Washington 1969, no. 19; Leningrad (St. Petersburg) 1989, no. 13; Edinburgh 1992, no. 53; London and The Hague 1999, no. 73; Hartford 2009, no. 3.

Selected Literature
Hofstede de Groot 1908–27, 6: no. 554; Valentiner 1931, no. 141; Bredius 1936, no. 51; Bauch 1966, no. 330; Gerson/Bredius 1969, no. 51; Tumpel 1986, no. A 72; Wheelock 1996, pp. 261–65; Corpus 2005, no. 18, pp. 498–507.

CAT. 35

Rembrandt van Rijn
Titus, the Artist's Son, 1660
Oil on canvas, 81.3 x 68.7 cm (32 x 27 in.)
Baltimore Museum of Art, The Mary Frick Jacobs Collection (1938.206)
PLATE 14

Inscriptions
On chair back to right: *Rembrand*[t] / *1660*

Provenance
(Gimpel and Wildenstein, Paris, by at least 1916); James Stillman, New York; C. C. Stillman, New York; (sale, American Art Galleries, New York, 3 February 1927, lot 25); (Duveen Brothers, New York); Mrs. Henry Burton Jacobs, Baltimore, 1927; gift to the Baltimore Museum of Art by Mary Frick Jacobs, 1938.

Selected Exhibitions
New York 1942B, no. 50; New York 1950, unnumbered; Baltimore 1954, no. 82; Baltimore 1968, no. 12; Chicago 1969, no. 15; Montreal and Toronto 1969, no. 15; Melbourne and Canberra 1997, no. 18.

Selected Literature
Hofstede de Groot 1908–27, 6: no. 707; Valentiner 1931, no. 146; Rosenberg 1948, 1: pp. 27 n. 22, 220; Bauch 1966, no. 430; Gerson/Bredius 1969, no. 707.

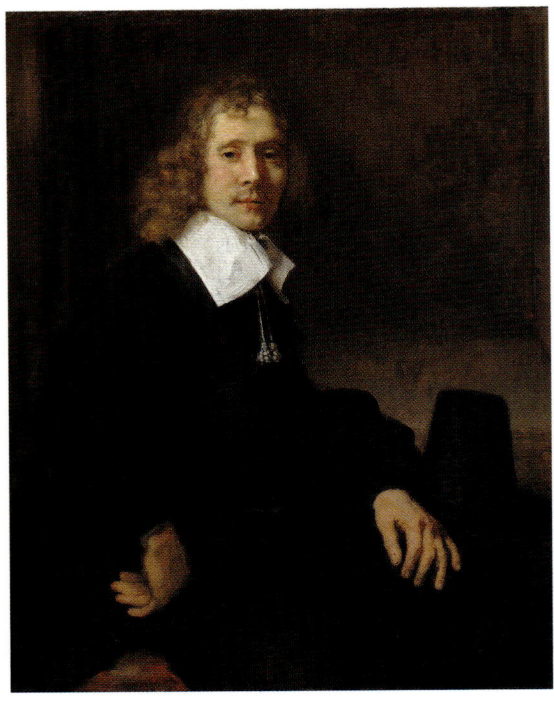

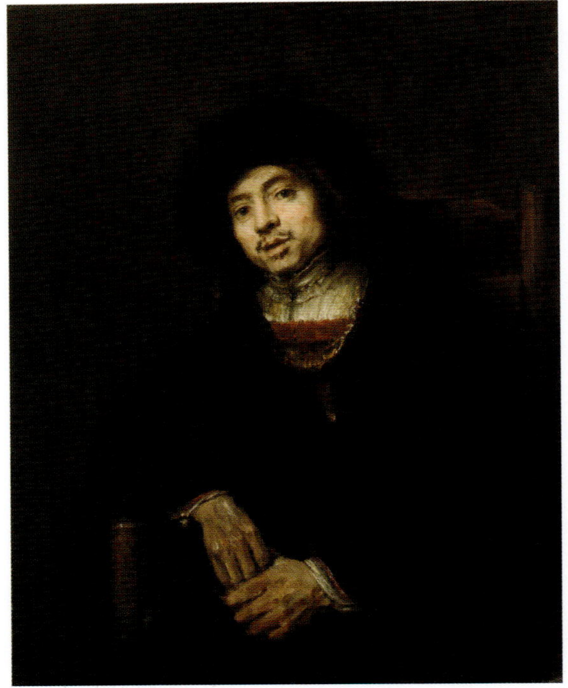

CAT. 36

Rembrandt van Rijn
A Young Man Seated at a Table (possibly Govaert Flinck), c. 1660
Oil on canvas, 109.9 x 89.5 cm (43 ¼ x 35 ¼ in.)
National Gallery of Art, Washington; Andrew W. Mellon Collection; 1937.1.77
PLATE 35

Inscriptions
At center right: *Rembrandt 166*[.]

Provenance
Count Carl Wachtmeister [Wachtmeister Trust], Wanås, Sweden, until 1926; (Duveen Brothers, New York and London); sold December 1926 to Andrew W. Mellon, Pittsburgh and Washington; deeded 28 December 1934 to the A. W. Mellon Educational and Charitable Trust, Pittsburgh; Andrew W. Mellon Collection, National Gallery of Art, 1941.

Selected Exhibitions
London 1929, no. 67; Amsterdam 1935, no. 29; San Francisco 1939, no. 88a; Washington 1969, no. 20; Leningrad (St. Petersburg) 1976; The Hague and San Francisco 1990, no. 53; Melbourne and Canberra 1997, no. 19.

Selected Literature
Hofstede de Groot 1908–27, 6: no. 784; Valentiner 1931, no. 159; Bredius 1936, no. 312; Berenson and Valentiner 1941, no. 203; Bauch 1966, no. 439; Gerson/Bredius 1969, no. 312; Tümpel 1986, no. 217; Wheelock 1996, pp. 265–70.

CAT. 37

Rembrandt van Rijn
Portrait of a Young Man in an Armchair, c. 1660–65
Oil on canvas, 104.1 x 85.1 cm (41 x 33 ½ in.)
Memorial Art Gallery, George Eastman Collection of the University of Rochester, N.Y. (68.98)
PLATE 36

Inscriptions
None

Provenance
Otto Beit (1865–1930), London; (Knoedler Galleries, New York); George Eastman (1854–1932), 1911; his bequest to the University of Rochester, N.Y., 1932; transferred to the Memorial Art Gallery, University of Rochester, 1968.

Selected Exhibitions
Detroit 1930, no. 65; Milwaukee 1964, unnumbered; Chicago 1969, no. 17; New York 1977, unnumbered.

Selected Literature
Hofstede de Groot 1908–27, 6: no. 782; Valentiner 1931, no. 148; Bredius 1936, no. 299; Bauch 1966, no. 433; Gerson/Bredius 1969, no. 299; Rosenthal 1979, pp. 4, 20, 33–34; Schwartz 1985, fig. 390 (as signed and dated 1660).

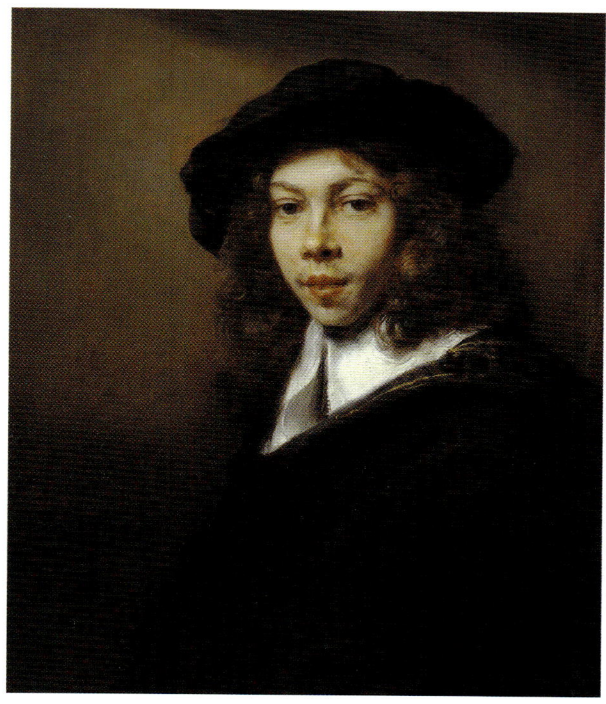

CAT. 38

Rembrandt van Rijn
Portrait of a Young Man, 1666
Oil on canvas, 71.6 x 62.8 cm (28 1/4 x 24 3/4 in.)
The Nelson-Atkins Museum of Art, Kansas City, Missouri
(Purchase Nelson Trust) 31-75.
PLATE 15

Inscriptions
At lower left: *Rembrandt f. 1666*

Provenance
(Duveen Brothers, London and New York, 1928–31); acquired by Nelson Trust, 1931, for the William Rockhill Nelson Gallery of Art, Kansas City.

Selected Exhibitions
Detroit 1930, no. 76; Melbourne and Canberra 1997, no. 26.

Selected Literature
Hofstede de Groot 1908–27, 6, no. 780; Valentiner 1931, no. 170; Bredius 1936, no. 322; Bauch 1966, no. 443; Gerson/Bredius 1969, no. 322; Schwartz 1985, p. 339, fig. 398; Tümpel 1986, no. 224; Wetering 2008, p. 194, fig. 234.

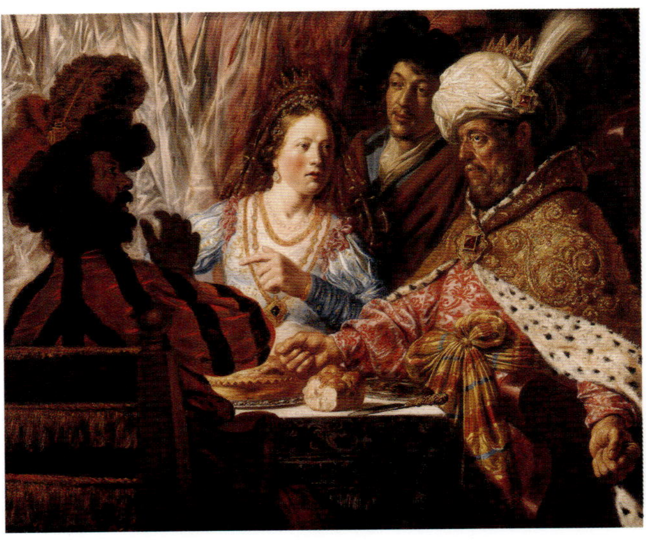

CAT. 39

Jan Lievens
The Feast of Esther (Wrath of Ahasuerus), c. 1625
Oil on canvas, 130.9 x 163.2 cm (51 ½ x 64 ¼ in.)
North Carolina Museum of Art, Raleigh, 52.9.55
PLATE 47

Inscriptions
None

Provenance
Charles A. de Burlet, Basel; (consigned in 1949 to Hans Schaeffer Galleries, New York); acquired by the North Carolina Museum of Art, 1952.

Selected Exhibitions
Raleigh 1959, no. 1; Oberlin 1963, no. 11; Montreal and Toronto 1969, no. 1; Leiden 1976, no. S29 (as follower of Rembrandt); Washington, Detroit, Amsterdam 1980, no. 31 (as Jan Lievens); Utrecht and Braunschweig 1986, no. 51; Berlin 1991, no. 52; Washington 2008, no. 6.

Selected Literature
Valentiner 1956, no. 65; Bauch 1966, no. A1; Gerson/Bredius 1969, no. 631 (as Jan Lievens); Schneider 1973, pp. 344, 349; Corpus 1982–86, 1: no. C2, pp. 446–60; Sumowski 1983, 3: no. 1181, pp. 1776, 1820; Gutbrod 1996, pp. 115–26, 134, 306, 374, 380 (b&w illus.); Weller 2009, no. 25, pp. 107–11.

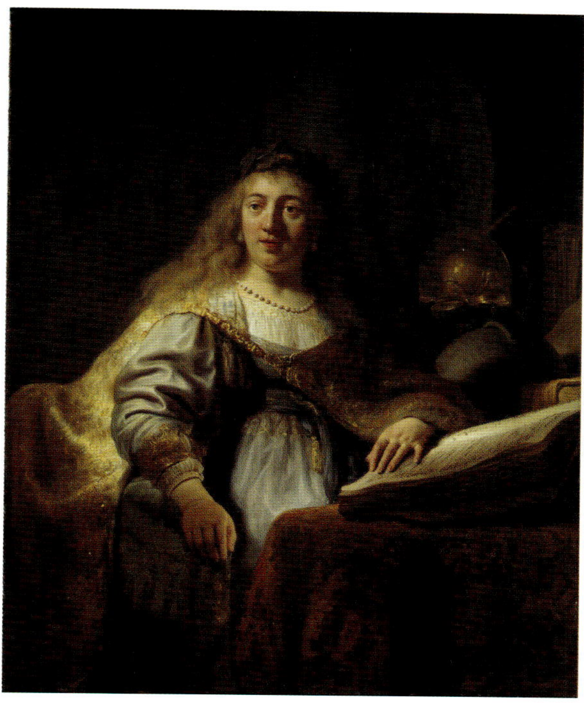

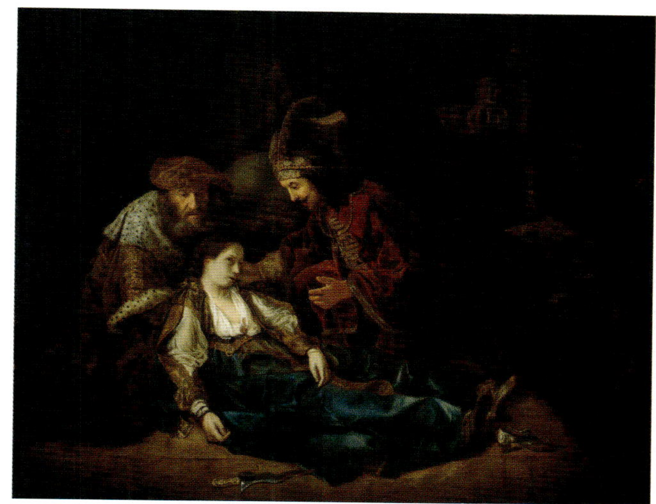

CAT. 40

Rembrandt van Rijn
Minerva in Her Study, 1635
Oil on canvas, 137 x 116 cm (54 x 45⅝ in.)
Private collection, New York
PLATE 50

Inscriptions
Center left: *Rembrandt. f. / 1635*

Provenance
(Sale, Christie's, London, 21 November 1924, lot 123); (with Lord Joseph Duveen, New York); Collection of Jules S. Bache, New York, 1929 (according to a photo mount for the picture in the Frick Art Reference Library, New York); auction sales and private collections in Munich, possibly the Netherlands, Stockholm, London, and Paris; Collection Baron Marcel Bich, Neuilly-sur-Seine, 1975–88; Ishibashi Foundation, Tokyo (on loan 1988–2001 to the Bridgestone Museum of Art, Tokyo); (Otto Naumann, Ltd., New York, 2001); acquired by the current owner, January 2008.

Selected Exhibitions
Amsterdam 1956, no. 28; Tokyo 1992, no. 6; Athens and Dordrecht 2000, no. 61; Madrid 2008, no. 20.

Selected Literature
Bredius 1936, no. 469; Bauch 1966, no. 259; Gerson/Bredius 1969, no. 469; Corpus 1982–89, 3: no. A114; Wetering 1997, p. 101 (fig. 129), pp. 105, 107, 124; Manuth and De Winkel 2002.

CAT. 41

Rembrandt van Rijn (follower of)
The Death of Lucretia(?), c. mid-1640s
Oil on canvas, 174 x 219.7 cm (68½ x 86½ in.)
The Detroit Institute of Arts, Gift of James E. Scripps, 89.44
PLATE 39

Inscriptions
None

Provenance
(Sale, Christie's, London, 12 May 1888, lot 10, as Rembrandt); bought by Deacon. James E. Scripps (1835–1906), Detroit; gift to the Detroit Institute of Arts, 1889.

Selected Exhibitions
Detroit 1930, no. 53.

Selected Literature
Detroit 1889, no. 47; Valentiner 1925–26, pp. 267, 270; Valentiner 1934, 2: xxix, xxxi, pl. 27 (as Jan Victors); Detroit 1944, no. 182; Sumowski 1983, 4: no. 1923 (as anon. Rembrandt school of the 1640s); Keyes et al. 2004, no. 75, pp. 184–85.

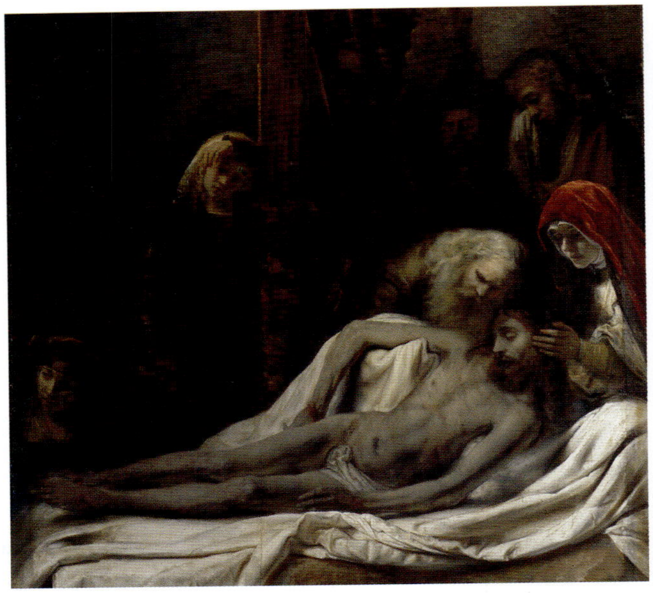

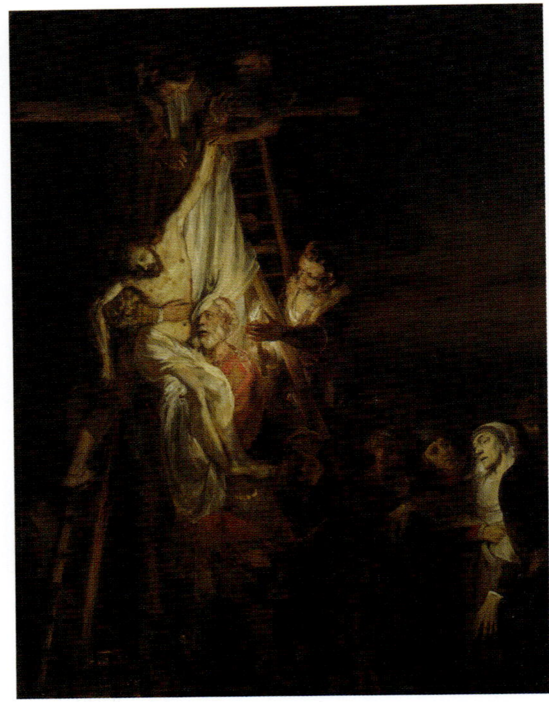

CAT. 42

Rembrandt van Rijn (workshop of)
Lamentation, c. 1645–50
Oil on canvas, 180.3 x 198.8 cm (71 x 78 1/4 in.)
The John and Mable Ringling Museum of Art, the State Art Museum of Florida, Sarasota; Bequest of John Ringling (SN252)
PLATE 46

Inscriptions
Bottom center right: *Rembrandt f. 1650* (added later?)

Provenance
(Sale, Christie's, London, 28 June 1929, lot 76); John Ringling (1866–1936), Sarasota, Fla.; bequest to the John and Mable Ringling Art Museum, 1936.

Selected Exhibitions
Detroit 1930, no. 53; New York 1940, no. 84; New York 1942B, no. 44; Raleigh 1956, no. 19; Montreal and Toronto 1969, no. 14; Chicago 1969, no. 24 (attributed to Rembrandt); Yokohama, Fukuoka, Kyoto 1986, no. 15 (as Rembrandt Workshop); Sarasota 1997, pl. 17.

Selected Literature
Hofstede de Groot 1908–27, 6: no. 137 (as possibly Rembrandt); Valentiner 1931, no. 103; Bredius 1936, no. 582, p. 25; Gerson/Bredius 1969, no. 582; Sarasota 1980, no. 116 (as school of Rembrandt); Sumowski 1983, 1: pp. 608, 610; Bikker 2005: no. R4, pp. 133–34.

CAT. 43

Rembrandt van Rijn (workshop of, probably Constantijn van Renesse)
The Descent from the Cross, c. 1650/52
Oil on canvas, 142 x 110.9 cm (55 7/8 x 43 5/8 in.)
National Gallery of Art, Washington; Widener Collection, 1942.9.61
PLATE 45

Inscriptions
None

Provenance
(Bachstitz Gallery, The Hague, 1921); inheritance from Estate of Peter A. B. Widener by gift through power of appointment of Joseph E. Widener, after purchase by funds of the Estate; National Gallery of Art, 1942.

Selected Exhibitions
Washington 1969, no. 12.

Selected Literature
Bachstitz Gallery 1921, 1: p. 5; Widener 1923 and subsequent eds., unpaginated; Valentiner 1931, no. 113; Bredius 1936, no. 584, p. 25; Rosenberg 1948, 1: pp. 134–35, 2: p. 186; Bauch 1966, no. 84; Gerson/Bredius 1969, no. 584; Corpus 1982–89, 2: pp. 628–30; Wheelock 1988, pp. 217–32; Wheelock 1996, pp. 300–309.

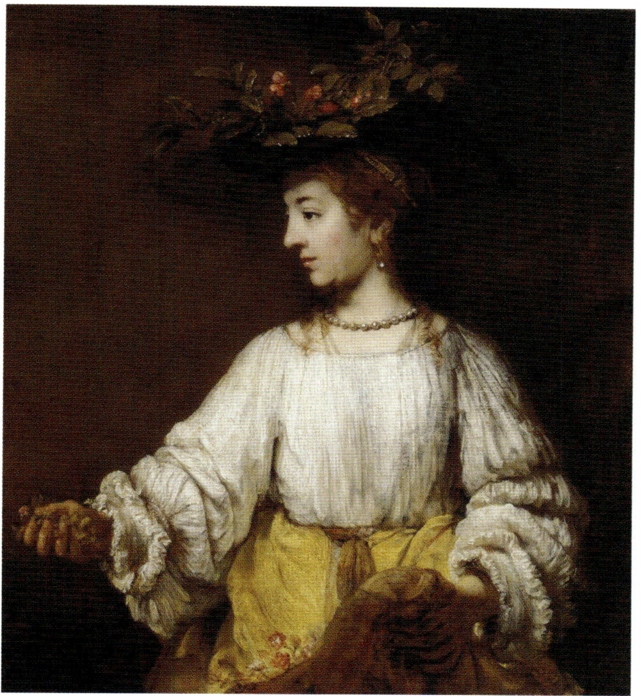

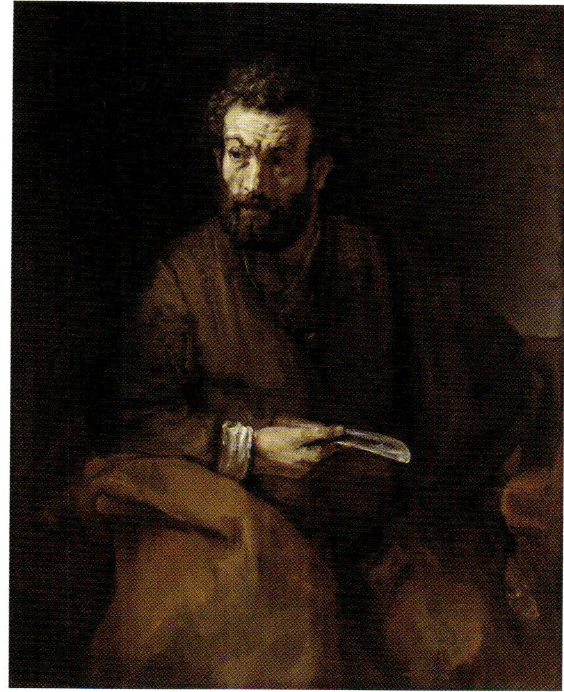

CAT. 44

Rembrandt van Rijn
Flora, c. 1654
Oil on canvas, 100 x 91.8 cm (39 ⅜ x 36 ⅛ in.)
The Metropolitan Museum of Art, New York; Gift of Archer M. Huntington, in memory of his father, Collis Potter Huntington (26.101.10)
Raleigh and Cleveland only
PLATE 44

Inscriptions
None

Provenance
(Duveen & Co., London and New York, from 1919); Mrs. Henry E. Huntington (formerly Mrs. Collis P. Huntington, d. 1924), New York; her son, Archer Milton Huntington (1870–1955), New York; gift to the Metropolitan Museum of Art, 1926.

Selected Exhibitions
New York 1942A, no catalogue; Cambridge 1948, no. 11; New York 1950, no. 20; Amsterdam 1956, no. 74; Berlin 1991, no. 41; Athens 1992, no. 13; New York 1995, no. 12; Edinburgh and London, 2001, no. 119; Boston and Chicago, 2003, no. 204; Moscow 2006; Madrid 2008, no. 33.

Selected Literature
Valentiner 1931, no. 124; Bredius 1936, no. 114; Bauch 1966, no. 282; Gerson/Bredius 1969, no. 114; Ainsworth 1982, pp. 62, 87, pls. 39, 40–42; Tümpel 1986, no. 111, pp. 273, 402; Liedtke 2007, pp. 661–69.

CAT. 45

Rembrandt van Rijn
St. Bartholomew, 1657
Oil on canvas, 122.7 x 99.7 cm (48 ⅜ x 39 ¼ in.)
The Putnam Foundation, Timken Museum of Art, San Diego, 51.001
Raleigh and Cleveland only
PLATE 43

Inscriptions
At center left: *Rembrandt / f. 1657*

Provenance
Prince Vassili Vassilievich Davidoff (1877–?), Kiev; (Thomas Agnew & Sons, London, and Duveen, New York, by 1912); Henry Goldman, New York, 1912 to 1937; estate of Henry Goldman, New York, 1937–47; (Wildenstein, New York, 1947–December 1951); acquired by the Putnam Foundation, San Diego, in December 1951.

Selected Exhibitions
Extended loan Metropolitan Museum of Art, New York, 1913–14; Detroit 1925, no. 22; Detroit 1930, no. 59; New York 1942B, no. 47; New York 1950, no. 18; Toronto 1951, no. 10; extended loan National Gallery of Art, Washington, 1952–65; Melbourne and Canberra 1997, no. 17; Washington and Los Angeles 2005, no. 3; Madrid 2008, no. 35; Los Angeles 2009, no. 13.

Selected Literature
Hofstede de Groot 1908–27, 6: no. 169; Valentiner 1921, p. 82; Bauch 1966, no. 217; Gerson/Bredius 1969, no. 613; Schwartz 1985, no. 352, p. 310; San Diego 1996, no. 16, pp. 90–94.

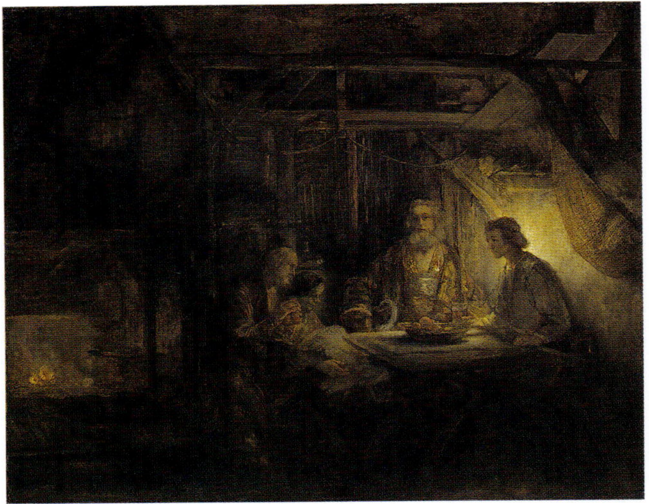

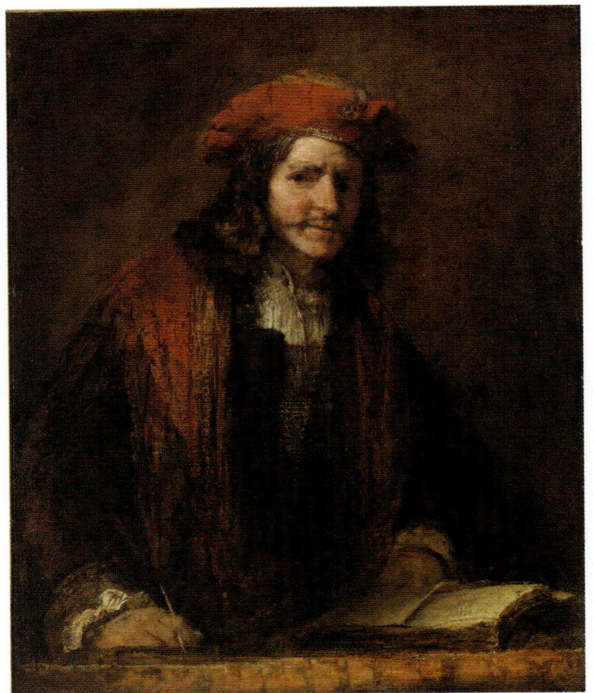

CAT. 46

Rembrandt van Rijn
Philemon and Baucis, 1658
Oil on panel, transferred from panel, 54.5 x 68 cm (21 ½ x 27 in.)
National Gallery of Art, Washington; Widener Collection, 1942.9.65
PLATE 41

Inscriptions
At lower left: *Rembrandt f. 1658*

Provenance
(Charles Sedelmeyer, Paris); Charles T. Yerkes (1839–1905), Chicago, by 1893; (sale, American Art Association, New York, 8 April 1910, no. 1160); (Scott & Fowles, New York); Otto H. Kahn (1867–1934), New York, by 1914; (Scott & Fowles, New York); Joseph E. Widener (1872–1943), Elkins Park, Penna., 1922; inheritance from Estate of Peter A. B. Widener by gift through power of appointment of Joseph E. Widener, after purchase by funds of the Estate; National Gallery of Art, 1941.

Selected Exhibitions
New York 1920, no. 9; Cambridge 1922, no catalogue; Washington 1969, no. 18.

Selected Literature
Yerkes 1893 and subsequent eds., no. 45; Bode 1897–1906, 6: no. 407; Hofstede de Groot, 1908–27, 6: no. 212; Widener 1913–16, intro. and page opposite pl. 37; Widener 1923 and subsequent eds., unpaginated; Valentiner 1931, no. 132; Bredius 1936, no. 481; Gerson/Bredius 1969, no. 481; Schwartz 1985, no. 373, p. 323; Wheelock 1996, pp. 247–52; Corpus 2010, no. 27, pp. 613–20 (as Rembrandt or pupil).

CAT. 47

Rembrandt van Rijn (attributed to)
Man in a Red Cap (an evangelist?), c. 1660–62
Oil on canvas, 102 x 80 cm (40 ¼ x 31 ½ in.)
Museum Boijmans Van Beuningen, Rotterdam, inv. 2113
PLATE 42

Inscriptions
None

Provenance
(Charles Sedelmeyer, Paris); P. C. Hanford, Chicago; (E. Fischof Gallery, New York); Charles Schwab, Pittsburgh, by 1909; (Duveen & Co., New York); (D. Katz, Dieren, the Netherlands); gift of the Vereeniging Rembrandt and 100 Friends of the Museum to the Museum Boijmans Van Beuningen, 1937.

Selected Exhibitions
New York 1909, no. 104; London 1929, no. 75; Detroit 1930, no. 69; Amsterdam 1935, no. 31; San Francisco 1966, no. 38; Brussels 1971, no. 86; Rotterdam 1988, no. 26; Melbourne and Canberra 1997, no. 32; Frankfurt and Kyoto 2003, no. 44; Washington and Los Angeles 2005, no. 13.

Selected Literature
Wurzbach 1906–11, 2: p. 410 (as attributed to C. Fabritius); Hofstede de Groot 1908–27, 6: no. 185; Valentiner 1921, pp. 219, 221; Bredius 1936, no. 618; Bauch 1966, no. 248; Gerson/Bredius 1969, no. 618; Tümpel 1986, no. 89; London and The Hague 1999, p. 214 n. 235; Giltaij 2009.

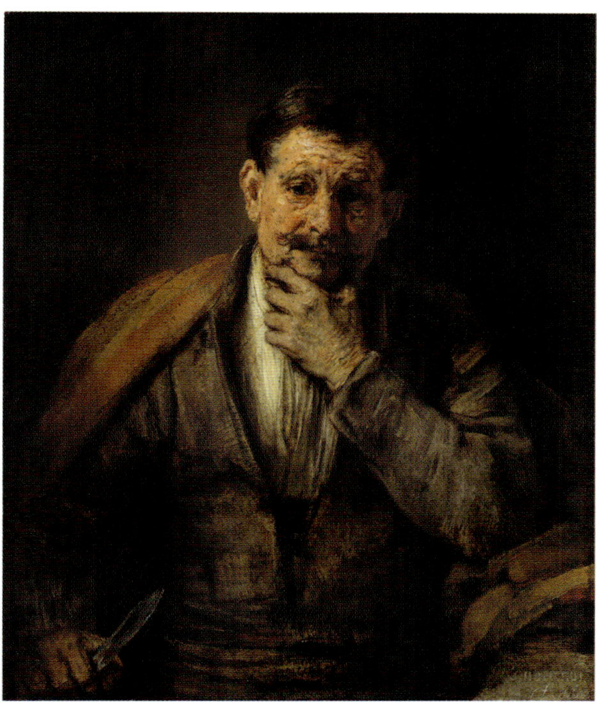

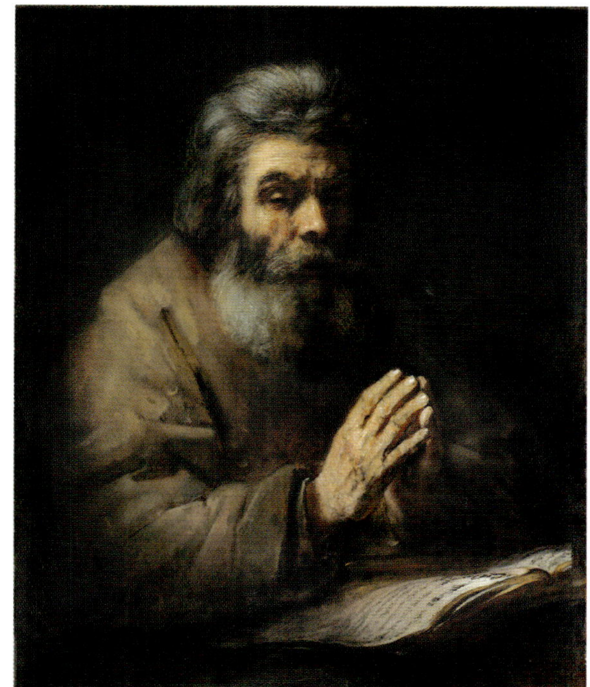

CAT. 48

Rembrandt van Rijn
St. Bartholomew, 1661
Oil on canvas, 86.7 x 75.6 cm (34 1/8 x 29 3/4 in.)
The J. Paul Getty Museum, Los Angeles, 71.PA.15
Cleveland and Minneapolis only
PLATE 48

Inscriptions
At lower right: *Rembrandt. f. 1661*

Provenance
(Sale, Sotheby's, London, 27 June 1962, lot 10); J. Paul Getty (1892–1976), Sutton Place, Surrey, England; gift to the J. Paul Getty Museum, 1971.

Selected Exhibitions
Minneapolis 1972, no. 43; Washington and Los Angeles 2005, no. 8; Los Angeles 2009, no. 6.

Selected Literature
Hofstede de Groot 1908–27, 6: no. 168; Valentiner 1921, p. 221; Bredius 1936, no. 615; Getty 1965, pp. 31, 113–19; Bauch 1966, no. 235, p. 13; Gerson/Bredius 1969, no. 615; Tümpel 1986, no. 83, p. 399; Melbourne and Canberra 1997, pp. 144–45.

CAT. 49

Rembrandt van Rijn (follower of)
Old Man Praying, c. 1661 or later
Oil on canvas, 87.3 x 72.1 cm (34 3/8 x 28 3/8 in.)
The Cleveland Museum of Art, Leonard C. Hanna Jr. Fund, 1967.16
PLATE 49

Inscriptions
At middle right: *Rembrand*[t] *f. 166*[1]

Provenance
Frau Charlotte Barreiss, Zurich; (sale, Sotheby's, London, 24 June 1964, lot 5); (Pinakos Inc., New York); acquired by the Cleveland Museum of Art, Leonard C. Hanna Jr. Bequest, 1967.

Selected Exhibitions
Amsterdam 1956, no. 89; Chicago 1969, no. 19.

Selected References
Hofstede de Groot 1908–27, 6: no. 194; Bredius 1936, no. 616; Bauch 1966, no. 234; Lee 1967; Gerson/Bredius 1969, no. 616; Cleveland 1982, pp. 260–62; Cleveland 1993, p. 193.

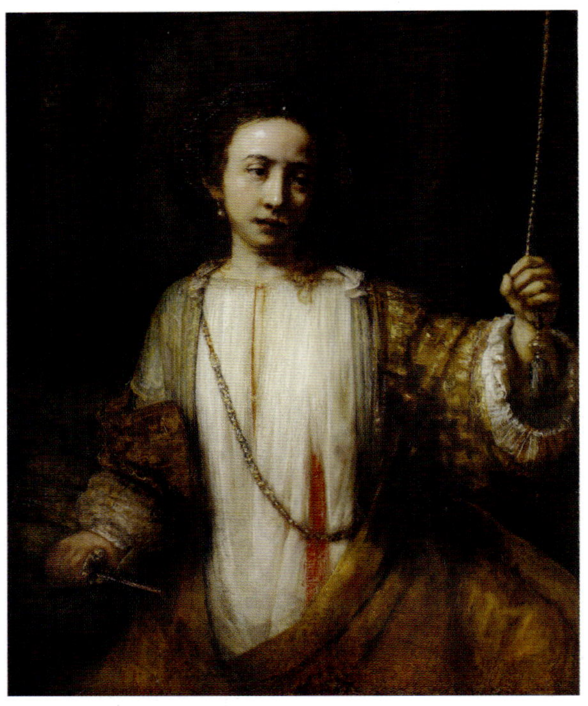

CAT. 50

Rembrandt van Rijn
Lucretia, 1666
Oil on canvas, 110.2 x 92.3 cm (43 3/8 x 36 3/8 in.)
Minneapolis Institute of Arts; The William Hood Dunwoody Fund (34.19)
PLATE 40

Inscriptions
Bottom left: *Rembrandt f 1666*

Provenance
(Henry Reinhardt and Sons, Inc., New York, by 1926); Herschel V. Jones (d. 1928), Minneapolis, 1927–28; Lydia Wilcom Jones, Minneapolis, by inheritance, 1928–34; acquired by the Minneapolis Institute of Arts, 1934.

Selected Exhibitions
Detroit 1930, no. 77; Chicago and Worcester 1935, no. 10; Chicago 1942, no. 34; Los Angeles 1947, no. 31; New York 1950, no. 28; Amsterdam 1956, no. 98; New York 1957, no. 4; Chicago 1969, no. 21; Washington 1991, unnumbered.

Selected Literature
Hofstede de Groot 1908–27, 6: nos. 220 and 220a; Valentiner 1931, no. 169; Bredius 1936, no. 485; Bauch 1966, no. 286; Gerson/Bredius 1969, no. 485; Edinburgh 2001, pp. 242, 244; Golahny 2003, pp. 148–56; Madrid 2008, p. 50.

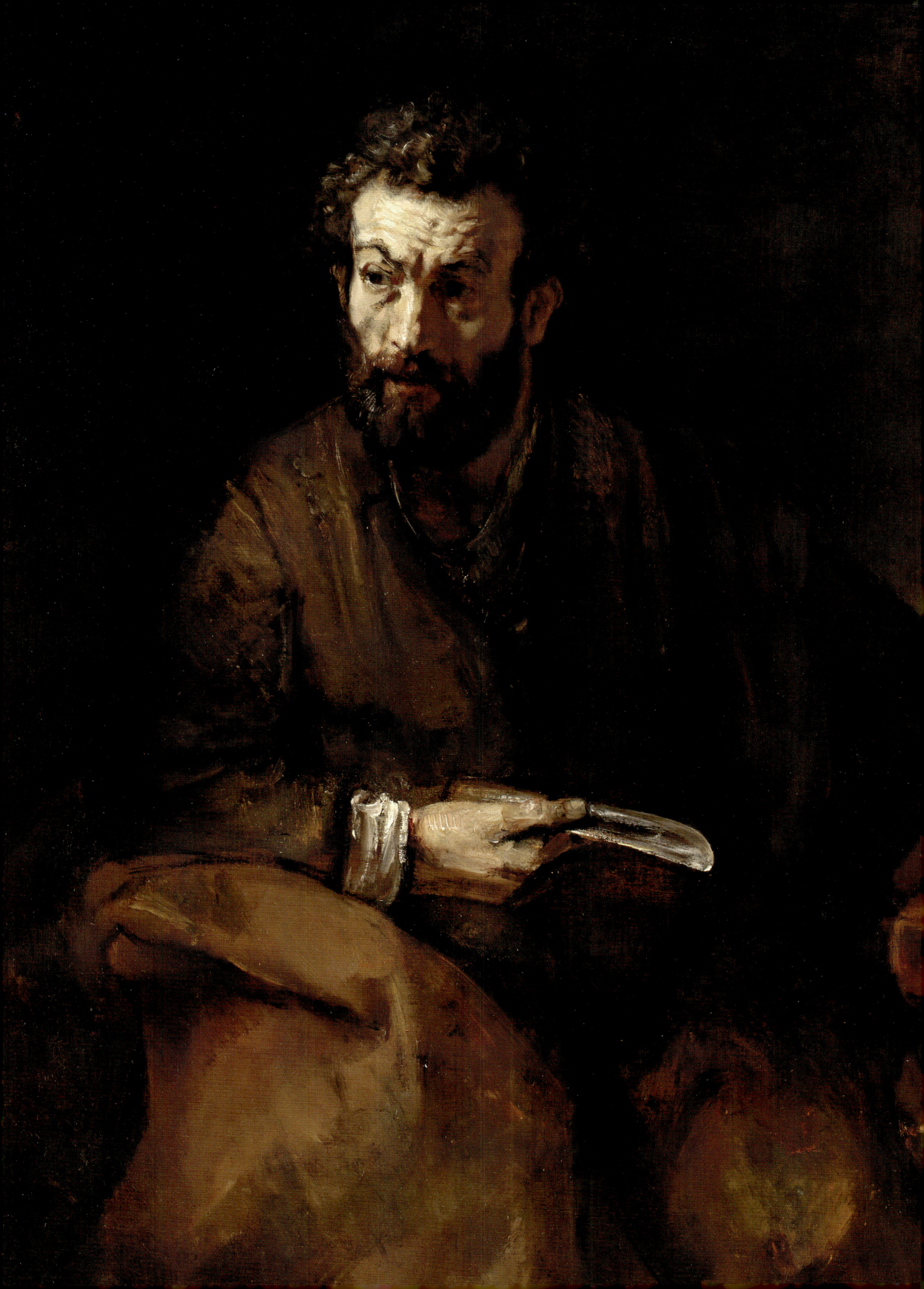

REMBRANDT PAINTING EXHIBITIONS IN NORTH AMERICA: 1892–2011

Exhibitions in North American museums largely devoted to paintings by Rembrandt between 1892 and 2011.*

1892 Chicago. The Art Institute of Chicago. *The Rembrandt of Pecq: Abraham Entertaining the Angels.*

1909 New York. The Metropolitan Museum of Art. *The Hudson-Fulton Celebration: Loan Exhibition of Paintings by Old Dutch Masters.* Exh. cat. by W. R. Valentiner.

1922 Cambridge, Mass. Fogg Art Museum, Harvard University. *Rembrandt Paintings, Drawings, and Etchings.*

1930 Detroit. The Detroit Institute of Arts. *The Thirteenth Loan Exhibition of Old Masters: Paintings by Rembrandt.* Exh. cat. by W. R. Valentiner.

1933 New York. M. Knoedler & Company. *Loan Exhibition of Paintings by Rembrandt.*

1935 Chicago. The Art Institute of Chicago. *Paintings, Drawings, and Etchings by Rembrandt and His Circle.* Exh. cat. Also on view at the Worcester Art Museum, Mass.

1937 New York. Schaeffer Galleries. *Rembrandt.* Exh. cat.

1942 New York. Metropolitan Museum of Art. *The Art of Rembrandt.*

1947 Los Angeles. Los Angeles County Museum of History, Science, and Art. *Loan Exhibition of Paintings by Frans Hals and Rembrandt.* Exh. cat. by W. R. Valentiner.

1948 Cambridge, Mass. Fogg Art Museum, Harvard University. *Rembrandt: Paintings and Etchings.* Exh. cat.

1950 New York. Wildenstein and Company. *Loan Exhibition of Rembrandt, Under the High Patronage of His Excellency, Dr. Eelco N. van Kleffens, Ambassador of The Netherlands.* Exh. cat.

1951 Toronto. Toronto Art Museum. *Rembrandt Exhibition.*

1956 Raleigh. North Carolina Museum of Art. *Rembrandt and His Pupils.* Exh. cat. by W. R. Valentiner.

1958 Indianapolis. John Herron Art Museum. *The Young Rembrandt and His Times.* Exh. cat. by Seymour Slive. Also shown at Fine Arts Gallery of San Diego.

1965 Washington, D.C. National Gallery of Art. *Exhibition of "Portrait of a Man in a Fur-lined Coat" by Rembrandt* (on loan from the Fuller Foundation, Boston).

1969 Chicago. The Art Institute of Chicago. *Rembrandt after Three Hundred Years.* Exh. cat by Egbert Haverkamp-Begemann et al. Also on view at the Minneapolis Institute of Arts and the Detroit Institute of Arts.

1969 Montreal. Montreal Museum of Fine Arts. *Rembrandt and His Pupils.* Exh. cat. Also on view at the Art Gallery of Ontario, Toronto.

1969 Washington, D.C. National Gallery of Art. *Rembrandt in the National Gallery of Art.* Exh. cat by Egbert Haverkamp-Begemann et al.

1973 New York. The Metropolitan Museum of Art. *Dutch Couples: Pair Portraits by Rembrandt and His Contempories.* Exh. cat. by John Walsh Jr.

1984 Kingston, Ont. Agnes Etherington Art Centre, Queen's University. *Pictures from the Age of Rembrandt: Selections from the Personal Collection of Dr. and Mrs. Alfred Bader.* Exh. cat. by David McTavish.

1991 Washington, D.C. National Gallery of Art. *Rembrandt's Lucretias.* Exh. booklet by Arthur K. Wheelock Jr. and George Keyes. Also on view at the Minneapolis Institute of Arts.

2000 Boston. Isabella Stewart Gardner Museum. *Rembrandt Creates Rembrandt: Art and Ambition in Leiden 1629–1631.* Exh. cat. by Alan Chong et al.

2003 Boston. Museum of Fine Arts. *Rembrandt's Journey: Painter·Draftsman·Etcher.* Exh. cat. by Clifford Ackley et al. Also on view at the Art Institute of Chicago.

2003 Indianapolis. Indianapolis Museum of Art. *Rembrandt Face to Face.* Exh. cat. by Stephanie S. Dickey.

2003 Washington, D.C. National Gallery of Art. *Rembrandt's Late Religious Portraits.* Exh. cat. by Arthur K. Wheelock et al. Also on view at the J. Paul Getty Museum, Los Angeles.

2008 Cincinnati. Cincinnati Art Museum. *Rembrandt: Three Faces of the Master.* Exh. cat. edited by Benedict Leca.

2009 Hartford. Wadsworth Atheneum. *Rembrandt's People.* Exh. cat. by Eric Zafran.

2009 Los Angeles. The J. Paul Getty Museum. *Rembrandt in Southern California.* Exh. cat. by Anne T. Woollett. Survey of Rembrandt paintings in various southern California collections.

2011 New York. The Frick Collection. *Rembrandt and His School: Masterworks from the Frick and Lugt Collections.* Exh. cat. by Collin B. Bailey (ed.).

2011 Philadelphia. Philadelphia Museum of Art. *Rembrandt and the Face of Jesus.* Exh. cat. by Lloyd DeWitt et al. Also on view at the Detroit Institute of Arts and the Musée du Louvre, Paris.

* For a listing of exhibitions devoted to all aspects of seventeenth-century Dutch art shown in American institutions between 1888 and 1991, see Lynn Federle Orr and Elise Brecall, in *Great Dutch Paintings from America* (The Hague and San Francisco 1990), pp. 494–98.

REFERENCES

Ainsworth 1982
Ainsworth, Maryan Wynn, et al. *Art and Autoradiography: Insights into the Genesis of Paintings by Rembrandt, Van Dyck, and Vermeer.* New York, 1982.

Allentown 1960
Hirsch, Richard T., and Fern Rusk Shapley. *The Samuel H. Kress Memorial Collection.* Allentown, Pa.: Allentown Art Museum, 1960.

Amsterdam 1898
Rembrandt: Collection des Oeuvres du Maître. Exh. cat., Rijksmuseum, Amsterdam. Amsterdam, 1898.

Amsterdam 1932
Schmidt-Degener, F. *Rembrandt Tentoonstelling.* Exh. cat., Rijksmuseum, Amsterdam. Amsterdam, 1932.

Amsterdam 1935
Schmidt-Degener, F. *Rembrandt Tentoonstelling.* Exh. cat., Rijksmuseum, Amsterdam. Amsterdam, 1935.

Amsterdam 1956
Van Schendel, A. *Rembrandt Tentoonstelling ter Herdenking van de Geboorte van Rembrandt op 15 Juli 1606.* Exh. cat., Rijksmuseum, Amsterdam; Museum Boymans, Rotterdam. Amsterdam, 1956.

Amsterdam 1969
Thiel, P. J. J. van, et al. *Rembrandt 1669/1969.* Exh. cat., Rijksmuseum, Amsterdam. Amsterdam, 1969.

Amsterdam 1991
Tümpel, Astrid, and Peter Schatborn. *Pieter Lastman: The Man Who Taught Rembrandt.* Exh. cat., Het Rembrandthuis, Amsterdam. Zwolle, 1991.

Amsterdam 1996
Schuckman, Christiaan, Martin Royalton-Kisch, and Erik Hinterding. *A Collaboration on Copper: Rembrandt and Van Vliet.* Exh. cat., Museum het Rembrandthuis, Amsterdam. Amsterdam, 1996.

Amsterdam 2002
Wetering, Ernst van de, et al. *The Mystery of the Young Rembrandt.* Exh. cat., Staatliche Museen, Gemäldegalerie Alte Meister, Kassel; Museum het Rembrandthuis, Amsterdam. Amsterdam, 2002.

Amsterdam 2003
Wetering, Ernst van de. *Rembrandt's Hidden Self-Portraits.* Exh. booklet, Museum het Rembrandthuis, Amsterdam. Amsterdam, 2003.

Amsterdam 2006A
Alexander-Knotter, Mirjam, et al. *De "joodse" Rembrandt: De mythe ontrafeld* [The "Jewish" Rembrandt: The myth revealed]. Exh. cat., Jewish Historical Museum, Amsterdam. Zwolle, 2006.

Amsterdam 2006B
Bull, Duncan, et al. *Rembrandt Caravaggio.* Exh. cat., Rijksmuseum, Amsterdam. Zwolle, 2006.

Amsterdam and Berlin 2006
Wetering, Ernst van der, et al. *Rembrandt—Quest of a Genius.* Exh. cat., Rembrandthuis, Amsterdam; Gemäldegalerie, Staatliche Museen Berlin. Zwolle, 2006.

Angel 1642
Angel, Philips. *Lof der Schilderkonst.* Leiden, 1642.

Antwerp 1992
Flemish Paintings in America: a Survey of Early Netherlandish and Flemish Paintings in the Public Collections of North America. Selected by Guy C. Bauman and Walter A. Liedtke. Antwerp, 1992.

Athens 1992
From El Greco to Cézanne: Masterpieces of European Painting from the National Gallery of Art, Washington, and The Metropolitan Museum of Art, New York. Exh. cat., National Gallery/Alexandros Soutzos Museum, Athens. Athens, 1992.

Athens and Dordrecht 2000
Schoon, Peter, and Sander Paarlberg, eds. *Greek Gods and Heroes in the Age of Rubens and Rembrandt.* Exh. cat., National Gallery/Alexandros Soutzos Museum and Netherlands Institute, Athens; Dordrechts Museum, Dordrecht. Athens and Dordrecht 2000.

Baltimore 1954
Rosenthal, Gertrude. *Man and his Years.* Exh. cat., Baltimore Museum of Art. Baltimore, 1954.

Baltimore 1968
Rosenthal, Gertrude, et al. *From El Greco to Pollock: Early and Late Works by European and American Artists.* Exh. cat., Baltimore Museum of Art. Baltimore, 1968.

Baltimore 1984
The Taste of Maryland Art: Collecting in Maryland 1800–1934. Exh. cat., Walters Art Gallery. Baltimore, 1984.

Bachstitz Gallery 1921
Gronau, G. *The Bachstitz Gallery.* 3 vols. Berlin, 1921.

Bartsch 1797
Bartsch, Adam. *Catalogue raisonné de toutes les estampes qui forment l'oeuvre de Rembrandt, et ceux de ses principaux imitateurs.* 2 vols. Vienna, 1797.

Bauch 1966
Bauch, Kurt. *Rembrandt Gemälde.* Berlin, 1966.

Behrman 1972
Behrman, S. N. *Duveen.* Boston, 1972.

Benesch 1954–57
Benesch, Otto. *The Drawings of Rembrandt.* 6 vols. London, 1954–57.

Berenson and Valentiner 1941
Berenson, Bernard, and W. R. Valentiner. *Duveen Pictures in Public Collections in America.* New York, 1941.

Berlin, Amsterdam, London 1991
Brown, Christopher, Jan Kelch, and Pieter van Thiel. *Rembrandt: The Master and His Workshop.* Exh. cat., Altes Museum, Berlin; Rijksmuseum, Amsterdam; National Gallery, London. New Haven, London, 1991.

Bikker 2005
Bikker, Jonathan. *Willem Drost (1633–1659): A Rembrandt Pupil in Amsterdam and Venice.* New Haven, London, 2005.

Birmingham 1951
Opening Exhibition. Exh. cat., Birmingham Museum of Art. Birmingham, Ala., 1951.

Bode 1897–1906
Bode, Wilhelm von, assisted by Cornelis Hofstede de Groot. *The Complete Work of Rembrandt*. Trans. by Florence Simonds. 8 vols. Paris, 1897–1906.

Bordeaux 1981
Profil du Metropolitan Museum of Art de New York: De Ramses à Picasso. Exh. cat., Galerie des Beaux-Arts, Bordeaux. Bordeaux, 1981.

Boston 1959
Alvan T. Fuller Memorial Exhibition. Exh. cat., Museum of Fine Arts, Boston. Boston, 1959.

Boston 2000
Chong, Alan, et al. *Rembrandt Creates Rembrandt: Art and Ambition in Leiden, 1629–1631*. Exh. cat., Isabella Stewart Gardner Museum, Boston. Zwolle, 2000.

Boston and Chicago 2003
Ackley, Clifford S. *Rembrandt's Journey: Painter Draftsman Etcher*. Exh. cat., Museum of Fine Arts, Boston; Art Institute of Chicago. Boston, 2003.

Boston and New York 1969
Rembrandt: Experimental Etcher. Exh. cat., Museum of Fine Arts, Boston; Pierpont Morgan Library, New York. Boston, 1969.

Bowron 1990
Bowron, Edgar Peters. *European Paintings before 1900 in the Fogg Art Museum: A Summary Catalogue including Paintings in the Busch-Reisinger Museum*. Cambridge, Mass., 1990.

Braunschweig 1979
Ekkart, Rudolf E. O., Sabine Jacob, and Rüdiger Klessmann. *Jan Lievens, ein Maler im Schatten Rembrandts*. Exh. cat., Herzog Anton Ulrich-Museum, Braunschweig. Braunschweig, 1979.

Bredius 1920
Bredius, Abraham. "An Unknown Masterpiece by Rembrandt." *Burlington Magazine* 36 (May 1920): 208.

Bredius 1936
———. *The Paintings of Rembrandt*. Vienna, 1936.

Broos 1983
Broos, Ben. "Fame Shared Is Fame Doubled," pp. 35–58. In *The Impact of a Genius: Rembrandt, his pupils and followers in the seventeenth century*. Exh. cat., Waterman Gallery, Amsterdam; Groninger Museum, Groningen. Amsterdam, 1983.

Broos 1993
———. *Intimacies & Intrigues: History Painting in the Mauritshuis*. The Hague, 1993.

Brussels 1971
Hoetink, H. R., and P. J. J. van Thiel. *Rembrandt en zijn tijd*. Exh. cat., Palais voor Schone Kunsten, Brussels. Brussels, 1971.

Bruyn 1991
Bruyn, Josua. "Rembrandt's Workshop—Function and Production," pp. 68–89. In Berlin, Amsterdam, London 1991.

Buffalo 1957
Trends in Painting 1600–1800. Exh. cat., Albright Art Gallery, Buffalo. Buffalo, 1957.

Burt 1977
Burt, N. *Palaces for the People: A Social History of the American Art Museum*. Boston/Toronto, 1977.

Cambridge 1922
Rembrandt Paintings, Drawings, and Etchings. Exh. cat., Fogg Art Museum, Harvard University, Cambridge. Cambridge, Mass., 1922.

Cambridge 1948
Rembrandt. Exh. cat., Fogg Art Museum, Harvard University, Cambridge. Cambridge, Mass., 1948.

Carstairs 1968
Carstairs, Charles. *The Frick Collection: An Illustrated Catalogue*. Princeton, 1968. Vol. 1, *Paintings: American, British, Dutch, Flemish, and German*.

Chapman 1990
Chapman, H. Perry. *Rembrandt's Self-Portraits: A Study in Seventeenth-Century Identity*. Princeton, 1990.

Chattanooga 1952
Opening Exhibition. Exh. cat., George Thomas Hunter Gallery of Art, Chattanooga. Chattanooga, Tenn., 1952.

Chicago 1942
Paintings by the Great Dutch Masters of the Seventeenth Century. Exh. cat., Art Institute of Chicago. Chicago, 1942.

Chicago 1969
Cunningham, C. C., et al. *Rembrandt After Three Hundred Years*. Exh. cat., Art Institute of Chicago; Minneapolis Institute of Arts; Detroit Institute of Arts. Chicago, 1969.

Chicago 1973
Cunningham, C. C., et al. *Rembrandt After Three Hundred Years: A Symposium: Rembrandt and His Followers*. Art Institute of Chicago. Chicago, 1973.

Chicago and Worcester 1935
Paintings, Drawings, and Etchings by Rembrandt and his Circle. Exh. cat., Art Institute of Chicago; Worcester Art Museum. Chicago, 1935.

Cincinnati 2008
Leca, Benedict. *Rembrandt: Three Faces of the Master*. Exh. cat., Cincinnati Art Museum. Cincinnati, 2008.

Clark 1966
Clark, Kenneth. *Rembrandt and the Italian Renaissance*. New York, 1966.

Cleveland 1982
Lurie, Ann Tzeutschler. *European Paintings of the 16th, 17th, and 18th Centuries*. The Cleveland Museum of Art Catalogue of Paintings. Cleveland, 1982.

Cleveland 1993
Chong, Alan. *European & American Painting in the Cleveland Museum of Art: A Summary Catalogue.* Cleveland, 1993.

Cohn 1986
Cohn, M. B. *Francis Calley Gray and Art Collecting in America.* Cambridge, 1986.

Constable 1964
Constable, W. G. *Art Collecting in the United States of America: An Outline of a History.* London, New York, 1964.

Corpus 1982–89
Bruyn, Josua, et al. *A Corpus of Rembrandt Paintings.* Trans. by D. Cook-Radmore. 3 vols. The Hague, Boston, London, 1982–89.

Corpus 2005
Wetering, Ernst van de, et al. *A Corpus of Rembrandt Paintings IV: The Self-Portraits.* Dordrecht, 2005.

Corpus 2010
Wetering, Ernst van de, ed. *A Corpus of Rembrandt Paintings V: The Small-Scale History Paintings.* New York, 2010.

Crenshaw 2006
Crenshaw, Paul. *Rembrandt's Bankruptcy.* New York, 2006.

Day and Sturges 1987
Day, Holliday T., and Hollister Sturges, eds. *Joslyn Art Museum: Paintings and Sulpture from the European and American Collections.* Omaha, 1987.

De Witt 2008
De Witt, David. *The Bader Collection: Dutch and Flemish Paintings.* Agnes Etherington Art Centre, Queen's University, Kingston. Kingston, 2008.

Denver and Newark 2001
Westermann, Mariët. *Art & Home: Dutch Interiors in the Age of Rembrandt.* Exh. cat., Denver Art Museum, Denver; Newark Museum, Newark, N. J. Zwolle, 2001.

Detroit 1889
Catalogue of the Scripps Collection. Detroit, 1889.

Detroit 1925
Catalogue of a Loan Exhibition of Dutch Paintings of the Seventeenth Century. Exh. cat., Detroit Institute of Arts. Detroit, 1925.

Detroit 1930
Valentiner, W. R. *Paintings by Rembrandt.* Exh. cat., Detroit Institute of Arts. Detroit, 1930.

Detroit 1944
Catalogue of Paintings. Detroit Institute of Arts. Detroit, 1944.

Dordrecht 1998
Schoon, Peter, et al. *Arent de Gelder (1645–1727): Rembrandts laatste leering.* Exh. cat., Dordrechts Museum; Wallraf-Richartz-Museum, Cologne. Ghent, 1998.

Edinburgh 1992
Williams, Julia Lloyd. *Dutch Art and Scotland: A Reflection of Taste.* Exh. cat., National Gallery of Scotland, Edinburgh. Edinburgh, 1992.

Edinburgh and London 2001
Williams, Julia Lloyd. *Rembrandt's Women.* Exh. cat., National Gallery of Scotland, Edinburgh; Royal Academy of Art, London. Munich, London, New York, 2001.

Eisler 1977
Eisler, Colin. *Paintings from the Samuel H. Kress Collection: European Schools Excluding Italian.* London, 1977.

Ekkart 2006
Ekkart, R. E O. "Rembrandt and Innovation in Amsterdam Portraiture." In Rembrandt—Wissenschaft auf der Suche Beiträge des Internationalen Symposiums Berlin 4. und 5. November 2006. *Jahrbuch der Berliner Museen* 51 (2009): 39–42.

Fort Worth 2009
Brettell, Richard R., and C. D. Dickerson III. *From the Private Collections of Texas: European Art, Ancient to Modern.* Exh. cat., Kimbell Art Museum, Fort Worth. New Haven, 2009.

Frankfurt and Kyoto 2003
Giltaij, Jeroen. *Rembrandt Rembrandt.* Exh. cat., Städelsches Kunstinstitut un Städtische Galerie, Frankfurt; Kyoto National Museum. Frankfurt, 2003.

Gerson/Bredius 1969
Bredius, Abraham. *Rembrandt: The Complete Edition of Paintings.* Revised by Horst Gerson. London 1969.

Getty 1965
Getty, J. Paul. *The Joys of Collecting.* New York, 1965.

Giltaij 2009
Giltaij, Jeroen. "Observations on the 'Man in a Red Cap.'" *Jahrbuch der Berliner Museen* 51 (2009): 157–60.

Ghent 2005
Van Cuyp tot Rembrandt de Verzameling Cornelis Hofstede de Groot. Exh. cat., Groninger Museum. Ghent, 2005.

Golahny 2003
Golahny, Amy. *Rembrandt's Reading: The Artist's Bookshelf of Ancient Poetry and History.* Amsterdam, 2003.

Gudlaugsson 1959–60
Gudlaugsson, S. J. *Gerard Ter Borch.* 2 vols. The Hague, 1959–60.

Gutbrod 1996
Gutbrod, Helga. *Lievens und Rembrandt: Studien zum Verhältnis ihrer Kunst.* Frankfurt am Main, 1996.

The Hague and London 2007
Ekkart, Rudi, and Quentin Buvelot. *Dutch Portraits: The Age of Rembrandt and Frans Hals.* Exh. cat., Royal Picture Gallery Mauritshuis, The Hague; National Gallery, London. Zwolle, 2007.

The Hague and San Francisco 1990
Broos, Ben, et al. *Great Dutch Paintings from America.* Exh. cat., Mauritshuis, The Hague; Fine Arts Museums of San Francisco. Zwolle, 1990.

The Hague and Schwerin 2004
Duparc, Frederik J., et al. *Carel Fabritius 1622–1654*. Exh. cat., Royal Cabinet of Paintings Mauritshuis, The Hague; Staatliches Museum, Schwerin. Zwolle, 2004,

Hammer 1985
Armand Hammer Foundation. *The Armand Hammer Collection*. Los Angeles, 1985.

Hartford 2009
Zafran, Eric. *Rembrandt's People*. Exh. cat., Wadsworth Atheneum Museum of Art, Hartford. Hartford, Conn., 2009.

Hartwell 2001
Hartwell, D. Myers. "Turning Copper into Gold: The William A. Clark Collection," pp. 13–26. In *Antiquities to Impressionism: The William A. Clark Collection, Corcoran Gallery of Art*. Washington, London, 2001.

Haskell 1970
Haskell, Francis. "The Benjamin Altman Bequest." *Metropolitan Museum Journal* 3 (1970): 259–80.

Hofstede de Groot 1908–27
Hofstede de Groot, Cornelius. *A Catalogue Raisonné of the Work of the Most Eminent Dutch Painters Based on the Work of John Smith*. Trans. Edward G. Hawke. 10 vols. London, 1908–27.

Houbraken 1753
Houbraken, Arnold. *De groote schouburgh der Nederlandsche konstschilders en schilderessen*. 3 vols. The Hague, 1753. 1st ed. The Hague, 1718–21.

Indianapolis 1937
Dutch Paintings, Etchings, Drawings, Delftware of the Seventeenth Century. Exh. cat., John Herron Art Museum, Indianapolis. Indianapolis, 1937.

Indianapolis 2006
Dickey, Stephanie S. *Rembrandt Face to Face*. Exh. cat., Indianapolis Museum of Art. Indianapolis, 2006.

Indianapolis and San Diego 1958
Carter, David G., and Seymour Slive. *The Young Rembrandt and his Times*. Exh. cat., John Herron Art Museum, Indianapolis; Fine Arts Gallery, San Diego. Indianapolis, 1958.

Ingamells 1992
Ingamells, J. "Rembrandt and the New Attributional Changes at the Wallace Collection." *Apollo* 135 (March 1992): 146–50.

Kassel and Amsterdam 2001
Wetering, Ernst van de, and Bernhard Schnackenburg. *The Mystery of the Young Rembrandt*. Exh. cat., Staatliche Museen, Gemäldegalerie Alte Meister, Kassel; Museum het Rembrandthuis, Amsterdam. Wolfratshausen, 2001.

Keyes et al. 2004
Keyes, George S., et al. *Masters of Dutch Painting: The Detroit Institute of Arts*. London, 2004.

Kingston 1984
McTavish, David. *Pictures from the Age of Rembrandt: Selections from the Personal Collection of Dr. and Mrs. Alfred Bader*. Exh. cat., Agnes Etherington Art Centre, Kingston. Kingston, 1984.

Kingston 1996
Manuth, Volker, et al. *Wisdom, Knowledge and Magic: The Image of the Scholar in Dutch 17th-century Art*. Exh. cat., Agnes Etherington Art Centre, Kingston. Kingston, 1996.

Kress 1994
Ishikawa, Chiyo, et al. *A Gift to America: Masterpieces of European Painting from the Samuel H. Kress Collection*. Exh. cat., North Carolina Museum of Art, Raleigh; Museum of Fine Arts, Houston; Seattle Art Museum; Fine Arts Museums of San Francisco. New York, 1994.

Lairesse 1707/1740
Lairesse, Gerard de. *Groot schilderboek. . . .* 2 vols. Amsterdam, 1707; 2nd ed. Haarlem, 1740.

Lee 1967
Lee, Sherman E. "Old Man Praying." *Bulletin of The Cleveland Museum of Art* 54, no. 10 (1967): 295–301.

Leiden 1956
Van Gelder, J. G., et al. *Rembrandt als Leermeester*. Exh. cat., Stedelijk Museum de Lakenhal, Leiden. Leiden, 1956.

Leiden 1976
Wurfbain, M. L. *Geschildert tot Leyden Anno 1629*. Exh. cat., Stedelijk Museum de Lakenhal, Leiden. Leiden, 1976.

Leiden 1991
Vogelaar, Christiaan, et al. *Rembrandt and Lievens in Leiden*. Exh. cat., Stedelijk Museum de Lakenhal, Leiden. Zwolle, 1991.

Leningrad 1976
Paintings from American Museums. Exh. cat., State Hermitage Museum, Leningrad; Pushkin Museum of Fine Arts, Moscow; Museum of Ukrainian Art, Kiev; Belorussian State Museum of Fine Arts, Minsk. Leningrad, 1976.

Leningrad 1989
Masterpieces of Western European Painting of the XVIth–XXth Centuries from the Museums of the European Countries and USA. Exh. cat., Hermitage, Leningrad. Leningrad (St. Petersburg), 1989.

Liedtke 1989
Liedtke, Walter. "Reconstructing Rembrandt Portraits from the Early Years in Amsterdam (1631–34)." *Apollo* 129 (May 1989): 323–31; 371–72.

Liedtke 1990
Liedtke, Walter. "Dutch Paintings in America: The Collectors and Their Ideals," pp. 47–50. In The Hague and San Francisco 1990.

Liedtke 1992
———. "Rembrandt and the Rembrandt Style." *Apollo* 135 (March 1992): 140–45.

Liedtke 1995
———. "Rembrandt's 'Man in a Gorget and Plumed Cap' in the J. Paul Getty Museum." *Burlington Magazine* 137 (July 1995): 458–62.

Liedtke 1996
———. "Reconstructing Rembrandt and His Circle: More on the Workshop Hypothesis," pp. 37–48. In *Rembrandt, Rubens and the Art of Their Time: Recent Perspectives*. Ed. by R. E. Fleischer and S. Scott Munshower. Papers in Art History from the Pennsylvania State University Press. University Park, 1996.

Liedtke 2004
———. "Rembrandt's 'Workshop' Revisited." *Oud Holland* 117 (2004): 48–73.

Liedtke 2007
———. *Dutch Paintings in The Metropolitan Museum of Art*. 2 vols. New Haven, London, 2007.

London 1929
Exhibition of Dutch Art, 1450–1900. Exh. cat., Royal Academy of Arts, London. London, 1929.

London and Amsterdam 2006
Lammertse, Friso, and Jaap van der Veen. *Uylenburgh & Son: Art and Commerce from Rembrandt to De Lairesse 1625–1675*. Exh. cat., Dulwich Picture Gallery, London; Rembrandt House Museum, Amsterdam. Zwolle, 2006.

London and The Hague 1999
White, Christopher, and Quentin Buvelot, eds. *Rembrandt by Himself*. Exh. cat., National Gallery, London; Royal Cabinet of Paintings Mauritshuis, The Hague. London, 1999.

Lopez 2007
Lopez, Jonathan. " 'Gross False Pretences': The Misdeeds of Art Dealer Leo Nardus." *Apollo* 166 (December 2007): 76–83.

Los Angeles 1947
Valentiner, W. R. *Loan Exhibition of Paintings by Frans Hals and Rembrandt*. Exh. cat., Los Angeles County Museum, Los Angeles. Los Angeles, 1947.

Los Angeles 2009
Woollett, Anne T. *Rembrandt in Southern California*. Exh. cat., J. Paul Getty Museum, Los Angeles, et al. Los Angeles, 2009.

Madrid 2008
Vergara, Alejandro. *Rembrandt: Pintor de Historias*. Exh. cat., Museo Nacional del Prado, Madrid. Madrid, 2008.

Manuth and De Winkel 2002
Manuth, Volker, and Marieke de Winkel. *Rembrandt's* Minerva in her Study *of 1635: The Splendor and Wisdom of a Goddess*. Otto Naumann, Ltd., New York. New York, 2002.

McQueen 2003
McQueen, Alison. *The Rise of the Cult of Rembrandt: Reinventing an Old Master in Nineteenth-Century France*. Amsterdam, 2003.

Melbourne and Canberra 1997
Blankert, Albert. *Rembrandt: A Genius and His Impact*. Exh. cat., National Gallery of Victoria, Melbourne; National Gallery of Australia, Canberra. Zwolle, 1997.

Milliken 1936
Milliken, W. M. "Mr. Severance's Gifts to the Museum." *Bulletin of The Cleveland Museum of Art* 23, no. 2, part 1 (1936): 17–27.

Milliken 1944
———. "Mrs. Prentiss's Gifts." *Bulletin of The Cleveland Museum of Art* 31, no. 3 (1944): 32.

Milwaukee 1943
Seventeenth Century Dutch Masterpieces. Exh. cat., Art Institute, Milwaukee. Milwaukee, 1943.

Milwaukee 1964
Great Art from Private Colleges and Universities. Exh. cat., Marquette University, Milwaukee. Milwaukee, 1964.

Milwaukee 1989
Bader, Alfred, and Isabel Bader. *The Detective's Eye: Investigating the Old Masters*. Exh. cat., Milwaukee Art Museum. Milwaukee, 1989.

Minneapolis 1972
The J. Paul Getty Collection. Exh. cat, Minneapolis Institute of Arts. Minneapolis, 1972.

Minty 2008
Minty, Nancy T. "Great Expectations: The Golden Age Redeems the Gilded Age," pp. 215–35. In *Going Dutch: The Dutch Presence in America, 1609–2009*. Edited by Joyce D. Goodfriend, Benjamin Schmidt, and Annette Stott. Leiden and Boston, 2008.

Moltke 1965
Moltke, Joachim Wolfgang von. *Govert Flinck, 1615–1660*. Amsterdam, 1965.

Montreal and Toronto 1969
Carter, David G., et al. *Rembrandt and His Pupils*. Exh. cat., Montreal Museum of Fine Arts; Art Gallery of Ontario, Toronto. Montreal, 1969.

Moscow 2006
Sadkov, Vadim, et al. *Rembrandt: His Predecessors and Followers*. Exh. cat., Pushkin Museum, Moscow. Moscow, 2006.

New Haven 1983
White, Christopher, et al. *Rembrandt in Eighteenth Century England*. Exh. cat., Yale Center for British Art, New Haven. New Haven, 1983.

New York 1890
Loan Collection of Paintings. Exh. cat., Metropolitan Museum of Art, New York. New York, 1890.

New York 1909
Valentiner, W. R. *The Hudson-Fulton Celebration: Catalogue of a Collection of Paintings by Dutch Masters of the Seventeenth Century*. Exh. cat., Metropolitan Museum of Art, New York. New York, 1909.

New York 1914
Loan Exhibition of Paintings by the Great Dutch Masters of the 17th Century. Exh. cat., Scott & Fowles, New York. New York, 1914.

New York 1920
Fiftieth Anniversary Exhibition. Exh. cat., Metropolitan Museum of Art, New York. New York, 1920.

New York 1925
Dutch Masters of the Seventeenth Century. Exh. cat., M. Knoedler & Co., New York. New York, 1925.

New York 1930
A Loan Exhibition of Sixteen Masterpieces. Exh. cat., M. Knoedler Gallery, New York. New York, 1930.

New York 1933
Loan Exhibition of Paintings by Rembrandt. Exh. cat., M. Knoedler Gallery, New York. New York, 1933.

New York 1939
McCall, George Henry. *Catalogue of European Paintings and Sculpture from 1300–1800. Masterpieces of Art.* Edited by W. R. Valentiner. Exh. cat., New York World's Fair. New York, 1939.

New York 1940
Pach, Walter. *Catalogue of European and American Paintings, 1500–1900.* Exh. cat., New York World's Fair. New York, 1940.

New York 1942A
The Art of Rembrandt. Exh. cat., Metropolitan Museum of Art, New York. New York, 1942.

New York 1942B
McCall, George Henry. *Paintings by the Great Dutch Masters.* Exh. cat., Duveen Galleries, New York. New York, 1942.

New York 1950
Wildenstein and Co. *Loan Exhibition of Rembrandt, Under the High Patronage of His Excellency, Dr. Eelco N. van Kleffens, Ambassador of the Netherlands, for the Benefit of the Public Education Association.* Exh. cat., Wildenstein Gallery, New York. New York, 1950.

New York 1957
Paintings and Sculpture from the Minneapolis Institute of Arts. Exh. cat., M. Knoedler & Co., New York. New York, 1957.

New York 1961
Twenty-fifth Anniversary: 1936–1961. Exh. cat., Schaeffer Galleries, New York. New York, 1961.

New York 1973
Dutch Couples: Pair Portraits by Rembrandt and His Contemporaries. Exh. cat., Metropolitan Museum of Art, New York. New York, 1973.

New York 1977
Sutton, Denys. *Treasures from Rochester.* Exh. cat., Wildenstein Galleries, New York. Rochester, 1977.

New York 1993
Frelinghuysen, Alice Cooney, et al. *Splendid Legacy: The Havemeyer Collection.* Exh. cat., Metropolitan Museum of Art, New York. New York, 1993.

New York 1995
Von Sonnenburg, Hubert, and Walter Liedtke. *Rembrandt/Not Rembrandt in The Metropolitan Museum of Art: Aspects of Connoisseurship.* Exh. cat., Metropolitan Museum of Art, New York. Vol. 1, *Paintings: Problems and Issues*, by Hubert von Sonnenburg; vol. 2, *Paintings, Drawings, and Prints: Art Historical Perspectives*, by Walter Liedtke et al. New York, 1995.

New York 2001
Orenstein, Nadine M., ed. *Pieter Bruegel the Elder: Drawings and Prints.* Exh. cat., Museum Boijmans van Beuningen, Rotterdam; Metropolitan Museum of Art, New York. New Haven and London, 2001.

New York, Toledo, Toronto 1954
Rousseau, T. *Dutch Painting: The Golden Age, An Exhibition of Dutch Pictures of the Seventeenth Century.* Exh. cat., Metropolitan Museum of Art, New York; Toledo Art Museum; Art Gallery of Ontario, Toronto. New York, 1954.

Oberlin 1963
Youthful Works by Great Artists: An Exhibition. Exh. cat., Allen Memorial Art Museum. Oberlin, 1963. Cat. in *Allen Memorial Art Museum Bulletin* 20, no. 3 (Spring 1963).

Orlers 1641
Orlers, Jan Jansz. *Beschrijvinge der Stadt Leyden.* Leiden 1641.

Peters 1988
Peters, Susan Dodge, ed. *Memorial Art Gallery: An Introduction to the Collection.* New York, 1988.

Pittsburgh 1925
Paintings by Old Masters from Pittsburgh Collections. Carnegie Institute, Pittsburgh. Pittsburgh, 1925.

Quodbach 2002
Quodbach, Esmée. " 'The Last of the American Versailles': The Widener Collection at Lynnewood Hall." *Simiolus* 29, nos. 1 and 2 (2002): 42–96.

Quodbach 2004–5
———. "Rembrandt's 'Gilder' is here": how America got its first Rembrandt and France lost many of its old masters." *Simiolus* 31, nos. 1 and 2 (2004–5): 90–107.

Raleigh 1956
Valentiner, W. R. *Rembrandt and His Pupils.* Exh. cat., North Carolina Museum of Art, Raleigh. Raleigh, 1956.

Raleigh 1959
Byrnes, James B. *Masterpieces of Art: In Memory of William R. Valentiner, 1880–1958.* Exh. cat., North Carolina Museum of Art, Raleigh. Raleigh, 1959.

Ringling Museum 1986
Great Paintings from the John and Mable Ringling Museum of Art. New York, 1986.

Rosenberg 1948
Rosenberg, Jakob. *Rembrandt.* 2 vols. Cambridge, 1948. Rev. ed. *Rembrandt: Life and Work.* Greenwich, Conn., 1964.

Rosenberg 1957
———. "Rembrandt's Portraits of Johannes Elison and his Wife." *Bulletin of the Museum of Fine Arts, Boston* 55 (1957): 3–9.

Rosenthal 1979
Rosenthal, Donald, ed. *The George Eastman Collection.* Exh. cat., Memorial Art Gallery, University of Rochester. Rochester, N.Y., 1979.

Rotterdam 1988
Giltaij, Jeroen, and Guido Jansen. *Een gloeiend palet: Schilderijen van Rembrandt en zijn school* [A glowing palette: Rembrandt and his school]. Exh. cat., Museum Boymans-van Beuningen. Rotterdam, 1988.

Saarinen 1958
Saarinen, Aline B. *The Proud Possessors: The Lives, Times and Tastes of Some Adventurous American Collectors*. New York, 1958.

San Diego 1996
Petersen, Nancy Ames, et al. *European Works of Art, American Paintings, and Russian Icons in the Putnam Foundation Collection*. Timken Museum of Art, San Diego. San Diego, 1996.

San Francisco 1939
Masterworks of Five Centuries. Exh. cat., Golden Gate International Exposition, San Francisco. San Francisco, 1939.

San Francisco 1966
Gerson, Horst. *The Age of Rembrandt: An Exhibition of Dutch Paintings of the Seventeenth Century*. Exh. cat., California Palace of the Legion of Honor, San Francisco; Toledo Museum of Art; Museum of Fine Arts, Houston. Boston and Haarlem, 1966.

Scallen 2004
Scallen, Catherine B. *Rembrandt, Reputation, and the Practice of Connoisseurship*. Amsterdam, 2004.

Schneider 1973
Schneider, H. *Jan Lievens: Sein Leben und seine Werke*. Rev. ed. with supplement by R. E. O. Ekkart. Amsterdam, 1973.

Schneider 1985
Schneider, C. "A New Look at the Landscape with an Obelisque." *Fenway Court* (1985): 6–21.

Schwartz 1985
Schwartz, Gary. *Rembrandt, His Life, His Paintings*. New York, 1985.

Schwartz 2006
———. *The Rembrandt Book*. New York, 2006.

Slive 1970–74
Slive, Seymour. *Frans Hals*. 3 vols. London, 1970–74.

Slive 1978
Slive, S. "Rembrandt at Harvard." *Apollo* 107 (June 1978): 453–63.

Smith 1829–42
Smith, John. *A Catalogue Raisonné of the Works of the Most Eminent Dutch, Flemish and French Painters*. 8 vols. and Supplement. London, 1829–42.

Sterne 1980
Sterne, Margaret. *The Passionate Eye: The Life of William R. Valentiner*. Detroit, 1980.

Stockholm 1992
Cavalli-Björkman, Görel, et al. *Rembrandt and his Age*. Exh. cat., Nationalmuseum. Stockholm, 1992.

Strauss and Van der Meulen 1979
Strauss, Walter, and Marjon van der Meulen. *The Rembrandt Documents*. New York, 1979.

Sumowski 1983
Sumowski, Werner. *Gemälde der Rembrandt-Schüler*. Vol. 4. Landau/Pfalz, 1983.

Sutton 1986
Sutton, Peter C. *A Guide to Dutch Art in America*. Washington, DC: Netherlands-American Amity Trust; Grand Rapids, 1986.

Sutton 1990
———. *Northern European Paintings in the Philadelphia Museum of Art from the Sixteenth through the Nineteenth Century*. Philadelphia, 1990.

Taft Museum 1995
The Taft Museum: Its History and Collections. Vol. 1. New York, 1995.

Talley 1989
Talley, M. Kirby, Jr. "Connoisseurship and the Methodology of the Rembrandt Research Project." *International Journal of Museum Management and Curatorship* 8 (1989): 175–214.

Thiel 1992
Thiel, P. J. J. van. "De Rembrandt-tentoonstelling van 1898." *Bulletin van het Rijksmuseum* 40 (1992): 11–93; 123–27.

Tokyo 1992
Brown, Christopher, ed. *Rembrandt, his Teachers and his Pupils*. Exh. cat., Bunkamura Museum of Art, Tokyo; Kawamura Memorial Museum of Art, Chiba; Yamaguchi Prefectural Museum of Art. Tokyo, 1992.

Toledo 2009
Bacigalupi, Don, et al. *Toledo Museum of Art Masterworks*. Toledo, 2009.

Tomkins 1970
Tomkins, Calvin. *Merchants and Masterpieces: The Story of the Metropolitan Museum of Art*. New York, 1970.

Toronto 1950
Fifty Paintings by Old Masters. Exh. cat., Art Gallery of Ontario, Toronto. Toronto, 1950.

Toronto 1951
Rembrandt Exhibition. Exh. cat., Toronto Art Museum. Toronto, 1951.

Tucson 1961
Twenty-five Paintings from the Collection of the Samuel H. Kress Foundation. Exh. cat., University of Arizona, Tucson. Tucson, 1961.

Tümpel 1986
Tümpel, Christian. *Rembrandt: All Paintings in Color*. Antwerp and New York, 1986.

Utrecht and Braunschweig 1986
Blankert, Albert, et al. *Nieuw Licht op de gouden Eeuw: Hendrick ter Brugghen en tijdgenoten*. Exh. cat., Centraal Museum, Utrecht; Herzog Anton Ulrich-Museum, Braunschweig. Utrecht, 1986.

Valentiner 1909
Valentiner, Wilhelm Reinhold. *Rembrandt: des Meisters Gemälde, mit 643 Abbildungen*. Klassiker der Kunst. 3rd ed. Stuttgart and Leipzig, 1909.

Valentiner 1920–21
———. "Die Vier Evangelisten Rembrandts." *Kunstchronik und Kunstmarkt* 56 (1920–21): 219–22.

Valentiner 1921
———. *Rembrandt Wiedergefundene Gemälde (1910–1920), in 120 Abbildungen*. Klassiker der Kunst. Stuttgart and Berlin, 1921.

Valentiner 1925–26
———. "Komödiantendarstellungen Rembrandts." *Zeitschrift für bildende Kunst* 59 (1925–26): 265–72.

Valentiner 1931
———. *Rembrandt Paintings in America*. New York, 1931.

Valentiner 1934
———. *Die Handzeichnungen Rembrandts*. 3 vols. New York, 1934.

Van Mander 1604/1618
Van Mander, Karel. *Het Schilderboeck*. Haarlem, 1604. 2nd ed. Amsterdam, 1618.

Veen 1997
Veen, Jaap van der. "Faces from Life: *Tronies* and Portraits in Rembrandt's Painted Oeuvre," pp 69–70. In Melbourne and Canberra 1997.

Veen 2006
———. "Hendrick Uylenburgh's Art Business Production and Trade between 1625 and 1655," pp. 117–205. In London and Amsterdam 2006.

Vey and Kesting 1967
Vey, H., and A. Kesting. *Katalog der Niederländischen Gemälde von 1550 bis 1800 im Wallraf-Richartz-Museum*. Cologne, 1967.

Vries 1989
Vries, Lyckle de. "Tronies and Other Single Figured Netherlandish Paintings." *Leids Kunsthistorisch Jaarboek* 8 (1989): 185–202.

Walker 1974
Walker, John. *Self-Portrait with Donors: Confessions of an Art Collector*. Boston/Toronto, 1974.

Walsh 1976
Walsh, J., Jr. "Child's Play in Rembrandt's 'A Lady and Gentleman in Black.'" *Fenway Court* (1976): 1–7.

Washington 1969
Rembrandt in the National Gallery of Art. Exh. cat., National Gallery of Art, Washington. Washington, 1969.

Washington 1978
The William A. Clark Collection. Exh. cat., Corcoran Gallery of Art. Washington, 1978.

Washington and Minneapolis 1991
Wheelock, Arthur K., and George Keyes. *Rembrandt's Lucretias*. Exh. brochure, National Gallery of Art, Washington; Minneapolis Institute of Arts. Washington and Minneapolis, 1991.

Washington 2000
Baer, Ronni, Arthur K. Wheelock Jr., Annetje Boersma. *Gerrit Dou 1613–1675: Master Painter in the Age of Rembrandt*. Exh. cat., National Gallery of Art, Washington; Dulwich Picture Gallery, London; Royal Cabinet of Paintings Mauritshuis, The Hague. New Haven and London, 2000.

Washington 2008
Wheelock, Arthur K., Jr., et al. *Jan Lievens: A Dutch Master Rediscovered*. Exh. cat., National Gallery of Art, Washington; Milwaukee Art Museum; Rembrandthuis, Amsterdam. New Haven, 2008.

Washington, Detroit, Amsterdam 1980
Blankert, Albert, et al. *Gods, Saints & Heroes: Dutch Painting in the Age of Rembrandt*. Exh. cat., National Gallery of Art, Washington; Detroit Institute of Arts; Rijksmuseum, Amsterdam. Washington, 1980.

Washington and Los Angeles 2005
Wheelock, Arthur K., Jr., et al. *Rembrandt's Late Religious Portraits*. Exh. cat., National Gallery of Art, Washington; J. Paul Getty Museum, Los Angeles. Washington, 2005.

Weitzenhoffer 1982
Weitzenhoffer, Frances. "The Creation of the Havemeyer Collection, 1875–1900." PhD diss., City University of New York, 1982.

Weller 2009
Weller, Dennis P. *Seventeenth-Century Dutch and Flemish Paintings*. Systematic Catalogue of the Collection, North Carolina Museum of Art. Raleigh, 2009.

Wetering 1997
Wetering, Ernst van de. *Rembrandt: The Painter at Work*. Amsterdam, 1997.

Wetering 1999
———. "The Multiple Functions of Rembrandt's Self-Portraits," pp. 10–37. In London and The Hague 1999.

Wetering 2002
———. "Rembrandt's Hidden Self-Portraits." *Kroniek van het Rembrandthuis*, nos. 1–2 (2002): 2–3, 8–25.

Wetering 2008
———. *Rembrandt: A Life in 180 Paintings*. Amsterdam, 2008.

Wheelock 1988
Wheelock, Arthur K., Jr. "The Art Historian in the Laboratory: Examinations into the History, Preservation, and Techniques of the 17th-Century Dutch Painting," pp. 215–45. In *The Age of Rembrandt: Studies in Seventeenth-Century Dutch Painting*. Papers in Art History from the Pennsylvania State University. Vol. 3. Edited by Roland E. Fleischer and Susan Scott Munshower. Pittsburgh, 1988.

Wheelock 1995
———. *Dutch Paintings of the Seventeenth Century*. The Collections of the National Gallery of Art Systematic Catalogue. New York and Oxford, 1995.

Whitehill 1970
Whitehill, W. M. *Museum of Fine Arts Boston: A Centennial History*. Cambridge, Harvard University Press, 1970.

Widener 1885
Catalogue of Paintings Forming the Private Collection of P. A. B. Widener, Ashbourne—near Philadelphia. Paris, 1885.

Widener 1913
Early German, Dutch and Flemish Schools. Notes by W. R. Valentiner and Cornelis Hofstede de Groot. Vol 1. of *Pictures in the Collection of P. A. B. Widener at Lynnewood Hall, Elkins Park, Pa*. 3 vols. Philadelphia, 1913.

Widener 1923
Valentiner, W. R. *Paintings in the Collection of Joseph Widener at Lynnewood Hall*. Elkins Park, Pa., 1923.

Williamstown 1960
Exhibit Twelve—Dutch and Flemish Masters. Exh. cat., Sterling and Francine Clark Art Institute, Williamstown. Williamstown, Mass., 1960.

Williamstown 1992
Kern, Steven. *List of Paintings in the Sterling and Francine Clark Art Museum*. Williamstown, Mass., 1992.

Winkel 2006
Winkel, Marieke de. *Fashion and Fancy Dress and Meaning in Rembrandt's Paintings*. Amsterdam, 2006.

Worcester 1936
Rich, Daniel Catton. *Rembrandt and His Circle: A Loan Exhibition of Paintings, Drawings and Etchings*. Exh. cat., Worcester Art Museum. Worcester, 1936.

Wurzbach 1906–11
Wurzbach, Alfred von. *Niederländisches Künstler-Lexikon*. 3 vols. Vienna and Leipzig, 1906–11.

Yerkes 1893
Catalogue from Collection of Charles T. Yerkes. Chicago, 1893.

Yerkes 1904
Catalogue of Paintings and Sculpture in the Collection of Charles T. Yerkes, Esq. New York, 1904.

Yokohama, Fukuoka, Kyoto 1986
Brown, Christopher. *Rembrandt and the Bible*. Exh. cat., Sogo Museum of Art, Yokohama; Fukuoka Art Museum; and Kyoto National Museum of Modern Art. Yokohama, 1986.

TRUSTEES

NORTH CAROLINA MUSEUM OF ART 2010–2011

INDEX

A

B

C

D

E

F

G

H

I

J

K

L

M

N

O

P

R

S

T

U

V

W

Y

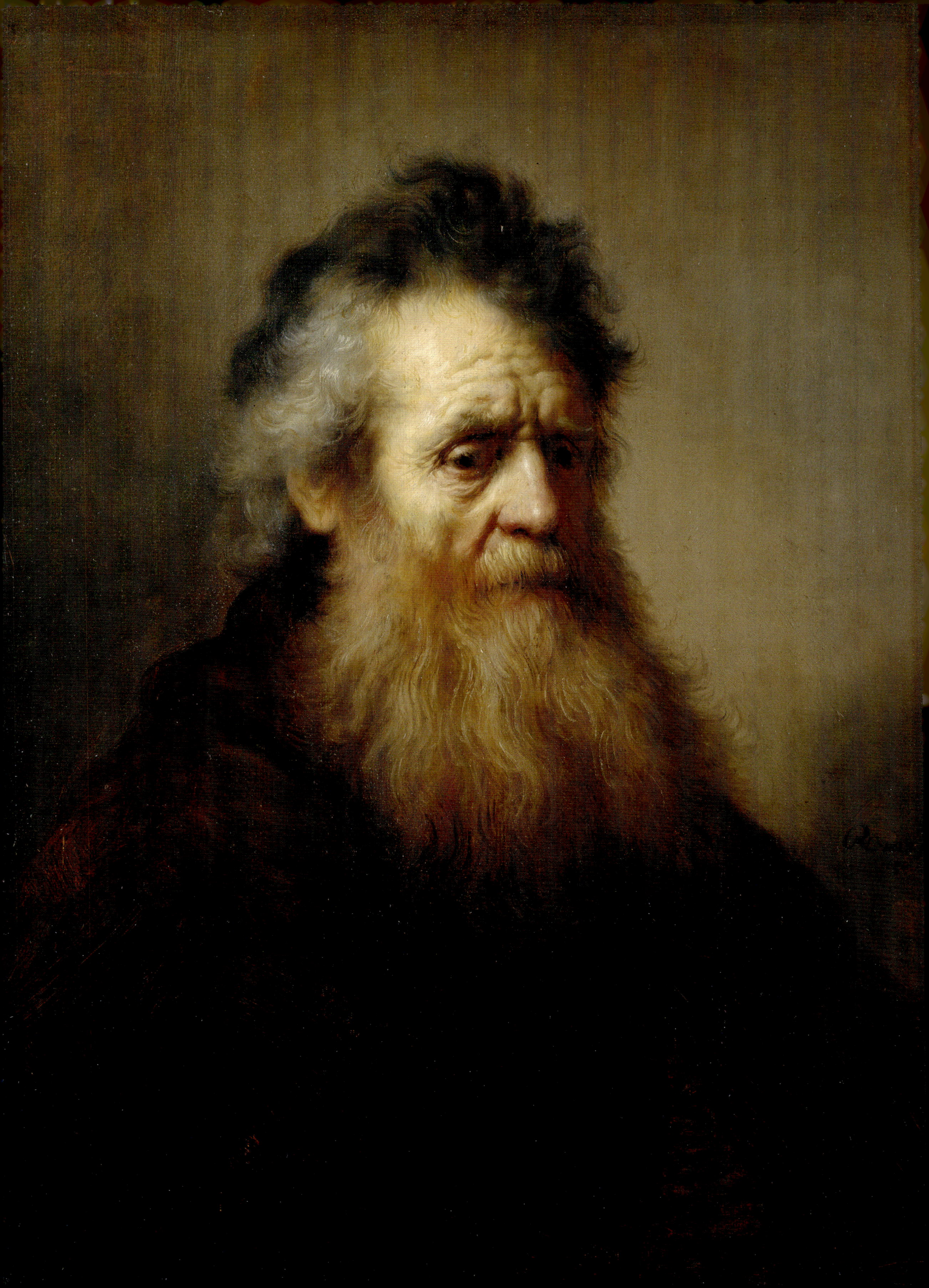

DETAILS

Half title: Detail of Rembrandt van Rijn, *Man in a Fur-lined Coat*, c. 1655–60 (cat. 32).
pp. 2–3: Detail of Rembrandt van Rijn, *Lucretia*, 1666 (cat. 50).
p. 4: Detail of Rembrandt van Rijn, *Self-portrait*, 1659 (cat. 34).
p. 8: Detail of Rembrandt van Rijn (workshop of; Isaac de Joudreville?), *Bust of a Young Man in a Gorget and Plumed Cap* (cat. 8).
p. 10: Detail of Rembrandt van Rijn, *Joris de Caulerij*, 1632 (cat. 11).
p. 12: Detail of Rembrandt van Rijn, *Portrait of Anthonie Coopal*, 1635 (cat. 20).
p. 14: Detail of Rembrandt van Rijn, *Portrait of a Young Man*, 1666 (cat. 38).
pp. 16–17: Detail of Jan Lievens, *The Feast of Esther (Wrath of Ahasuerus)*, c. 1625 (cat. 39).
p. 18: Detail of Rembrandt van Rijn, *Study of an Elderly Woman in a White Cap*, c. 1640 (cat. 26).
pp. 30–31. Detail of Rembrandt van Rijn (workshop of), *Portrait of a Young Woman*, 1632 (cat. 13).
p. 32: Detail of Rembrandt van Rijn, *Self-portrait (Study in a Mirror)*, c. 1629 (cat. 4).
p. 57: Detail of Rembrandt van Rijn (workshop of), *Portrait of a Man*, c. 1655–60 (cat.33).
pp. 58–59: Detail of Rembrandt van Rijn and workshop, *Portrait of a Woman*, 1635 or earlier (cat. 21).
p. 60: Detail of Rembrandt van Rijn, *Self-portrait with Shaded Eyes*, 1634 (cat. 17).
pp. 86–87: Detail of Rembrandt van Rijn, *Old Man with a Gold Chain*, c. 1631 (cat. 7).
p. 88: Detail of Rembrandt van Rijn, *The Operation (Touch)*, c. 1624/25 (cat. 2).
pp. 110–11: Detail of Rembrandt van Rijn (workshop of; Ferdinand Bol?), *Portrait of a Young Man in a Broad-brimmed Hat*, 1643 (cat. 27).
p. 112: Detail of Rembrandt van Rijn, *Man in a Fur-lined Coat*, c. 1655–60 (cat. 32).
pp. 126–27: Detail of Rembrandt van Rijn (circle of), *Young Man with a Sword*, c. 1633–45 (cat. 24).
pp. 140–41: Detail of Rembrandt van Rijn, *Minerva in Her Study*, 1635 (cat. 40).
p. 142: Detail of Rembrandt van Rijn (follower of), *The Death of Lucretia*(?), c. mid-1640s (cat. 41).
pp. 170–71: Detail of Rembrandt van Rijn (attributed to), *A Scholar by Candlelight*, c.1628/29 (cat. 3).
p. 177: Detail of Rembrandt van Rijn, *Portrait of the Reverend Johannes Elison*, 1634 (cat. 18).
p. 201: Detail of Rembrandt van Rijn, *St. Bartholomew*, 1657 (cat. 45).
p. 202: Detail of Rembrandt van Rijn, *Portrait of a Man in a Red Doublet*, 1633 (cat. 16).
p. 222: Detail of Rembrandt van Rijn, *Portrait of an Old Man*, 1632 (cat. 14)

PHOTO CREDITS

Photo © The Art Institute of Chicago: cat. 7.
Bildarchiv Preussischer Kulturbesitz/Art Resource, NY: figs. 12, 13, 49, 66, 67.
The Bridgeman Art Library Nationality: cats. 4, 41 and figs. 40, 88.
© The Cleveland Museum of Art (digital images): cats. 6, 21, 33, 49.
From Corpus 2005, fig. 74 on p. 140: fig. 14.
© The Educational Alliance, Inc./Estate of Peter Blume/Licensed by VAGA, New York, NY (art), Imaging Department © President and Fellows of Harvard College (photographs): cats. 5, 30; © The Educational Alliance, Inc./Estate of Peter Blume/Licensed by VAGA, New York, NY (art), © President and Fellows of Harvard College, Rick Stafford (photograph): cat. 14.
Mitro Hood: cats. 29, 35.
Kunstmuseum des Landes Niedersachsen Fotonachweis: Museumsfotograph: fig. 25.
Erich Lessing/Art Resource, NY: fig. 50.
The Metropolitan Museum of Art/Art Resource, NY (digital images); cats. 9, 10 and figs. 2, 4, 30, 31, 33, 36, 37, 59, 68, 73, 85, 92. © The Metropolitan Museum of Art/Art Resource, NY (digital image), Malcolm Varon (photograph): cat. 44.
Jamison Miller: cat. 38.
© 2009 Museum Associates/LACMA/Art Resource, NY (digital image): cat. 15.
© 2011 Museum of Fine Arts, Boston (photographs): cats. 18, 19 and fig. 10.
National Gallery, London/Art Resource, NY: figs. 24, 87.
Courtesy National Gallery of Art, Washington: cats. 23, 36, 43, 46.
North Carolina Division of Archives and History and the *News and Observer*, Raleigh, NC: fig. 1.
Photography Incorporated, Toledo: cat. 32.
Réunion des Musées Nationaux/Art Resource, NY: fig. 77.
The Royal Collection © 2010 Her Majesty Queen Elizabeth II: fig. 9.
Scala/Art Resource, NY: fig. 16.
© Sterling and Francine Clark Art Institute: cat. 28.
Wadsworth Atheneum Museum of Art/Art Resource, NY: cat. 22 and figs. 5, 72.
Robert Wedemeyer: cat. 25.
From Ernst van de Wetering, *Rembrandt: A Life in 180 Paintings* (Amsterdam: Local World, 2008), fig. 189 on p. 149: fig. 71.
From Winkel 2006, fig. 20 on p. 64: fig. 61, and fig. 21 on p. 65: fig. 62.